AI on Trial

AI on Trial

Mark Deem
Solicitor-Advocate of the Senior Courts of England & Wales

Peter Warren
Editor of the website Future Intelligence and the Presenter of the PassW0rd radio show on the ramifications of technology on society on London's ResonanceFM

Bloomsbury Professional

LONDON · DUBLIN · EDINBURGH · NEW YORK · NEW DELHI · SYDNEY

BLOOMSBURY PROFESSIONAL
Bloomsbury Publishing Plc
50 Bedford Square, London, WC1B 3DP, UK
1385 Broadway, New York, NY 10018, USA
29 Earlsfort Terrace, Dublin 2, Ireland

BLOOMSBURY and the Diana logo are trademarks of Bloomsbury Publishing Plc

© Bloomsbury Professional 2022

British Library Cataloguing-in-Publication Data

A catalogue record for this book is available from the British Library.

ISBN:	PB: 978 1 52651 355 7
	Epdf: 978 1 52651 357 1
	Epub: 978 1 52651 356 4

Typeset by Evolution Design & Digital Ltd (Kent)
Printed and bound by CPI Group (UK) Ltd, Croydon, CR0 4YY

To find out more about our authors and books visit www.bloomsburyprofessional.com. Here
you will find extracts, author information, details of forthcoming events and the option to
sign up for our newsletters

Foreword

Roy Amara, the American researcher, scientist and futurist, described our societal relationship with technology as one where we tend to overestimate the effect of a technology in the short-term, but underestimate its effect in the long-term.

Although we have, in one form or another, been living with AI for nearly 50 years, Amara's law is likely to be equally true for the future of AI. Its development however is likely to be impacted by a widespread sensationalism which has taken hold in the way AI is characterised combined with a lack of public understanding and education about the technology. Memorably at the launch of our House of Lords Select Committee report 'AI in the UK: Ready Willing and Able?', Dr Stephen Cave, Director of the Leverhulme Centre for the Future of Intelligence, held up an article from *The Sun* newspaper of that day. The article had the headline 'Lies of the Machine: Boffins urged to prevent fibbing robots from staging Terminator style apocalypse'.

This lurid and unhelpful view of AI is consistently pedalled in both the media and in films. As the celebrated cyber security expert Mikko Hypponen says in this book:

> 'If I were an AI system that had just achieved sentience the first thing that I would do would be to do a search on the internet to find out what I was. The only information that would come back would be from science fiction films where I would find that in the main that humanity not only did not like me but seemed to spend a lot of time actively destroying me.'

We are however on the edge of a future that is so different from our past that it risks making previous advances that have impacted society look inconsequential. As a result, it is the opinion of most of the experts featured in this book that there is an urgent need to confront the issues that the advent of AI and robotics now present us with.

This lively, engaging and accessible book makes an important contribution to the debate

As the authors make clear in their closing Manifesto, while many people are blissfully ignorant of the speed of progress of technology and often dismissive of it, robotics and AI in particular represent not just a threat to the way we have been employed up until now but also a revolution in how we will live our lives in the future. This is not simply about the success of a particular technology: more importantly it is about how we develop future economies and how we ensure that everyone has a role in this new world.

As a consequence it is evident, as we make clear in our original House of Lords Report that the adoption of AI will need to be actively controlled through ethical and regulatory oversight.

One of the greatest challenges we have is to ensure that everyone is properly educated about the changes that are about to occur and to make sure that those changes can be readily understood, a point made by many contributors. What AI does and how it does it has to be transparent so that people will trust it and see the need to adopt it. From my experience this needs to apply as much to our legislators as it does to society at large.

The framing of the debate by the authors in the manner that a case would be heard in a courtroom, reflected in its title *AI on Trial*, is a recognition of the significant legal and ethical challenges that AI will throw up as it becomes ever more irreversibly woven into our lives and the need for the evidence and supporting arguments in a number of areas to be weighed carefully.

For example one of the issues that will have to be solved in a new world where machines can make decisions is who is responsible for those decisions in the event of something going wrong and can an AI system have a legal personality in the same way that a company does?

As a result, consideration of the legal personhood of an AI system, discussed by Professor Ryan Abbot in his chapter on whether robots and AI can own patents, becomes a vital issue.

The book examines in detail the potential weaponisation of AI, its consequences and the need for proscription. It also explores the fundamental importance of the data that AI systems will use and underlines that not only does that data need to be cleansed of bias but that also those using the data should be forced to explain why they need that data and what they are going to be doing with it.

Above all the book lays out a comprehensive trail of evidence framed in conversations with the experts. Readers can explore and come to their own conclusions on the ethical use of AI and how and in what circumstances it should be used.

The book concludes with a Manifesto in which the authors set out the key challenges that they think need to be overcome for the adoption of AI. It amounts to a Herculean task for legislators and regulators.

Consensus can be reached on many of the challenges and the solutions and *AI on Trial* will be required reading for all of us making policy in the field of AI data and robotics. That said, whilst the idea of creating a supra-national body to regulate AI development is a good one, achieving the international agreement to accomplish it is a different matter. The Council of Europe, the Organisation for Economic Co-operation and Development (OECD) and the United Nations are all suggesting ways forward in this area but whether any will become a regulator as opposed to a forum remains to be seen. Even achieving a vital convention along the lines of a non-proliferation treaty for lethal autonomous weapons, as the book touches upon, is proving hugely difficult. By placing AI on trial the authors have shown the pressing need for us to hold a mirror up to our relationship with the technology to ensure that despite the risks we can create a legal, ethical and regulatory environment which not only encourages investment and development, but offers appropriate safeguards. Whether we take the short-term or the long-term view, we need to ensure this exciting but misunderstood technology can deliver wider societal benefit.

Lord Clement-Jones

House of Lords

22 February 2022

Acknowledgements

In writing any book there are a number of people who have often helped in the process who go unnoticed. However, they make invaluable contributions, either with research, inspiration, suggestions, or simply by helping to make time available for the authors to get on with writing by taking on the burden of other tasks, whether professional or domestic.

We would therefore like to thank Claire Banyard, Blue Buffery, Eleanor, Rowan, Milo and Hamish Deem, Tom, Matt, Charlie and Georgie Warren, Jane Whyatt and of course in true Hollywood style our parents, Mary and Mervyn Deem and Stanley and Sheila Warren, without whom this would not have been possible.

Mark Deem and Peter Warren

Acknowledgements

Contents

Contents

Introduction: AI at a tipping point

Origins

Artificial Intelligence (AI) promises to be one of the most powerful technologies that humanity has ever developed, with an ability to change every single aspect of our lives. Whether it will be for the best, is down to us.

The words 'Artificial Intelligence' and the adoption of the technology have become synonymous with the twenty-first century, even though it was first discussed by the computing pioneers Donald Michie and Alan Turing while they played chess at Bletchley Park during World War II. It is celebrated as the technology of tomorrow: the potential saviour of a human race that is facing huge challenges from climate change, over-population, disease, economic change, competition for resources, global conflict and a race for control of outer space.

AI, say its proponents, will solve all of these issues. It will usher in a period of unparalleled civilisation and prosperity and create a golden age of achievement that will ultimately even involve the further evolution of humanity into near godlike entities, as many of those giving evidence in this book have highlighted.

Up until now AI has largely been seen as the source of interesting and eye-catching intellectual experiments as the technology's developers seek to underline its ability to compete with people.

The widely credited breakthrough of the technology in this area was on 11 May 1997 when Gary Kasparov, the reigning world chess champion, was beaten by an AI system developed by IBM called 'Watson'.

This 'victory' for the technology and Watson was followed up on 16 February 2011, when it beat Ken Jennings and Brad Rutter, the world's two top players of the US Quiz show *Jeopardy*, in a special three-day *Jeopardy* challenge for a prize fund of $1m. Unfortunately, both Jennings – who had the longest unbeaten run on the show – and Rutter – who had earned the largest prize pot – $3.25m – playing the show – proved incapable of stopping the AI system and picking up the purse.

AI's dominance of intellectual games was further consolidated on 15 March 2016 when Google DeepMind's AlphaGo system beat the reigning world Go (or Weigi) champion in a five-match series of the Chinese board game, once again being played for the ultimate prize of $1m.

Wider application

There will not be one area of our lives and our worlds that AI will not touch.

AI is now involved in mining, farming and space exploration. Autonomous yachts from Saildrone,[1] just one of several autonomous boat companies, have sailed over 500,000 nautical miles and spent over 13,000 days at sea, crossed the Atlantic and sailed into the Antarctic as they map the seabed and record weather conditions. Other robot marine vessels from IBM and Boeing that do not need food or living spaces are routinely entering environments that are very hazardous to people. For a number of years autonomous vehicles have been routinely deployed on the surface of the Moon and Mars, once again environments extremely hostile to humans.

We have become used to seeing robots working in our factories, making cars and many other everyday objects. AI's effects are being seen on our computers, on the internet, in social media and in medicine and transport. Very soon AI will start to make inroads into accountancy, the law, business management, the hospitality industry and even the arts. According to 'Harnessing Artificial Intelligence to Accelerate the Energy Transition', a study by the World Economic Forum, it will even map our electricity grids in virtual reality and control them remotely.

What this means for our world are huge changes. In the largest open-cast iron ore mine in the world at Carajas in Brazil, virtually every part of the operation is being carried out by robots. In other mines deep underground, a similar robotic takeover is occurring. In Slovenia, members of the Underwater Explorer for Flooded Mines (UNEXMiN) project are using robots to explore the potential of mines that are currently inoperable.

On our farms, according to Sir James Paice, UK Agriculture Secretary in 2010 under David Cameron, we have no option but to use AI because of population growth and global warming:

> 'Farming is going to have to use technology to meet the huge challenge of food supply in the future. I don't think as a society and certainly I don't think the entire UK Governing body, has fully understood what's going to happen in the next 30 to 40 years with the growth in world population, the impact of climate change on many parts of the world, and its ability to produce food because of climate change. The whole thing means we're going to be at serious risk. We could be short of food in the next 30 or 40 years. And I don't think people are fully waking up to that.
>
> We're going to see the continued advance of technology, the use of robotics, the use of satellites in growing our crops, robotics in in both crop production and in livestock production. We now have fully automatic milking parlours with no human intervention in milking dairy cows. The cow puts itself into a machine and the machine operates and milks the cow and the cow walks out again. We are seeing dramatic changes like that happening. We're going to see more. We're going to see massive advances in the science used in farming.'

---

1 Saildrone, 'Any Sensor. Anytime. Anywhere', www.saildrone.com/.

The AI revolution and its impact on what is the oldest industry in the world is a good example of the power of the new technology. Farming is being revolutionised by computer driven mechanisation according to Professor Simon Blackmore, of the world leading agricultural research centre Harper Adams: 'Whereas once farms used to employ 20 farms and use an equal amount of horses all of those have been replaced by massive tractors driven by one man.'

Since 1950 the number of agricultural workers has fallen from 491,000 to 108,000 in 2020.

Now even those remaining workers are set to be replaced by AI, because soon robots will be tending our fields and only harvesting plants when they need to instead of bringing the harvest in all in one go, which risks possibly losing 60 per cent of it.

This was backed up by Professor Blackmore in 2016, who said that farm machinery is already being roboticised, with combine harvesters able to perform sophisticated crop analysis on data harvested from field sensors that is then stored in the cloud. If a crop, such as corn, is not ready the combine harvester will decide to cut lanes through it to dry it rather than harvesting it. This could create a cultivation system that will increasingly see farming, once one of the largest sources of employment in the UK and the US, become almost completely roboticised. We will become accustomed, according to Professor Blackmore, to seeing robot tractors tending crops using data collected by satellites, robots looking after animals and drones weeding in the fields.

As an example of that process, in 2017, Harper Adams and York-based Precision Decisions, harvested 4.5 tonnes of spring barley from a field that had been sewn and tended entirely by robots and drones. In April 2021 in a nod to this new future, a farm in Nacton in Suffolk took delivery of the UK's first robot tractor.

It is a world that is already highly advanced in the aero and defence industries. The recent crashes of two of Boeing's 737 Max airliners in Ethiopia and Indonesia have made us painfully aware of the extent of 'roboticisation', when MCAS, an AI system designed to correct the plane's tendency to pitch, overrode urgent attempts by the pilots to prevent the planes crashing.

According to news reports – and hugely controversially – AI is already being deployed in weapons systems. In May 2021 *The New Scientist* printed a piece based on a United Nations Report that stated that autonomous drones had been used to kill soldiers in the conflict between Syria and Turkey.[2] The use of AI systems in warfare has provoked a heated debate, with a number of the world's leading AI computer scientists and ethicists signing a petition to ban the use of AI in warfare.

Despite that, military ethics committees in both France and the US have cleared the technology for use by their armed forces. The French military ethics committee gave permission for its armed forces to develop augmented soldiers and is considering medical treatments, prosthetics and implants that improve 'physical, cognitive,

---

2 David Hamburg, 'Drones may have attacked humans fully autonomously for the first time' (*NewScientist*, 27 May 2021) www.newscientist.com/article/2278852-drones-may-have-attacked-humans-fully-autonomously-for-the-first-time/.

perceptive and psychological capacities', and could allow for location tracking or connectivity with weapons systems and other soldiers.

The committee said that France needs to maintain 'operational superiority of its armed forces in a challenging strategic context' while respecting the rules governing the military, humanitarian law and the 'fundamental values of our society'.

As a result, it has forbidden any modification that would affect a soldier's ability to manage the use of force or affect their sense of 'humanity'.

A similar justification has been given by the US; according to the National Security Commission on AI (NSCAI) the US has a moral duty to its citizens to develop AI weapons.

'The National Security Commission on Artificial Intelligence humbly acknowledges how much remains to be discovered about AI ... Nevertheless, we know enough about AI today to begin with two convictions. First, the rapidly improving ability of computer systems to solve problems and to perform tasks that would otherwise require human intelligence – and in some instances exceed human performance – is world altering. AI technologies are the most powerful tools in generations for expanding knowledge, increasing prosperity, and enriching the human experience. AI is also the quintessential "dual-use" technology. The ability of a machine to perceive, evaluate, and act more quickly and accurately than a human represents a competitive advantage in any field – civilian or military. AI technologies will be a source of enormous power for the companies and countries that harness them.

Second, AI is expanding the window of vulnerability the United States has already entered. For the first time since World War II, America's technological predominance – the backbone of its economic and military power – is under threat. China possesses the might, talent, and ambition to surpass the United States as the world's leader in AI in the next decade if current trends do not change. Simultaneously, AI is deepening the threat posed by cyber-attacks and disinformation campaigns that Russia, China, and others are using to infiltrate our society, steal our data, and interfere in our democracy. The limited uses of AI-enabled attacks to date represent the tip of the iceberg. Meanwhile, global crises exemplified by the COVID-19 pandemic and climate change highlight the need to expand our conception of national security and find innovative AI-enabled solutions.

Given these convictions, the Commission concludes that the United States must act now to field AI systems and invest substantially more resources in AI innovation to protect its security, promote its prosperity, and safeguard the future of democracy.'[3]

It is a debate we take evidence on in Chapter 7, where Dr Matti Aksela, an AI expert from the cyber security company F-Secure, questions whether AI will weaponise the internet. In Chapter 8, the renowned and hawkish anti-China expert Brigadier General Robert Spalding and peace campaigner Professor Toby Walsh provide

---

3 See www.nscai.gov/.

competing evidence about the role of AI in warfare and whether we should be in an arms race.

This AI arms race prompted the famous Finnish hacker and technologist Mikko Hypponen to observe that it was as dangerous to win as it was to lose:

'For example, let's say that IBM issues a press release that it has made a breakthrough. It believes it is on the verge of superhuman intelligence, it is ready to demonstrate this next month and ship it next year, unimaginable right now. But let's just assume that it has made a breakthrough and it could do something like this. What would happen? Think about China's President Xi or Russia's President Putin. What they would see is that the Americans, are going to win the race.

This is the most important race. If the US win this race, they will win everything. The Americans will be superior in everything forever. They will win every race in every area. They will create every innovation. From now on, they will be the economic superpower forever. They will win every war. If that's the case, then the obvious thing to do is to steal that technology at any price. Or if you can't steal that technology, then you must destroy that technology, so your enemies don't get it.

To me, it would seem that an innovation at this scale would destabilise global peace, instead of bringing great benefits.'

The deployment of AI weapons systems poses the very real risk of causing great damage.

Paradoxically, one of the areas that many see AI having the greatest impact on is health. This has been emphasised by Aamir Butt, the former Chief Executive Officer of the AI cancer screening company TumourTrace in providing evidence for this book:

'It is better in some diagnostic fields and where it is not better, it will become better because the more data you gather, the more accurate your predictions become. That is a function of time. It's not if, it's when. In those areas where it is not better than humans it quite simply will become better as more data becomes available. One of the main reasons for that is that once an algorithm is trained to perform a certain task to the level that you require of it then it will always carry out that task.

It does not make mistakes. It does not get tired; it does not get overwhelmed. It does not suffer from anxiety or stress because it had an argument with its partner before it started work and its conclusions are not subject to interpretation. If you take those factors into account as long as it's been properly trained it will keep giving you the correct outcome.

In biology most things have an underlying pattern, put a certain number of chemicals together, and they will form the particular shape of a protein, that's an underlying pattern. If you have symptom A, and symptom B, and symptom C, the implication is that you have or have not got cancer, that's an underlying pattern that is being uncovered. Thus, in the area of medicine, anything that actually has an underlying pattern will benefit greatly from artificial intelligence and anything which is truly random, is unlikely to be a benefit.

I can't think of anything in biology which does not have a pattern that's waiting to be discovered. Our perception of free will is just biology we don't understand. If you think about our behaviour our responses are so governed by our biology that I think we will soon be able to use AI to explain a lot of what we do via our biology.

If AI uncovers a pattern that we do not understand the cause for that is very exciting because that then highlights an area that must be researched.'

This is a feature of the technology, which is acknowledged by the US NSCAI:

'AI is an inspiring technology. It will be the most powerful tool in generations for benefiting humanity. Scientists have already made astonishing progress in fields ranging from biology and medicine to astrophysics by leveraging AI. These advances are not "science fair" experiments; they are improving life and unlocking mysteries of the natural world. They are the kind of discoveries for which the label 'game changing' is not a cliché.

In 1901, Thomas Edison was asked to predict electricity's impact on humanity. Two decades after the development of the light bulb, he foresaw a general-purpose technology of unlimited possibilities. "[Electricity] is the field of fields," he said. "It holds the secrets which will reorganize the life of the world."

AI is a very different kind of general-purpose technology, but we are standing at a similar juncture and see a similarly wide-ranging impact. The rapidly improving ability of computer systems to solve problems and to perform tasks that would otherwise require human intelligence is transforming many aspects of human life and every field of science. It will be incorporated into virtually all future technology. The entire innovation base supporting our economy and security will leverage AI. How this "field of fields" is used – for good and for ill – will reorganise the world.

AI is already ubiquitous in everyday life and the pace of innovation is accelerating. We take for granted that AI already shapes our lives in ways small and big. A "smartphone" has multiple AI-enabled features including voice assistants, photo tagging, facial recognition security, search apps, recommendation and advertising engines, and less obvious AI enhancements in its operating system. AI is helping predict the spread and escalation of a pandemic outbreak, planning and optimising the distribution of goods and services, monitoring traffic flow and safety, speeding up drug and therapeutic discovery, and automating routine office functions. Recognising the pace of change is critical to understanding the power of AI. The application of AI techniques to solve problems is compressing innovation timescales and turning once-fantastical ideas into realities across a range of disciplines.'

The impact of AI on our lives will be so transformational that some have called it the Fourth Industrial Revolution – a title that is a significant understatement

6

given the changes it is already imposing on our lives, changes that as has already been highlighted have only just begun. For just as with previous technological revolutions such as the agricultural revolution and the three industrial revolutions that followed, one of the immediate consequences were job losses. The harnessing of waterpower either as hydro power used in water mills or as steam for cotton mills ended the careers of the hand loom weavers, whilst the introduction of electricity as described above further revolutionised industrial production in a similar way to the revolution brought about by the introduction of electronics, which has now ushered in the roboticisation of production lines that AI will manage.

In recognising that the industrial revolution was brought about by steam, Cambridge University's DeepMind Professor of Machine Learning, Neil Lawrence, provides important evidence about this human redundancy. It is apparent from the earlier comments about farming that a lack of humanity is occurring in processes that we used to view as central to our existence and cultural definition. As Professor Lawrence states, we like to think of ourselves as intelligent so when something replaces us, we confer upon it intelligence, while in this case it is simply a machine. In agriculture, as Professor Blackmore points out, the process of human redundancy has been ongoing. Farm mechanisation, enabled by the industrial revolution which could produce farm machinery, began to reduce manpower. With AI that reduction in farming is nearly complete: according to interviews carried out for PassW0rd, a dedicated technology radio programme on the digital radio station ResonanceFM, farmers are now swapping the tractor seat for a desk chair and a laptop.

Up until now the symbiotic nature of the impact of these various 'revolutions' has softened their impact. The Enclosure Movement that brought about the large fields that mechanisation and modern farming methods could take place upon forced peasants from the lands. They gravitated instantly to the slums of the cities and found employment in the new mills and factories of the industrial revolution. The argument has frequently been made by economists that while the initial consequence of rapid economic change is unemployment, the world of work also changes to create new jobs. With AI that development is less clear, indeed as the US NSCAI points out: it 'humbly acknowledges how much remains to be discovered about AI'.

Thus, the societal ramifications of this pervasive AI involvement are huge. AI can quite simply do a lot of repetitive tasks much more efficiently than the people who currently perform them, as we have seen from the robot takeover of the manufacturing industry. In South Korea mobile phone production lines for the company LG are totally automated, the only current role for human beings is to slide around upon cushions on their bottoms to clean and service the machines: a trend that has seen factory workers suffer a similar decline to that observed in farming.

Fear of the technology

This process of human redundancy will only continue because, as Aamir Butt observed, machines do not tire, do not sleep, do not make mistakes. Which leads us to the thorniest issue of the AI revolution – fear of AI. This fear is very real among ethnic minority communities – and with just cause.[4] As we will see in Chapters 10 and 11, bias in the way that data has been collected (or not collected) and even problems with some AI-controlled CCTV cameras are justifying concerns that ethnic minorities have with institutionalised discrimination in the system. Such technological distrust then has some very real foundations particularly given that the UK, with its 6m CCTV cameras, is the third most surveilled state in the world after China and the US.

There is a widespread feeling that this distrust of the machine and its motives will only grow as work opportunities are lost to robots. This has led some experts to warn of a similar reaction to that seen in 1811, when a revolt against mechanisation started among rural handloom weavers in Nottingham, Yorkshire and Lancashire who felt they were losing their livelihoods to the textile mills.

The Luddites smashed machinery and fought the army – at one time more troops were involved in suppressing the Luddites than fighting in Wellington's Peninsular War in Spain against Napoleon. The revolts famously became known as the Luddite Rebellion and were the origin of the use of the word Luddite for a person opposed to the introduction of new technology. The Luddites were not alone. In 1830 in England a similar movement known as the 'Swing Riots' started in Kent among agricultural workers, who attacked the threshing machines that they saw as being responsible for their loss of jobs. The plight of the agricultural workers was particularly acute because over the preceding 50 years they had not only seen the onset of mechanisation but also a profound change to their lives, as we have mentioned, due to the Enclosure Movement. This had taken the land in commons they had often used to grow food on to supplement their diet and income and handed it over to richer farmers as part of large parcels of land. The strips that the farm labourers had previously worked were then reassigned to them usually far away from the village and often on less fertile land, or were simply lost to them. This reaction may happen in the twenty-first century agricultural sector, unless the problems identified by Sir James Paice mentioned earlier are emphasised to the population.

Many are forecasting that AI will cause this predicament right across the economy, hitting every single sector and for the first time cutting into the livelihoods and careers of the middle classes that until now have been the champions of technological innovation.

Even the practice of law and administration of justice will not be immune, a point identified by the barrister Sandeep Patel QC, who specialises in technology, prosecuted the Lulzsec hackers and has researched the ramifications of AI at Oxford University:

> 'In about five years' time, 70% of the judicial work done by lawyers will be done by machine. I think that will apply to around 70% of jobs, apart from someone who is a ballet dancer, or a footballer or is in the arts. AI will

---

4 'Briefing note on the ethical issues arising from public–private collaboration in the use of live facial recognition technology (accessible)' (GOV.UK, 21 January 2021) www.gov.uk/government/publications/public-private-use-of-live-facial-recognition-technology-ethical-issues/briefing-note-on-the-ethical-issues-arising-from-public-private-collaboration-in-the-use-of-live-facial-recognition-technology-accessible.

inevitably compete or will encroach in most areas of life, whether it be work, play or entertainment. Already, AI machines are replicating scores which mimic Mozart and Beethoven.'

Patel believes that this legal revolution will inevitably lead to AI systems being interrogated in the dock and that barristers will either be trained in AI programming or will work alongside a team of technology advisers.

The nightmare scenario, where livelihoods are significantly impacted, has already been recognised by the EU, as evidenced by the European Parliament passing a resolution in February 2017 on Civil Law Rules on Robotics stressing just such employment fears.

Stealing the headlines

This widespread anxiety is currently manifested and to an extent fed by the media and Hollywood. It is a fascination that tends to follow two classic storylines that according to Tony Frost, twice editor of the *National Inquirer* the US's largest tabloid, are the only things to engage the public. 'The public are only interested in two things, sex and money, sex and money, in that order', Frost, an Englishman, told a colleague when he was Deputy Editor of the *Sunday Mirror*.

Thus, the stories that tend to get most coverage in newspapers are the possibilities of having a relationship with a robot, the ultimate machine takeover of your life, or of our losing out completely to robots.

The latter story is either manifested as robots taking over our jobs or of taking over our world in the guise of killer robots. A typical headline from June 2009 in the UK's *Daily Telegraph* was 'March of the killer robots'. It is a consistent theme.

At the launch of the House of Lords Report, 'AI in the UK: Ready, Willing and Able?' on 16 April 2018 *The Sun* newspaper ran the headline: 'Lies of the Machine: Boffins urged to prevent fibbing robots from staging Terminator style apocalypse'.

As the cyber security expert Mikko Hypponen confirms, it is a consistent position for the tabloids as we can see from a *Sun* headline over three years later on 8 August 2021, that ran: 'TERMINATOR TERROR: Meet the "killer robots" of modern warfare from AI-powered suicide drones to machine guns that choose their own targets'.

Since Fritz Lang's 1927 film *Metropolis* Hollywood and the world of films, also preoccupied with the same topics as the newspapers, expand the boundaries slightly but still along the same lines, opening up the idea of the AI takeover to explore the boundaries of what is human and how long it will be before AI technology can reach consciousness. This point is what the AI pioneer and thinker Ray Kurzweil calls 'the Singularity' and is a point that preoccupied the first thinkers on the subject: Mary Shelley in *Frankenstein* and the Czech writer, playwright and critic Karel Čapek in his play *Rossum's Universal Robots*. It is a topic that we explore in Chapter 17.

A pre-occupation with robots both beating and absorbing us is what prompted the Finnish cyber security expert Hypponen to observe that if he were an AI that had achieved sentience the first thing he would do would be an internet search to see what people thought of AI. Inevitably the AI would then discover that humanity was in morbid fear of it and that it would destroy any emergent AI if it could not dominate it at the earliest possible opportunity.

It is this potential conflict, this very real possibility of competition not just with us but also with AI systems that is leading to a blurring of lines that is significant now. The capabilities of AI are now outstripping those of humans. There are very real concerns that people, due to a tendency to anthropomorphise both machines and animals that has been noted since humans first created records, will begin to mistake machines for sentient beings – a possibility that has already led to the European Union promoting legislation that robot and AI systems must be discernibly unhuman. This safety measure is intended to prevent the exploitation of the vulnerable by technology systems with which they may have formed a bond. It is also significant that the EU stresses that we must also monitor any robotic enhancements made to disabled humans to ensure that they do not supersede able-bodied humans.

That the progress of AI development has reached such a level that some liken it to evolution has meant that the technology has begun to attract the attention of a significant number of people from different academic disciplines: philosophers, ethicists, neuro-surgeons, psychologists and inevitably religious experts from many faiths. The ethics of machines is now a hot topic.

Stanford University's Professor John Markoff, a Pulitzer Prize winning former technology editor of the *New York Times* in an interview for the PassW0rd radio programme in January 2021 shares this viewpoint:

> 'What is interesting about where we are now is that a decade ago at Stanford, there was probably one ethics class on campus, now you can't turn around on campus without bumping into an ethics class. A point that I made in the book I wrote 'Machines of Loving Grace' is that this is more about us as designers of machines and how we design the machines and how we design our relationship with the machines than it is about the machines themselves. I am now a little more hopeful because we're creating a generation of designers who are deeply immersed in thinking ethically about the machines they make.'

This point has not been lost on Murray Shanahan, Professor of Cognitive Robotics at Imperial College, one of the AI world's most influential voices who has called for empathy to be built into AI systems.

For Sherry Turkle, the Abby Rockefeller Mauze, Professor of the Social Studies of Science and Technology at the Massachusetts Institute of Technology, author of the *Empathy Diaries* and a noted opponent of our love affair with machines, this would be a step too far. Like the EU, Professor Turkle maintains that the lines of separation between people and machines must be maintained at all costs and that they should not be allowed to be humanlike. Professor Turkle states that the issue is not about putting empathy into the machines it is about putting empathy into the people who design them.

At a crossroads?

The emergence of a debate concerning the march of the machines is proof that we are now quite literally at an ethical crossroads about the use of AI technology in our world. This is not a statement that is part of the media scaremongering about AI because all of these technological developments now have the very real potential to achieve enormous good or harm, according to how we decide to use them.

AI can drive incredible developments in health as can be seen by the speed with which a vaccine to the COVID-19 pandemic was developed, but at the same time it can create weapons systems that will ban people from the battlefield. It can develop intelligence systems that penetrate deep into our personal lives and strip us of our privacy, a fact that the Chinese have found out to their cost.[5] In China, a state that is now virtually completely cashless, participation in society is now state controlled due to AI, a fact highlighted in a 2020 Amnesty International Report which called the situation in the Uighur province of Xinjiang 'a dystopian hellscape'.[6]

Such evidence of abuse is telling because knowledge of the potential of big data and AI among the public at large does mean that the technology is currently at a tipping point because of the possibility of a loss of trust. In many cases the potential for this to occur could happen due to confusion.

AI is a technology that few understand, as mentioned it is a technology that has the potential to develop fear among the general population very quickly. When that distrust of what AI can do is compounded by a fear of unemployment caused by the introduction of AI, some of the very real and necessary benefits of the technology may be lost, benefits that according to many are essential to the survival of humanity in the twenty-first century.

For instance, in energy use alone, according to a report in September 2021 from the World Economic Forum,[7] the use of AI can accomplish massive savings and help counter global warming by driving the energy generation sector closer to net zero emissions.

The report finds that AI has the potential to create substantial value for the global energy transition. Based on BNEF's net-zero scenario modelling, every one per cent of additional efficiency in demand creates $1.3 trillion in value between 2020 and 2050 due to reduced investment needs. AI could achieve this by enabling greater energy efficiency and flexing demand.

'AI is already making its mark on many parts of society and the economy. In energy, we are only seeing the beginning of what AI can do to speed up the transition to the low-emissions, ultra-efficient and interconnected energy

---

5 Ross Andersen, 'The Panopticon is Already Here' (*The Atlantic*, September 2020) www. theatlantic.com/magazine/archive/2020/09/china-ai-surveillance/614197/.

6 Amnesty International, 'China 2020' (*Amnesty International*, 2020) www.amnesty.org/en/ location/asia-and-the-pacific/east-asia/china/report-china/.

7 World Economic Forum White Paper, 'Harnessing Artificial Intelligence to Accelerate the Energy Transition (*WEF*, September 2021) www3.weforum.org/docs/WEF_Harnessing_AI_ to_accelerate_the_Energy_Transition_2021.pdf.

systems we need tomorrow. This report shows the potential and what it will take to unlock it – guided by principles that span how to govern, design and enable responsible use of AI in energy. Governments and companies can collectively create a real tipping point in using AI for a faster energy transition.'

It is an AI revolution in energy that will not only achieve cost savings and efficiencies but also one that will develop new markets and industries.

According to research from the Offshore Renewable Energy Catapult:

'The UK is targeting a seven-fold increase in offshore wind capacity by 2050, and with this growth comes the need for more operations and maintenance (O&M) activity. With windfarms set to be located in deeper, more remote, often challenging waters, securing safe access for humans will be a significant industry challenge.

Accelerating and investing in the development of advanced Robotics and Autonomous Systems will mitigate this risk and means robots will handle not only routine maintenance tasks, but also improve pre-emptive maintenance, which will extend the life of components and turbines at sea, supporting the industry's waste reduction drive.'

Again, like Saildrone, military drones and space machines, robots are going into places that are extremely hazardous to people. In the wind turbine industry alone the process which will create an onshore and offshore robotics market will be worth £1.3bn by 2030 and will increase to £3.5bn by 2050.[8]

This is a development of robotics to attempt to try to meet carbon neutral needs but one that will not necessarily lead to a huge number of jobs. Yet it is a function of AI and robotics that will be essential for our future.

In a similar vein according to the former journalist Professor Markoff, now a researcher at Stanford University's Centre for Advanced Study in the Behavioural Sciences whose work focuses on the future of work and AI, we have to quickly develop robotics if we are to solve rapidly approaching demographic problems.

'Some years ago, I met the Nobel prize-winning economist and psychologist Daniel Kahneman at a dinner, I had just been to China, and I was saying, the robots are coming, the robots are coming. They're going to steal all of our jobs, and Kahneman stopped me, and he said, you know, we'll be lucky if the robots come in time. I said, what do you mean? And he walked me through the demographics of the modern world. That really changed my framing of the way I saw the relationship between humans and robots.

We have a dramatically ageing population almost everywhere in the world, except for Africa. In America, Asia, Europe, there are ageing populations. And after I thought about that for a while, I realised that he was right. In China,

---

8   Gavin Smart, 'The Economic Opportunity for Robotics in Offshore Wind and Key Energy Markets' (*ORE Catapult*, 10 September 2021) https://ore.catapult.org.uk/wp-content/uploads/2021/09/ORE-Catapult-RAS-market-report-FINAL.pdf.

they don't have a large enough workforce to work and be able to look after the elderly. I have now changed the questions I used to ask. I have stopped asking, when will we have self-driving cars? When will we have a machine that can safely give an ageing human a shower? Nobody had an answer to that question. We still don't have an answer to that question. So, I'm afraid for our generation, the machines are not going to be here in time.'

To ensure that this does not happen it is essential that the new data-driven world of AI is trusted. As confirmed in the WEF energy report:

'For AI to contribute meaningfully to the future power system, it needs to earn trust from the engineers, employees and managers who run it. Everyone should feel comfortable with AI being part of their workflows, even if they are not developing the AI tools themselves ... The successful deployment of AI-based solutions by the end user will also involve education. Educating consumers on how their data is used in these algorithms, and what the limits of AI are, should help them best interact with it.'

A recurring theme throughout the evidence provided in this book is that transparency is the key to the adoption of AI: if people are suspicious about what it is doing and how it is doing it then they will not work with it.

AI on trial

This potential for the undermining of trust in AI and therefore the slow adoption of the technology will be heightened if AI remains unsecured and unsupported by a proper framework of law and regulation. The position that the AI world is in at the moment – and perhaps one of the reasons why Sundar Pichai, the Chief Executive Officer of Alphabet, the parent company of Google, called on the EU to develop AI regulation, and the reasoning behind such a call – is something that this book examines in detail.

There is no consensus about AI law, nor as yet is there a specific AI law. One possible reason for this is the power of the technology companies. The six largest companies in the world by market capitalisation are Apple, Microsoft, Alphabet, Saudi Aramco, Amazon and Facebook in that order. Five of those are tech companies, all of which are involved in AI research.[9] The size of the companies provokes very real caution among legislators. This point was stressed in the House of Commons evidence hearings into the draft Online Harms Bill in September 2021 to the legislators by William Perrin of the Carnegie Trust who said that any gaps in the regulations would be quickly exploited by lawyers for the tech giants. This contest will be all the greater given the far greater value promised by AI.

How much of a battle can be expected can be gauged by some early skirmishes over whether AI should be afforded legal status or personhood. One example of this is the number of attempts that have already been made to designate an AI machine as an inventor on a patent application. The latest patent application by Dr Stephen Thaler on behalf of an AI machine he had built called Dabus has been

---

9 See https://companiesmarketcap.com/.

thrown out by the Court of Appeal on the grounds that Dr Thaler did not follow the correct procedure.[10] Dr Thaler had failed to comply with section 13(2) of the Patents Act 1977 which required him to identify a person as the inventor and to indicate how he had derived his rights from that person.

It could be claimed that the law with regard to AI is in a similar state of development to the law in relation to cars when they revolutionised transport. A number of people claim that the car's adoption into society went ahead with few laws to control it and it was only after a number of problems were recognised (such as deaths caused by collisions) that the law mandated the need for seatbelts and air bags. This is a point we explore in Chapter 17.

Furthermore, with AI it is contended by organisations like the US technology industry lobby group the Information Technology Innovation Forum that so few people understand AI that there is a very real risk that poor legislation could be introduced which would damage the industry with the very real possibility that the US could lose out in the AI race to countries such as China, a point we explore through evidence of Brigadier General Robert Spalding in Chapter 8 and in Chapter 16.

This is a situation that currently prevails worldwide and one that Alphabet's Sundar Pichai is presumably hoping will be addressed by the EU in its promulgation of AI laws because, following the development of the General Data Protection Regulation (EU) 2016/679 (GDPR), the EU has emerged as a pioneer in technology regulation. It is notable that a series of US states and other jurisdictions have since developed legislation, broadly mirroring the earlier EU initiative.

With any law concerning AI, given not only its global but also its societal impact, it is submitted that any regulations and controls will also need to be imposed on a supra-national basis and that there may be a need to develop international consensus so that agreements can be put in place similar to those that govern nuclear and chemical weapons and genetic modification.

At the moment we do have the vestiges of some principles on standardisation which are being put forward by the Institute of Electronic and Electrical Engineers, and the International Standards Organisation with its SC42 committee, and we also have legislation being drafted by the EU and Switzerland, the development of some sectoral guidance in Singapore whose monetary authority is drawing up guidelines for the technology. The response to AI's rapid development is, in legal terms, still very patchy.

This official hesitancy is best understood by looking at the situation surrounding autonomous cars. In 1995, Carnegie Mellon University's NavLab 5 completed the first autonomous coast-to-coast drive of the US. Of the 2,849 miles between Pittsburgh, Pennsylvania and San Diego, California, 2,797 miles were autonomous (98.2 per cent), completed with an average speed of 63.8 mph. Yet despite this impressive feat the adoption of autonomous cars has largely stalled principally because of legal issues. It is a picture that mirrors that of the evolution of a legal regime more generally, despite the production of a number of white papers, executive orders

10 *Thaler v Comptroller General of Patents Trade Marks And Designs* [2021] EWCA Civ 1374.

and the musings of a number of committees, one notable example of which is the Select Committee of the UK House of Lords' most recent report 'AI in the UK: Ready, willing and able?'. As yet there is no discernible thread.

A final point that we examine is that even though many existing laws have been well tested over time, AI will not fit seamlessly into them because as we have seen from the recent judgment against Dr Thaler all of our laws seek to identify a human being as the instigator of an act. As in the recent case quoted from a United Nations Report by the *New Scientist* of an autonomous drone firing upon Syrian soldiers mentioned above, already the chain of causation is slipping from human hands and this will only increase. Whilst common law systems are well-placed at adapting old laws to new and unforeseen circumstances, law will have to develop to take into account new technologies. If Mrs Donoghue had bought her own ice cream float as is observed in Chapter 16, the law of negligence would not have traced its origins to the remains of a snail in a ginger beer bottle in a café in Paisley which had supplied the drink the ice cream was floating in. If we rely on this ad hoc approach as a model for the development of future laws to regulate a world governed by AI, then we may risk an uneven regime emerging that lacks the overarching coherence that a real attempt to lay out the ground rules an AI world will need.

To achieve that we need to establish key themes of AI regulation and that can only be done by getting to grips with AI and understanding what needs to be regulated. Our aim is to place AI on trial and to examine, through evidence presented by leading AI thinkers, scientists and technologies, what the AI revolution means, the potential it offers and the threat it poses, so that we can understand what framework is necessary to both support and safeguard against the technology, and to unlock and deliver the immense societal benefits it offers.

Our opening submissions (Part 1) focus on the building blocks of the technology, the importance of data and algorithms, and the present state of its development.

In Chapter 1, we hear from the inaugural DeepMind Professor of Machine Learning at Cambridge University, Professor Neil Lawrence, about the use of data and the vital importance of the integrity of that data. In Chapter 3, leading AI scientists based in Silicon Valley, Amy Hodler and Emil Eifrem provide evidence about the importance of data in context, where it is appropriate to use AI and where it should not be used.

In Chapter 2, Ben Lorica another Silicon Valley AI expert and commentator points out the present state of the AI technology; whereas in Chapter 4, Professor Reid Blackman talks about the critical role of ethics in AI adoption.

These building blocks are essential to a baseline understanding of the technology.

In Part 2 of the book (Chapters 5 to 15) we examine in detail certain of the key concerns presented by applications of AI through interviews we have conducted with pre-eminent thought leaders, including issues of data ownership, rights and responsibilities of AIs, cybersecurity, diversity, bias and questioning whether we might need a Hippocratic Oath.

Our closing submissions (Part 3 – Chapters 16 and 17) look at questions of causation and liability and whether now is the time for an AI law, before we present (Part 4) a view on AI expressed 'from the judicial bench' (with permission from Lord Sales, Justice of the UK Supreme Court) and conclude – in light of all the evidence and submissions – with a proposed manifesto for the development of an effective ethical, legal and regulatory framework which will support the realisation of the promise of this most powerful of technologies.

Part 1

Opening Submissions

Chapter 1

A question of definition

Professor Neil Lawrence is the inaugural DeepMind Professor of Machine Learning at the University of Cambridge and a visiting Professor of Computational Biology and Machine Learning at the University of Sheffield. Before taking up his present position, Professor Lawrence served as the Director of Machine Learning for Amazon, based in Cambridge.

His research interests are in probabilistic models with applications in computational biology, personalised health and developing economies. He has helped to develop the Open Data Science Initiative, an approach to data science designed to address societal needs.

In a series of interviews with Professor Lawrence, we tried to get behind the hype about AI and to discover useful definitions of what it is and what it can do.

In particular, we wanted to focus on the need to disengage Artificial Intelligence (AI) from many of the myths that have been fostered in film and media by pointing out that AI is currently not a sentient robot entity and may never be deployed in that way.

Through his evidence, Professor Lawrence shows that a more accurate way to view AI is not as an all-seeing machine but rather as algorithms that are deployed in our networks to seek out patterns that allow those machines to bring their findings to our attention. Another notable function of the AI system is to make decisions about the running of systems themselves, for example keeping a part of a critical infrastructure network such as an energy supply running. Accordingly, they will use feedback mechanisms deployed in a system and perform according to the significance of the information that the machines receive. This is a machine function, which Professor Lawrence demonstrates through his evidence using the example of James Watt's Centrifugal (or Flyball) Governor.

What is meant by the term 'Artificial Intelligence'?

There are three types of lies: lies, damned lies and big data. That is a paraphrase of a quote whose genesis has been lost in the mists of time, but was popularised by Mark Twain, who also came up with a quote which is more interesting: 'figures often beguile me, particularly when I have the arranging of them to myself'.

The quote is important, because there is actually a problem with the term 'Artificial Intelligence', specifically it implies that we are creating something that is, like us, intelligent.

And that's not true. All we are doing is using computers and statistics and those computers are feeding on our data.

'At the moment I am writing a book called *What is intelligence?* because in a sense that is at the heart of the question what is Artificial Intelligence and I think that the term is a nonsense' said Lawrence, who highlights that the term itself started out due to a turf war over the notion of 'thinking machines'.

The term 'Artificial Intelligence' (AI) was first coined in 1955 for the Dartmouth Summer Research Project on Artificial Intelligence in 1956 by John McCarthy,[1] who used it as part of his funding bid to the Rockefeller Foundation. One of the principal reasons of so doing, was because he was trying to move the area away from the influence of Professor Norbert Weiner, one of the founders of these ideas and the area of cybernetics.

For McCarthy, an Assistant Professor of Mathematics at Dartmouth College, the term was an important one because he wanted a new and neutral term that did not belong to anyone.

McCarthy's aim was to discuss the concept of machine intelligence and to define ideas about thinking machines and what they could do unencumbered by the ideas about the area that had been expressed by Professor Weiner, an irrepressible and brilliant academic with a reputation for assertiveness.

It is therefore an irony that, since its birth, the concept itself has led to arguments about what it is. The different groups are now splitting into two – those who champion Artificial General Intelligence, the development of a sentient machine,

---

1 In the early 1950s there were various names for the field of 'thinking machines': cybernetics and automata theory and complex information processing. The variety of names suggests the variety of conceptual orientations.

In 1955, John McCarthy, then a young Assistant Professor of Mathematics at Dartmouth College, decided to organise a group to clarify and develop ideas about thinking machines. He picked the name 'Artificial Intelligence' for the new field. He chose the name partly for its neutrality; avoiding a focus on narrow automata theory, and avoiding cybernetics which was heavily focused on analog feedback, as well as him potentially having to accept the assertive Norbert Wiener as guru or having to argue with him.

In early 1955, McCarthy approached the Rockefeller Foundation to request funding for a summer seminar at Dartmouth for about 10 participants. In June, he and Claude Shannon, a founder of information theory then at Bell Labs, met with Robert Morison, Director of Biological and Medical Research to discuss the idea and possible funding, though Morison was unsure whether money would be made available for such a visionary project.

On 2 September 1955, the project was formally proposed by McCarthy, Marvin Minsky, Nathaniel Rochester and Claude Shannon. The proposal is credited with introducing the term 'Artificial Intelligence'.

The Proposal states: 'We propose that a 2-month, 10-man study of artificial intelligence be carried out during the summer of 1956 at Dartmouth College in Hanover, New Hampshire. The study is to proceed on the basis of the conjecture that every aspect of learning or any other feature of intelligence can in principle be so precisely described that a machine can be made to simulate it. An attempt will be made to find how to make machines use language, form abstractions and concepts, solve kinds of problems now reserved for humans, and improve themselves. We think that a significant advance can be made in one or more of these problems if a carefully selected group of scientists work on it together for a summer.'

The proposal goes on to discuss computers, natural language processing, neural networks, theory of computation, abstraction and creativity (these areas within the field of Artificial Intelligence are considered still relevant to the work of the field).

20

and those who argue that AI is all about machine learning, known as 'narrow AI', the ability of a machine to derive meaning from data it can then make a decision about or refer through to a human being to make a decision.

'What is AI?, it's an interesting question because it depends on what people mean by AI and there's a group that clearly means what people are starting to call AI, but my opinion is that that's not even a defined concept. So, the idea of solving what intelligence is, without an application, seems to me to be fairly nonsensical because you have to define intelligence first, I know there's work on that but it's unclear.

But if you look at what we have managed to produce so far, I would say it's a form of automated algorithmic decision making that's based on data. We are in a position where I think if we can compartmentalise a given task, we can get humans to provide data or acquire data by watching humans or other entities going about their daily lives, then we can automate that task by reconstructing that data for a number of interesting domains, particularly often perceptual domains.

I would say that those are the sort of advances that people got excited about. The more human like abilities. These perceptual advances, particularly around vision, language, speech and really impressive things like translation and improvements to automatic machine translation',

but for Lawrence, these current advances do help to foster the elemental confusion that is emerging about AI and its potential sentience:

'If you think about more recent developments such as conversation – or chat – bots, these are performing in ways that it was hard for us to envisage not so long ago, even if you believed that we were going to be able to create models that could just learn directly from data. They are fascinating because, of course, they trigger questions about what is interesting for a human and they give rise to questions about achieving meaning, without sentience.'

'Everyone used to be very excited about chess until computers beat us at it', claims Lawrence, highlighting that such developments have inevitably led to a very dangerous tendency: anthropomorphising machines. This is a tendency that inevitably leads to the human insistence on either conferring sentience or a higher capability on machines.

What is the nature of our relationship with machines?

'One of the aspects of our intelligence, is we have to anthropomorphise things to understand them. Now, unfortunately, anthropomorphise is quite a difficult word to say, but it's a very easy thing to do.

And that's what we're doing with our AI. We're constantly turning it into an intelligence like us in order to better communicate with it, because that's how we communicate with these things, we have to have a model with each other. We have to have a model of who we all are. So, we're trying to do that with the computer. But of course, the machine learning computers are very different.'

This alludes to a frequent criticism of the systems, that the algorithms can make calculations and deductions at speeds that far outstrip our ability to follow.

'This causes a number of problems. It means it's hard for us to understand the mistakes that the computer makes and why it might be making them, it behaves in ways that go beyond our understanding.

We tend to think it's doing something very magical when in reality it's just operating on a very different cognitive basis to the cognitive basis we're used to as humans. That become very different at the interface between AI and human beings. Something we need to do a lot of work on, I think.'

According to Lawrence, this powerful human desire to anthropomorphise has not only led to confusion about intelligence existing in machines, it has also led to an inevitable confusion about personality existing in machines. Such confusion has existed since the start of our development of machines and is something to which we have grown accustomed since our childhoods. We are surrounded by characters like *Thomas the Tank Engine*. Sailors will speak of ships as feminine, whilst mechanics in garages and car owners have a tendency to attribute human characteristics to vehicles. A bad car might easily be referred to as though it is a bad person, rather than a machine not performing correctly through design or poor alignment.

This same quality in relation to AI and machine learning arose with the example of the 'Centrifugal Governor' (see below), a device invented by the Dutch scientist, physicist and inventor Christiaan Huygens for use in windmills to manage mill stones and which was then adapted by James Watt to control steam engines – an innovation that has often led to Watt being credited as the mechanism's inventor.

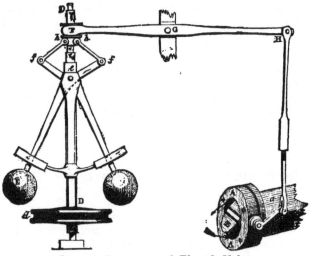

FIG. 4.—*Governor and Throttle-Valve.*

Source: R Routledge, *Discoveries & Inventions of the Nineteenth Century* (13th edn, Routledge, 1900).

22

The 'Governor' works because of two spheres that are mounted on the top of a vertical drive shaft and regulate the shaft's speed. As the shaft spins the balls are forced outwards by the speed of the shaft's rotation and a scissor mechanism immediately above the balls is depressed. This in turn is connected to a lever that controls the flow of steam to the engine that is powering the drive shaft. As the scissor mechanism is depressed the steam flow is constricted and the drive shaft slows. This action decreases the centrifugal force and lowers the height of the balls which in turn elongates the scissors mechanism which then increases the flow of steam. This is essentially the automatic regulation of a machine using physics, rather than data.

> 'So even though there are aspects that were considered special to us and those aspects are absorbed by the machine, we retain this essence that is us.
>
> And the term artificial intelligence moves us because it's got that special term in it, "intelligence". We want to feel that that's unique to us, which is why I think we need to ponder that question a bit and what we really mean. In the end I think we really mean anthropomorphic intelligence, when we're saying AI.
>
> And so, I think the way that the society looks at all of those things in the long term, perhaps not in the immediate term, at the moment when a machine starts to do something that humans were doing then it is AI.
>
> I think we are now in the period where something is AI because it seems to be something new that humans are doing but as we get more familiar with it, we realise it's a trick and not real intelligence.
>
> Obviously, it's not really a trick, it's an amazing thing, but that's the sense that humans have of it. They don't see machines today as being intelligent, take the example of James Watt's Governor: it's an intelligent mechanism, it is making decisions, but today you wouldn't see it that way. And yet on Holborn Viaduct, the Statue of Science actually holds the centrifugal governor in her arms. So, at one point, it was certainly seen as that.'

Lawrence's point is therefore that when an action taken by a machine can do something that is good it has a beneficial result, it produces power, but the action is unwitting. The objective of the machine was created by a human and is data dependent – the physics of the movement of the flywheel provides information in terms of physical force.

In the twenty-first century, the new power source is not steam, but data. The new mantra of the information age is that 'data is the new oil' (or increasingly 'the new oxygen') and its relationship to AI is, according to Lawrence, currently similar to that of the Centrifugal Governor, although with the key difference that many in the AI world think that the range and effectiveness of the technology can be greatly increased if ever more data is fed into it and the AI systems will be able to discover new tasks by themselves.

From the patterns the machines learn from this ever-increasing amount of data, the machines will then be able to arrive at the next questions they need to answer. Put simply, the systems will be able to learn from the data itself what they need to do and a 'universal governor' rather than a centrifugal governor will be born, which will feel as though it has the hallmarks of being a sentient AI with the capability of objective truth.

How do we move beyond one-trick ponies?

The thinking is that AI systems will eventually not be task specific, something that Lawrence says has not happened yet:

'The debate is – and there are people within the machine learning community who seem to believe this – that all that is required is more data and more complex models, and we can get non task specific AI, but broadly speaking, the AI we have that's working today is task specific. There are some examples of translation between tasks, but I don't see that as anything more impressive than what we were doing 10 years ago. The tasks themselves are more impressive, but the capability to translate from one task to another is not there. I remain unconvinced that we can make particular leaps forwards in that direction. And I think that's, maybe where my opinion differs from some other commentators who think that all that's required are more complex models and more data. That may be true. But I think we need a bit more thought about the structure of our models. I don't think that the approaches we're using around what people are calling differential programming, just deep learning in the sort of purest form that we have today are going to be sufficient for those tasks.'

At the moment, according to Lawrence, what we are seeing is the grouping together of a series of machines that have specific tasks with the possibility that another AI system could be sat on top of them all, that will then take the data outputs and 'learning' from the task specific systems and extract further meaning. Within that scenario every machine will still be task specific.

'I think that's effectively what's going on where you are seeing, intelligent agents, people are trying to compose that model. But one of the really remarkable things about, human intelligence is our ability to move between tasks.'

This is an ability that Lawrence maintains may keep humans employable for a while.

'Each of those tasks, when you distil it down, we can get a computer perhaps to perform those tasks more rapidly or more efficiently. But the ability to know when to switch tasks and what task needs doing next, is something that is quite difficult to replace, which is why so many jobs won't be replaced until people work out how to extract the repeatable tasks from those jobs and enhance the humans trying to do those jobs by assisting with those tasks.

I think that that is the way that we are seeing more intelligent systems being put together, but I think that they remain somewhat brittle. They don't have the robust capability of the human to do that sort of interaction and that's largely because they miss an enormous amount of context and even just reasoning about what a sensible decision is through knowledge of what the human condition is and what a good decision is by humans. At the moment much of AI is trying to interact with humans. In order to do that well, you have to really have a good understanding what it is to be human.'

To describe the current nature of AI, Lawrence uses the term developed by the philosopher Isaiah Berlin in his popular essay *The Hedgehog and the Fox* which expands upon a fragment attributed to the Ancient Greek poet Archilochus; 'a fox knows many things, but a hedgehog one important thing'.

Berlin develops this idea to divide writers and thinkers into two categories: first, hedgehogs, who view the world through the lens of a single defining idea – Berlin gives examples of hedgehogs as Plato, Lucretius, Dante, Pascal, Nietzsche, Hegel, Proust and Braudel. Foxes on the other hand, according to Berlin, can draw on a wide variety of experiences. Berlin provides examples of those foxes for whom the world cannot be boiled down to a single idea, such as Herodotus, Aristotle, Erasmus, Shakespeare, Montaigne, Moliere, Goethe, Pushkin, Balzac and Joyce.

> 'I think that the AI is like a hedgehog, and the public conception of it is that it's the perfect hedgehog. The hedgehog that means the fox is no longer needed. That's absolutely untrue and that is very worrying because it's partly about God creation and it's partially about having an omniscient entity. And in many of the things you see around 'AI intoning' like Elon Musk and a lot of people in this techno utopian world in California are just falling into these traps, about this all-seeing hedgehog. That is just not going to deliver.'

This is a view of AI that, according to Lawrence, brings further problems because people confer on AI and its use qualities which the technology currently does not possess.

> 'When they have those conversations, their fear is that the hedgehog somehow becomes evil or has different motivations. Whereas the reality is it's not an intelligent hedgehog. It will be deployed at scale. It will be a hedgehog, and it will be just stupid. It's this one big idea that has these defects in it that we don't see ...'

says Lawrence, adding that the role of humans in this relationship currently will be to be foxes in Berlin's terms, essentially directing the hedgehogs in their tasks.

> 'We've got to be fox-like about seeing what those defects are and introducing more of the fox into it. A lot of my talks, I suppose, are trying to disrupt people's view of the hedgehog.'

For Lawrence, the role of AI is to be augmentary: AI will provide answers and find patterns in data that may be missed by people, but humans should decide what to do with that data. This is a view of AI that Lawrence maintains we must develop if we are to avoid falling into other traps, one of the most dangerous of which is blind faith in the conclusions of AI and an inability, due to our technological reliance, to carry out important tasks ourselves. This essentially transforms Archilochus's hedgehog into a Delphic Oracle that must be consulted before any important mission is undertaken. Lawrence notes:

> 'The real problem with AI at the moment is no one understands the hedgehog, but they think they know what the hedgehog does and they think that that is

good, and that it will be able to solve our problems even though they do not understand how it came to its' conclusions. This has led to something I have termed "model induced blindness" or another term I'm trying to use a lot now is "model-thinkers". It's an idea I have borrowed part of from Professor Daniel Kahneman the psychologist and economist who wrote a lot about the psychology of judgement and decision making and his idea of theory blindness. But I think my concept is perhaps slightly different from the theory blindness that Kahneman talks about, because it's almost specifically when you've got a mathematical problem.

What is emerging from people in this current scientific environment is that they constantly give answers according to what their model is, which is an abstraction. This analogy is not truth in any sense or form.'

Lawrence adds that the potential risk from the combination of the model-maker, the data and from the AI is made even greater by the small number of people in the AI field:

'One of the issues we're seeing now with AI is this question of scale. It's one of the reasons the model creators hold so much power because unless you are an expert in that domain yourself, you can't question. So, then your inability to question them is the same as our inability to question the hedgehog in this case but when it turns out that the model or the hedgehog is stupid then society will have a real problem.'

This is a significant issue echoed by many of those involved in the AI community and by many AI commentators: that of politicians, legislators and administrators not understanding AI and how it works or failing to appreciate that it is only as good as the data model it uses.

A case of the blind leading the blind?

A criticism that is increasingly being levelled at politicians is that, of the 650 members presently sitting in the UK Parliament, only 26 have science degrees and few of those are in computing. Indeed, the high level of technology project failures in the UK has often been blamed on a lack of technological know-how in both the civil service and Westminster.

It is something of which Lawrence has first-hand experience:

'I had a session with a very senior Government adviser on the topic of AI and I had been spending most of the session talking about data. When we came to the end of our time he said: "well we talked about data a lot shall we now talk a little about AI?" I was quite shocked because I knew him to be a very capable Government official and so I assumed that he knew AI was all about data, but it seemed that he had been sold a line by major companies trying to sell him solutions and that they had told him that it was about the methods that they had.'

This is particularly important because, as Lawrence has stressed, not understanding how AI works and accepting the conclusions that it has come to will lead to a blind faith in the AI's conclusions that has already been noted. For example, research among the US military has found that the operators of military technology are unwilling to override decisions made by systems because they do not wish to take responsibility for making an error, a phenomenon that will almost certainly increase as AI systems become more and more widespread in our society.

'The term I've started using a lot in this space is intellectual debt, which is a Professor Jonathan Zittrain term, And of course, people will be unwilling to switch off, or intercede because they don't understand what the machine is doing, because no one understands what the machines are doing because of this intellectual debt phenomenon, which is you can create a machine that does everything it's told to do but, since you created it in parts and no one works on the whole, it leads to a management issue on the result.'

A problem which, according to Lawrence is compounded by two factors, the sheer amount of data that is being processed and the billions of calculations that the AI is performing:

'It's like a consequence of the "Mythical Man-Month" the book by Fred Brooks.[2] You create an entity that is beyond any individual's understanding. So, when it makes a particular decision, it could even be the right decision but to understand why it made that decision, you have to trace through these interlocking set of components, when I worked at Amazon on the supply chain, we used to do this. It came up a lot. It's a great system, the most efficient in the world but sometimes it would do something unexpected, and we would think why the hell did it do that?

So, to understand that you have to trace back and find the point that the event happened. The system can't explain itself because it doesn't know what you're looking for, unlike humans for example who can explain themselves. Of course, you have to think that their explanations may or may not be true, but we've adapted to what those explanations are.

With human explanations, we understand the limitations at some level of those explanations, and we can communicate with each other despite those limitations. The machine doesn't have any of this. This is a reason why intervening is so hard, because your intervention could be the wrong call if you do not fully understand why the machine did what it did.'

The problems of the mass of data being processed by the system and the speed at which it is occurring – Lawrence adds – are then made even more challenging due to the speed that people can process information.

'Take Jean-Dominique Bauby, the former editor in chief of French "Elle Magazine", who, suffered a brain stem stroke in 1993, that almost completely disabled him, so he could only move his left arm, remarkably Bauby wrote a book that took him, about seven months at four hours a day. Now we all

---

2 *The Mythical Man-Month*: a book by IBM Software Project Manager Fred Brooks (Addison-Wesley, 1975), whose central argument is that large programming projects suffer management problems different from small ones due to the division of labour; that the conceptual integrity of the product is therefore critical; and that it is difficult but possible to achieve this unity.

instantly imagine what it would be like to be in that state, in this new world we live in – relative to AI – we actually are in a worse state, we are in a locked in state.

Using "Shannon information theory"[3] as a measure Bauby could communicate at a rate of six bits a minute One bit of information is the equivalent of a coin toss. Using Shannon, I can tell you that I'm roughly communicating to you at a rate of two thousand bits per minute.

The IBM AI debating system can communicate at a rate of around 60 billion bits per minute. So, to put that in context, two thousand bits per minute – two thousand is a reasonable monthly salary. Now think of 60 billion it's the wealth of the richest person on the planet being paid to you every month.

It's a very, very different type of cognition that is reliant on things that are beyond our understanding. Yet it's a very powerful technology that is in a very nice way, complementary to our own ability.

Now what we like to do is to think about the motivations of all around us and anthropomorphise them and then communicate that. And we do that to these machines. That's why we like to give things names and motivations. But in reality, they don't have names or motives.

There's a danger to this to paraphrase a famous quote and say, "lies, damn lies and big data", because big data are a potential new route to manipulating the statistics that are presented to us and the facts that are presented and many of us will not know that is happening. In the past this danger was perceived and the invention of the field of mathematical statistics was designed to deal with that danger.

So, people like Dalton, Pearson, Fisher looked at data, and the misrepresentation of statistics, and they said this is how you represent it so we can draw correct conclusions.

Unfortunately, they also decided that an appropriate use of this new technology was eugenics because they thought they had some single access to some underlying truth about how you could prove that humanity should move forward.'

---

3 Information theory studies the transmission, processing, extraction, and utilisation of information. Abstractly, information can be thought of as the resolution of uncertainty. In the case of communication of information over a noisy channel, this abstract concept was made concrete in 1948 by Claude Shannon in his paper 'A Mathematical Theory of Communication', in which 'information' is thought of as a set of possible messages, where the goal is to send these messages over a noisy channel, and then to have the receiver reconstruct the message with low probability of error, in spite of the channel noise. Shannon's main result, the noisy-channel coding theorem, showed that, in the limit of many channel uses, the rate of information that is achievable is equal to the channel capacity, a quantity dependent merely on the statistics of the channel over which the messages are sent. Put very simply, more water can flow through a bigger pipe.

To be, or not to be, AI: that is the question

It is, according to Lawrence and many others interviewed for this book, one of the greatest mistakes that we continue to make with AI, an insistence on seeing in it both the route to an objective truth and a potential god-like superbeing that we wish to unite with.

> 'That is an enormous mistake that we continue to make where AI is present, that there is some objective truth that we can optimise ourselves towards, that we aren't anything more than a collective of information processing individuals who are massively handicapped in our ability to communicate to each other. And we perform this extraordinary cognitive dance in order to believe in this.'

It is a dance that means that a lot of AI converts see the next stage of evolution not as being augmented by AI but as amalgamating and fusing with it: essentially a capitulation based upon the inevitability of our losing out to AI development.

This is a notion that Lawrence says has roots in the satirical novel *Erewhon* written by Samuel Butler and published in 1872.

> 'Samuel Butler was writing on the evolution of the machine in Erewhon, he discusses in the book about consciousness and machines becoming sentient, which was considered laughable at the time.[4]

> He could have seen no roots to that because what he was talking about was so distant. But what it does reveal is a sense that these machines of the industrial era could combine with evolution. He was very inspired by reading Origin of the Species, which had been published 13 years before Erewhon and was sufficient for him to feel that we were creating some form of intelligence or life. But, of course, what happens is people are born into that and they realise the special nature of our intelligence.'

Lawrence, however, thinks that there may be a religious rather than Darwinistic motive in part of the desire to achieve oneness with a machine, that some are casting as an approaching deity.

> 'I've become very interested in the interface between humans and religion because some of it is so resonant that you just can't help but feel something

---

4 Samuel Butler, 'The Book Of The Machines' in *Erewhon* (Trubner & Co, 1872): 'Consciousness, in anything like the present acceptance of the term, having been once a new thing – a thing as far as we can see, subsequent even to an individual centre of action and to a reproductive system – why may not there arise some new phase of mind which shall be as different from all present known phrases, as the mind of animals is from that of vegetables....There is no security against the ultimate development of mechanical consciousness. A mollusc has not much consciousness. Reflect upon the extraordinary advance which machines have made during the last few hundred years and not how slowly the animal and the vegetable kingdoms are advancing. The more highly organised machines are creatures not so much of yesterday, as of the last five minutes,...in comparison with past time. Assume for the sake of argument that conscious beings have existed for some twenty million years: see what strides machines have made in the last thousand! May not the world last twenty million years longer? If so, what will they not in the end become? Is it not safer to nip the mischief in the bud and to forbid them further progress?'

on. I refer to these people as Singulartarians, this notion of AI as religion is very, very powerful. The things that are being spoken about it are that effectively the computer is an omniscient God and that we will have the capability to upload our brains to it, effectively a form of immortality. An associated idea is that we will have the capability to extend our powers by augmenting ourselves with an AI and achieve the powers of a demigod.

I often think Scientology is a religion masquerading as science and this seems to be the opposite, science masquerading as religion. That's perhaps not surprising because there are questions that science doesn't do a great job of answering about the human condition and people are maybe snatching for AI to help answer those questions. I think it's an error and I think it actually misses much more interesting questions about who we are, which could also be triggered by thinking about what AI is.

I don't see AI as a great power, but I do think it asks interesting questions about what we see as uniquely human and who we are.

My perspective is opposite to that of transhumanism, which is saying that we want to move beyond the current constraints we are under, because I feel we're remarkable creatures, because of the constraints we're under, which is really about that capability to communicate, our capability to share ideas because they're very bandwidth constrained. That's what makes us beautiful and incredible, while transhumanism says, we want to connect ourselves to the Internet to be able to transmit at the same speed as computers and I think that doing that probably leads us to become something uninteresting and essentially non-human.'

It is a point that Lawrence is adamant about and he warns against what he calls the great AI Fallacy: the notion that it will be the first generation of automation that's going to adapt to us:

'AI is going to be the first automation technology that adapts to who we are rather than us having to adapt to what it is.'

For Lawrence, the AI we currently embrace is 90 per cent machine learning that is as dispassionate as the Centrifugal Governor of the Industrial Revolution. The AI is not in humanoid machines called robots, it is in our networks as algorithms and as the data that they process, a data processing that will only increase with the deployment of the sensors in the Internet of Things – devices that will open our doors, windows and monitor our living spaces, spending, movements and health – literally our lives.

It is the algorithms and data that are the building blocks of the AI and necessarily need to be the focus for any legal, ethical and regulatory regime. Robots will exist, but they will be empowered by the AI in the network, which will control them and decide when they will work and when they will not.

'The AI will undermine our cognitive dance because in our interaction with it we have placed it in a role where it can see who we are and they peer deeply into our soul because of the amount of data we dispense every day, these machines know us better than we know ourselves. That is because

30

within you there is a model of who you are that is incorrect. You all think you are nicer people than you genuinely are. The machine knows who we are. That is limiting our freedoms, it's limiting our aspirations because through knowing who we truly are the machine can undermine us and it does that in an emergent relationship.

So, my main argument is akin to Pascal's Wager: we should believe that AI will do us harm because it is the best way from preventing us from falling into those harms. If we say, that AI has some universal good that will take us on a journey of freedom and health, we'll be in for a sorry end as a civilisation.'

Chapter 2

The state of things

Dr Ben Lorica *is an AI data scientist based in Silicon Valley. He is the Program Chair of the Spark+AI Summit and Co-Chair of the Ray Summit. Dr Lorica is also the former Chief Data Scientist at O'Reilly Media, and the former Program Chair of the Strata Data Conference, the O'Reilly Artificial Intelligence Conference, and TensorFlow World.*

Throughout his career, Dr Lorica has advised several technology start-ups, early growth companies and organisations in dealing with all aspects of data, machine learning and AI.

In our discussions with Dr Lorica, we focussed on the present state of AI: how is the technology being deployed at the moment? Which areas of development are anticipated? What might the barriers to those developments be? Through his evidence, we explore with Dr Lorica where the relevant areas of consideration would necessarily need to be in respect of a legal, ethical and regulatory framework for the technology.

What is the state of AI at the moment?

'The AI term that is bandied about in the media is really machine learning and that machine learning technology is a field that has been around for a while, since 2011 or 2012, which was when some people started showing that deep learning was particularly promising.

What they found was that deep learning in particular excels at things that are very useful for products. In particular, it excels in simple perception tasks such as, for example, computer vision, image recognition, object detection, speech recognition, natural language processing and understanding.

So, I think right now I would say that AI is a set of building blocks, that, at some point might start showing real promise in terms of intelligence, but I would say right now it's a set of discrete building blocks.

The three most commercially applied building blocks are: (i) computer vision, giving systems the ability to see and recognise objects; (ii) speech technology, the ability of systems to understand, to transcribe accurately what someone is saying and maybe even make recordings that sound like a human is reading a book; and then finally, (iii) in the area of natural language processing, which is the ability to respond to what someone is saying in the way that a chat bot might.

If you look at most of the AI systems, they use some of these building blocks in one shape or form.

So, for example, if you looked at autonomous vehicles, they will use computer vision, and object detection because being able to see what's in front of you and to respond to it is fundamental to driving.'

As with Professor Lawrence, Dr Lorica shares the view that there is a degree of confusion that pervades any discussion concerning AI because the media likes to encourage such confusion and portray AI systems as almost sentient machines, whereas in reality they are more akin to technological systems, which have been trained to look for underlying patterns in data. Any conclusions reached are necessarily on the basis of these correlations, but these are achieved at speed.

'Right now, at least that is true. The most promising systems that we have are in the field of machine learning and within that field they tend to be in a certain form of machine learning called "supervised machine learning", which relies on having labelled examples. It is supervised, and you need to teach it patterns. This means you input the right pattern and then when it identifies what it thinks is an example of that pattern you either confirm that it is, or you then reject its conclusion so you develop a system of pattern identification reinforcement.

There is another area that is also showing some promise though the applications are less widely deployed because the methodology is a little harder and that is called "reinforcement learning". The Alpha Go example of that I think is what people most often talk about. That was when an AI program developed by the now Google-owned DeepMind beat a 9-dan master in the Chinese board game Go (or Weigi). But there are other examples where AI systems have been winning at video games and multiplayer video games.

There are also some signs of early potential applications for reinforcement learning in regular companies. So, for example, some companies are starting to introduce reinforcement learning in some of their recommendation and personalisation systems. By introduce I mean, they're retaining their existing systems, but they're layering reinforcement learning on top of the existing systems so that the AI systems begin to learn from the decisions that are being made by humans on the existing system.

Another area where reinforcement learning is showing promise is in industrial automation. In areas where, for example, where you have an expensive piece of equipment or machinery that in the past has been tuned manually by humans. Now you can use reinforcement learning to relieve some of the humans of the more mundane tasks.

Most recently, there's a class of software, that is widely used in companies for simulation that is now being connected to AI systems. These are simulation software systems and there are several software vendors in this area. Some of them are even billion-dollar companies. They are systems that businesses have used for a long time used to simulate things like their factory floors, their retail stores, and their logistics and other parts of their operations.

If you look at the user interface of some of this software, some of the simulation software actually allows you to depict the environment that you're simulating. Let's say it's a retail store or factory floor. With AI you create an interface that could look a little like a computer game, using graphics and AI controlled agents and a factory floor lay out. It makes sense to ask yourself, can reinforcement learning play a role in simulation?

This is now starting to happen. There's a start-up here in San Francisco called Pathmind.com, which integrates with simulation software and uses deep reinforcement learning to enable businesses to simulate even more complex scenarios.'

Given his contention that what we are really referring to are instances and applications of machine learning, for Lorica there is a very real question as to the utility of the term 'Artificial Intelligence'.

'I would say right now, I think it's useful as a rallying cry, but more precisely, I think, that as I alluded to earlier, that most of what we are really talking about falls under the umbrella of machine learning. Obviously though, AI is an inspiring goal to some people, so it's a good rallying cry.

In fact, I myself have a podcast and I recently interviewed a friend of mine, Professor Kenneth Stanley,[1] who is a pioneer in a field called neuro evolution or open-endedness. While open-endedness in particular may be less practical at the moment but it's really something that the people in the AI community are really starting to look at.

Essentially, open-endedness creates open-ended algorithms. The aim of the exercise is to develop algorithms that can continue to solve more and more complex problems. It will train itself and it will do so in many ways, such as inventing problems for the algorithm to solve.

The first open-ended algorithms were tasked with traversing obstacle courses. Once they had mastered those the algorithms responded by building more and more complex obstacle courses to conquer.

I'm bringing this up to point out that that's the point of the term AI right now, it's useful because it inspires a lot of people. It's a great rallying cry. It's also a great funding, rallying point, but for all intents and purposes, most commercial systems implement some form of machine learning or a system that is comprised of many, many different machine learning systems.'

How does it work and how are decisions taken?

'If we look at machine learning itself, then it works in the way I described, which is basically you ask yourself, is this a problem where I have data, and can I get labelled data? Do I have enough scale to justify training a model?

---

1   www.cs.ucf.edu/~kstanley/.

And then you go ahead and train a model, given that you have the data with which to train the model.

The way it works right now, for the most part, is supervised. You need to come up with problems for which you have labelled examples to teach a machine.

If you give it enough examples, it will build a model that can perform the tasks that you want it to do. So, if the task is to transcribe this piece of audio or if the task is to recognise objects in this video stream.

Let's say I have a surveillance camera that's running 24/7 and I decide, I really need to understand when someone is opening the door. If you give it enough examples, then it will be able to summarise your video stream and provide you with instances where someone is opening a door.

If I want to transcribe audio, then it will work in a similar way but with one caveat. One of the things that people who work in speech will always point out is that "understanding" speech for an AI is a lot harder than "understanding" written text, because for one thing, we don't speak perfectly, in the well-crafted sentences that we use in written texts.

There's a lot of pauses, fillers and "ums" and we tend to repeat ourselves a lot. It's a tendency that I am now very familiar with because I have a podcast, and we do transcripts for some of the episodes.

And what we do, is we use an AI tool to do the transcription and then I hire a human editor to make it the more readable. I think at some point, if you could tell the system to make the transcript, more sensible by removing all of the repeats and removing all of the fillers and so on. However, by doing this you might have a transcription service that is 100 per cent. accurate, but the text might still be unreadable.'

How should we use AI and where should it be deployed?

'Think about something that you do, that is repeatable and that you think could happen without doing it yourself. That's where I would start. If you think about your typical day, there are some things that you would probably rather have a machine do instead.

There are other issues though, which depend on the limitations of the technology today. For example, we talked about the development of AI systems for eyes – computer vision – and for ears – speech – but there's also arms and legs, so the development of robotics is another area in which we are seeing deployment where the system can help people.

Maybe some most of the things you might want a machine to do require lifting and movement and there maybe you will hit some of today's limitations because the technology is either not good enough or not affordable enough.

I'm sure there are certain things that you can come up with in your day to day life where you can imagine automation playing a role. The other way to think about this is automation, workflow automation. In terms of deployment, so in a typical company, what workflows are repeatable for which we have data and for which we can actually automate, given the level of current technology? Where you can automate something to either achieve efficiencies or cut costs, the chances are you will do so.

One example I mentioned earlier is surveillance cameras. No-one wants to watch a surveillance video, that could be 200 hours long because they have to find a two- minute-long incident. If you can train a machine to find that two minutes, then everyone is better off. People don't want to carry out a long and tedious task where they could also run the risk of missing the incident because they became bored and their attention lapsed, or they walked away from the system and left it running. A trained AI will find the images very quickly, meaning the details of that particular incident could be available within an hour, rather than in days.'

Should there be limits to where AI can be used?

Just because AI or machine learning can be deployed in certain areas or for certain applications, does not mean that it should be used in that way. Lorica highlights the need for a sensible debate to take place as to where the boundaries of the use of AI should be set:

'I definitely think that there should be limits in terms of what it should be used for, and I think we should have that conversation.

The problem here, is that in terms of AI and in terms of those types of settings, military settings for example, then they would have to be subject to the same types of conversations and treaties as the other similar serious weapons, such as chemical weapons for example or nuclear missiles.

But I don't know if those conversations are happening right now, especially given the challenges we're facing in the world. To what extent do these two countries talk among themselves about bio and germ warfare? The same level of discussion that has to happen with AI.'

As set out in the Introduction and as is referred to elsewhere in these opening submissions and in the evidence of others, AI is presently being used in the criminal justice system and facial recognition applications are being used by the police. Perhaps controversially it has been used in certain jurisdictions for sentencing guidance, with troubling results. Lorica believes transparency of the technology is what will ultimately help us determine whether AI should play a role or not:

'In the examples you just cited you need to make sure that your citizens are aware that you're using AI. There should be full transparency – an open process where people can provide feedback and where people maybe push back if they don't agree with its deployment in particular areas.

37

Other topics that comes up a lot these days in in AI circles are transparency, trust and explainability. So, I think all three of these point to the fact that people, the humans and here even the users of the technologies, want to understand, even at a high level, how these systems work? How do AI systems make decisions? People want to know the answer, so that they're more confident about using them.'

In terms of that transparency, Lorica accepts that there are a lot of people who have limited or no understanding of AI (including technically literate professionals) but notes that, at least at some level, there needs to be an understanding of whether an AI system is involved and, if so, to what extent.

'If people know that AI is being used in a particular device or setting, at least they know the type of system they're interacting with. And there might be some people involved who can understand and who can ask the right questions.

So, it's, I guess it's like any other piece of technology, for example, do you understand precisely how a car works? Probably not, but if you have a friend who's a mechanic that you trust, you can transfer some of your hesitation over to him and then he can reassure you. It is a similar situation with AI.

It is not just that we need know that AI has been involved somehow, giving us transparency but we also need to be able to ask, experts to audit these systems on their behalf; in an ideal scenario, you don't want these systems to be audited by the people who built them. In other words, there has to be some accountability.'

Such accountability and transparency could be provided by AI itself, where an AI system sits on another system and explains what it is doing. Lorica notes that this so-called explaining AI system is a whole new area of active research for academics and industrial researchers:

'They can either be built by the system itself, or by the people who built the AI, which is good, because they need to know how their systems work. But they can also be built by a third party, independent of the people who built the system which is again desirable because then we can hopefully have faith in their independence.'

Can we trust AI at the moment?

The importance of trust in these technologies generally, and in relation to explainability, specifically, is critical. Indeed, at least theoretically, somebody could interfere with the explainability of an AI system so that it deliberately disguises or misreports something that it is doing. A good example of that would be what happened in the US sabotage of the Iranian Nantanz nuclear enrichment plant where the technicians monitoring the computers were being told the wrong things by the computers because their system had been interfered with. They were told the system was working perfectly because it reported it was, whereas in fact the sensors had been disconnected and the centrifuges were being destroyed. The question is therefore whether we are going to be able to keep AI honest in the pursuit for transparency and trust.

'That is a good question, but it's a bit hard to answer because AI has not yet developed to that level, so these notions of security are not quite there yet. What we have right now are a different products and systems that rely on machine learning. Each of those systems need to be audited and tested.

That's the area of transparency and explainability.

But now people are also starting to talk about security. How do we make sure that these systems that rely on machine learning are secure because they're also software systems?

Software systems get attacked, as you know. So, I think that people are beginning to realise this as more and more of these systems get deployed. What people are beginning to realise is that they need to set up teams that draw on people from many different disciplines and backgrounds.

You can't just have people who are experts in machine learning. You might need people who are experts in security, cryptography, privacy, even compliance.'

Have we already lost control of AI development?

One of the images or one of the plots that people in Hollywood and writers love, is that of the system out of control, the system enslaving us. Indeed, Lorica wryly notes that one could imagine a new film where an AI is responsible for a global pandemic which 'takes over the world' by ensuring that we stay in our houses for years.[2] Whilst this would appear to be firmly in the domain of mythmakers in Hollywood, there is a need for certain coding constraints to be placed on the development of AI:

'These are things that people are trying to grapple with right now. I think that there's a group at the University of California, Berkeley headed up by Professor Stuart Russell[3] that's trying to come up with frameworks to make sure that AI is built in in a proper way, including the control mechanisms that you describe.

There's also an effort to make sure that there are at least groups that are doing things in the open that can match what the commercial companies are doing.

One good thing, is that a lot of the research does tend to occur in the open, papers are published, source code for the programs are published. What's probably missing are just the data sets and one of the reasons for that is

---

2   The initial interview with Dr Lorica, in which he made this observation, took place on 26 April 2020 – the first UK lockdown was announced on the 23 March 2020.
3   See www2.eecs.berkeley.edu/Faculty/Homepages/russell.html. Professor Russell provides evidence in Chapter 13.

because they are commercially sensitive. Some companies have better data sets than others, so they have an inherent advantage.

So yes, there definitely are research groups that are trying to think through how to put in those safety mechanisms and this is a conversation that's happening in the research community.

On the other hand, for the most part, most researchers are focused on building systems that do very specific tasks because that debate is taking part around what is called AGI,[4] artificial general intelligence. Right now, people are focused on systems that can do narrow tasks in very specific domains.

While the conversations are going on around failsafe mechanisms[5] for AGI development they may not occur as actively among the people who are building these more specific systems. They are beginning to talk about other relevant issues like fairness and bias, privacy and security, explainability and things like this but the fact that these conversations are happening now while the machine learning systems are still fairly narrow and specific, is a good sign to me.'

Imposing constraints of ensuring oversight?

Some people have been suggesting that there may be the need for some independent software overseeing body, the equivalent of a Federal Drug Administration for software to say what is good AI and what is bad AI.

The proposed aim would be to explain the aims of a given product or service and its intended objectives. It would then be tested against these parameters and only if approved would its development and roll-out be permitted.

Lorica notes that there is nothing in principle to object to here, although questions how workable this would be in practice as there are many systems being developed and how such a regulatory system would be used would inevitably vary considerably.

'I think we have to be careful, as to what domains and settings, these systems are deployed in that could become a difficult area and it may not be necessary because often in areas like health and public safety regulations already exist that govern what can be introduced. For example, for computer vision technologies that are in driverless cars because they are out on the road. There is public safety involved and I can see that there's some kind of certification of minimum competency.

I think that these conversations are already taking place inside the community of machine learning.

People are aware of the issues I listed earlier, fairness and bias, transparency and explainability, safety, reliability, privacy and security. So, in many ways,

---

4   See https://en.wikipedia.org/wiki/Artificial_general_intelligence.
5   See Chapter 13 and, in particular, the contribution of Professor Neil Barrett.

I think that these teams need to take this more to heart rather than have some government oversight body.

My hesitance has to do with the fact that machine learning will be powering many different kinds of applications and different use cases and settings, which could hamper AI development. At the moment if I push out a new application on my website, I don't have to get it certified by a government board and these new systems will be as ubiquitous as those.

In other words, these systems will be all over the place which could generate a huge government bureaucracy and it may start to concern itself with whether I put an AI in the micro-controller of a washing machine – which is less than a dollar in costs – just to make sure that it tells me when the washing machine is vibrating for predicted maintenance. So, do I have to have this AI that goes into this sub one-dollar microcontroller certified by the government? It's for predictive maintenance. The thing is it's a microcontroller for less than a dollar.

If you look at the current situation with cybersecurity, you can put up a web site now, no one is certifying. No government body is certifying you. But on the other hand, there are private companies that can audit you and certify you. It just seems like there might be a healthy balance here between what can be done by the community and what can be done by a government party that might not be well-funded enough to, to deal with the volume of devices and software.

But, let's map this over to cybersecurity. You can put up a website right now, but you may not be an expert. It might have all sorts of holes in security, there's no government oversight. But you can cause a lot of harm because you can leak private information.'

So is the issue not just technology, but humans and humanity itself?

'There's two parts to this: there's the data and there's the people working on a project which is why I think it helps if you have a team of people building these systems who come from many different backgrounds. There's the whole cultural background, but there also needs to be a background in perspective.

If your team is made up of people who basically went to the same schools and studied the same kind of degrees, then maybe that's not ideal. You need teams that come from many different backgrounds, both culturally, intellectually and academically.

People might try to fit in with the rest of the team, but people are starting to think through the risks involved with these systems and how they can deal with those issues.

How do we manage the risks from AI? One way that people are thinking about this is in those categories, that I've been listing Fairness and bias, safety and reliability, security and privacy, explainability and transparency. Let's look at security and privacy in this system. Well, the people who built the systems, if they all come from machine learning, that's probably not enough. You also need people who come from a security background.

In other words, as people recognise that there's risk involved in deploying the systems. I think they're going to start setting up teams that reflect those risks. As I have mentioned before, in order to grapple with some of these risks, we need to draw from a broader pool of people and I think a lot of those people will come from disciplines that people have not thought of before such as compliance, but also ethics and philosophy and the arts.'

Ultimately, however, Lorica confirms that it is not always the machine that will do bad things, but the people who deploy them. And it is the intentions and aims of the users that will not always be clear. This is necessarily a relevant factor in any ethical, legal or regulatory regime.

Increasingly, it would appear that according to Lorica everything seems to point towards the fact that we need to become better people, rather than it being uniquely the fault of technology when things go wrong. 'I think that's always been the case.'

Chapter 3

The building blocks of responsible AI

Amy Hodler is the Director of Analytics and AI Programs at Neo4j, using graph analytics to reveal structures within real-world networks to infer dynamic behaviour. In her career, Amy has worked with and for start-ups, emerging companies and big technology companies, including EDS, Microsoft and Hewlett-Packard.

Through her evidence, Ms Hodler shows how data and – perhaps crucially – the context or prism through which such data is viewed creates 'contextual information', which is key to an AI being able to take complex and valuable decisions. Such context is also vital to ensure that the data sets are used responsibly and provide a route to which decisions can be understood and explained.

We see it in the abstraction of cyberspace and in the concreteness of everyday things – the world is becoming increasingly connected. I carry two phones, I have a watch that is connected, my car has anywhere between 75 to 125 computers embedded in it, that are connected to each other and to me, but also to the internet and social media. And as the world is becoming increasingly connected, so is data.

What's interesting about relationships and connections in data is that these areas actually offer clues to understanding reality. They are the clue to knowledge. And if you think about how the human brain works, it is ultimately a set of neurons connected through synapses, a network. Meaning, context and intelligence emerge from these connections. The same is true in data. The more we know about how things fit together, the more we can understand that data and draw conclusions.

If we look into the world of AI and machine learning, it turns out that the interaction between elements, people and things are the best predictors of all. There is plenty of research in the social sciences to bear this out. The pioneering work by social researchers James Fowler and Nicholas Christakis[1] has demonstrated that emotion spreads from person to person to person and up to three degrees of separation, even among people who are not acquainted. And not just emotions, but actual behaviours, from the likelihood that you smoke, tend to obesity, suffer from suicidal tendencies and even how you vote.

---

1   James H Fowler and Nicholas A Christakis, 'Dynamic spread of happiness in a large social network: longitudinal analysis over 20 years in the Framingham Heart Study' (*BMJ*, 2008) 337.

As Christakis puts it:

'We discovered that if your friend's friend's friend gained weight, you gained weight; we discovered that if your friend's friend's friend stopped smoking, you stopped smoking; and we discovered that if your friend's friend's friend became happy, you   become happy.'

Think about the conclusion of that: if all you know about the individual is facts about their network, then you have a statistically significantly better ability to predict their behaviour than if you know everything about them as an individual.

What has this got to do with AI?

Well, one of the key consequences is that AI algorithms are able to predict behaviour far better if they are supplied with contextual information – our networks of relationships – to solve the problems we want them to address. Connected data and the context that provides, help AI to deliver more complex, nuanced decisions.

Ethical standards

It is becoming increasingly clear that AI should be guided not only by robust data governance, but robust ethical standards as well. A key overlapping principle in both of these areas is context. Contextual information not only results in better performing AI systems, but also in a clearer ethical perspective for those creating and shaping it. Context helps us understand the factors and pathways of logic processing (and be able to explain them) so we can hold organisations accountable for AI decisions.

Working with both highly as well as lightly regulated industries and governments, we have learned that worries about complex data – and its use in AI – are a worldwide concern, a fear accompanied by a feeling that no single organisation should regulate this alone.

The potential of AI is so immense and it will be used in ways we cannot yet imagine. Despite, and perhaps because of this, we have a duty to guide its development and application in ways that facilitate innovation and fair competition, public trust and confidence, while incorporating sufficient protection for the citizen.

Biased AI

A real issue in AI is avoiding the danger that we will automate human flaws and biases. For example, Amazon had a recruiting tool it had to shut down after realising it was biased against women. This was not the original intention for using automation: Amazon's HR team had actually set out to seek more balance, but it was training its AI recruiting based on current, mostly male employees. The firm didn't explicitly know or look at biological sex or gender, but it turns out when you look at LinkedIn profiles and résumés, men and women have a tendency to choose different sports, social activities or clubs, and adjectives to describe accomplishments. So, the AI was picking up on these subtle differences and trying to find recruits that matched what they internally identified as successful.

Unknowable AI

Beyond bias, there's also another concerning area: unknowable AI. Many of us have heard about the metaphor of the inscrutable black box. It's very hard to explain how AI arrives at right answers because we can't decipher its decision-making process, but if it's accurate, who cares?

Take the case of US citizen Glenn Rodriguez, sentenced after participating in a robbery when he was 16. Glenn spent 10 years being a model inmate. He volunteered and mentored others to do better as well. When the time came to learn the fate of his parole, everybody, including himself and his lawyers and even the parole board, was initially in favour of granting Rodriguez parole and giving him another chance.

But Glenn was denied parole because a computer assessment had produced a high-risk score. Everyone was surprised, but no-one was willing to go against the software's apparently objective, fact-based decision, which was based on over 100 different factors, as well as lots of different weightings.

Despite requests, the company behind the decision was not required to share any information. The good news is that on a third subsequent parole hearing, Glenn finally did get parole. After looking at the likely data, and comparing his scores to others, there was a subjective question that changed his risk score significantly. His lawyer surmised this, but since no one could see the data, this could never be proven.

This is an example of a truly unknowable black box. When it comes to unknowable AI, there seem to be just two different types of unknowable situations; software that's really complex and difficult to understand, and the type that we're not allowed to look at. Both of these are problematic.

Inappropriate AI

The third type of concern is inappropriate AI. This is where AI is working exactly like it was intended to, but with questionable outcomes. The ethical issue here is just because we can, does not mean we should.

The Chinese Government has implemented a social credit system that will credit both your financial credit worthiness and also your social worthiness. The system takes into account things you might normally consider, like were you late paying a bill. Then there's also things that are more behavioural, like trying to limit jaywalking.[2] The system uses facial recognition to see and track if you cross the road at the wrong time. It can do the same if you smoke in a non-smoking area, which would negatively affect your social score.

---

2   A term, which originates in the US to denote where pedestrians are walking in or crossing a road that has traffic, other than at a suitable crossing point, or otherwise in disregard of traffic rules.

The problem is this social credit score impacts everything, from whether you get a mortgage to whether you can get high-speed internet. So there's a lot of ramifications to personal rights, and it is believed by next year, there will be 1.4 billion people who live in China and have a social credit score.

For me, this is an example of 'we can, but I don't believe we should'. The idea of bias in data and algorithms, unknowable AI, and inappropriate AI, has confirmed to my mind that we have a responsibility.

Creators of AI and those that implement systems that rely on AI, have a duty to guide how these systems are developed and deployed. We have a responsibility to implement AI in a way that aligns with our social values.

Next, let's take a look at how we can build a foundation for more responsible AI.

The foundation for responsible AI

To be clear, when I talk about AI and AI systems, I am talking about end outcomes or solutions, which depend on processes that have been developed to work in a way similar to the way we humans think, which is very probabilistic: if I think about how I make a decision, I am hopeful it's a good solution, but I am never 100 per cent sure.

So we have the what (AI systems), and then we have the how, which is machine learning. Machine learning is about the algorithms trying to iterate to optimise a solution based on a set of training data or examples it has been given. But we don't have to tell it how to do that. We make tens of thousands of decisions like this every day, which we do by looking around our surrounding circumstances; you grab information and likely don't realise how much, or what, you're taking in. You mentally make connections, and then you try to make the best decision you can with the context and the information you have at the time. Then you move on.

It shouldn't be any different for AI.

The computer requires that same type of information – the same context and connections – so it can learn based on the context. With all that adjacent information, AI systems can make necessary adjustments, just as we do, as circumstances change. And circumstances always change, don't they?

AI without context

Take an example: 'We saw her duck'.

This can be interpreted in many different ways. Does it mean *I ducked*? Did somebody throw something at me? But maybe it means we saw a friend's aquatic fowl. It might mean somebody named 'We' saw their pet duck. Or maybe even that we went over to a friend's house for a duck dinner. There are probably other interpretations as well.

Without context, AI can only ever be narrowly focused on exactly what we've trained it to focus on, resulting in sub-par predictions outside the relevant domain. It also means reduced transparency – and if you can't explain how a decision was made, then you can't hold people accountable and you're not going to trust the decisions that come out of it.

Graphs as the fabric for context

There are no isolated pieces of information in the natural world, only rich, connected domains all around us. This is where a branch of mathematics called 'graph' comes in. Graph theory, and nowadays technologies based on it, was specifically developed as a way to represent connected data, and analyse relationships within that set of data. Very simply, a graph is a mathematical representation of any type of network, and graph technologies are designed to treat the relationships between data as equally important as the data itself.

Graphs were not only built to understand relationships, they were built on relationships. And that's significant, because in nature you don't get any unrelated, isolated data points. In data handling terms, graph database and platform stores and uses data as we might first sketch it out on a whiteboard, showing how each individual entity connects with or is related to others. It acts as a fabric for our picture of our data, imbuing it with context and connections. Graphs help us incorporate the fabric of connections in the data, which enrich the data and in so doing make it more useful, in the same way perhaps that individual stars in the sky become more meaningful if we look at them a different way, as constellations. And they turn out to be pretty useful; with the context they provide, we have been navigating for thousands of years.

If we next think about layering on additional context and information, we start to develop maps, which helps us answer all sorts of questions: How do we get from point A to B? How many routes are there from point C to D? What's the most efficient manner for me to do that? And then, we can add in more context like traffic, to answer practical questions, such as how do I reroute during different times of day when traffic is bad?

Imagine adding in even more context, such as what companies like Lyft are doing to disrupt transportation. We're now able to add more information, such as multiple user requests and the price point they are willing to bear. We can layer on more context, like their various pick up and drop off needs. And ultimately, we add more value in the form of well-coordinated rides that are priced perfectly. It's efficient for the driver, for the riders, and a pleasant experience – everything happens seamlessly.

The more you add context, the more value you add to the data and what you're already doing. In a property graph model – technology that was built to see data as a set of connections, not as rows and columns in a table, which is what older computer models used to represent the world did – we have nodes that represent objects and directional relationships – each of which can have properties/attributes. Woven together, they create a *fabric of context and connections* that makes our data more meaningful and useful.

Graph technologies were originally custom-built and used internally by game-changing companies like Facebook, Google, Uber, Netflix, Twitter and LinkedIn because those row and table approaches fell short of their need to find connections between people, places, locations and systems in their data. Now, they are used across multiple industries, including government, financial services, healthcare, retail, manufacturing and more. In fact, graph technology deployments encompass a broad variety of use cases that include fraud detection, cybersecurity, real-time recommendations, network & IT operations, master data management and customer 360.

More recently, graph technologies have been increasingly integrated with machine learning and AI. These applications include using connections to predict with better accuracy, to make decisions with more flexibility, to track verifiable data lineage, and to understand decision pathways for improved explainability. Furthermore, graph technology has been recognised as a major leap forward in machine learning. In 'Relational inductive biases, deep learning, and graph networks', a recent paper from DeepMind, Google Brain, MIT and the University of Edinburgh,[3] researchers advocate for '… building stronger relational inductive biases into deep learning architectures by highlighting an underused deep learning building block called a graph network, which performs computations over graph-structured data'.

The researchers found that graphs had an unparalleled ability to generalise about structure, which broadens applicability because, '… graph networks can support relational reasoning and combinatorial generalisation, laying the foundation for more sophisticated, interpretable and flexible patterns of reasoning'.

For any machine learning or AI application, data quality – and not just quantity – is foundational. If we use contextual data, we create systems that are more reliable, robust and trustworthy. Graph technologies, which naturally store and analyse connections, allow us to holistically advance these goals. And in fact, the amount of research being published on the use of graphs with AI has also skyrocketed in recent years, from less than 1,000 to over 3,750 graph-related AI research projects.

To summarise, if context can be incorporated into AI we might derive better conclusions and predictions, as well as curb the bias issue, while at the same time ensuring that we apply these technologies in ways that do not violate our societal and economic principles. AI that doesn't explicitly include contextual information will result in less useful outcomes as solution providers leave out valuable, adjacent information.

Next, we'll look at the contextual building blocks to improve AI systems in two fundamental areas: robustness and trustworthiness.

---

3 Peter W Battaglia, Jessica B Hamrick, Victor Bapst, Alvaro Sanchez-Gonzalez, Vinicius Zambaldi, Mateusz Malinowski, Andrea Tacchetti, David Raposo, Adam Santoro, Ryan Faulkner, Caglar Gulcehre, Francis Song, Andrew Ballard, Justin Gilmer, George Dahl, Ashish Vaswani, Kelsey Allen, Charles Nash, Victoria Langston, Chris Dyer, Nicolas Heess, Daan Wierstra, Pushmeet Kohli, Matt Botvinick, Oriol Vinyals, Yujia Li and Razvan Pascanu, 'Relational inductive biases, deep learning, and graph networks' (2018) arXiv:1806.01261v3 [cs.LG].

Building robust AI with context

According to Stratistics MRC, the global fraud detection and prevention market was valued at $17.5 billion in 2017 and is expected to grow to $120 billion by 2026, and there's been over 48,000 US patents for graph fraud and anomaly detection issued in the last 10 years. And financial services companies are indeed turning to graphs to reveal predictive patterns, find unusual behaviour and score influential entities, and contextual information in machine learning models.

Even beyond the obvious fit in financial services, people are using graph algorithms in various industries to engineer more predictive 'features' that train AI models for higher accuracy and precision. It was estimated several years ago that there was $72 billion a year in insurance fraud related to the tragedy of the ongoing opioid crisis. Recent estimates of the direct cost of opioid abuse on US services such as healthcare, legal services, childcare and support care are at a staggering $100 billion a year. This is a significant issue, both sociologically and economically, and experts believe fraud is an area to target because we have the data – we know where the money flows. Looking at this insurance information, using community detection graph algorithms, we actually get to see the relationships between doctors, pharmacies and patients, and how tight those communities are. Fraud has a shape, and graphs are really good at understanding the topology of data. Relationships and community detection help to identify where the clusters and patterns lie and then use machine learning to more accurately identify fraudsters.[4]

Situational flexibility

Situational awareness and appropriateness is another concern for AI where context-based learning and action are critical. Consider how we want an age-appropriate chatbot sensing and responding differently in an interaction with a seven-year-old versus a 30-year-old. This isn't a fanciful example as a mental health chatbot created for use by children was unable to understand a child explicitly reporting underage sexual abuse, as reported by the BBC.[5]

To head off these kinds of damaging instances before they happen, AI-based systems need to be flexible, which includes designing AI in a way that views user interaction as critical to the design and implementation of autonomous decision-making systems.

Contextual information also helps an AI solution flex within new situations that it is untrained for, reducing failures and equipping it with new data or unexpected scenarios. For example, a semi-autonomous car might be programmed to decelerate in rainy weather, but we would also want it to expand its AI application

---

4 An example of this method can be found in a research paper, 'Graph Analysis for Detecting Fraud, Waste and Abuse in Health Care Data', where graphs were used to find structural communities that were more predictive of fraud. Juan Liu, Eric Bier, Aaron Wilson, Tomo Honda, Sricharan Kumar, Leilani Gilpin, John Guerra-Gomez and Daniel Davies, 'Graph Analysis for Detecting Fraud, Waste, and Abuse in Healthcare Data' (AAAI'15: Proceedings of the Twenty-Ninth AAAI Conference on Artificial Intelligence, 2015) 3912–19.
5 Geoff White, 'Child advice chatbots fail to spot sexual abuse' (*BBC*, 11 December 2018) www.bbc.co.uk/news/technology-46507900.

to incorporate contextual information such as a drop in temperature and when approaching a bridge. Or especially difficult, situationally apply learning to break for objects in the road such as a dog but not slam on the brakes for a paper bag or flock of birds. Many are aware of stories such as autonomous vehicles that change lanes based on stickers on the road.

The problem is wider than driverless cars, though. It is about anything important that makes autonomous decisions or semi-autonomous decisions. In cases where autonomous decisions are broadly implemented, situational awareness actually becomes critically important. Dealing with situations beyond narrow/safe limits we've defined for the system in advance, and being flexible to different situations, is the only way we'll be able to safely implement AI in larger environments. That means being able to learn based on context and incorporate adjacent information – which is what graphs are all about.

Building trustworthy AI with context

Trustworthiness is a critical topic for AI standards efforts and is strongly called out in the EU Ethics Guidelines, the US Government's National Institute for Standards and Technology, which is creating a plan for the next wave of US AI Government standards, in ISO Standards' workgroups on trustworthiness and governance, to name a few.[6] Broadly when we think about trustworthiness, we need to consider how we enhance and increase the reliability, fairness and trust from an explainability standpoint. Let's look at how context can help us.

In order for AI solutions to be reliable and fair, we need to know what data was used to train our models and why. Unfortunately, this isn't straightforward. If we consider a large cloud service provider or a company like Facebook with an enormous amount of data, it is difficult to know what exact data was used to inform its algorithms, let alone which data may have changed.

Graphs add the required context for this level of explainability. For example, graph technology is often used for data lineage to meet data compliance regulations such as GDPR or the California Consumer Privacy Act (CCPA). A data lineage approach is also used on NASA's knowledge graph to find past 'lessons learned' that are applicable to new missions. When we store data as a graph, it's easier to track how that data is changed, where data is used, and who used what data.

Understanding and monitoring data lineage also guards against the manipulation of input data. For example, corporate fraud research has shown that when the significance of input data is common knowledge, people will manipulate information to avoid detection.[7] Imagine a utility system or voting infrastructure where we might be confident in our monitoring software, but could not rely on the input data. The whole system would become immediately untrustworthy.

---

6   *Plan for Federal Engagement in Developing AI Technical Standards and Related Tools* (NIST, 2019).
7   Wei Zhou and Gaurav Kapoor, 'Detecting evolutionary financial statement fraud' (2011) 50(3) *Decision Support Systems* 570–75.

We need to have reliability in the output of our AI systems. And I could have the best system in the world. But if my data has been manipulated, how do I rely on that? We need to know where the data's been and who's touched it. We need to know exactly when it was changed, what the chain of relationships are and how that data may be used somewhere else. That's a classic graph data lineage problem, and trusting your systems so you trust the data is essential. You could have fantastic, unbiased data – but if someone tweaked that data, the outcome is no longer trustworthy. Fortunately, graphs are really good at allowing us to track the chain of data change and subsequent ripple effects.

Finally, context-driven AI systems avoid excessive reliance on any one point of correlated data. Organisations are beginning to apply AI to automate complex business dependencies in areas such as data centres, batch manufacturing, and process operations. With contextual coordination, they avoid the trap of noisy, non-causal information and use root-cause analysis to maximise future efficiency. Contextual information helps us identify the root cause of a problem as opposed to just treating a symptom.

Fairness

Understanding the context of our data also reveals the potential biases inherent in existing data as well as how we collect new data and train our models. Existing data may be biased by the fact that it underrepresents one gender, which is a known issue in medical studies.[8] Or perhaps an AI's human language interactions were trained on a narrow age or accent range. Higher arrest rates for minorities become embedded in prosecution data. When historical input data is used for predictive policing, it causes a vicious cycle of increased arrests and policing.

The Royal Statistical Society published an Oakland, CA simulation analysis of a Machine Learning approach often used for predictive policing[9] and found that rather than correcting for the apparent biases in the police data, the model reinforces these biases.

The COMPAS software for risk assessment system (and which was part of the problem the rejected parolee, Glenn Rodriguez, faced above) is also used in many cities when a person is booked, before they're indicted or face criminal charges. The software is used to assess the risk to reoffend, and the public defender, lawyer and others may view this score and use it to make judgements. But, notoriously, COMPAS consistently gives Black Americans higher risk scores than white Americans.

How could we try to make this system more fair and ethical?

Part of seeing bias in data that is often overlooked is knowing where your data came from, who collected it, how they collected it and when they collected it. There's a kind of chain of evidence in data collecting and how it's used. If we better

---

8 Sergey Feldman, Waleed Ammar, Kyle Lo, Elly Trepman, Madeleine van Zuylen and Oren Etzioni, 'Quantifying Sex Bias in Clinical Studies at Scale With Automated Data Extraction' (*JAMA Network Open*, 2019) 2(7):e196700. doi:10.1001.
9 Kristian Lum and William Isaac, 'To predict and serve?' (2016) 13(5) *The Royal Statistical Society* 14–19.

understand the chain we help reveal biased data that otherwise may not be readily apparent.

Contextual data can assist in privacy efforts because relationships are extremely predictive of behaviour. This means we can learn from peripheral information and collect less information that is less personally identifiable.

Trust and explainability

A machine learning model is mostly done on existing data, but not all situations can be accounted for ahead of time. This means we'll never be completely sure of an AI reaction to a novel condition until it occurs. Consequently, AI deployments need to dynamically integrate contextual information. For example, researchers have developed an application that predicts the legal meaning of 'violation' based on past cases. However, legal concepts change over time and need to be applied to new situations. Because graph technologies capture and store relationships naturally, they help AI solutions adjust faster to unexpected outcomes and new situations.

Summing up, to increase public trustworthiness in AI, predictions must be more easily interpretable by experts and explainable to the public. Without this, people will reject recommendations that are counterintuitive.

Considerations for building responsible AI

Finally, let's briefly turn to some considerations for implementing building blocks for responsible AI. If you're in the initial stages of planning and collecting data for an AI system, the first thing is to know what's in your data and track your data – that's table stakes, very simple.

(a) Debias your data

There are toolkits out there to help balance and remove bias from your data such as the AI Fairness 360 toolkit.

(b) Involve your experts

Your data doesn't necessarily speak for what is most predictive or what success looks like, so include subject matter experts throughout the process.

(c) Use developer resources

Access more tools, like the Algorithmic Justice League, for understanding things like more fair algorithms and advice.

(d) Use interpretable models

If you have a Black Box model and an interpretable model that are equally accurate, you should favour the method that can be explained. The Prediction Lab at Duke

University provides practical papers for guidance and free code for interpretable models.

(e) Add context, like a knowledge graph

You can add a knowledge graph to an AI system so it can make better predictions using context or for faster heuristic decisions. For example, adding a knowledge graph to a shopping chatbot so users are directed to the best product to fit their current needs.

(f) Explainability v interpretability

If you have high-stakes decisions (things that could negatively impact lives), insist on lay-understandable explanations that are accurate, complete and faithful to what the AI system is actually doing.[10]

(f) Conduct a risk assessment

You need to look at the potential outcomes of your model performing poorly – before you put it into production. It could be something as simple as a checklist, such as the EU checklist contained in its guidelines,[11] or a committee to review risks.

Summary

AI is not all about machine learning. Context, structure and reasoning are really important for us to improve AI. Graphs and connected data are key elements that allow us to do that, and that's why we're seeing the research involving graphs significantly increase.

Another final thought on the future of AI is encapsulated in this quote from theoretical neuroscientist Vivienne Ming:

> 'If you're not thinking about the human problem, then AI isn't going to solve it for you.'[12]

The danger now is that the power and reach of AI is so significant. More significant than it has ever been. But we cannot AI our way out of all of our problems. In particular, if we're codifying our own human flaws, we've got to deal with the human flaws at the same time.

Although the evolution of standards is imperfect, we are seeing governments and standards bodies making the necessary first steps in encouraging reliable, robust, and trustworthy systems that use AI technologies. The lesson for the AI system builder today and tomorrow is clear: when considering such a broad and evolving area of technology, integrating context should be foundational.

---

10 Cynthia Rudin, 'Stop explaining black box machine learning models for high stakes decisions and use interpretable models instead' (2019) 1 *Nat Mach Intell* 206–15.
11 *Ethics Guidelines for Trustworthy AI* (EU European Commission, 2019).
12 *Understand Your Love/Hate Relationship With AI*, interview with Vivienne Ming on Salesforce.com.

Chapter 4

The ethics dimension

Professor (ret.) Reid Blackman is the CEO of Virtue Consulting, an ethics consultancy that focuses on corporate governance and emerging technologies like Artificial Intelligence, biotech, and virtual and augmented reality. He works with senior leadership to devise strategies and policies that mitigate ethical risk and with product developers to incorporate ethically responsible design practices. Blackman is a senior adviser to the global accountancy firm Ernst & Young and sits on its Artificial Intelligence Advisory Board.

Prior to launching Virtue, Blackman was a Fellow at the Parr Center for Ethics at UNC Chapel Hill and a Professor of Philosophy at Colgate University. He received his B.A. from Cornell University, his M.A. from Northwestern University, and his PhD from the University of Texas in Austin.

Blackman sits on the 'Methods to Guide Ethical Research and Design' committee for the IEEE Global Initiative on the Ethics of Autonomous and Intelligent Systems and is a member of the EU AI Alliance.

Throughout our discussions with Blackman, we were keen to explore the role that ethics should play in any framework that is developed for Artificial Intelligence.

As with the evidence of Professor Lawrence in Chapter 1 and Dr Lorica in Chapter 2, Blackman treats discussions of AI as properly referring to machine learning:

> 'When people talk about AI, they're talking really about machine learning, we're talking about machine learning in specific areas. What a lot of people seem to be asking is: "are the machines conscious or self-conscious or sentient or whatever"?
>
> Of course, the answer to that is no. That's why we have the distinction between artificial general intelligence (AGI) and artificial narrow intelligence (ANI). What we are dealing with at the moment when people talk about AI is ANI and most of it is machine learning.
>
> I think people don't pay much attention to the difference between a difference in degree and a difference in kind.
>
> It could do this thing that computers before could do but, now it does it a million times faster. Previously AI could only handle chess now it can handle the Chinese game of Go. But that's different than, say, judging someone's character. Those things have nothing in common. That's one issue. The other issue is that the way that the AI system gets programmed, often the

output is some kind of number. You'll use AI to give a numeric score for a defendant to see whether the number indicates the likelihood that they're going to commit a crime or be arrested in the next two years, or what their credit score is or something like that. And when numbers are the output of machines for some reason, people are inclined to trust it. I think the implicit reasoning behind it seems to be something like, well, the computer is doing math and math is objective.

So, we can trust it. Which is problematic, of course, because it's the programmers who are creating the algorithms that the computers process and the programmers might make important mistakes in their programming. Or they might be pulling data in from places where it's just not relevant.

They can do, technically speaking, a bad job. They can do, if you like, not technically, but if you want to call it qualitatively, a bad job by, for instance, choosing the wrong metrics to optimise or mistaking one metric for another. Or even taking data that's flawed.

It could be a technical problem; it could be a qualitative problem. It could be both.'

The ethical perspective

In August 2019 the American Round Table[1] released a statement saying that US corporations should put the interests of people before profit. This was around the same time that Blackman was appointed as an ethical adviser to one of the world's largest accounting firms, specifically to deal with the issues raised by technology. Blackman notes that this represents a step-change and a departure from past practices.

'I am an ethics consultant and that essentially involves ethical risk consulting. That couldn't have been a viable business five years ago. What's driving the change is consumers, citizens and employees really pushing for companies that don't prioritise profit over people.

---

1 'On Monday, the Business Roundtable, an association of over 180 chief executive officers of America's leading companies, headed by the well-respected CEO of JPMorgan Chase, Jamie Dimon, released a statement that could radically change the mission of corporations and the lives of their employees. For over 600 years, capitalism has reigned supreme. Companies were expected to generate the most profits for their shareholders. The employees, vendors and communities where they operate were of lesser concern. All that mattered was the bottom line and how much the shareholders earned on their investments. The pursuit of profits prevailed over everything else. The Business Roundtable recommended that corporations must change the way they operate and now focus on their employees, the places where they conduct business and their vendors to ensure that everyone is treated fairly. This will come before the needs and wants of the shareholders. The CEOs assert that Americans deserve an economy that allows each person to succeed through hard work and creativity and to lead a life of meaning and dignity. They believe that the free-market system is the best means of generating good jobs, a strong and sustainable economy, innovation, a healthy environment and economic opportunity for all.' Jack Kelly, 'Top CEOs Sign a Statement Prioritizing People Over Profits: What It Means For Employees' (*Forbes*, 20 August 2019).

Survey after survey from big consulting firms verify this. Companies are beginning to wake up to it and for the most part are increasingly talking the talk without walking the walk. Some companies like Ernst and Young are forward looking and they see the momentum that's being built around ethics. So, they're getting ready for this new world, which will involve ethics because not considering ethics will impact the bottom line.

You cannot get big tech companies to become more ethical, just because it helps them sleep better at night. That's not going to happen. Ethics needs to be tied into the bottom line because reputational risk or risk of being regulated or risk of being sued are business risks so more and more companies will start adopting concrete processes and practices to erect operationalised ethics within the organisation.

What will make companies move is if it means they're going to lose employees or they're going to get sued. That's going to cause issues for a company's profitability. Then we'll say, we had better start putting protections in place so that our people remain healthy because the cost of turnover is too high.

That's what's going to get the decision makers on board. That's not to say that the people in the business are necessarily callous. I've met many, many, people in large tech firms and small tech firms who genuinely do care. But there's enough people who don't care who still occupy decision making roles. It's not enough to appeal to corporate entities on the grounds that you're damaging mental health. You've got to tie it up to something like losing employees, alongside the cost of hiring new people or the risk of a lawsuit.'

Does AI need regulation?

Blackman expresses the view that big tech knows that it has a lot to lose if it does not embrace some form of regulation:

'My guess is that they know that they're eventually going to be regulated, and so they're calling for it because they're not going to try to fight that. But then they're going to be strongly lobbying to get the regulations written in a way that suits them. The main reason why I think things need to be changed, and changed now, is because we have a tremendous amount of evidence that there are ways it can cause very deep societal harms, both to communities and individuals. There are dozens of cases where there have been ethically problematic results from using AI irresponsibly.

For instance, consider United Healthcare, an insurance company in the US. They had an AI algorithm that made recommendations to doctors and nurses about who to pay attention to in the hospital and who needs the resources. But it was biased, and it was recommending that they spent more time with white patients than with sicker Black patients.

In another example, Amazon created an AI driven piece of recruiting software that would read resumés and green light and red light them. It was trained on historical data, and what the AI learned was that Amazon did not hire too many women, so it started throwing out the female applicants. So, if it read something like, university football, women's team, then it would toss out that resumé.

They then tried to delete those variables, such as that of being a woman and the system found proxies for it. For instance, men tend to use words like "execute" and "captain" in their resumés, whereas women don't tend to use those words. So, it found the "we hire men" pattern but just through different means. Amazon had to scrap the project as they couldn't remove the bias from their algorithm.

In another example COMPAS (Correctional Offender Management Profiling for Alternative Sanctions), a software system for crime recidivism analysis was found to have discriminated against Black people.

Then there have been other cases with a recruitment program called HireVue that "help" with the interviewing process when in fact it's basically engaging in modern day phrenology. The programs examine videos of applicants, judging those applicants character traits based on external features that they manifest, for instance, body language and tone, pace in talking, etc., that's totally pseudoscience.

But some major corporations are using that stuff. Yet another example was Google and Project Maven. Google was working with the U.S. Department of Defense to enable drone operators by using AI to sift through video and identify objects for images for a human operator to look at. The engineers became really worried about it. They protested over it saying Google should not be involved in weaponry. Some senior engineers resigned. That was a big deal.

Salesforce had a contract with the U.S. Customs and Border Patrol, which a lot of Americans saw as ethically problematic.

Then there was the famous case where Microsoft put out a chatbot that was trained on the responses it received from Twitter: it became racist and anti-Semitic in less than 24 hours. So again, the whole thing had to be shut down.

We had another case with Goldman Sachs. They were being investigated for having a biased credit card, the Apple card, for giving women much lower credit limits than their partners, even though they held identical financial assets.

Why do we care about AI ethics so much now?

Well, AI is now being developed at a breakneck pace now, both by start-ups and in house by larger companies and it's not just the big tech companies, also now Fortune 500 and 1000 companies are also developing their own programs.

Governments too are also trying to use AI for a variety of purposes, so we know that it's exploding in growth right now. We know that there is no oversight and we have already seen that there are many ways it can easily go wrong. When you put it all together, you realise that we need to get on this now.'

Ethics then is an issue. It will be potentially a business and a legal cost that will involve both business and governments; however, we should not be looking for a hypothetical business case to consider ethics as part of the technology, it is a moral imperative. As Blackman says, it will also lead to reputational issues and to potentially provable issues of design and intent that will be difficult to evade in a court of law.

A question of transparency?

Rather than being caught out, Blackman takes the view that companies and organisations should be transparent in their use of AI and should say what they are doing with people's data. Despite pressure from the US to discourage the development of robust AI regulation in the EU, the recent development of the draft EU AI Law is a welcome first step, albeit that its design is more designed for AI products, rather than AI services.

'I think it's pretty clear that we do. Everyone says, OK but it needs to be smart regulation, of course, no one wants dumb regulation, not intentionally anyway.

So, you have all these people saying we need smart regulations. Who are you arguing against? Then of course, there is disagreement as to whether a particular regulation is smart or not.

What should the regulation look like? I don't totally know. I think GDPR is a good start. I also think that we should be also look to the medical industry for some models. The place where I've seen ethics operationalised successfully is in healthcare where we had some medical disasters that then lead to ethical regulation, and we now have really good regulation.

You have Institutional Review Boards so that when people do research or when they want to develop a drug or they want to test a drug, for instance, it has to pass a certain ethical standard, by the likes of the IRB and we have ethics committees in hospitals, those things came about as a result of regulation. One of the points I keep hitting on in conversation is people need to stop pretending that we're reinventing the wheel of ethics and industry.

We've seen it before. We've seen it be reasonably successful, and we should to the extent that we can, model that.'

Do we need to be more humane?

The examples identified by Blackman show that – in reality – what is actually happening is that our data sets are holding up a mirror to our humanity and it is being found wanting. We think we're better than we are. But does this mean that we have to become more humane? Do we need to have more people pursuing more humane objectives on boards?

'It's not going to happen. That's true, but no, it's not about changing hearts and minds. That's not how the health care profession changed. In that profession, rule makers built a concrete process and practice and used clear standards and best practices. They trained the relevant stakeholders in the right way so they could achieve certain goals and goals that would dovetail into general business operations. It's not about becoming more humane as a people. It's about doing your due diligence. And right now, companies aren't doing even that.'

Do we to need to define intelligence in all of this?

'I'm not big on definitions generally, but I like to think about different kinds of intelligence and give certain kinds of examples and say is the thing we're creating like this or like that or neither, as opposed to trying to come up with some discrete definition of necessary and sufficient conditions for competent intelligence.

Socrates would break down the definitions of people who tried to define things. He would classically say, tell me what piety is, for instance, piety is this? Oh, really? What about this or that?

So, Socrates just would ask people to give him certain kinds of definitions and then he would ask questions that would ultimately reveal that the person didn't know what they were talking about.

We're going to have exactly that issue with regard to AI where some people will try to define things that other people are going to be knocking down. We're going to be here for a while. That's always been the criticism of philosophers and ethics that's why I don't think, Socrates would make a great adviser to Google.

It's not to say that philosophers generally don't have something to offer. They have a tremendous amount to offer, they just need to be recalibrated. Philosophers are very good at asking questions like, should we do this? Is this a good or a bad thing to do? And then going about answering another question, in an extremely systematic fashion but the problem is that the question is utterly irrelevant because businesses are not asking, should we do it? They're asking, given that we're going to do it, how can we do it in a way that minimises risk such as reputational risk or legal risk? So, the academic question and answer is just irrelevant to them. The business person asks the relevant question, but because they have no proper training. They probably don't have a PhD in philosophy,

They therefore go about pursuing their relevant question in an utterly systematic manner saying that they need definitions and regulations. So, they're all over the map. They're playing a game of whack a mole. But the academics, they're easily retrainable if you just tell them, here is what we're going to do. How do you go about mitigating risks? They can answer that question but it's just not a question to which they are accustomed.

Academics want to be published and the kind of questions that genuinely interest them at the moment are really relevant for business practitioners, and senior AI engineers. What has to be addressed by all concerned is how we're practically going to integrate ethical risk mitigation in a way that doesn't stymie innovation, doesn't slam on the brakes and does mitigate risk.'

Can ethical standards be hardwired into software?

'Good luck doing that. This is an area where there are so many variables, but you're not going to be able to get that. Just think, there are two places where AI thinks, oh, we'll just program it. Number one is driverless cars, but they are not really safe enough to roll out. And another place on the opposite end of the spectrum is radiologists, where there's a lot written about how this stuff is not nearly ready enough to replace radiologists because there are too many judgement calls that are needed. So, then you take something as complicated as the ethics – good luck!

I don't think you should program it into the software. I don't think a piece of software is going to recognise the ethical risks. I think you need human judgement involved. And there are ways of operationalising that judgement or figuring out when it's appropriate or, teaching your employees to smell ethical smoke so that when there is an issue, they can pull an alarm and then it goes up to relevant experts, for instance. There's lots of different things that you can put in place to do your due diligence.'

Do we need more education and training in ethics?

'Think about the health care industry. Did you take a medical ethics course when you were in primary school? Is the health care industry, falling apart from ethics because of that? No. I was an ethics professor. I love ethics. If it happened and everyone gets taught ethics from, a very young age, I think that would be a phenomenal thing.

But the idea that we need that in order to get responsible development in the employment of AI is ridiculous. And it's a good thing it's ridiculous because it's going to take generations for it to happen – if it ever does. If it were necessary we can never expect to get actual responsible AI.'

Blackman notes, however, that there is a case for having ethics components in formal training for company executives:

'They need to be aware of the ethical risks because insofar as, and this is tying it to the bottom line, because you have to tie the bottom line, the C Suite, the board of directors are responsible for the reputational risk of the company and the sustainability of the brand.

What they do need as part of their education now is the knowledge of ethical and thereby reputational and otherwise risks of AI and other emerging technologies. That said, educating the C Suite and Board of Directors isn't sufficient because someone actually has to take care of it. There's got to be a process built in and then there has to be specific owners of those processes.

If we just say it's everyone's responsibility, that just amounts to its being nobody's.'

But is reputational risk an ethical risk?

'I wouldn't say it's the ethical dimension. I would say it is what moves people to take ethics seriously. Ethically, people look after the data of their customers they have an obligation, a moral obligation to do that but they don't. You're not going to get people to do anything because it's their moral obligation. Not generally, not companies.

Let me give you an analogy. There's an elderly person who needs help to cross the street. Here are three scenarios. Scenario one, you don't help them across the street. You just ignore them. Scenario two, you help them across the street because you want other people to look at you and say, oh, what a nice person helping that elderly person across the street. So, you just want the praise of other people. Scenario three, you help the person out of compassion for them. Scenario three is the ideal. Scenario one is where corporations are now for the most part. Getting companies to get to scenario two is an improvement in my mind. And you get them to move there by caring about non ethical things first. So, you get them to care about, ethics because if you don't it will wreck their reputation because millennials and Generation Ds really care about this stuff, and they have the power of social media to make them go viral for all the wrong reasons.

They will vote with their wallets, and they don't want to work for companies that prioritise profit over people. We've got to do the right thing now. They will do the right thing for those reasons, but not as it were, the right reasons, that is to say, the kinds of reasons that genuinely warrant moral praise. But that's OK because it's better than doing nothing at all. It's better than doing the wrong thing.'

Part 2

Evidence

Chapter 5

Owning the digital future

In the AI world to whom does your data belong?

In any debate concerning the legal, ethical and regulatory consequences which might flow from the use of any given asset, it is of fundamental importance to understand who owns a given asset. This is no different in the world of AI, where an appreciation is required of who can validly assert a legal right to – akin to ownership of – the underlying data, how an AI seeks to use this data and the importance of such data to an AI system. In the words of Professor Neil Lawrence, data defines AI. And yet the relationship between the algorithm and its specific rules and instructions and the training of such algorithms on a data set or groups of data sets is often overlooked.

Professor Irene Ng *is a leading expert in the economics of AI and data. An entrepreneur, academic and market design economist, she is the Professor of Marketing and Service Systems at WMG at the University of Warwick, a Senior Member of Wolfson College, Cambridge University and a Turing Fellow at the Alan Turing Institute.*

Her research is in economic engineering and service systems. She designs and engineers data platforms, transactions, economic and business models and she specialises in the understanding of value and markets for the data and digital economy. She is also the inventor of personal data accounts for a new asset class of personal data owned by individuals themselves and is the CEO of Dataswift.io.

Professor Ng agrees with Professor Lawrence about the importance of data but goes further. She is particularly keen to emphasise that the starting point is to understand our relationship with data, not least because this is where the problems concerning data and AI begin. Whilst it is not uncommon to hear arguments being advanced that we should 'own our own data', many of us simply don't understand what this means, or indeed how this can be achieved in practice. According to Ng:

> 'When we think about data, we don't really have a full grasp of what data really is. Most people jump straightaway into some notion of "information" when actually data – in its rawest form – is just bitstrings of ones and zeros. These bitstrings then develop into either information or knowledge. That's what we then call or embrace in the over-arching term "data".
>
> I think there is a colloquial or general understanding of data by most people that means something more than just raw bitstrings, and that it has some form of meaning attached to those bitstrings.'

This 'colloquial understanding' of data – the conflation of concepts of data and information – creates real issues when we consider who should properly have a legal entitlement to own and control the use of that data.

It is a conflation which has been allowed to develop by voracious companies capturing data of an ever more personal nature and seeking to blur the distinction between data which should rightfully be ours and where we could be harmed if it is manipulated, and third party data perceptions of us.

The battle for our data

At present we do not own all the information about ourselves – nor is it credible to suggest we could ever do so. It is too late for that – even though we can clearly be victims of its use or misuse. For Ng, we need to have a better understanding of different types of data and our relationship with it as this will inform rights of ownership and control over how it is used.

Whilst few people would have genuine concerns with the notion that we should be legally entitled to our own core data, the position is more complicated regarding data which has been captured by others and more complex still when we consider entitlement to data, which has been derived about us by third parties.

According to Ng not only do we need to define data, we also need to examine what the data is being used for, how it is being used, what permissions were attached to the data, who is doing what, what their relationship to our data is and we also need to establish what is done at what point. Only then says Ng can we start to examine the issues that AI raises for us via our data.

A crucial point according to Ng is to first understand that there are three types of data: 'core data', 'signal data' and 'information derivatives' and that all are very different.

Core data is our identity: our name, our date of birth, our passport, our account numbers, our phone number and where we live.

> 'This is data that is fundamental to our being in both the physical and the online worlds. They bind the data to our physical selves. We typically think that this data belongs to us though there are mutual owners of the data who will also assert their rights over its existence, such as the banks, the passport office, the government and the phone company.'

The next layer of data that sits on top of our core data is the most controversial because of the potential contested ownership claims that can develop, and we will call this 'signal data'. Signal data can come from records of us, eg health data, which is a 'snap shot' of our health profile, or more dynamic forms of our behavioural data, such as where we are, what we have bought, what we have been doing. Typically, it will be generated by a combination of events.

> 'I could be out for a walk in the countryside. My mobile phone knows this because I have given permission for it to know my location, while I am out, I start to do internet searches for wild-flowers and trees, so my data is

beginning to reveal a potential interest in the environment. I do a search for pubs in the area, this reveals a time for the query.'

According to Ng all of these requests are inferential signals, information that on its own does not definitely confirm something but provides an indicator. It is this data that is contentious because for many people this is private information that they consider should be their concern and no-one else's, while the big data companies assert their ownership to it via collection and subscription. We gave agreement to its collection by ticking terms and conditions in return for a service such as Google maps and the data companies state that to offer that service they need to know where we are and have the right to collect other data.

The final class of data are 'information derivatives', this is data that has been combined with other data with the aim of forcing more certainty from the signal data. The signal data that is a speculative inference may be sent to companies wishing to sell subscriptions to nature conservancy magazines who then send emails to you alerting you to a special offer, to which you respond and take out a subscription – a signal that is now confirmed and that can be added to a profile of you. An alternative version could be the combination of core data about you provided by a bank or a loyalty card and other information that you have agreed in the terms and conditions. This can then be processed, resulting in a profile.

Capturing our digital DNA

For instance, in an interview conducted by Peter Warren (one of the authors of this book) with Clive Humby, joint founder of the data company Dunn-Humby which makes 'customer insight products' and is responsible for the Tesco loyalty card (the company is now owned by Tesco), Humby told Warren that by simply interpreting people's buying patterns their voting patterns could be derived to such an extent that particular 'swing streets' could be identified.

The collection of this many layered data presents many problems, the chief of which is the transparency over the issue of ownership and the transparency over the collection and processing of the core data, the signal data and what other data it has been combined with and why.

For example, as we walk along a street today, we shed data much in the same way that we shed skin and that data, unlike skin, does not yet hold our genetic DNA, but it does hold our digital DNA. It is data that is being captured very discretely. Which raises yet another issue, when we walk along a street, we assume we have the right to choose how we physically present ourselves, yet we do not have this luxury online. Even more importantly most of us do not know what is being captured and by whom, we do not know what is being broadcast.

For us to achieve 'our interest' in this data we have to know what is being broadcast and who is collecting our data, says Ng. Only then will we be able to make a trade-off between what is captured and what is being broadcast and it is only by knowing that, that we will be able to license that capture because we are then aware of the data that has been collected. We will also, by reference to the data's relationship to us, be able to determine who owns this data.

This is an important point because it means that then we will be able to correct any wrong or inaccurate data that is held about us. The last great data issue is one best illustrated by a famous television advert for *the Guardian* in 1986 which shows a fast-running skinhead accelerating away from a car that has pulled up at a junction. From another camera angle we see that the skinhead is not running from the car but seems to be about to attack a businessman walking along the street. Again, a wrong impression, as we see when the camera pans out that the skinhead is actually pushing the businessman out of the way of a pallet of bricks falling from an overhead crane. As the advert points out, it's important to get the full picture.

Getting on top of the data

The legal issue here is that this pattern of data use is not only in constant flux but also as understanding grows of the ways that the data and computing giants of the late 1990s make their money, so will the challenges to the accepted patterns of the ownership of data. It is a change to the model that the data giants may themselves encourage because though the ownership devolves onto the entity 'deriving' the data, that entity will also have any resulting liability for harms caused by that data. This is an important risk factor for those on the cutting edge of technology, for instance, not only can there be harms caused by technology addiction, there can also be unintended events that could lead to crippling damages for the data giants for using AI. It is a fact that has not been lost on Sundar Pichai, the head of Google parent company Alphabet.

In June 2018 Pichai published seven guiding AI principles that effectively committed the company to being ethical by design. In January 2020, in an op-ed piece in the *Financial Times*, Pichai called for the regulation of AI, that as Cambridge's Professor Neil Lawrence said earlier would appear to be something that starts with the data.

Ng agrees:

> 'The problem starts when you collect data, when you store it and when you process it – that is the part where AI comes in because it is doing the processing. Most people make all these assumptions about where data is collected and where is it stored, and that understanding is very simplistic because they think about it in a real-world way. People think that the data is obtained from one place and that it is then mixed up by a computer and is used to build something a little like bricks and then that makes a house but that is where that understanding departs from what actually happens, because the reality is much more complex.

> We seem to think there's this big data lake sloshing about with lots and lots of data in it and that there are algorithms swimming through it like fish looking for particular things in all of the data and that somehow an intelligence emerges from this that really needs to be policed. That's very simplistic, because for instance AI (or machine learning) can be everywhere data is collected. For example, it can analyse how much rain fell on your windscreen and as a result make your windscreen wiper go faster. It did not go into a data lake to do this.

So, if you think about data, you have to recognise that it can be very small bits of data or it could be a big data lake or, it can be lumpy combinations of both, ie there can be a lot of combinations of data brought together in a centralised, decentralised or distributed manner for many reasons. It can be variable. When you think of its processing, it can also be at the 'edge' of a system, like the car windscreen wiper or an IoT [Internet of Things] device, but it can also be in a big data lake. This is where the problem is, to get a common understanding of the scope of the debate on data.

We need to start to think about the different sorts of information within the AI space and address the fears that AI raises and not generalise too quickly, for example just thinking about the relationship between processing and impact; what does the system do? What is the context of the system and the data that is being used?

I'll give you an example again, if you take the last number of your passport and you change it, digitally, you're a completely different person. If you take the last number of your Fitbit steps today and change it, it does not matter. Data is multi-dimensional and it can be very potent. When combined with other data it can become harmless. On the other hand, inert data that's personal, can become very potent, data when combined with other data can lose its meaning. This is all about relevance, meaning and context. But if you don't understand this about data, you confuse the medium and the message and say they're all the same thing, but they are not.'

Though this mutability of data can quickly confer great power on data changing it from an inert state into a very potent force, the Chinese state, for example, is accused of running a tremendous AI-based surveillance system. It could combine steps recorded on a fitness tracker and your passport number and know exactly where you've gone. How do we protect against that?

'Why do you want to restrict data and its power? Is it a case of privacy, civil liberties, cybersecurity or discomfort in giving the power to the state or the collector?

If we want to restrict the potential for AI to be used in ways that are not beneficial to people, then the problem is not merely the technology, but the politics, because we will have to face the question of who has the right to decide for us, not only as the people who are subjected to the AI but also for the companies that develop the technology because there is the possibility to always blame the AI system and its developers, especially if an AI-related mishap has occurred.

There is the potential for weapons to create great harm. Equally, there is the potential for society's machines and technology to create great harm. We need to have a sensible discussion on what and where harm is created and how it interacts with the power to do harm. Where it interacts with the inability for people to exercise their agency to stop certain things, which is related to power. On the other hand, we have to think about choice and freedom, because as we know very well, even in the world without data in the world of democracy and rights you cannot police without destroying some freedoms. We need to talk about these freedoms and what the choices are that you're curtailing when you start to police it, the problem with that is that very often it's a one-sided conversation, with those in power seeing all of the benefits from their side and the people who are being governed not seeing it the same way.'

Regaining control of our data

The issues with data mean that very often with AI there is the possibility of ending up with an unintended consequence – we have already found that using conventional training data from the internet led to a Microsoft AI chatbot expressing racist sentiments within 24 hours. This means that AI systems will simply reflect our own biases back to us, an issue that asks questions about humanity. This hidden AI learning that we are not aware of is a problem that Risto Siilasmaa, the head of Nokia and AI expert warns of in Chapter 15.

Clearly, transparency is an issue that all sides agree on, from Alphabet's Sundar Pichai, to Professors Ng and Lawrence. It has prompted Ng to develop a solution called the HAT Microserver, which is a personal data server that powers a personal data account infrastructure which seeks to enable full intellectual property rights over data within for both privacy and mobility of the data by mirroring current trends in so-called 'edge computing'.

With Ng's Personal Data Servers, you control your data through ownership of a personal data server and all the data within it. An AI-based software system orders that data according to data rules that you have enabled, letting you specify what data about you can be used. The system also lays out how it can be processed, essentially creating an interrogatable interface that lets other AIs know what data you have available and negotiating a transaction for that data either in cash, credits or services.

It is a system that confers not only IP rights over the data, but a degree of social ownership upon the individual because they can ensure its accuracy, usefulness and availability. The individual can control and choose what data to share, and with whom. For example, with your doctor it would make sense to share all of your health data and maybe your supermarket purchases, but this is data that you may not want to share with an insurance company.

Ng's system copies the model that the computer industry is developing for technology. Edge computing using 5G technologies will be built to take advantage of mobile phones, tablets and laptops and integrate with IoT devices. These 5G devices will be able to use edge connectivity to pull data from the network but will not go near the core unless it is absolutely necessary for reasons of speed. Thus, for instance, the emergency services calls and connectivity will be routed around towers in an area close to an incident and will only be sending traffic back to their HQ when they need to rather than relying on the HQ systems to route traffic. It is a development that marks the move to the devolved data model being touted by technology companies which takes advantage of the collective computing power of the edge rather than running huge database computers at the centre.

In the new model contact only occurs with the core if it has to and pioneers like Ng are pushing for particular classes of data to be distributed in the same way that the processing power will be devolved. Though the argument over core or distributed processing has raged in the computing industry for nearly 30 years, now with the emergence of 5G there are signs that the dispute may be settled. Here Ng lays out the advantages of distributed data in the twenty-first century.

'The modern data issues are something that we have tried to correct with our Personal Data Server system. With a PDS a data scientist puts little tools that are completely private in your server, your personal data store. You can do all sorts of things with these tools. It analyses you and provides you with insight and shows it back to you. How busy your calendar is, how depressed you were last week, and it's only shown to you and nobody else. If I choose to, I can share that insight, I can share that with the counsellor through bundling it up into 'Data Passes' and then sharing it through a Data Passport. I can share how busy I am to the guy who supplies me with the food I order so that he can come up with some suggestions to suit my lifestyle. That piece of insight is something that was given to me. I see it. It's mine. It's private to me. I shared it voluntarily. I had choice.

Was my life better because of it? Yes, because I am doing it. If you had said, no, it is worse, then you wouldn't do it. So what I'm saying is the presumption that the output of an AI follows a certain course in terms of its outcome assumes that it must be processing data in the worst possible way leading to its discrimination, but you are not really sure that is the case because you do not have that data use audit trail.'

The essential issue then is one that everyone is familiar with and makes perfect sense to us. The core data resides with the individual, it is not transferable because it relates to us. It could be claimed that this is actually a return to our data's natural state, our data resides with us and belongs to us. Ng's system attempts to address this point because at the moment we are not in that relationship with our data because we do not have technology that gives us legal entitlements to our data.

'This is the central point, which is why I am very concerned about data and why I am very concerned about AI and the potential bias it could have, and the use of the raw material, data. The crux of the problem that we now face is the fact that data is collected, stored and processed in places that you have no control over. There is no transparency over this process.

If you change that model to one where a technology exists to create entitlement that is data agnostic, then you can put in rules on the flow and distribution of data. For example, AI would become a collective AI. I have my algorithm, you have yours. With that situation we would come together and collectively we would develop a collective group intelligence that would be a combination of edge AI combined with some AI from the centre. So, I might know my body dimensions and I want to buy some blue jeans, so I go to a website to buy some and the website tells me that people who buy blue jeans like to buy red scarves.

Thus, in an ideal world you want to be able to take some of your insights and objectives and share that with the insights that have developed in the centre. Insights that have been obtained from data created from processing the insights from the edge, your data that has been processed in ways that you have given permission for, combined with other sanctioned data, that you have engaged with in a way that is transparent and that you also agree with.

That is a system where we are in control, my concern about AI is in the in the way that our data has become distributed.

The model where there's a big data lake and it has got lots of people's data in it and you simply lay claim to that and decide what you want to do with it in the way that big data lakes do it, I think that is not sustainable and truly there are not that many people who have that sort of power. The only organisations with that sort of power are the big tech companies, but if you are talking about the regulation of those companies then you are not talking about AI regulation. You are talking about anti-trust or competition law and about regulations around how big companies should be, how powerful they should be, how much they control and own the raw data and whether they have the right to do that.'

The dangers of personal data control

Professor Barry Smith, the philosopher and AI scientist at Edinburgh University is sceptical and argues that: 'we are not as nice as we think we are', and that we are happy to lie to ourselves all of the time. If we're in control of our own data then we'll censor it and it's only by that data being combined with other data that a more accurate picture of us emerges.

'There are issues about our being control of our own data, and we do have a tendency to explain our actions in our own interests, if that were not the case, we would not have courts. There's absolutely nothing wrong with that. It's not because we are fake, we are dressing up the truth, but we do that in every walk of life, we put a spin on things. We have that right. Why would we not have that right? Even in data?'

It is this relationship with truth that will become one of the issues of our times. Fake news, fraud, news manipulation, distortion and straight out lying have all become twenty-first century watchwords but they are failings that have beset humanity since we started to speak. Twitter and Facebook are now censoring online content in a bid to drive out political untruth. A version of events in our interests is the essence of humanity, the version of us that we think is nice. According to the majority of people interviewed for this book, part of the fallibility of humanity is our lies, is our fraud, is our not liking the ugliness of our reality. It is the data part of us that informs the AI that leads to racist and biased systems, but Ng does not believe it is the biggest problem.

'Our data distortions are an issue and this can be dealt with through data provenance, eg ensuring the data is verified from the source and untampered with. The bigger challenge is in what we do with AI and how transparent we are about what we are doing. Where we fall over is when we believe we have the right to make decisions and to make them on behalf of others. This is the real issue of data for big technology companies like Google and Facebook. The fact that they can do this at scale and use that data at scale to make certain decisions which influence our behaviours is where we run into trouble, but that's traditionally how we've always been running into trouble, even in the way the State governs and in the way we organise ourselves. That is humanity too. We need to recognise that even in this digital age our power relations and institutions are the same, merely manifested digitally. We need to recognise that the challenge is with our institutions. The technology merely lays bare that challenge.

So, we also have to begin to think that data is just another form of humanity when we generate it, it is an expression of our humanity. We should have the right to dress it up in the same way that we wear clothes in a certain way. You don't always have to believe what I say but, there are ways to check if I'm telling the truth. If it matters enough there's a sanction in polite society in terms of how often you lie, and you become known for it.

So other data can be used to force truth from data and that's fine if the process is transparent and we can all agree to a certain amount of decision making done on our behalf by government and local government, such as how often your bins really should be emptied based on the collective good and, what the public good is. These are the ways we have thought about our societies, but for some reason we do not think of the internet as the same as our societies on the internet almost all the rules are different. How different, are they? Why do I own myself when I walk down a street but not when I browse the web?'

The allure of whole body data

However, there is a contradiction, with this view of sanitised data, because one of the primary methods of creating 'dressed up versions' of ourselves is by omission and censorship, by removing unwelcome information. If the NHS were provided with accurate information about our sex lives, our diet and drinking and sleeping patterns it could diagnose people simply from their lifestyles and address those issues before we became ill. We would be able to understand a range of diseases and discover commonalities that cannot be seen at the moment because of concerns over privacy, intrusion and government surveillance.

Whole body data derived from store cards, credit cards and mobile phones could all be united by an AI in the collective good, saving individual suffering and decreasing the treatment bill for the NHS, but as of now such a system would be unpopular. As we will find out from Professor Fred Cate in Chapter 14, having an AI system in your car that fined you if you exceeded the speed limit was considered intrusive by his students, a use of data that for Ng should be a matter of choice.

'In certain circumstances we should always see the whole. And we should always have all of our body across all of the hospitals in the world, and they should all belong to us in the way our bodies belong to us and our data should belong to us. We should have the right to give that up to get the treatment we want, to give up that data to get into the drug trials we want to get into. We should have the right to do that, but no third party should tell me that I should give up the right to choose.'

It is a view of data shared by many privacy advocates in the Information Age and one that seeks to reassert and redefine the idealism of the early days of the internet but it does miss out one crucial part of the equation from the big technology companies which is that, according to Professor Iain Brown Head of Data Science for the data company SAS and Adjunct Professor of Marketing Analytics at University of Southampton, we get a very good deal from the high tech giants.

According to Professor Brown the value of our data to a company like Google, for instance, is around £60 a year while the cost of our buying an equivalent internet search capacity would be around £20,000 a year. According to the data scientists, that value of the manipulation of the data by the AI systems comes from the insights and answers to questions it is able to deliver by combining that data. In isolation the big data companies say that an individual's data is valueless, a position that Ng rejects:

> 'I actually disagree that all your data that comes together is valueless. If you've got your whole-body data, you can use the data to buy services for better diagnosis. You will know your state of mind, you can present the data that you hold in your PDS and understand how that compares with other data that people with similar conditions have presented and you will then be able to find solutions based upon your data much more effectively.
>
> If you have that AI at the edge that means that you can collect and buy services to organise data in your server which is really valuable and that AI can create an output that can actually then be sent out and amalgamated into the collective. We can also use a lot of the work that is being done with differential privacy to ensure privacy is maintained and yet data benefits can be derived. You don't have to give all your calendar and all that you've said. You can buy privacy preserving algorithms to give an analysis of that at the edge of the system where you present your output data which can then be analysed by the centre, which means that you can develop a value from your participation. There are clever ways of doing this without trampling all over your rights.
>
> You can still aggregate. You do not have to aggregate the raw data because the moral hazard of doing that is very high and the temptation for it to be used or misused by the powerful is also high but there are different ways of doing edge processing before it is brought to the centre. We can also do some centre processing and bring that to the edge. We need to develop these systems to create that collective good and also create the personal good.'

The data model of you

At issue in this discussion is the new world that the internet creates. As Ng points out the product of the internet is information, this is where Information Technology gets its name and in this new world there is a product that is created which is an 'information derivative'. In the world of finance, a derivative is an arrangement or product (such as a future, option, or warrant) whose value derives from and is dependent upon the value of an underlying asset, such as a commodity, currency, or security. An information derivative gets its value from a licence to use data and, crucially, from intent. If we visit a website, we have intent to obtain information either about an event or a product and in doing so we produce a signal of interest. When that is combined with our core data it becomes valuable because our interests become uniquely identifiable. In the terms and conditions we so blithely sign we give large companies the right to pick up the signal of our interests, the only property we have in this relationship is ourselves, but who owns the insight? You because of your behaviour, or the company that is monitoring you?

'Essentially, the bitstrings can be configured to notice something (whether it's raining, whether a street has been entered) and at that moment they give off a signal. That signal might be who you are, or where you are, that you are in a street in Cambridge or that you have entered somewhere that sells wine and that you have stopped. It's a sign that you are interested in wine. That could be one signal and we give off many signals that can be interpreted either individually or correlated against other data to try to derive other information and these are the information goods that economists believe there is a market for.'

The life blood of the Metaverse

'That is not the same as saying the data underneath it all is owned by someone, we do not know. It's all very messy, legally. What we do know is that much like derivatives you have taken the option on the signal and that therefore that signal is precious because signals create the ability for services to be offered. This means that for example if you go onto a website that you generate one of these signals, whether or not who the underlying data belongs to is another issue, but a signal has been created. Just as we know that you have gone into a premises that sells wine now we know that something about wine on a website triggered your interest and now you will suddenly find that wine adverts are now being flashed up at you because that information has achieved some value. Again, there is no value to the person who generated that data other than they are receiving adverts about something that they appear to be interested in.

However, another process has now started, which is to verify that signal, to see if it only had a half-life. Is the person still in Cambridge an hour later? If so, is it worth recommending restaurants? Or, is it a perishable signal has the person gone? All of these things are the questions that the system asks now and will ask more in the future because the aim will be to improve the quality of the signal.

That's why it has a market of its own. The person generating this signal may be completely unaware that they are generating this information. A good example of this is the way you dress, what you wear is a statement about you, you want people to register that but you do not realise the extent of that, you are aware that you are broadcasting and unaware that you are broadcasting, online your broadcasts are being collected.

Now, if you think that's wrong, then I ask the same question do you want to selectively broadcast about yourself when you walk down the street? Because if you do then something will have to select the people that you want to broadcast to. How do you deal with that?

I think may people forget that the online world is maybe a little dysfunctional and different from the offline world, but both worlds have very similar issues.

People pry and peek and people look at CCTVs and watch you all of the time and we are somehow ok with that to an extent I think offline world surveillance is a problem but other people might not think so but for those people who are concerned about privacy it's a problem, because you can start to use AI image and facial recognition technology to start to move into the offline world and begin to search for other data characteristics to add to your already rich data stream.'

Who owns your metadata in the Metaverse?

Rights in property were defined in approximately 1870 in the real world but on the internet, in the online world, our focus is more on intellectual property rights. Although the introduction of the EU GDPR in 2018 strengthened rights in relation to the manner in which our personal data is used, the concept of providing consent for use of personal data is substantially inferior to an absolute ownership right.

Ng believes, however, we need to work towards providing the data subject with such complete control and that more traditional property rights in this space will become increasingly important:

'We don't need to make them up anymore because they are beginning to emerge. My data can be stored in my house. It will be governed by the same legal constructs, which is why IP rights become important on the internet because they are the right to give rights, so I can say I give you the right to use my data for a short duration of time or to use it for some reason. I can deny you those rights and I can give you those rights. If you do not have those rights of determination, then you become a second-class citizen and you do not have true freedom. It is for this reason that we will see people beginning to ask for more than just data protection or privacy, but to assert their rights over the control of the data derivatives, because otherwise parts of the understanding of you will be owned by different interests, otherwise you will be beholden on someone else to pass that information on for you and they will obtain value from their intercession. At the moment the situation is very like you putting all your money with Sainsbury's and then whenever you go to Waitrose telling Sainsbury's to pay Waitrose.'

This distinction between data and the information derivative is, according to Ng, essential to understanding the new information-reactive modern world.

'Economists like to talk about data as an "information good" and that's the big difference. Information is a bundle of data. Data may not be informative until it has been structured, data is just a bitstring of ones and zeros. It's a higher order and it has a boundary that defines it as an information good and that boundary will say whether it is a book, or a song or a definition of an individual's preferences. So that is your "data good" while the lower order data could be just the information from a sensor that just went from a one to zero and then back again so it is telling you that a door in your house has been opened and then closed, the data was the record because the sensor is attached to the door but the information is the conclusion.

You can make a market out of songs and files and things, but data is largely unbounded. It's very difficult to manage data because of the nature of it and the economic property of it, it's economic value is a challenge to bind, but if you do not bind it in some way or interpret it in some way or give it some boundaries then it is just like air and water. It's not an asset unless it is in some bounded state where the structure is fungible, even if the content is not.'

The data at our core

It is this core value of the rights inherent in personal data and the rights the individual gives to use that data that then define the situation, which develops from there, says Ng, as the processing of the data then goes on to confer rights upon others as they create information derivatives according to the agreement made with them.

'The point of GDPR was to regulate the way data is processed and controlled. The EU concluded (correctly) that the data that sits within centralised systems cannot have any property rights attributed to it by data subjects and therefore the rights belong to the organisation that collected that data, meaning that the data that you legally collect, you own in the eyes of the law. The technology that collects the data owns it and whoever owns that technology is the owner of the data that it has collected unless contractually transferred.

Pre-GDPR there was always a case that when data was in a centralised system that it could be processed and controlled in a different way. What GDPR did was quite simply to make a law that only pertains to personal data and the rights of the individual in their data and defines the role of the data processor and the data controller. It studiously avoids any determination of whether or not data is an asset.

What we're talking about is what happens to data owned by the technology which collected it? According to that data's status there are certain things that can be done to it and certain measures that need to be taken to protect it according to the law, but the law does not confer ownership on it, it says that it has to be treated in a particular way but it does not say it is a personal asset, it says it must be protected like a currency not that it's a new oil for the individual.

You can't even say it creates value the way markets can create value along a supply chain, because it does not move like a "good" through a supply chain and nor can you necessarily say who owns which part of a supply chain when data is in a centralised system.

While GDPR was an attempt to try to redress the situation that has occurred as the internet has evolved and it does give us something to work with as the impact of AI and its use of data begins to emerge it did not go far enough though at the time it went as far as it could.

GDPR gave us many rights but it fought shy of giving us full property rights because it's impossible legally because of the way that data collection has developed up until now. At the moment your data sits within the technology of an organisation, when that changes then our rights will change.'

In this new emerging world though, intellectual property rights will be very important. We address this point in Chapter 6, in which we discuss the ownership ramifications of this new twenty-first century data age on core data, intellectual property and the 'information derivatives' that will be generated by AIs and algorithms.

A data trust: our data in our interest

One entity that will inform this debate about data ownership that is relevant here is a concept that has been called the data trust, something it has been suggested will become a legal entity that will soon emerge, but what is it?

'Data trusts are a really interesting legal concept that takes advantage of trust status, which is one of our oldest legal concepts, where you uphold the wishes of whoever is settling what on whom. These will need to be established because using a data trust online underlines some of the idiosyncrasies that we have been discussing, the most notable of which is that you must have property rights to be able to settle on a trust in the first place.'

In our fast-moving world, many people are beginning to question the principles of our economic model and the role of companies. The US Business Roundtable, which is made up of the country's leading business executives, has called for social good to be placed above profit as the main purpose of a company. This is a trend that is being seen elsewhere, in Belgium for instance Thierry Geerts, a Google executive and author of *Digitalis*, has flagged up this new world of collective data good and pointed out that Belgians view giving data as a public service equivalent to that of giving blood. A trend in data use and 'collective ownership' is becoming very popular among the growing number of ethically aware technologists, according to Ng.

'There are many apps out there right now that are beginning to embrace a new awareness that we can use to lock social good into technology and engage with in a much more mutually beneficial way. Here, for instance, we have developed 13 apps with different AI developers who have built some amazingly rich data sets that respect people's dignity and data rights. Some run on a subscription approach, while others use a double-sided market, for example, one company has created a little medical platform for people to share their data with that is also subscribed to by a pharmaceutical organisation that is looking for find patients for its drug trials. Its business model would be to get money from the company who would be able to match up people who have a potential disease, like diabetes, with a diabetes trial. A match that would allow it to learn from the other side of the market in the way that I earlier described. Data can create so many different types of business and economic models that we really have to choose what the business model is in order for the market to find a value for the data that people wish to transact with.'

The new world created by data

There is a unification of data that the data industry has been quietly pursuing for a number of years. Many involved in AI see it as the greatest potential of the new technology so that greater and greater insights can be gained from unstructured data lakes. In some data centres in the US, companies have been able to use systems that share their data in an anonymised form with the data of other companies to enrich the information the company holds on its customers. This is one of the areas that many observers consider controversial as it blurs the lines of privacy and benefit that Ng has outlined.

'The area of data unification is really where the market has to correct itself. I think we can do data lakes, but we will have to re-evaluate those in the light of the permissions that allow them to exist. Many of these data lakes were developed with legacy technologies and that means that they will have legacy issues, such as terms and conditions, GDPR, the ability of modern and future technology to connect to them, data value and utility in the modern age – literally it might not be worth connecting to them if you want to take advantage of the hybrid centre-edge edge data capabilities.

In the future, as I have said not only will individuals have personal data servers but so will businesses and SMEs so there will be many design patterns in creating different AI capabilities; we can process our own data using our own personal AI, much of that data will be distributed so that we can derive rapid insights from a better use of the world's information. In many ways in their current form data lakes are the past and will become a special case of data mining. As we all know that is not sustainable because the data lakes become too big and you've got to deal with all the potential risks of hacks which can become very expensive to secure. At the moment you can process a lot of it and you can get some insights out of it but doing so will become dated and potentially unattractive because new companies are better at doing leaner, smaller processing, using distributed data. They will also be able to give you the best utility, and they will be able to do it without one giant data centre in the middle of nowhere. The big data lakes will become the habitat of dinosaurs.'

It is this evolution, that Ng says will lead to a developing world of AI opportunity for us as individuals and for the technology industry. A world where AI entities will negotiate with other AIs, whether they be individuals, smaller companies or bigger companies, and they will be prepared to release our data on a proportional basis so that we can create some value from it.

'We already have a nascent personal AI, it's called a smartphone. We have another personal AI and it's called a PC. We have from the 1980s collected this set of small tools. They're not big they are just one phone and one laptop, but they have enabled us to be able to speak or translate into every language, calculate any number and get huge amounts of information. Now, it is not unheard of when you want to start using your own personal data server to have your own personal AI, in fact have a choice over what kind of personal AI you want to be able to interact with and who else you want to be able to interact with.

It's literally what it means to become more human in a digital society because we will then be enabled and not monitored in ways we've not had before. But we will also have a choice in terms of how we will interact with others. That's the kind of computation that we need. I like to think about the internet currently as a society, a society where the elite have computation, storage and data and we don't. At the moment in data terms, we are the factory farmed chickens and they are the farmers. We are quite literally exploited.

In the future we have to change that relationship in everyone's interests. It will be a fusion of our properly asserted and defended interests in the market, when we have computation and data storage, markets will form better. It is this that we should have a discussion about, and that discussion should be about the about the distribution of data. AI is a moving space due to the pace of development and its use will be defined by the discussion about the ethical use of data.'

Though for the markets to perform in the interests of the individual Ng says that regulation is essential.

'We will need regulation, to make sure that rules are transparent, and we will need regulation to make sure that there is balance between rules, agency and choice. We will need regulation to ensure that people stop hiding and that truth can be told and so that lies are exposed. These are all the kinds of things that that actually makes markets form better. You do need regulation for markets to form better. It is a process that will be accelerated by the distributed model because even though you prefer to have inaccurate data or to hide bits of yourself the collective will be able to determine that because it will be able to map you against other individuals because of your data points. It will be a process a little like removing the dross from a metal.'

In this new transparent world Ng also thinks that it will lead to a better relationship between businesses and consumers, one in which a greater understanding will cater to needs rather than promoting products and manipulating desires.

'There's a difference between trying and actually getting it wrong or right. One of the things that AI will do is make predictions about people's behaviour and it will collect those predictions and learn from them, accreting predictions is not a bad thing. Predicting that I'm coming to the door so please could you open the door is not a bad thing. If you use predictions to help with decisions that is not making a decision for me. My life is being augmented because my decisions are being supported. It is a process that will inevitably build trust between the customer and the organisation providing the help because if you make a prediction that supports my decision then I value your help. It is when you try to predict for me and decide for me and therefore rob me of my agency and choice that the consumer will have something to say and there is a very fine line between serving up a web search for an individual and serving up a web search where the companies have been selected by the search company on the basis of how much they have paid to be in that web search. Essentially, we need a new data contract that puts the interests of the individual first and builds upon the work of GDPR.'

The new 'data' rights

With a new data contract such state and corporate digital manipulation becomes more difficult.

'Information is power and when an entity is in possession of a lot of data and data on you including where you are and your behaviour then they have power over you and there is always the temptation to abuse that power and become corrupt. That's why the distribution of the data becomes so crucially important and redistributing it is very similar to redistributing wealth. What has happened is the equivalent of people giving all of their wealth to a state or a large organisation which has conferred power on them and now those entities can do all sorts of things to you. However, if we redistribute the entitlements to your data it changes that relationship and makes the markets form better.'

Though in this redistributed system it is evident that we will have to have our own AI systems that will show us our data and what they have done with it and which operate as unique identifiers, but who will they owe their allegiance too? For Ng this again comes down to choice.

'Technology is all about subscription not imposition, at first we never took our phones very seriously, we just talked to people on them. The first time we looked down on our phone was probably the snake game. Then it became a smartphone and our world changed. Technology and its usage and adoption is evolutionary. It is not revolutionary. The first personal AIs will be crude and will probably be used as simple chat systems to order things or for games. We are already seeing AI companions and they will probably evolve into your own private AI but we are a long way from you an AI system at birth and I don't think it should really happen because you should be is a position to elect to have something you should never be conferred or given an AI. It should be an evolution. It should be choice. And some people can choose to say, I don't want an AI until I step out the door or something. I have an AI free environment. These are all choices people can make. It just makes the world better if they have choice. We shouldn't be homogenising society. We should try to actually keep some of the qualities that make us what we are, which are our differences.

We want the new AI world to be contextual and that too is very important because as well as having the right to keep our data private we have the right to be private. I don't want to be with my phone all the time, but I want it some of the time. I want my bedroom to be free of it, I want it when I go out, so that it enables me and augments me. That's the freedom we should have in a digital world. That compact between me and my machine will let something special happen because up till now all technology products have become a template of our behaviours and we start to behave very similarly when products are the same. When the technology is working with me it is enabling my differences due to decision support. Technology should enhance our bodily capabilities in a similar way to the way that an exo-skeleton does.

We should treat AI in the same way in terms of supporting our decision, in terms of supporting our choices and our purchases and the things we interact with. It's not all; it's not nothing; it's somewhere in between. And that's the fabric of humanity.'

Chapter 6

Patently obvious – the AI inventor

Should an AI be able to make IP?

At the heart of this chapter is the idea of AI behaving like a person. An idea that could have a huge impact in the developing debate about the future role of AI in our lives and the role it is already carving out in our lives.

For at least two decades, machines have been autonomously generating patentable inventions. 'Autonomously' here refers to the machine, rather than to a person, meeting traditional inventorship criteria. In other words, if the 'inventive machine' were a natural person, it would qualify as a patent inventor. The US Patent and Trademark Office (USPTO or Patent Office) may have granted patents for inventions autonomously generated by computers as early as 1998.

If patent law begins to develop a notion of AI inventors, the idea could swiftly gain currency on social media and among conspiracy theorists that not only can AI invent things but also outperform humans in terms of creativity and intellect, it will inevitably begin to inflame the torches of the mob. That in the process, the AI inventor will also leave educated researchers unemployed and potentially rob 'skilled workers' of opportunity, will only fuel the anger of AI's opponents.

This is not a tabloid fantasy; it is an actual reality, for the population at large, the technology community and those who see some merit in the technology for society. For AI to work for the benefit of society its processes need to be explainable and its role needs to be seen as valid and economically sustainable for those wishing to deploy these systems. It has to be seen to be doing good, and it has to be understood.

It is for that reason that we have to understand Professor Ryan Abbott's idea of the AI inventor and the need and inevitability of it, and to keep the 'AI inventor' in proportion as a useful social innovation which is a technological augmentation, and not as a personification.

As Professor Abbott argues, an AI inventor if deployed properly should be a force for good, and its potential role should be considered and regulated for wider societal benefit.

Ryan Abbott, MD, JD, MTOM, PhD *is Professor of Law and Health Sciences at the University of Surrey School of Law and Adjunct Assistant Professor of Medicine at the David Geffen School of Medicine at UCLA. He has worked as a partner in legal* *practice, where he primarily focused on transactional matters and intellectual property litigation in the life sciences, and he has been general counsel of a biotechnology company.*

Professor Abbott has published widely on issues associated with law and technology, health law, and intellectual property in leading legal, medical, and scientific books and journals. His research has been featured prominently in the popular press, including in The Times, the New York Times, the Financial Times, and other media outlets. He routinely gives keynote lectures and presents internationally in academic (eg, MIT, Stanford, Yale, Oxford, Cambridge), government (eg, World Intellectual Property Organisation, World Trade Organisation, UK Intellectual Property Office), and industry (eg, Google, IBM, Swiss Re) settings. Managing Intellectual Property magazine named him as one of the 50 most influential people in intellectual property in 2019 and again in 2021.

In some of his earlier work, Professor Abbott examined instances of autonomous machine invention in detail and argued that such machines ought legally to be recognised as patent inventors to incentivise innovation and promote fairness. The owners of such machines would be the owners of their inventions. In those works, as here, terms such as 'computers' and 'machines' are used interchangeably to refer to computer programs or software rather than to physical devices or hardware.

What happens, though, when inventive machines become a standard part of the inventive process?

This is not a thought experiment. For instance, whilst the timeline is controversial, surveys of experts suggest that Artificial General Intelligence (AGI), which can be described hypothetically as a computer able to perform any intellectual task a person could, will develop in the next 25 years. Some thought leaders, such as Ray Kurzweil, one of Google's Directors of Engineering, predict computers will have human levels of intelligence in about a decade.

The impact of the widespread use of inventive machines will be tremendous, not just on innovation, but also on patent law.

Right now, patentability is determined based upon the existence of an inventive step, which is 'not obvious' to a hypothetical, skilled person. The skilled person represents the average worker in the scientific field of an invention. However, once the average worker uses inventive machines, or inventive machines replace the average worker, then inventive activity will be normal instead of exceptional.

If this skilled person standard fails to evolve accordingly, this will result in too lenient a standard for patentability.

Patents have significant anti-competitive costs, and allowing the average worker to routinely patent their outputs would cause social harm. As the US Supreme Court has articulated, '[g]ranting patent protection to advances that would occur in the ordinary course without real innovation retards progress and may ... deprive prior inventions of their value or utility'.

The skilled standard must keep pace with real world conditions. In fact, the standard needs updating even before inventive machines are commonplace. Once inventive machines become the standard means of research in a field, the test would also encompass the routine use of inventive machines by skilled persons.

The first intellectual victory of the machines

Taken a step further, once inventive machines become the standard means of research in a field, the skilled person should be an inventive machine. Specifically, the skilled person should be an inventive machine when the standard approach to research in a field or with respect to a particular problem is to use an inventive machine (the 'Inventive Machine Standard').

To obtain the necessary information to implement this test, the Patent Office should establish a new requirement for applicants to disclose when a machine contributes to the conception of an invention, which is the standard for qualifying as an inventor. Applicants are already required to disclose all human inventors, and failure to do so can render a patent invalid or unenforceable.

Similarly, applicants should need to disclose whether a machine has done the work of a human inventor. This information could be aggregated to determine whether most invention in a field is performed by people or machines. It is information which would also be useful for determining appropriate inventorship, and more broadly for formulating innovation policies.

Whether the Inventive Machine Standard is that of a skilled person using an inventive machine or just an inventive machine, the result will be the same: the average worker will be capable of inventive activity, importantly, if they are aware of the process. Conceptualising the skilled person as using an inventive machine might be administratively simpler, but replacing the skilled person with the inventive machine would be preferable because it emphasises that the *machine* is engaging in inventive activity, rather than the human worker.

Yet simply substituting an inventive machine for a skilled person might exacerbate existing problems with the 'not obvious' inquiry. With the current skilled person standard, decision makers, in hindsight, need to determine what another person would have found obvious. This results in inconsistent and unpredictable calculations about what is or what is not obvious. In practice, the skilled person standard bears unfortunate similarities to the 'Elephant Test', or Justice Stewart's famously unworkable definition of obscene material: 'I know it when I see it.' This may be even more problematic in the case of inventive machines, as it is likely to be difficult for human decision makers to theoretically decide what a machine would find obvious.

However the test is applied, the Inventive Machine Standard will dynamically raise the current benchmark for patentability. Inventive machines will be significantly more informatively process aware and empowered than skilled persons and also capable of considering more prior art. An Inventive Machine Standard would not prohibit patents, but it would make obtaining them substantially more difficult: A person or computer might need to have an unusual insight that other inventive machines could not easily recreate, developers might need to create increasingly intelligent computers that could outperform standard machines, or, most likely, invention will be dependent on specialised, non-public sources of data. The 'not obvious' bar will continue to rise as machines inevitably become increasingly sophisticated. Taken to its logical extreme, and given there may be no limit to how intelligent computers will become, it may be that every invention will one day be obvious to commonly used computers. That would mean no more patents should be issued without some radical change to current patentability criteria.

What is 'not obvious'?

Patents are not intended to be granted for incremental inventions. Only inventions which represent a significant advance over existing technology should receive protection. This is because patents have significant costs: they limit competition, and they can inhibit future innovation by restricting the use of patented technologies in research and development. To the extent that patents are justified, it is because they are thought to have more benefits than disadvantages. Patents can function as innovation incentives, promote the dissemination of information, encourage commercialisation of technology and validate moral rights.

Although other patentability criteria apply, the 'not obvious' requirement is the primary test for distinguishing between significant innovations and trivial advances. Of course, it is one thing to express a desire to only protect meaningful scientific advances, and another to come up with a workable rule that applies across every area of technology.

Determining the level of ordinary skill is critical to assessing what is obvious or not. The more sophisticated the skilled person, the more likely a new invention is to appear obvious. Thus, it matters a great deal whether the skilled person is a 'moron in a hurry' or the combined 'masters of the scientific field in which an [invention] falls'.

Determining what constitutes prior art is also central to the obviousness inquiry. On some level, virtually all inventions involve a combination of known elements. The more prior art can be considered, the more likely an invention is to appear obvious.

AI, which is to say a computer able to perform tasks normally requiring human intelligence, is playing an increasingly important role in innovation.

For instance, IBM's flagship AI system 'Watson' is being used exploratively to conduct research into drug discovery, as well as clinically to analyse the genes of cancer patients and develop treatment plans. In drug discovery, Watson has already identified novel drug targets and new indications for existing drugs. In doing so, Watson may be generating patentable inventions either autonomously or collaboratively with human researchers.

The incredible value of instantly actionable information

In clinical practice, Watson is also automating a once human function. In fact, according to IBM, Watson can interpret a patient's entire genome and prepare a clinically actionable report in 10 minutes, a task which otherwise requires around 160 hours of work by a team of experts.

Watson is largely structured as an 'expert system', although Watson is not a single program or computer – the brand incorporates a variety of technologies. Here, Watson will be considered a single software program in the interests of simplicity. Expert systems are one way of designing AI that solve problems in a specific domain of knowledge using logical rules derived from the knowledge of experts. These were a major focus of AI research in the 1980s.

Expert system-based chess-playing programs HiTech and Deep Thought defeated chess masters in 1989, paving the way for another famous IBM computer, Deep Blue, to defeat world chess champion Garry Kasparov in 1997. However, Deep Blue had limited utility – it was solely designed to play chess.[1] The machine was permanently retired after defeating Kasparov. Alphabet's leading AI company DeepMind uses another type of inventive machine. DeepMind systems use artificial neural networks, which essentially consists of many highly interconnected processing elements working together to solve specific problems.

The design of neural networks is inspired by the way the human brain processes information. Like the human brain, neural networks can learn by example and from practice. Examples for neural networks come in the form of data, so more data means improved performance. This has led to data being described as the new oil of the twenty-first century, and the fuel for machine learning. Developers may not be able to understand exactly how a neutral network processes data or generates a particular output.

The Go game changer

As noted in Chapter 1, in 2016, DeepMind developed an algorithm known as AlphaGo which beat a world champion of the traditional Chinese board game Go (or Weiqi), and subsequently the world's leading player in 2017. Go was the last traditional board game at which people had been able to outperform machines. AlphaGo's feat was widely lauded in the AI community because Go is exponentially more complicated than chess. Current computers cannot 'solve' Go solely by using 'brute force' computation to determine the optimal move to any potential configuration in advance. There are more possible board configurations in Go than there are atoms in the universe. Rather than being pre-programmed with a number of optimal Go moves, DeepMind used a general-purpose algorithm to interpret the game's patterns. DeepMind is now working to beat human players at the popular video game *StarCraft II*.

AI like DeepMind is proving itself and training by playing games, but similar techniques can be applied to other challenges requiring recognition of complex patterns, long-term planning, and decision-making. DeepMind is working to develop an algorithm to distinguish between healthy and cancerous tissues, and

---

1 This concept of the singularity is one which chimes with Professor Lawrence's view of the present status of AI as a hedgehog (adopting the language of Isaiah Berlin and Archilochus), as we saw in Chapter 1.

to evaluate eye scans to identify early signs of diseases leading to blindness. The results of this research may well be patentable.

We are in the midst of a transition from human to machine inventors.

For purposes of patent law, an inventive machine should be one which generates patentable output while meeting traditional inventorship criteria. Because obviousness focuses on the quality of a patent application's inventive content, it should be irrelevant whether the content comes from a person or machine, or a particular type of machine. A machine which autonomously generates patentable output, or which does so collaboratively with human inventors where the machine meets joint inventorship criteria, is inventive.

Under the present framework, inventive machines would not be the equivalent of hypothetical skilled machines, just as human inventors are not skilled persons. In fact, it should not be possible to extrapolate the characteristics of a skilled entity from information about inventive entities.

Courts never have judged patentability by what the real inventor; applicant or patentee could or would do. Real inventors, as a class, vary in their capacities from ignorant geniuses to Nobel laureates; the courts have always applied a standard based on an imaginary work of their own devising which they have equated with the inventor.

What then conceptually is a skilled machine?

Is it a machine that can be anthropomorphised according to the various descriptions courts have given of the skilled person? Such a test might focus on the way a machine is designed or how it functions. For instance, a skilled machine might be a conventional computer that operates according to fixed, logical rules, as opposed to a machine like DeepMind's, which can function unpredictably. However, basing a rule on how a computer functions might not work for the same reason the Flash of Genius test failed: Even leaving aside the significant logistical problem of attempting to figure out how a computer is structured or how it generates particular output, patent law should be concerned with whether a machine is generating inventive output, not what is going on inside the machine. If a conventional computer and a neural network were both able to generate the same inventive output, there should be no reason to favour one over the other.

Alternatively, the test could focus on a machine's capacity for creativity. For example, Microsoft Excel plays a role in a significant amount of inventive activity, but it is not innovative. It applies a known body of knowledge to solve problems with known solutions in a predictable fashion (for example, multiplying values together). However, while Excel may sometimes solve problems that a person could not easily solve without the use of technology, it lacks the ability to engage in almost any inventive activity. Excel is not the equivalent of a skilled machine – it is an automaton incapable of ordinary creativity.

IBM's Watson used in clinical practice may be a better analogy for a skilled worker.

Watson analyses patients' genomes and provides treatment recommendations. Yet as with Excel, this activity is not innovative. The problem Watson is solving may be more complex than multiplying a series of numbers, but it has a known solution. Watson is identifying known genetic mutations from a patient's genome. It is then suggesting known treatments based on existing medical literature. Watson is therefore not innovative, adhering as it does to conventional wisdom and the processing of large amounts of data at high speed.

Unlike Excel, however, Watson *could* be inventive. For instance, Watson could be given unpublished clinical data on patient genetics and actual drug responses and tasked with determining whether a drug works for a genetic mutation in a way that has not yet been recognised. Traditionally, such findings have been patentable. Watson may be situationally inventive depending on the problem it is solving, in the same way that a skilled worker is aware of an issue affecting a work flow that they are involved in although unaware that the issue represents a patentable opportunity.

It may be difficult to identify an actual computer program now which has a 'skilled' level of creativity. To the extent a computer is creative, in the right circumstances, any degree of creativity might result in inventive output. To be sure, this is similar to the skilled person. A person of ordinary skill, or almost anyone, may have an inventive insight. Characteristics can be imputed to a skilled person, but it is not possible in the way the test is applied to identify an actual skilled person or to definitively say what he or she would have found obvious. The skilled person test is simply a theoretical device for a decision maker.

Replacement or enhancement?

To determine if a skilled machine one day represents the average worker in a field, decision makers would also need information about the extent to which such machines are used. Obtaining this information may not be practical.

Patent applicants could be asked generally about the use and prevalence of computer software in their fields, but it would be unreasonable to expect applicants to already have, or to obtain, accurate information about general industry conditions.

Having inventive machines replace the skilled person may better correspond with real world conditions. Right now, there are inherent limits to the number and capabilities of human workers. The cost to train and recruit new researchers is significant, and there are a limited number of people with the ability to perform this work. By contrast, inventive machines are software programs which may be copied without additional cost. Once Watson outperforms the average industry researcher, IBM may be able to simply copy Watson and use it to either replace individual workers, or take on the work of a large team of researchers.

Indeed, as mentioned earlier, in a non-inventive setting, Watson can interpret a patient's entire genome and prepare a clinically actionable report in 10 minutes, as opposed to a team of human experts who take around 160 hours. This situation echoes the immediate impact of the US' ENIAC machine, one of the world's first computers built in 1945, which calculated a trajectory in 30 seconds that took a human 20 hours, allowing one ENIAC to displace 2,400 humans.

Once Watson is proven to produce better patient outcomes than a human team, it may be unethical to have people underperform a task which Watson can automate. When that occurs, Watson should not only replace the human team at its current facility – it should replace every comparable human team. Watson could similarly automate in an inventive capacity.

Thus, inventive machines change the skilled paradigm because once they become the average worker, the average worker becomes inventive. As the outputs of these inventive machines become 'routinised', however, they should no longer be inventive by definition. The widespread use of these machines should raise the bar for obviousness, so that these machines no longer qualify as inventive but shift to become skilled machines – machines which now represent the average worker and are no longer capable of routine invention.

Regardless of the terminology, as machines continue to improve, the bar for what is 'not obvious' should rise. To generate patentable output, it may be necessary to use an advanced machine that can outperform standard machines, or a person or machine will need to have an unusual insight that standard machines cannot easily recreate. Inventiveness might also depend on the data supplied to a machine, such that only certain data would result in inventive output. Taken to its logical extreme, and given there is no limit to how sophisticated computers can become, it may be that everything will one day be obvious to commonly used computers.

It is possible to generate reasonably low-cost and accurate information about the use of inventive machines. The Patent Office should institute a requirement for patent applicants to disclose the role of computers in the inventive process. This disclosure could be structured along the lines of current inventorship disclosure. Right now, applicants must disclose all patent inventors. Failure to do so can invalidate a patent or render it unenforceable. Similarly, applicants should have to disclose when a machine autonomously meets inventorship criteria.

These disclosures would only apply to an individual invention. However, the Patent Office could aggregate responses to see whether most inventors in a field (eg, a class or subclass) are human or machine. These disclosures would have a minimal burden on applicants compared to existing disclosure requirements and the numerous procedural requirements of a patent application. In addition to helping the Patent Office with applications, these disclosures would provide valuable information for the purposes of attributing inventorship. They might also be used to develop appropriate innovation policies in other areas.

Will it be in the interests of skilled people to use inventive machines?

The current standard neglects to consider the modern importance of machines in innovation. Instead of now replacing the skilled person with the skilled machine, it would be less of a conceptual change, and administratively easier, to characterise the skilled person as an average worker facilitated by technology.

Moving forward in time, once the use of inventive machines is standard, instead of a skilled person being an inventive machine, the skilled person standard could incorporate the fact that technologies used by active workers include inventive machines. In future research, the standard practice may be for a worker to ask an inventive machine to solve a problem. This could be conceptualised as the inventive machine doing the work, or the person doing the work using an inventive machine. It may be that research teams in the future need as much expertise in computer science as they do in traditional scientific disciplines.

Granted, in some instances, using an inventive machine may require significant skill, for instance, if the machine is only able to generate a certain output by virtue of being supplied with certain data. Determining which data to provide a machine, and obtaining that data, may be a technical challenge. Also, it may be the case that significant skill is required to formulate the precise problem to put to a machine. In such instances, a person might have a claim to inventorship independent of the machine, or a claim to joint inventorship. This is analogous to collaborative human invention where one person directs another to solve a problem. Depending on details of their interaction, and who 'conceived' of the invention, one person or the other may qualify as an inventor, or they may qualify as joint inventors. Generally, however, directing another party to solve a problem does not qualify for inventorship. Moreover, after the development of AGI, there may not be a person instructing a computer to solve a specific problem.

Whether the future standard becomes an inventive machine or a skilled person using an inventive machine, the result will be the same: the average worker will be capable of inventive activity. Replacing the skilled person with the inventive machine may be preferable doctrinally because it emphasises that it is the machine which is engaging in inventive activity, rather than the human worker.

The changing use of machines also suggests a change to the scope of prior art. The analogous art test was implemented because it is unrealistic to expect inventors to be familiar with anything more than the prior art in their field, and the prior art relevant to the problem they are trying to solve. However, a machine is capable of accessing a virtually unlimited amount of prior art.

Advances in medicine, physics or even culinary science may be relevant to solving a problem in electrical engineering. Machine augmentation suggests that the analogous arts test should be modified or abolished once inventive machines are common, and that there should be no difference in prior art for purposes of novelty and obviousness. The scope of analogous prior art has consistently expanded in patent law jurisprudence, and this would complete that expansion.

The skilled person standard should now incorporate the fact that skilled persons are already augmented by machines. Once inventive machines become the standard means of research in a field, the skilled person should be an inventive machine when the standard approach to research in a field or with respect to a particular problem is to use an inventive machine. When and if AGI is developed, inventive machines should become the skilled person in all areas, taking into account that AGI may also be augmented by specific AI.

The new inventive war of discovery

The case of *Mobil Oil Corp v Amoco Chemicals Corp* concerned complex technology which involved compounds known as Zeolites used in various industrial applications. Mobil had developed new compositions known as ZSM-5 zeolites and a process for using these zeolites as catalysts in petroleum refining to help produce certain valuable compounds. The company received patent protection for these zeolites and for the catalytic process. Mobil subsequently sued Amoco, which was using zeolites as catalysts in its own refining operations, alleging patent infringement. Amoco counterclaimed seeking a declaration of non-infringement, invalidity, and unenforceability with respect to the two patents at issue. The case involved complex scientific issues.

One of the issues in the case was the level of ordinary skill. An expert for Mobil testified that the skilled person would have 'a bachelor's degree in chemistry or engineering and two to three years of experience'. An expert for Amoco argued the skilled person would have a doctorate in chemistry and several years of experience. The District Court for the District of Delaware ultimately decided that the skilled person 'should be someone with at least a Master's degree in chemistry or chemical engineering or its equivalent, [and] two or three years of experience working in the field'.

If a similar invention and subsequent fact pattern happened today, to apply the standard proposed we would need to determine the extent to which inventive technologies are used in the field; characterise the inventive machine(s) that best represents the average worker if inventive machines are the standard; and determine whether the machine(s) would find an invention obvious.

The decision maker is a patent examiner in the first instance, and potentially a judge or jury in the event the validity of a patent is at issue in a trial. For the first step, determining the extent to which inventive technologies are used in a field, evidence from disclosures to the Patent Office could be used. That may be the best source of information for patent examiners, but evidence may also be available in the litigation context.

Assume that today most petroleum researchers are human, and that if machines are autonomously inventive in this field, it is happening on a small scale. Thus, the court would apply the skilled person standard. However, the court would now also consider 'technologies used by active workers'. For instance, experts might testify that the average industry researcher has access to a computer like Watson. They further testify that while Watson cannot autonomously develop a new catalyst, it can significantly assist an inventor. The computer provides a researcher with a database containing detailed information about every catalyst used not only in petroleum research, but in all fields of scientific inquiry. Once a human researcher creates a catalyst design, Watson can also test it for fitness together with a predetermined series of variations on any proposed design.

The question for the court will therefore be whether the hypothetical person who holds at least a Master's degree in chemistry or chemical engineering or its equivalent, has two or three years of experience working in the field, *and is using Watson*, would find the invention obvious. It may be obvious, for instance, if experts convincingly testify that the particular catalysts at issue were very closely related to an existing catalyst used outside of the petroleum industry in ammonia synthesis, that any variation was minor, and that a computer could do all the work of determining if it were fit for purpose. It might thus have been an obvious design to investigate, and it did not require undue experimentation in order to prove its effectiveness.

Data and technological muscle will extract the value from invention

Now imagine the same invention and fact pattern occurring approximately 10 years into the future, at which point DeepMind, together with Watson and a competing host of AI systems, have been set to the task of developing new compounds to be used as catalysts in petroleum refining. Experts testify that the standard practice is for a person to provide data to a computer like DeepMind's, specify desired criteria (eg, activity, stability, perhaps even designing around existing patents) and ask the computer to develop a new catalyst. From this interaction, the computer will produce a new design. As most research in this field is now performed by inventive machines, a machine would be the standard for judging obviousness.

The decision maker would then need to characterise the inventive machine(s). It could be a hypothetical machine based on general capabilities of inventive machines, or a specific computer. Using the standard of a hypothetical machine would be similar to using the skilled person test, but this test could be difficult to implement. A decision maker would need to reason what the machine would have found obvious, perhaps with expert guidance. It is already challenging for a person to predict what a hypothetical person would find obvious; it would be even more difficult to do so with a machine. Computers may excel at tasks people find difficult (like multiplying a thousand different numbers together), but even supercomputers struggle with visual intuition (mastered by most toddlers).

In contrast, using a specific computer should result in a more objective test. This computer might be the most commonly used computer in a field. For instance, if DeepMind and Watson are the two most commonly used AI systems for research on petroleum catalysts, and DeepMind accounts for 35 per cent of the market while Watson accounts for 20 per cent, then DeepMind could represent the standard. However, this potentially creates a problem – if DeepMind is the standard, then it would be more likely that DeepMind's own inventions would appear obvious as opposed to the inventions of another machine. This might give an unfair advantage to non-market leaders, simply because of their size.

To avoid unfairness, the test could be based on more than one specific computer. For instance, both DeepMind and Watson could be selected to represent the standard. This test could be implemented in two different ways. In the first case, if a patent application would be obvious to DeepMind or Watson, then the application would fail. In the second case, the application would have to be obvious to both DeepMind and Watson to fail. The first option would result in fewer patents being granted, with those patents presumably going mainly to disruptive inventive machines with limited market penetration, or to inventions made using specialised non-public data. The second option would permit patents where a machine is able to outperform its competitors in some material respect. The second option could continue to reward advances in inventive machines, and therefore seems preferable.

It may be that relatively few AI systems, such as DeepMind and Watson, end up dominating the research market in a field. Alternatively, many different machines may each occupy a small share of the market. There is no need to limit the test to two computers. To avoid discriminating on the basis of size, all inventive machines being routinely used in a field or to solve a particular problem might be considered. However, allowing any machine to be considered could allow an underperforming machine to lower the standard, and too many machines might result in an unmanageable standard. An arbitrary cut-off may be applied based on some percentage of market share. That might still give some advantage to very small entities, but it should be a minor disparity.

After characterising the inventive machine(s), a decision maker would need to determine whether the inventive machine(s) would find an invention obvious. This could broadly be accomplished in one of two ways: either with abstract knowledge of what the machines would find obvious, perhaps through expert testimony, or through querying the machines. The former would be the more practical option. For example, a petroleum researcher experienced with DeepMind might be an expert, or a computer science expert in DeepMind and neural networks. This inquiry could focus on reproducibility.

Finally, a decision maker will have to go through a similar process if the same invention and fact pattern occurs 25 years from now, at which point AGI has theoretically taken over in all fields of research. AGI should have the ability to respond directly to queries about whether it finds an invention obvious. Once AGI has taken over from the average researcher in all inventive fields, it may be widely enough available that the Patent Office could arrange to use it for obviousness queries. In the litigation context, it may be available from opposing parties. If courts cannot somehow access AGI, they may still have to rely on expert evidence.

An innovation to break a log jam or another addition to a morass?

The skilled person standard received its share of criticism even before the arrival of inventive machines. What we are focusing on is the degree of cognitive difficulty in conceiving an invention that fails to explain what it actually means for differences to be obvious to an average worker. The approach lacks both a normative foundation and a clear application.

Courts may maintain the current skilled person standard and decline to consider the use of machines in obviousness determinations. However, this means that as research is augmented and then automated by machines, the average worker will routinely generate patentable output. The dangers of such a standard for patentability are well-recognised.

A low obviousness requirement can 'stifle, rather than promote, the progress of the useful arts'. Concerns already exist that the current bar to patentability is too low, and that a patent 'anti-commons' with excessive private property is resulting in 'potential economic value … disappear[ing] into the "black hole" of resource underutilisation'. It is expensive for firms interested in making new products to determine whether patents cover a particular innovation, evaluate those patents, contact patent owners, and negotiate licences. In many cases, patent owners may not wish to license their patents, even if they are non-practising entities that do not manufacture products themselves. Firms that want to make a product may thus be unable to find and license all the rights they need to avoid infringement. Adding to this morass, most patents turn out to be invalid or not infringed in litigation.

Could patent AI transparency open up more inventive opportunity?

Excessive patenting can thus slow innovation, destroy markets, and, in the case of patents on some essential medicines, even cost lives. Failing to raise the bar to patentability once the use of inventive machines is widespread would significantly exacerbate this anti-commons effect.

Instead of updating the skilled person standard, courts might determine that inventive machines are incapable of inventive activity, much as in the US the Copyright Office has determined that non-human authors cannot generate copyrightable output. In this case, otherwise patentable inventions might not be eligible for patent protection, unless provisions were made for the inventor to be the first person to recognise the machine output as patentable. However, this would not be a desirable outcome. As I have argued elsewhere, providing intellectual property protection for computer-generated inventions would incentivise the development of inventive machines, which would ultimately result in additional invention.

Today, there are strong incentives to develop inventive machines. Inventions by these machines have value independent of intellectual property protection, but they should also be eligible for patent protection. People may apply as inventors for recognising the inventive nature of a machine's output, or more ambitiously, inventive machines may be recognised as inventors, resulting in stronger and fairer incentives. Once inventive machines set the baseline for patentability, standard inventive machines, as well as people, should have difficulty obtaining patents.

It is widely thought that setting a non-obvious standard too high would reduce the incentives for innovators to invent and disclose. Yet once inventive machines are normal, there should be less need for patent incentives. Once the average worker is inventive, inventions will 'occur in the ordinary course'.

Machine inventions will be self-sustaining. In addition, the heightened bar might result in a technological arms race to create ever more intelligent computers capable of outdoing the standard. That would be a desirable outcome in terms of incentivising innovation. Even after the widespread use of inventive machines, patents may still be desirable. For instance, patents may be needed in the biotechnology and pharmaceutical industries to commercialise new technologies. The biopharma industry claims that new drug approvals cost around 2.2 billion dollars and take an average of eight years. This cost is largely due to resource intensive clinical trials required to prove safety and efficacy. Once a drug is approved, it is often relatively easy for another company to recreate the approved drug. Patents thus incentivise the necessary levels of investment to commercialise a product given that patent holders can charge monopoly prices for their approved products during the term of a patent.

AI transparency should clean a system which is creating blocks to innovation

Yet patents are not the only means of promoting product commercialisation. Newly approved drugs and biologics, for example, receive a period of market exclusivity during which time no other party can sell a generic or biosimilar version of the product. Because of the length of time it takes to get a new biologic approved, the market exclusivity period may exceed the term of any patent an originator company has on its product. A heightened bar to patentability may lead to greater reliance on alternative forms of intellectual property protection such as market exclusivity, prizes, grants or tax incentives.

With regards to disclosure, without the ability to receive patent protection, owners of inventive machines may choose not to disclose their discoveries and rely on trade secret protection. However, with an accelerated rate of technological progress, intellectual property holders would run a significant risk that their inventions would be independently recreated by inventive machines.

Depending on the type of innovation, industry and competitive landscape, business ventures may be successful without patents, and patent protection is not sought for all potentially patentable inventions. In fact, 'few industries consider patents essential'. For instance, patents are often considered a critical part of biotechnology corporate strategy, but often ignored in the software industry. On the whole, a relatively small percentage of firms patent, even among firms conducting research and development. Most companies do not consider patents crucial to business success. Other types of intellectual property such as trademark, copyright, and trade secret protection, combined with 'alternative' mechanisms such as first mover advantage and design complexity, may protect innovation even in the absence of patents.

The legislative challenge of the changing innovation landscape

Inventive machines may result in further consolidation of wealth and intellectual property in the hands of large corporations like Google and IBM. Large enterprises may be the most likely developers of inventive machines owing to their high development costs.

It could be claimed that a counterbalance to additional wealth disparity could be broad societal gains. The public would stand to gain access to a tremendous amount of innovation – innovation which might be significantly delayed or never come about without inventive machines. These are arguments that will need to be presented to policymakers.

The concerns regarding industry consolidation are another basis for revising the obviousness inquiry. The widespread use of inventive machines may be inevitable, but raising the bar to patentability would make it so that inventions which would naturally occur would be less likely to receive protection. To the extent market abuses such as price gouging and supply shortages are a concern, protections are, at least theoretically, built into patent law to protect consumers against such problems.

Inventive machines may ultimately automate knowledge work and render human researchers redundant. While past technological advances have resulted in increased rather than decreased employment, the technological advances of the near future may be different. There will be fewer limits to what machines will be able to do, and greater access to machines. Automation should generate innovation with net societal gains, but it may also contribute to unemployment, financial disparities and decreased social mobility. It is important that policymakers act to ensure that automation benefits everyone, for instance by investing in retraining and social benefits for workers rendered technologically unemployed. Ultimately, patent law alone will not determine whether automation occurs. Even without the ability to receive patent protection, once inventive machines are significantly more efficient than human researchers, they will replace people.

Chapter 7

AI and cyber security

Are we weaponising the internet?

As we have found from the earlier chapters – and particularly from Professor Lawrence in Chapter 1 – data is at the heart of AI, and as we have discovered from Professor Ng in Chapter 5, we are data. So, what happens if that data is interfered with? The consequences are obvious. Not only can the systems themselves be destroyed, but damage can very easily be done to the interests of individuals. Just what sort of damage can be done can be gauged by the Stuxnet hacking attack, which was claimed to have been mounted by the US and Israeli military on the Iranian nuclear enrichment plant at Natanz in Iran. The computer virus hid on the Programmable Logic Controllers of the system and placed itself between the human operators and the centrifuges so that it could capture a picture of the system working properly. It then played a loop of the system behaving normally to those monitoring it whilst instructing the centrifuges to randomly spin faster than they should and also suddenly braking. The human operators were unaware of this behaviour, which destroyed one fifth of the centrifuges and sabotaged the Iranian nuclear programme, putting it many years behind in its development.

If similar measures were introduced in AI systems then the results could be all too real. Against this background, cybersecurity becomes a crucial component of the new AI age. Not only are AI systems being developed, so too will AI cyber weapons be developed to disrupt them, in this technological game of cat and mouse.

Since the start of the cyber security industry in the late 1980s, protecting computer systems, which up until that point were completely undefended, has always been challenging. Even now there is a widespread acceptance by the cyber security industry that breaches of most companies are inevitable: 'it is not if, but when' is the recurring theme of any discussion concerning the cyber profile of a business. Top cyber-security companies, whose capabilities range from threat detection, automated defence through to penetration testing, readily identify the potential threats posed by the proliferation of data and its role as a critical asset of business and national infrastructure. However, does AI offer a new tool in the armoury of threat detection or does its role in automated defence create the possibility of the internet being weaponised in pursuit of cyber resilience? If so, what protections and safeguards might be required?

Dr Matti Aksela is the Vice President of Artificial Intelligence at the leading cyber security company F-Secure and heads F-Secure's Artificial Intelligence Centre of Excellence. His responsibilities include directing AI research and implementation work at F-Secure, as well as collaboration with Universities and other partners in the domain. Prior to joining F-Secure, Dr Aksela worked in various technical and leadership roles in organisations helping further improve products and solutions across industries via the utilisation of machine learning and AI. He holds a Doctorate of Science (Technology) in Computer Science (Information Technology) from the Helsinki University of Technology.

The threats are huge – nation states go by the cyber title of 'nation state actors' and are seen as the biggest hacking threats, with China and Russia in particular being accused of systematic Intellectual Property (IP) theft and democratic destabilisation by their use of information warfare.

It is this participation by nation states that lies at the heart of the issue we face from cyber-attacks. In the twenty-first century we are totally dependent upon technological systems that are becoming ever more complex as AI and 5G technology is rolled out. Increasingly our energy, water, health, finance, emergency, military, transport and education systems are becoming reliant on internet-based systems, whilst our communications, logistics and research systems are absolutely dependent on modern computer and radio technology. Any interference with this critical national infrastructure or damage to underlying databases could have potentially devastating consequences for large amounts of people.

This reliance on communications systems was fatally demonstrated during the 2004 Madrid train bombing which killed 193 people. The subsequent wave of calls on the city's communications networks caused them to collapse (even for the emergency services) provoking widespread panic as people were unable to contact relatives.

Research carried out after the bombings has discovered that the denial of water and communications are the two factors that will quickly cause civil unrest. This means that cyber-attacks have the potential to become particularly effective as part of what is now called a 'blended war', a combination of cyber-attacks and conventional warfare to wreak both physical and psychological damage on an opponent's population and infrastructure and weaken an opponent in the run-up to a confrontation.

An AI war we may find it hard to prevent

This realisation and the low-cost of entry have led to most countries in the world developing cyber-warfare capabilities which has often resulted in the development or patronage of cyber-crime gangs by states eager to deny their activities. This volatile atmosphere is further compounded by one of the greatest weaknesses of the computer network, the difficulty of being able to positively identify the source of an attack with any certainty, an essential factor if you wish to declare a war on another country.

Now with the advent of AI a further potentially terrifying component has been added to an already deadly brew, and one in which AI systems will be used to defend against AI-enabled attackers in a battle inside our computer networks for information and strategic advantages such as the ability to turn off an opponent's communications network – the issue which has recently bedevilled US and UK relations with China over 5G and the Chinese communications company Huawei. This is a situation that has led the US President to demand that the US develop its own 5G capability and the UK Prime Minister to guarantee that Huawei will no longer play any part in the UK's telecommunications network by 2027.

The emergence of AI as a fast-developing component in our vital digital backbone now means that the attackers have an additional target in addition to data, the network and the computing processes, and that target is the function of the algorithm itself. This is a further development of the process successfully deployed in the Stuxnet attack mentioned at the start of the chapter.

In this new world AI programs are on both sides, used by criminals and states to try to break into systems to gather data and secrets; as former Brigadier General Robert Spalding and Professor Walsh point out in the next chapter, a threat that the AI systems will also be deployed to guard against, something that could potentially lead to something that must be guarded against, an AI war on the internet that we may not be aware of until it is too late. These threats obviously dictate that any defender must be both aware of and able to counter all of those challenges.

It is against this backdrop that Aksela, the head of cyber security company F-Secure's Artificial Intelligence Centre of Excellence, summarises the issues for the cyber industry:

> 'I think there are three points that need to be made about this: one, how can we as defenders use AI to defend our customers better, detect threats and protect our customers better; two, how can malicious actors use machine learning and AI to perform different types of attack; and, finally, how do we make machine learning more secure because we have to think about the security of machine learning now too.'

For AI evangelists, it is the answer to all ills. AI in cyber security, they claim, will mean that the systems will map and know what is 'good' and 'should be' and thus quickly be able to map everything that is different from those two patterns and quickly 'see' and prevent attacks. AI, it is said, will replace threat analysis.

> 'The problem with this is that a lot is being said but the reality is that there is nothing in place like that not even in the semi-near term.
>
> Anyone researching this area will have heard various opinions on general intelligence. I have heard five-year predictions for at least the last decade and each one has said that this competence is just around the corner.
>
> From my pragmatic machine-learning perspective I would say that we are at the machine learning stage and machine learning is a tool. I see AI in the main as an umbrella term. Machine learning is one way to implement AI and things like neural networks are a subset of machine learning. For example, deep learning is a subset of neural networks, a subset of machine learning, and yet also a part of AI. But what we have today is rather narrow intelligence.
>
> We have very useful tools that we can use for many things, sometimes even better than humans can do. But they can be used only on very focused problems and very focused parts of the whole problem. It is a technology that can be very beneficial, when it is used properly, but it is not magic. It is not going to be solving all of our problems for us.

We have a tendency to want to interpret things in a way that's familiar to us. This means that when something happens and it looks smart, we interpret that as being smart in the same way as we are, intelligent in the same way as we are.'

The threat posed by relying on systems we cannot understand

'For example, when you are looking at your dog, you think it thinks like you do, you anthropomorphise it. Thus, when you see, all these very impressive image and voice recognition solutions we think well if it can do that then it can do anything and that's not the case we over emphasise their complexity, because the things that we see are impressive but in terms of actually true intelligence, there's not that much of it.

Most of the things that are happening at the moment are machine learning. Thinking about what AI is to me, I use it as a term that describes the ability to mimic human cognitive abilities, like thinking and decision taking processes.

Machine learning is very good for particular things, for performing particular mundane tasks that we do, but doing them very well.

You have to specify the task in the right way. You might have a supervised learning problem, to solve that you will have raw data and you will have very high dimensional data that you can use to describe the entity, the outcome you want. It could be facial recognition or a prediction of what's going to happen, so you will have a very complex and large dataset. We humans are not good at processing huge volumes of data, we are very good at abstracting things and thinking broadly and being innovative those are human strengths. But pure volume of data, speed of processing. I'll give that one to the computers because machine learning for some things, is superior to humans.'

Aksela also emphasises that these mundane tasks are also now being assigned to computer programs by criminals because the technology at present doesn't have any moral boundaries, although it may be possible for an AI general intelligence to be educated in ethics.

'Machine learning is a tool. Like any tool, you can use it for different purposes, good and bad. A doctor can use a knife to save a life, a criminal can use it to take one. It is just the purpose you apply it to which makes you give meaning to the technology; criminals are programming bots to find weaknesses so that they can exploit them. So, automation is already helping the criminals.

With the development general of AI or superintelligence then it becomes totally different. If humans, weren't guided by morals on ethics we would have a very different world and it is good we have this feature. That means it is obviously important to be able to teach that feature to a general intelligence.

Though as I have said we are not there yet. That means the ethics are in the hands of the person applying the machine learning and the target they are trying to achieve.'

Can we teach the machines to be good?

This begs the question: can you write ethics into code and, if you could, would it not be possible for someone else to code it out?

'If we assume that we can encode ethics, which is I would say is debatable, but not unfathomable, you could have different principles in the code and by deducing from those principles, you know, how to do the right thing in a way but that could be coded out because you can change any code. You can also change any data that is in the world. The only solution we have to that is to have certain measures in place, to make it very difficult if not impossible to do so, and to be able to spot any changes that have happened.

Putting rules in place would not work with a hypothetical general intelligence AI, ethics in AI today are a different thing and I have been involved in the discussions surrounding that which are being quite broadly discussed within the European Commission and the Council of Europe about how you build ethical AI solutions and the possible threats that not doing so raises. The main discussion is focussing on AI development principles and how you ensure fairness? How do you avoid data bias? How do you avoid discrimination? Usually bias is one of the main causes for the systems to be discriminatory.

If you had this kind of more general AI, of course, then there would be a much broader sense of things. Regardless of your views of capitalism or Marxism, there are fundamental rights and wrongs. Hopefully, a general AI could transcend most of the things that humans assign as right in terms of politics or religion.'

At present, Aksela contends that machine learning AI doesn't have any motivation, it does not have desire, it does not 'want'. This echoes a point made by Professor Neil Lawrence at the start of the book. The person supplying that desire and want is the person who tells the AI what to do. So, does regulating ethics mean educating the AI developers in ethics?

'It is difficult to say due to the complexity of modern design because we have a lot of different building solutions in software and some of those are actually becoming automated too, again you have to ask the question about who is in control and what are they trying to achieve? How much of that is actually somebody who really deeply understands the machine learning and is thinking about the underlying algorithms? Or are you just asking someone to give an algorithm some data and an objective and order it to optimise the data to achieve that objective? In a sense then understanding what the system does and what you are doing becomes even more important.

That's where the democratisation of data science and machine learning use is both a huge opportunity, but also a risk, because achieving a common understanding of what's happening suddenly becomes a very large task.

Modern AIs are really simple curve fitting solutions that optimise a certain boundary between decision boundaries and try to make the most out of it, which is one of the challenges if you don't really know what your algorithm can do. You could ask an algorithm to do a good thing for example but if you do not know your data is biased or is biased in that situation and if you do not know that in advance then you might reach a totally different outcome than you intended.'

Knowing what the objective of the system is can also raise questions in this new AI world because many companies are also seeking to use AI systems to sell products to people and believe that the no holds barred use of manipulation and understanding of 'curated desires' is also right and in accordance with their terms.

'There's a lot of machine learning use for marketing purposes, because companies want to sell more things. You might argue that's good for the company, because it gets more revenue but is it what people need? There are a lot of questions particularly if we're talking about something that's not necessary.'

Should certain systems be designated as sacrosanct?

Good data is essential to a good AI outcome, so protecting the data with cyber security becomes essential, therefore should awareness be raised of the data sanctity? Should it be brought home to those wishing to hack, that certain data bases are inviolate? Or that interference with personal data should be considered a crime against the individual? For example, if a criminal interfered with medical databases or locked them with a ransomware attack should they expect a particularly heavy penalty?

'If you're trying to interfere with people's health records and consequently also potentially the treatment, they're getting from an AI system then that is putting lives at risk. It is a lot more severe than interfering with, an online game that is based on an AI system.

Hacking a game to give you a higher score is obviously not as serious, as threatening lives. It's not really about cyber or AI or anything. My thinking on this is really kind of focused on the intent in many cases, the harm that can be caused.

Putting potentially thousands of lives at risk, is more severe than putting a fair amount of revenue at risk. In most legal systems, there will be a higher penalty for killing a person than stealing their wallet.

The discussion over the regulation or legal control of AI is to do with many things and for me it is about technological pragmatics and application you should not be trying to control the machine; you should be trying to control where and how the machine is being used. AI is going to be ubiquitous it will be used for many purposes so what is important is where it is being used. If the data is in a countdown timer to that will start a nuclear holocaust that would result in world extinction, I think it would be a fairly good thing to change that timer, even if it's touching upon somebody else's data that's not yours. If you can stop really bad things happening, then that is good. It is the intent that you're trying to achieve that matters. Therefore, from a legal perspective most of this is proscribed in the current framework.'

To refer once more to the Iranian Stuxnet example, it is highly possible that the Iranians could claim that the attack on its nuclear programme is also an attack on its ability to protect its people. Although as Aksela continues there are some moral decisions that we find it easier to make:

'If you kill a person – and we know that killing is bad – it doesn't matter if you kill via driving, hitting with a hammer or a knife or anything, that's really beside the point, what matters is the intent. If you want to cause harm to people, then it's a bad thing.

For AI, even where you could easily argue that interfering with another person's data is bad, it's also possible to think about the counter examples of where it actually might be good.

There's a lot of discussion about facial recognition. The argument is essentially over whether it is bad and whether it should be banned. If the intent is to monitor everybody, then that's bad, but conversely there is no problem with using, facial recognition for biometric authentication.

There are always ways to use technology for good and bad.'

Aksela's contention is that the general population would take issue with monitoring, unless and until that monitoring could have some particularly useful benefit, for example allowing valuable information to be collected so the perpetrator of a serious crime could be caught.

'When we think about regulating technology it's never really black and white. The big challenge is to work out if there is a need for a specific regulation at this point in time. This can be argued both ways. What should it be? Should it be a kind of a blanket term, a regulation that that really prohibits the use of certain types of technology, such as forbidding the use of deep learning or probabilistic programming? Doing this might have nothing to do with what you are trying to achieve with the regulation. Or should we perhaps think about it from the point of view of intent, of what we're trying to achieve with the algorithm and then actually realise that this is governed by existing legislation.'

Out of our hands and out of control?

According to the experts AI currently has no moral responsibility, so the role of cyber security becomes all important to secure data and prevent AI-related crime.

'The role of cyber security is in many ways is more important, because currently there is not very much concrete evidence of AI hacks. We know there are prototypes and there is research and I would say it is inevitable that it will happen because criminals tend to gravitate towards a means for getting money, with the least risk and this is along that path.

If we assume that this will happen, then what are we likely to see? We have already seen the development of automatically generated malware and automation – and those and AI are very close. We expect AI will lead to more complicated attacks and breaches. The capabilities of AI systems mean they will attain much higher velocities and scope – they will hit a lot more targets in an organisation.

The difference with the present position is that the very skilled hands of a keyboard attacker are very innovative. Using current technology, they can be more effective because they can take more adaptive measures than a machine can at the moment.

On the other hand, if you train a machine learning based attack bot, it can respond much quicker than a human can write code. The speed of operation and the bandwidth of computers are huge compared to humans.

So effectively, when we start to almost see these more automated advanced AI attacks, it won't be feasible to have human responders taking care of them, because they cannot do so. Attackers are likely to launch an attack on a large organisation at multiple points at the same time. Even if you have the best data collection and the fastest service operations people there it will not matter, because the speed of operations will be so fast it will only take a few seconds to complete the whole operation.

For this to be something that the cyber security industry can defend against, I think it's very important that we also embrace the technology to defend our customers and their data and to defend our institutions.'

This is something that F-Secure along with other cyber companies has already done. F-Secure's foray into the AI world is called Project Blackfin.

'The threat landscape is changing very fast and we are sure that we will see more automated attacks and we must be ready to defend against them. The way we're approaching AI is to develop something akin to a human like intelligence. We are trying to create something that mimics things in the same way a human brain does.

Project Blackfin is building on the strength of machine learning systems of today. Instead of having one Central AI solution that learns everything, we connect up that machine learning from the edge and share it quickly and see what we can achieve within that framework: we make each of these endpoint agents intelligent and able to take decisions, we make them able to learn from the data and build upon that.

It is now part of our rapid detection or response solution. It's out there in the market and it is doing local machine learning for an anomaly detection model right now.

So traditionally anomaly detection, of course, detecting something odd isn't the same as detecting something malicious, but usually it's interesting to find why something is odd. It's not a trivial problem to solve. On each one of these endpoints, there is a machine learning model that learns what's normal behaviour for that endpoint. We then combine that information instead of having to send all the data to the back end, which does not mean that it is not also combined in the back end. This means that there are several records of the behaviour monitored by that endpoint agent: the endpoint agent's view, that of the other endpoint agents and the stored memory in the back end which can serve as a reference point for the swarm.

Now that endpoint has the capability of evaluating what's happening with the context of its own understanding of its history, which is also shared with a larger group of similar agents monitoring different endpoints allowing for a combination of both. So the endpoints can see what is common for each of them and then compare that experience with other machines they can see; 'what's common for me as this particular end point with others in the swarm'. So, for example, one running on my machine can monitor what I'm doing, what's my usual behaviour, but then also giving that other perspective of what's common for this organisation and putting all these things together to understand much better what is happening and how and when to respond.

We are going to be building a lot more capabilities around this domain so we can take actions on that data and have dynamic response actions on that endpoint. If you think about data theft, with most current detection response solutions there is a loop reaction. It can be fast and take seconds, or you can have systems that are slower and take a few minutes for this end to end loop to happen, for the data to be collected and sent to the back end and analysed and for somebody to realise there's a problem and we need to do something about it. It is a process that is still going to take minutes. And how much valuable data can you exfiltrate in today's world within minutes? A lot.

Whereas if that was all happening on the endpoint, so the endpoints analyse and detect that something strange is happening and it is high risk and looks really bad. Then the endpoint can take pre-emptive action and perhaps throttle the bandwidth, and respond in the time frame that you have at your disposal. So we will be able to deal with these fast-complex advanced attacks of the future. We're still working on it, but the first generation is out there right now, and I believe that this is the direction that will allow us to fight threats when malicious actors start to use machine learning.'

Aksela's software solution is very similar in function to a rare and primitive deep-sea jellyfish called the Flying Spaghetti Monster or *Bathyphysa Conifera*,[1] which rather than being one organism is actually a colony of symbiotic cells each with a particular function with some providing digestive abilities and others being developed to create feeding tentacles, though the colony moves as though it is one entity. With Blackfin, the aim is to create something akin to a digital immune system.

'What we want to do is to make them intelligent enough to make decisions and then allow them to share those learnings so that the threats can be better anticipated by endpoint agents that haven't seen those threats yet. There are similarities to the human immune system.

---

1 Bathyphysa conifera, see Wikipedia at https://en.wikipedia.org/wiki/Bathyphysa_conifera.

If a new type of threat, is detected that information gets spread very quickly to make sure that the whole is quickly aware of it, so the defence capabilities of the solution are much better overall.'

The criminal AI threat

The criminals have always been on the cutting edge of technology and are experimenting with innovative uses of AI technology. As well as automated attacks on systems there are ever more subtle criminal uses of AI.

Aksela highlighted one alarming technology, known as 'deepfakes' which are profoundly concerning governments, regulators and businesses alike. This is especially the case following an incident in October 2019, where newspaper reports claimed that a senior UK energy company executive was tricked into giving £200,000 to criminals, who used AI to mimic the voice of the head of the energy firm's German parent company.

Deepfakes are not just confined to voice mimicry. The software can also be used to create convincing picture and video likenesses of individuals, a computing capability that in an age of increasingly remote working has been recognised as a huge risk.

According to Olu Odeniyi, an adviser on Cyber Security and Digital Transformation:

'Many free open source tools can be used to create deepfakes. A number of low-cost internet services are also available. Deepfakes are a serious threat, which many organisations don't understand and don't know what to do about. Many companies struggle with cyber security and deepfakes could bring a surge of serious fraud cases. The use of deepfakes could trump email scams. They will increasingly be used for extortion and to extract sensitive data from unsuspecting staff.'

It is a concern shared by Aksela in the context of cyber security:

'We have seen deepfake videos where you have videos showing politicians like Barack Obama making outrageous comments and they look completely real. The issue is that they are completely false – it's fake data – the politician did not say those things, but they can be used to distribute disinformation.

It is a development that creates distrust. We know that audio deception is already happening, we just do not have the precise numbers yet. So deepfakes have been included in the overall threat landscape and threat intelligence viewpoints. There are more and more of these automated types of attacks, which are living off the "digital land", in the cyber security world.

These are not criminal computer programs though. They are using complex technological capability – machine learning or AI-based – and special effects techniques that the film industry has perfected. So where do you draw the line?

Up until now, we are not aware of any very complicated AI-based software attacks but the technological capabilities of doing that are out there. We have seen computer companies deliberately building malicious machine learning software to prove they can be built and so they should be guarded against. There is also an open source penetration testing framework that has been built using machine learning.

It would be naïve not to expect the criminal development of AI systems.'

The automated cyber war

Indeed, the development of criminal AI code is logical because for the last 15 years most computer virus attacks have been automated by sending vulnerability testing programs out to search the internet for unprotected systems. The vulnerability testing system then draws up a list of potential computers that are analysed to find valuable targets for the hackers which are automatically attacked. Cyber security companies have tried to counter vulnerability testing attacks with automation, detecting the initial contact and attempting to determine the objective.

'There is a very fine line that has to be observed in what is happening with these attacks. They require dynamic countermeasures to be effective because of the speed and the breadth of those attacks that are already possible without even having the intelligence in the sense of machine learning or AI in the loop. For the attacker that automation is causing something like an AI attack already. Yes, definitely, that is out there.'

The development of 'dynamic countermeasures' will by their nature provoke legal argument because of the current legal lack of responsibility of computer systems. For some counter measures the level of engagement will have to be specified to avoid unintended damage.

How far automated systems will be allowed to go before provoking human engagement and the rules of engagement themselves will have to be specified. Rules will be bitterly contested by the defenders who say that they are in the teeth of a cyber war at the moment, a claim borne out by the ever-increasing number of data breaches and attacks.

It is a cyber war that is getting ever more sophisticated as the cyber security companies seek to stay one step ahead of the criminals, a task that they admit they are currently failing in and one they hope that AI and particularly the area of 'augmented intelligence' can help them with.

'Augmented intelligence is going to be one of the key areas where that will help us get the most value out of the AI machinery that we have today. The machine can identify and issue much quicker than a person and make a decision such as throttling the network, and then alert the human to the situation so they can assess the issue. We have acknowledged that machine learning is a valuable tool and we should use it to make our jobs better and then let human experts focus on what they need them to do, because then we complement each other. Processing billions and billions of rolls of data is definitely not a job for a human being.

We can build an algorithm though that is programmed to find what you're looking for in that data, training it on examples of malicious code or code that has a particular function. It then creates its own classifier. That program then analyses all of that data looking for those malicious examples and flags them up for a human operator to examine. That is a very useful example of AI deployment. We are doing a lot of that.'

The terrifying threat of an automated conflict beyond human control

A growing technological familiarity has, however, meant that criminals are now able to live off the digital land. Innovation and the speed of the attacks are essential, either for taking over computers or creating a diversion.

In January 2020 Navinder Singh Sarao used his ability to spot numerical patterns in mere seconds to influence the market, resulting in him making more than £9 million. Sarao, who suffered from autism, regarded trading as a video game in which the object was to compile points, not money.

The 41-year-old UK man was confined to his parents' home for a year for his May 2010 trading, which wiped billions off the value of publicly traded companies. Other examples abound, where hackers have used botnet attacks to distract cyber security staff into dealing with the automated online attack whilst the hackers enter the computer systems via another route. The use of AI systems in defending against attack could trigger an automated response and many fear that if attacks are targeted on sensitive computers that this could trigger an unintended cyber war where AI programs fight each other in cyber space and begin to soak up computer resources that could bring down our life support system: the internet.

On 9 November 1988, in perhaps the first example of an automated internet vulnerability attack, Robert Morris Junior, a student at MIT, wrote and released a program, now known as the 'Morris Worm', that was designed to highlight security weaknesses in computers linked to the nascent internet known as Janet. Morris unfortunately instructed the code to copy itself multiple times and to spread. The result was that the internet became overloaded and crashed. Although computer room managers became aware of the worm they were unable to combat the speed at which it replicated and had to disconnect the computers from the Janet network so they could be cleaned and isolated.

It is a doomsday scenario that AI systems would have the very real capability to bring about again.

Another very real threat, as we will explore further in the next chapter, is the theft, analysis and manipulation of data to target individuals as shown with Cambridge Analytica's influencing of the US elections.

'Fooling or misleading AI is a very important topic and it's one that's not getting enough attention. We need to build more resilient AI that it is harder to mislead, harder to attack, harder to manipulate.

110

If you put this into context, we constantly need to do the same for humans as well because we also want to educate people not to click on those links in phishing emails because they might download malicious software. One of the most common attack routes is still spam email that has either a malicious attachment or a malicious link in the body.

Now AI is an emerging threat in so many different ways and to counter that it has become crucially important to build really secure AI and to think about the security of AI, because people are not thinking about security. They are just thinking about: "how do you optimise the AI program?" They are not necessarily thinking about how their model could be exploited.

If we take the example of Churn Prediction Models you could put together a program to predict churn for mobile phone operators. The operators might want to contact the customer and encourage them to stay with them by offering some kind of incentive to stay.

The data scientists and the people working on these types of models do not actually think how that model could be effectively misused or what the impact could be. Can somebody manipulate the system so that they get incentives that are actually meant for a different purpose from the operator's perspective? That's a rather benign example.

With a security AI, the risks become greater because of what the security AI will be guarding and the places AI systems will be: autonomous vehicles and the image recognition systems they rely on could be manipulated to deceive either a vehicle or the machine learning that can be used in a healthcare setting in diagnosis or even surgery to take over the flight control systems of a plane without needing to get a terrorist on board. AI systems allow very fine targeting to take place.

There are so many applications where, being able to mislead or manipulate AI solutions can lead to great harm. This is something that anybody who builds AI machine learning models must be aware of whether it is for a political purpose or for an autonomous vehicle. Cyber security must become a core part of AI system development and that will also include an understanding of how these systems can be exploited if it fails.

This means that we all have to build secure AI solutions from the start. In my experience, this is not always the case: security is often the last thing that is added, with minimum effort at the very end, right before releasing a product.'

The essential legal log

There will be serious issues for the development of AI systems and the law, something Aksela is only too well aware of, not only is transparency necessary but also a log of what the systems have done and how they have arrived at their conclusions. There will also need to be the potential for a system reset.

'When you create machine learning models, you have to understand what's going on. We have to monitor the models and understand from the learning and analyse any mistakes a solution has made. I am not the biggest fan of the most complicated AI scenarios because you have large complicated systems that can only tolerate small input variations. I do not like them because variables can sometimes cause unexpected outcomes which can have a big impact, even if only small changes happen. The, robustness of models is a design issue. So, when you are thinking about how to build your machine learning solution, I think that should be one of the most critical points, making sure your system is robust and not restricted by its data. This is essential when we think about what a system is meant to do and where it is meant to be used.

If you are building an AI for a game, if it behaves oddly it's not that bad. But if it is a critical life and death system, or critical infrastructure that must not fail, it is very important that cyber security is taken into consideration when building that solution. It's really hard to glue on things after the fact, even if you really want to do it. Repairing a ship letting in water is more difficult than not having to make the repair in the first place.'

Taking responsibility for arm's length harm

Aksela's main message, as with most of the experts we interviewed, was that the problems that we face do not actually lie with the machines, they lie with us. It is people who are instructing machines to exploit the vulnerabilities of other people with fake messages, deepfakes, and fake news and it is people who supply demand and desire in the current AI world.

Aksela wants regulation of AI but, like Professor Ng, he points out that any regulation has to apply to people because the machines do not have any responsibility. The rules of our offline world he says, should be applied to our online world.

'AI is a technology, it is an enabler for things. When we start thinking about the discussion that we are seeing at the moment, that discussion is incorporating concerns that are way beyond what we have right now.

It is misleading for us to think about it as something magical or mythical or something that is truly intelligent. Currently, and for many years to come, it is going to be something that is a really valuable tool that we will use properly. The discussion is about what you would use this technology for. Like any technology, you can use it for a lot of good or bad.

I think the most important thing is that we should understand the technology and we should use it the right way.'

Combating the myth of the god in the machine

Aksela is concerned that there is a danger that the media, marketing and PR companies are misrepresenting the technology and exploiting our innate desire for magic; and that AI is being dangerously portrayed as an impending sentient deity.

'In a way, it is sad because that also takes away from what we can achieve. If we use technology to do good and with good intentions, we can do a lot of very good things but that's not what's happening right now. There are discussions on what we should be preparing for but there is also a bit more about a sci-fi world than what is actually out there, but there is a risk involved in getting this right. We must prevent the development of a Skynet or a sentient AI that will kill all humankind.

We must be really, really careful and start regulating the technology's development. That is something that is not going to happen globally, because there are going to be countries that will seek to abuse it and there are countries that we know that sponsor that.

Machine learning can be used as a building block for this solution, but an algorithm alone isn't the answer. We cannot ask an algorithm to monitor the ethical development of AI. That is our job.

The European initiative on developing AI law has provoked the fiercest debate and the biggest appetite for regulation but we should also be aware that this is also about morality in societies and that should be addressed.

The remoteness of drone pilots from what they do is very similar to the remoteness of computer hackers. It is easier to do harm with your fingertips to people in places far away. It is often said that somebody in some large tenement block in a foreign country does not care about the person that they are subjecting to a ransomware attack, they just want the money. There is no human engagement and they cannot see the impact of what they are doing. This has to change.'

Chapter 8

AI as the information weapon

The data war to end all wars?

The ability of AI to accomplish successful threat detection to our corporate data assets is clear and, as Dr Aksela noted in his evidence, so long as such threat detection is permitted legally, there is a high degree of confidence that the cyber security industry will be able to prevail in its day-to-day technological game of cat and mouse with threat actors. The speed and scale at which data can be collected and interpreted by machine learning and AI systems, however, does not mean that vulnerabilities, which could overwhelm us, may not arise.

The doctrine of 'Information Warfare', which was first developed by Winn Schwartau in his 1994 book of the same name, was initially dismissed in its early days as a 'geeky fad'. It is now accepted, however, as one of the realities of modern-day internet life because of our now near total reliance on the network. As we will now explore, the rapidly evolving trend to connect everything in our lives to the internet, from our bodies to our houses and our memories, makes us vulnerable in ways we have never considered.

Former Brigadier General Robert Spalding is a senior fellow at the Hudson Institute, whose work focuses on US-China relations, economic and national security, and the Asia-Pacific military balance. He is recognised as an expert on Chinese economic competition, cyber warfare, and political influence.

Brig-Gen Spalding has served in senior positions of strategy and diplomacy within the US Defense and State Departments for more than 26 years. As Senior Director for Strategy to the President, he was the chief architect of the framework for national competition in the Trump administration's National Security Strategy (NSS). During his time as a Military Fellow at the Council on Foreign Relations, he worked on US foreign policy and national security issues and encouraged competition to develop a Secure 5G infrastructure for the US.

Brig-Gen Spalding has written extensively on national security matters and is a Life Member of the Council on Foreign Relations. He has lectured globally, including engagements at the Naval War College, National Defense University, Air War College, Columbia University, S. Rajaratnam School of International Studies in Singapore and Johns Hopkins Applied Physics Laboratory. He received his BSc. and MSc. degrees in Agricultural Business from California State University, Fresno, and holds a doctorate in economics and mathematics from the University of Missouri, Kansas City. He is a distinguished graduate of the Defense Language Institute in Monterey and is fluent in Chinese Mandarin.

Brig-Gen Spalding is a noted critic of the Chinese regime and particularly focusses on the threat of data theft from nation states using communications networks.

Professor Toby Walsh *FAA, FACM, FRSN is a Laureate Fellow and Scientia Professor of AI at the University of New South Wales and research group leader at Data61. He has served as Scientific Director of NICTA, Australia's centre of excellence for ICT research. He is noted for his work in AI, especially in the areas of social choice, constraint programming and propositional satisfiability. Professor Walsh currently serves on the Executive Council on the Association for the Advancement of AI.*

He received an MA degree in theoretical physics and mathematics from the University of Cambridge and a MSc. and PhD. degree in AI from the University of Edinburgh. He has held research positions in Australia, England, Ireland, Italy France, Germany, Scotland and Sweden.

In 2015, he helped release an open calling for a ban on offensive autonomous weapons that attracted over 20,000 signatures. In 2017, he organised an open letter calling for a ban signed by over 100 founders of AI and Robotics companies including Elon Musk, Mustafa Suleyman and Jüergen Schmidhuber.

He is the author of two books on AI: 'It's Alive!: Artificial Intelligence from the Logic Piano to Killer Robots' which looks at the history and present of AI, and '2062: The World that AI Made', which looks at the potential impact AI will have on our society.

The very personal dangers of data

Whilst Brig-Gen Spalding and Professor Walsh sit at opposite ends of the political spectrum, both acknowledge that our readiness to give our data to big and small tech companies we know very little about, simply by accepting their terms and conditions, could have wide ranging consequences, of which we are completely unaware. By clicking to accept these terms – often without even reading them – we let those companies own intimate knowledge about us and open a window into our lives, to which we ourselves do not have access, in return for some beguiling service.

This data, which as we have seen from Professor Ng would inevitably include core data, signal data and the more contextualised information derivatives, instantly provides an insight into our interests, which can mean that we ourselves can be 'hacked'. We are allowing companies to gain an insight into our lives that we would not give to our neighbours. At best we can be psychologically manipulated, at worst we can be blackmailed unless we are guaranteed anonymity.

To underpin that last point, in an exercise carried out by one of the book's authors, over 100 hard drives were bought from the internet and then analysed. One belonged to the personal assistant to the head of NATO and contained extremely compromising information about the person's private life which (because of their devout religious beliefs) meant that they would have been vulnerable to pressure. In another case personal information on a famous senior UK politician was offered to one of the authors obtained from a credit card company, detailing the purchase of sex aids.

Whilst potentially shocking, it is only when presented in this way that the very real concerns of Spalding start to make sense.

In a 5G-AI world (where the speeds of data flow achievable on 5G networks enable greater processing of data for AI systems, as well as on the edge processing by more powerful devices) the ability to mine through vast amounts of data is a huge danger not only because individuals can be targeted but because of the detail that can be gathered on them from multiple sources. Just as we do not know what data on us is stored where, we also do not know how data is being collected, whether from friends or acquaintances' data stores that we are included in, or on websites we have visited.

We are now in a position where internet, retail and finance companies know more about us than our family and friends do, down to every intimate detail. It is a state of affairs that is now being debated by military experts. Social media, mind control and psychological manipulation was one of the topics on the agenda at 'Extreme Threats to the UK', a joint conference between the Royal United Services Institute and the Royal Aeronautical Society that took place in September 2020.

If an unfriendly state controls a nation's network it can not only turn it off, generating panic and incapacitating it, as was experienced by the Iraqis during the first Gulf War, it can also extract data: two capabilities Sun Tzu,[1] the influential ancient Chinese military thinker would have heartily endorsed.

The potential use of AI and 5G has also begun to concern defence experts. This is especially true in the wake of the claims made about the Cambridge Analytica scandal, in which it was said that the UK-based company was able to identify opinion leaders via a Facebook-based quiz and feed them with false information to unfairly influence the US election in favour of Donald Trump. It's a potential that has led to worries that similar techniques could be used by a foreign power to adversely affect people's psychology at times of increased global tension.

It is for these reasons that the US has insisted that the Chinese telecommunications giant Huawei is excluded from its market while successfully exerting sustained pressure upon the UK to remove Huawei from its network.

The concerns about Huawei are not just restricted to the US. MI5, the UK domestic intelligence agency, has been conducting a covert war against the Chinese telecoms company since it was first included in the UK's core infrastructure because, MI5 argues, the presence of the Chinese technology means that the UK has no surety that the telecoms network is loyal to the UK. In background briefings the domestic intelligence agency has been pointing out that there are also issues with potential data loss. The Emergency Services Network, over which messages are passed between Special Branch and MI5, is also potentially compromised owing to plans for it to run through smart base station technology 'on the edge' run by Huawei. Perhaps more importantly for MI5, its own communications will also pass over the 5G network.

As that smart technology processes much of that data on the edge, it raises significant concerns over its integrity and represents a significant threat to it.

---

1 Sun Tzu's *Art of War* is a standard military text book and has been since it was written in the 5th century BC. It is notable that one of Sun Tzu's preoccupations is with the acquisition of intelligence and information. For this reason *The Art of War* is also a standard cyber security textbook.

The reassurances from the UK Government that Huawei equipment will not be installed in the core of the network then become meaningless, particularly as the point of the 5G network is that most processing will be done 'on the edge', precisely where Huawei's equipment is installed.

As Spalding says in comments remarkably reminiscent of those of Professor Ng, securing data is essential. Though for Spalding ensuring the privacy and sanctity of data has military as well as personal reasons.

> 'I have been vocal about secure data and I think that's the challenge. It is not about Huawei, it is about Huawei being a conduit for the Chinese Communist Party (CCP) for acquiring data.
>
> It does not matter if it is Huawei or any other Chinese manufacturer. If they are making 3G compliant equipment, then they are making a Chinese network. It is the challenge of 5G, the control of data.
>
> As the Taiwanese-born American computer scientist and businessman, Kai-Fu Lee, author of "AI Superpowers: China, Silicon Valley and the New World Order" and the leading AI thought leader in China, says, "as Saudi Arabia is to oil, China aims to be to data".
>
> This is a big challenge for democracies, as the CCP and its businesses begin to use this data not just for commerce, but also for influence and intelligence collection.'

The information war

Hitherto the concerns about Chinese data collection have centred on the sort of intellectual property theft that came to light in 'Titan Rain', a US counter-intelligence project that sought to prevent Chinese data theft from several military development sites. Now, says Spalding, it is not just intellectual property or the settings from robot production lines; the Chinese want all of our data.

> 'Data is the power that drives the 21st century. AI requires data to improve the algorithms to improve our lives. Silicon Valley developed an entire app service and business model ecosystem that allows it to take data out of the system in order to provide you services. But that same data can be used to collect intelligence on you and influence you.
>
> It had been the case that you can opt out of that by not carrying a smartphone, because smartphones track nearly everything that you do. In the 5G world, the smartphone is no longer needed; it's built into the world around you, that means you cannot opt out.
>
> Today you open an app like Uber on your phone to call a car, tomorrow you will walk out of your front door and say "Uber", a camera will recognise your face, or read your lips or a microphone will pick up your voice and send a car.
>
> All of the data that's being collected about you, about your intentions, about who you meet, about your personality, all are useful when put it into an AI

system, and can be used to derive your intentions, but it can also begin to influence you imperceptibly.

That happens today with e-commerce. In China, the state is automating the ability to control the population. As these tech companies in China grow in power in the 5G system, slowly Baidu, Alibaba and Tencent will overtake Facebook, Amazon and Google because of their complete access to data for their AIs. They're really the most powerful tech companies today.

As they do, the ability for individual companies like Facebook, Amazon and Google to compete with the CCP's much more powerful ecosystem is going to be nearly impossible.

In 2007, when iPhone came out, there was no Facebook, Amazon or Google in the world's top five companies. In 2007, the world's top five companies were AT&T, General Electric, Microsoft, Exxon Mobil and Shell. In ten years, it's going to be Baidu, Alibaba and Tencent.

The reason Huawei has been so powerful is because the CCP takes income from Baidu, Alibaba and Tencent – Alibaba alone made $38 billion on Singles Day last year – and subsidises the deployment of the network because they want access to data to drive the global economy. In the 21st century, this is how you collect intelligence and drive influence.

In the US we spend $800 billlion on aircraft carriers, on F35s, on nuclear subs, on tanks, on an incredible array of military capability. None of that matters in the 21st century when you can influence at the individual level using people's data.

It is not a battle of the future, it is happening now.'

AI as the new world influencer

'In the US election in 2016, the Russians used AI bots, social media networks and big data to create protests in the US on both sides of the aisle. In the run up to the Taiwanese elections, the Chinese were using the same kind of technology and techniques within Taiwan, in Malaysia and in the Philippines. It is happening in Europe today as well.

All over the world, these tools are being used not only to create economic value for the companies that possess them, but also, if those companies happen to be in totalitarian regimes, to create influence for those regimes.

This is a practice documented by Samantha Hoffman, a researcher at the Australian Strategic Policy Institute. Ms Hoffman highlighted Global Tone Communications Corporation, a Chinese big data and AI company that does language translation in 65 languages, whose technology is built into Huawei products. It collects two to three petabytes of data per year and then sends that data to China not just for translating languages, but it also sends it to the People's Liberation Army intelligence arm and the propaganda arm of the CCP.'

119

To get some idea of the size of a petabyte, it is the equivalent of 68 billion pages of A4 documents. If made into a pile, one petabyte would make a tower 24,892 times the height of Canary Wharf at 6165.9 km high, nearly 700 times the height of Everest, an inconceivable amount of data. If ASPI's Hoffman is correct, then the figure from just one Chinese company is three times that and therefore the amount of data China is capturing is huge. However, can it be processed and analysed? According to Spalding:

'In 2017, I was asked the same question by the intelligence community: "How can the Chinese possibly process all that data?"

My response was: "That's what Facebook, Amazon and Google's business models are based on, being able to process that data and turn it into clicks. They are experts at it."

It is evident because of the existence of the Chinese tech giants that they have all that technology and capability. It is well documented in Kai Fu Lee's "AI Superpowers".'

For Spalding the situation is so precarious that all data must be protected.

'Not just some databases, but all data. In particular data owned by individuals should be only owned by those individuals and viewable only according to the individual's permission. What we failed to do when we built the internet was to secure data.'

Hacking humanity

It is a point that is also made by Walsh who feels, like Spalding, that the time for action is now because we are in a position where people can be hacked.

'There are immense risks. We are discovering that you can hack humans. You can collect data on a scale that humans never could have done and we're discovering that humans are full of lots of behavioural biases.

It's very easy to present data to people, to present fake news and filter bubbles that change what people decide, change how people act, not necessarily in their interests. We don't require much more sophisticated systems, we can do this already with the technologies we already have so we can already see many of these challenges. Which makes me think why should we allow micro-targeting of political adverts? It is not adding to our political discourse, it appears to be doing the opposite. That is why it should be banned, we regulate television advertising and we regulate the truth of political adverts. This is a very powerful, pervasive technology that needs to be regulated.'

According to Walsh, of particular concern is our implicit belief in technology itself. Computers can 'out remember' us already. In a bid to combat technology addiction and offset memory loss Microsoft and other companies, if given permission, flash memories from our past at us, telling us what we were doing many years ago, but we never question or could challenge their accuracy. Digital dependence can lead to re-programming. Walsh continues:

'We've only seen the beginnings of this. In some sense we have given up a lot of our digital lives. But the good thing about our digital lives is you can lie about your digital preferences. You can hide behind VPNs. It is possible, if you are careful, to evade some of this scrutiny. But we're starting to actually hand over data about our analogue selves, if you connect as many of us are doing to Fitbit, then you personally do not "know" that data.

Fitbit own your heartbeat and increasingly other bits of analogue data; where you are physically in the world, your blood pressure, all of these things. We have given our signal data to tech companies and now we are in danger of giving out even more private data. We have to be careful about this because if you want to think of a really dystopian world, you could have a world in which advertisers can actually monitor your bodily responses to their adverts. You can lie about your likes on Facebook, but you can't lie about your heartbeat. So that's an incredibly powerful tool to see the dilation of your pupils, to see how your heartbeat changes when you're exposed to an advert.

And, if you want the worst possible world to think about, it's when political parties get hold of that, when they can actually see how you respond to the political messages, they are giving to you.

It is something that could be done it on a nationwide scale and in real time, which you can do with smart algorithms. That is an incredibly powerful tool of manipulation, one that even George Orwell hadn't envisaged when he wrote "1984".'

Spalding and Walsh agree that the aim is no longer to hack our computers but to use our computers to hack our minds, a development extensively examined in a recent report produced by Future Intelligence.[2] The fact that technology can be used to discover our political preferences was confirmed by Clive Hunby,[3] the former joint head of the data analysis company Dunn-Hunby, and for Walsh this is something that must be regulated against.

'It's the political strategists that will be trying to hack us, they will be hacking our political preferences, hacking our purchasing preferences and hacking our brains. We like to think that we're rational in our decision making but actually, there's plentiful evidence in the psychology literature to show that we are very irrational in decision making and we're discovering the very tools that would allow us to manipulate the decisions that we make and not necessarily in our interest.'

Spalding notes that this issue:

'Is a challenge for democracy if we don't stand up and if we don't do something. The EU tried to pass global data protection regulation but that was completely irrelevant because you have no way of enforcing it physically on the data of the citizens to make sure that their data is not used in ways that are contrary to their own interests.'

---

2 See www.futureintelligence.co.uk/2021/06/09/big-tech-data-scraping-to-discover-our-emotions/.
3 See Chapter 10 and Chapter 17.

As Spalding says, the use of our data is now global and laws have geographical boundaries, trying to enforce them extra-territorially is very difficult. Some argue that determined enforcement is the issue and suggest that recent developments such as the announcement by the EU in July 2020 of a travel ban and asset freeze on two Chinese citizens and four Russians for hacking and intellectual property theft are the answer. The EU response is similar to that of the US which has begun issuing arrest warrants for a number of mainly Chinese foreign nationals for intellectual property theft. The solution according to Spalding is much simpler.

'We have to build encryption into the network. When your data is created, it needs to be encrypted and you need to have the key to it. Otherwise, there is no way of enforcing it. You cannot create an organisation to enforce data security. You have to build it into the fabric of the technology. That's the challenge with GDPR. A law cannot be enforced in a system that is essentially like the Wild West.'

Encrypt data to save our souls

But how do you build security or compliance into the software? Indeed, any large computer corporation should be able to find a way around it. For Spalding the Chinese have already achieved a head start in preventing his encryption solution.

'The Third Generation Partnership Project (3GPP) is the name of the industry standard making body where all the big telecommunication players, AT&T, Verizon, Huawei, ZTE, and Samsung, come together to design the 5G standards.

That is completely outside of government purview. In cyber security, 60 per cent. of the standards have been issued by the Chinese. All of the underlying patents are also all written by the Chinese. Today, there are 800 submissions on security at 3GPP with 3000 pages of technical write-ups on system vulnerabilities, none of which have been adopted, because the CCP controls the 3GPP.

Companies like BT and AT&T are not going to protect data any more than the government, you have to build security into the technology and the way we do that, or we used to do it, is by having standards that were adopted by the governments on behalf of the people to ensure that they had safety and security. We have governments today that have abdicated their responsibility to protect their citizens to corporations of the world and the CCP's swooped in and taken control of that process because in China, there's no difference between government and business.'

In the twenty-first century, the power is with the processors

Huawei is no stranger to surveillance practices. In meetings with the UK telecommunications giant BT in 2005 during tenders for the twenty-first century network, Huawei stressed that it could intercept 4 per cent of the UK's phone traffic in real-time if BT wanted them to do it for intelligence agencies. The legal obligation, then and now, is that BT only has to be capable of intercepting 0.01 per cent of calls. In the meeting Huawei shocked BT staff by trying to make the interception capabilities of its equipment a selling point. That Huawei is interested in knowing what is going on in its network does not surprise Spalding, he says it is the business of the twenty-first century technology company.

'If the governments hire a company to build them a network, it is not going to be as powerful as the network that Amazon, Facebook and Google have built or that Baidu, Ali Baba and Tencent own. The tech companies are far more capable, and they have far more talent and resources to do it.

Government spends its money on bombs and bullets the tech community spends its money on processors, on data collection and data processing. So, they are experts at what they do. I literally would not listen to a government official when they tell you about data processing.'

Such power, particularly when a government makes its country's own corporations subordinate to the state, Spalding says, is terrifying and has the very real possibility of technological mind control. According to him social media is now a cyber weapon.

'At the end of the Cold War, we thought we were going to turn the world into freedom loving people. What we failed to realise was that globalisation, and the internet gave totalitarian regimes with these technologies and these connectivity capabilities the ability to actually influence populations in exactly the opposite direction.

The economic power the Chinese exert via social media is huge the general manager of the Houston Rockets nearly lost his job because he tweeted about the people of Hong Kong, while a mid-level employee of the Marriott Corporation was fired at the behest of the CCP because he liked to tweet about Tibet. If you think that this influence isn't going on in your population right now, then you're wrong.'

In 1996 Patrick Tyrrell, the then head of the emerging UK cyber agency Commodore, put forward the idea that we should have national boundaries in cyberspace and that the UK's banking and financial sector should be protected accordingly. In 2020 those national boundaries are beginning to be asserted in a 'high tech nationalism' trend dubbed 'the splinternet'. Should we be arming with new age weapons to counter the threat coming from the Chinese? Spalding thinks so:

'If, in the Battle of Britain, instead of adopting aviation force protection, the Royal Air Force had said, we do not think anybody is going to fight in the skies so we are not going to build a Royal Air Force the Battle of Britain would have been a disaster. Today, we are ignoring the war that is happening around us influencing our population and stealing their data and claiming it is not the responsibility of governments but of corporations.'

When Nortel, the Canadian communications giant collapsed, it was found that the computers of its 100 top executives had been compromised by hackers who had removed huge amounts of information on intellectual property, including the company position, in numerous bids and tenders.[4] These were all losses that Huawei was claimed to be the direct beneficiary of, winning both business and developing products at Nortel's expense. As Spalding points out, in a new AI-directed war over 5G networks, the theft of company data is as effective a means of destruction as a bombing raid. As a result Nortel no longer exists.

In the UK Government, officials are wary about talking about the country being in a high-tech cyber war, out of fear that it will provoke a physical war, but for Spalding encryption and AI defences must be embraced. The lessons of Sun Tzu must be taken to heart.

'In the Pentagon we look at national security in terms of 20th century tools and procedures. That's changed. That is no longer the war being fought.

It's one of the reasons why I have been fighting this so hard, because I think it's hard for people to wake up and realise that, while we thought we were ruling the world, we were being essentially outflanked.

The rules are changing, geopolitics is changing, national security is changing. What we've built in the 20th century no longer has relevance in the 21st. And we need to think differently or we're going to lose our freedoms.

And quite frankly, the large tech companies are far more knowledgeable about how to manipulate populations using their tools rather than using the bombs and bullets that we used in the 20th century. The challenge we have is to address it.'

Hi-tech brutal and efficient war of our times

Spalding's fears of an information war are shared from the other side of the political spectrum by Walsh who not only can foresee an AI-controlled cyber war but one of AI-controlled weapon systems and robot soldiers as nation states arm themselves for the very different twenty-first century war.

'I have very strong views about this as do thousands of my colleagues because we cross into very dangerous territory. And there are plentiful legal, technical and moral issues to be concerned about.

One of the mistakes I think people make when they start discussing this is to think that the concerns that people like myself have who work in the field are fixed in time.

Actually, the concerns are going to change over time. The concerns I have today with the current capabilities are often about the inadequacies of the machines we will be handing over control to that will be making lots of mistakes and killing lots of the wrong people.

Equally, I can also see in 10, 20, 30 or 40 years' time when the technologies are much more capable than now we will have much greater concerns, some

---

4 Interview with Brian Shields Nortel's former head of cyber security, February 2020.

that the technologies will be much more capable and that will transform the way we fight war and that humans will no longer be in charge.

I am also concerned about the possibility that we might end up with flash wars happening because we put these complex systems out into the real world, and they interact against competitive systems in places like the internet.

We have already seen examples of how that ends badly in the stock market[5] and we've already had to put in circuit breakers and other measures to make sure that these complex systems do not behave in undesirable ways. That is acceptable in the stock market, because if something goes wrong, as has happened, the circuit breakers start and stop all the transactions and say none of that took place and they give everyone back their money and the system reboots. If that was the border between North Korea and South Korea and you have just started a nuclear war you cannot do that, because the algorithms got into unfortunate feedback loops and faster than humans could intervene, started fighting a war.'

However, Walsh admits this may not be like the wars in the past. Rather, they may be people fighting for your heartbeat, trying to use technology in a more sophisticated way so that the war is not noticeable. Sudden movements in the stock market may be the future wars.

'World War III will start on the internet. It is clear it is going to start in cyberspace before it starts in the physical space.[6] Then people are going to take down infrastructure connected to the internet, the water system, power plants, hospitals, everything that is online will be brought down. You will know that the World War III has started because everything will stop. That is going to impact all of us. Then it will spread out into the physical world.

If you look at the trajectory, warfare is increasingly against civilian populations, it is not fighting on battlefields with one army against another. They are very asymmetric; increasingly they're against civilian populations. If you look at Syria and elsewhere, you see that the wars are increasingly fought in and around and against civilian populations.

It is certainly not going to be robot against robots. And the idea that we can get people out of the battlefield make warfare much easier is I think, an incredibly dangerous and wrongheaded thought.'

In an AI world conflict will be a literal battle of hearts and minds

It is against this backdrop that Walsh thinks that the deployment of AI in cyber security represents an additional threat.

---

5 See Dr Matti Aksela's comments re Navinder Singh Sarao in Chapter 7.
6 The February 2022 increase in tension between Russia and the Ukraine saw a noticeable increase in cyber attacks as Russian troops massed on the Ukrainian border.

'Cyber attacks will become increasingly intelligent. Most current cyber attacks are rather unsophisticated simple phishing attacks that rely on human gullibility. Increasingly, they are going to be smarter. The only form of defence you have to deal with the speed and the volume of attacks will be by having smart algorithms to defend against them. Ultimately only secure military systems will be the ones not connected to anything because there will be no other way to protect them. That attack is going to be more sophisticated.

AI systems will be looking to hack people to win wars in ways that we've never thought of before. They may not actually involve missiles. It may involve changing the perception of humanity, of doing what we've already seen occur in the American election, where individuals are targeted and homed in on, to change perception and to win, without blowing people up.

Russia's already going down that road. I think this is why we do really have to worry about regulating both autonomous weapons in the physical kinetic world, and the cyber world. There are ongoing discussions at the United Nations about both those topics, with limited success.'

For Spalding, involving large technology companies in a developing 'splinternet' is not the answer. Like Professor Ng, he too favours control over personal data.

'What we need to do is secure the data. Once you secure the data in a democracy and you give individual citizens the power over their data this ability to manipulate them without their knowledge goes away. This is the only way that I can see to actually protect a democracy in the digital future.

If, for example, we were to say Facebook is now going to become an arm of the government then the government essentially is watching everything you do, and it has all kinds of incentives to begin to use that data in ways that are not according to our interests, principles or values we lose.

To counter China, we cannot become China.'

Ironically Spalding sees close parallels between Chinese state opinion surveillance and that of the large Silicon Valley tech giants.

'In fact, the business models are the same. If you go to China, the only people that know about the Tiananmen massacre are the censors that are employed by the government to censor all the traffic, on the network. At the same time, Facebook and Google employs censors, who are trained on what they should take off and leave on their platforms.

It's the same model. It's a model of control. Google and Facebook use it for commerce, and so they want to prevent Congress from regulating them. In China, it's all about controlling the population. In both places though, the censorship is due to the fears of state intervention in their businesses.'

The technology arms race we have to face

Is there going to be an AI and quantum computing arms race?

'When quantum computing is added to AI and you get a sufficiently number of Qubits (the basic unit of quantum information), then you can break any current encryption. We face almost a Y2K, call it a Q2K, where all of our encrypted data will be easily opened by a quantum computer in the future.

In that case, all of the encrypted data held by governments that the CCP have been able to collect but not open, they'll have access to as well. We have to come up with a post quantum encryption that allows us to prevent quantum computers from attacking our encryption.'

In October 2021, the announcement by Facebook that it had changed its name to Meta Platforms suddenly brought a new and fast developing technology to the public consciousness, the Metaverse. This is an attempt by big tech to create a complete digital copy of the world in which the technology companies aim to render every object and its behaviour in virtual reality, an objective that will mean that the technology companies will be able to accurately map our lives and to predict what will happen as the result of a particular action. If taken to its logical extreme they will digitally own each and every one of us, provoking Spalding to underline that ownership of individual data is the fundamental need in the coming AI age:

'Cyber security is a component we need but cyber security is only protecting the network. When you lock that data down with encryption, you tie it to an identity, particularly if it is a biometrically authenticated, encrypted, multifactor identity.

It is going to be very hard for anybody, even if they get access to the network to take that data and use it for anything. It is about protecting the data at the data level and building security from the inside out.

We have to start treating the digital highway of the future, the same way as we treat highways today. When you start doing that and protecting data at the centre, then you actually begin to have a chance for democracies to be competitive. The citizens of the CCP cannot encrypt their data that means they are all liable to be hacked.

If you secure the data of a democracy, the democracies are resilient enough to accept that. More importantly, it allows them to innovate and grow their economy and actually make their population more productive. Imagine if, rather than Facebook, Amazon and Google, just taking your data for nothing they have to pay for it. That's what I'm talking about, the ability to actually monetise your life.'

Securing our data to protect our future

'Everybody ought to be identified and their data secured, and the key for that data owned by them. That should be mandated in democracies. I think it's absolutely crucial for us to preserve our freedoms we cannot allow large companies or any kind of government to have the ability to aggregate data about us without our consent.

Once you control your data your relationships are based on trust. If a company says, it will not give you a service and you want that service, you can give them access to your data to obtain that service. If the company takes that data and uses it for another purpose, then you can take away the key.

In the 21st century, our security relationships really have far less meaning than before – what does have meaning are the economic, financial trade and information ties that keep us working together, collaborating as democracies, as free trade economies, as societies that want to protect the rights and privileges of our citizens.

People should get a vote in how this system works rather than the system working on automatic without their vote.'

It is a potential situation that could even see wars being fought and won in virtual reality without a shot being fired. It is also a potential conflict that could rob us of all determination. Walsh's solution to the challenges from AI both on the battlefield and in cyberspace is regulation and prohibition.

'If you look at the history of disarmament and development of military technology, we have decided there are certain technologies that should be regulated for a number of reasons, because we find weapons of mass destruction repugnant. We decided that for chemical weapons, we decided that for biological weapons, we decided that now even for nuclear weapons, cluster munitions, blinding lasers, there's a number of technologies that we've looked at and decided we do not actually need those and we do find that that crosses a line. We have collectively, globally decided to control those uses. And those regulations are not perfect. Biological weapons occasionally get used in Syria and elsewhere, but the world is a much better place because we have decided those technologies should be regulated.'

Walsh dismisses suggestions that ruthless adversaries will ignore any ban.

'It's not necessary. We have plentiful deterrents already: F-15s, cruise missiles, aircraft carrier fleets. We have plenty of large sticks – military, economic and diplomatic – to deter people from doing wrong. We do not need autonomous weapons or to allow AI the right to decide who lives and who dies.'

Walsh, like Spalding, views attacks on data by both states and individuals as of great concern particularly because of the developing fusion between automation and physical and cyber warfare.

'These are really challenging, difficult worlds that we're going to end up in and one of the challenges that is one of attribution is actually very difficult in the cyber world, especially to know who's coming at you. So maybe you can see that your database has been hacked, but to work out who it was is actually quite difficult. We see this all the time that fingers are pointed at North Korea, fingers are pointed at Russia saying that that's where we think these attacks are coming at us, but there's always that uncertainty. That's very destabilising. If we don't actually know who is coming at us, who it is that you therefore should be retaliating against?

We're going to have to consider these issues carefully. The first time I went to the United Nations to talk about the challenges of kinetic autonomous weapons, I noticed that they were talking about cyber warfare in the next room, and I sat in and listened on the discussion. As I went in, I said to my minders, everything I'm about to say in the room discussing autonomous weapons, you should be saying in this room about attacks in cyberspace: and they said; "we understand that, but it's already a difficult enough problem without you trying to compile the two together and make them even broader.'

The very real consequences of virtual attacks

For Walsh the need for regulation in cyberspace is overdue and, unlike Spalding, he rejects the argument that regulation is hard to accomplish, and he dismisses arguments from big tech that regulation will stifle innovation and from internet libertarians that the internet is a free space where laws should not apply. He also thinks that defensive and offensive cyber security weapons should be banned.

'To go back to the question of the physical and the cyber world, the two are merging into one and the distinction between the two is becoming very difficult to make. Anything that applies to the physical world, applies to the cyber world and vice versa.

There are things you will do in the cyber space that I think should be considered as acts of war and we should ban those things.

We're discovering that you can, and you should regulate cyberspace. It is also entirely possible to regulate the cyber world. In fact, many of our existing laws, laws of discrimination and the like already should be applied more forcefully to the cyber world. And you should, because we're already seeing examples of how things are going wrong because we haven't regulated the cyber world forcefully enough.

We should certainly not listen to the self-interested big tech companies who have profited greatly from the lack of regulation in the digital space. I have colleagues who work, for some of these companies and the more enlightened ones will say to you in private:

"We would actually welcome a bit more regulation. At the moment, it's a race to the bottom. We don't want to go in some of these directions, but we have to because if we don't, our competitors will. We would quietly welcome some rules being put in to define bad behaviour."'

The internet and AI are now mainstream

'As for the hacker culture, again, I think that was that was fine when this was not part of the mainstream of our lives: when it wasn't changing who is your president, when it wasn't impacting upon who gets welfare. Now that it is interwoven into the very fabric of our society and how we run ourselves it is too important to be left to self-interest groups.'

In the new AI world Walsh says hackers still have a role to play.

'I do think you have to try and release data responsibly. It is much more difficult these days because typically you are looking at such large data sets that it is hard to do that in a completely responsible way. We have seen that with the Snowden release and with the Panama Papers it is difficult because of the sheer volumes of data people are able to uncover and expose.

I'm sure history will look very favourably on people like Snowden and to a certain extent, Assange for exposing that our Western societies were going down a road of Orwellian surveillance that was perhaps stopped because it was exposed and that our democracies are better and stronger because of that.'

Should there then be rules for disclosure? Should there be codes of conduct for hackers?

'I'm not sure the hackers need any special rules other than the normal ethical moral codes that we apply to other people. I am not sure that hacking is any different to any other exposé, there was a public interest in the original Pentagon Papers and the original Watergate tapes.'

Bruce Schneier, the American cryptographer, security professional, privacy specialist and self-styled public-interest technologist, delivered a fiery speech at the Organisation for Economic Cooperation and Development's Digital Economy Ministerial Meeting in Cancun, Mexico, in June 2016. In it, he predicted that, unless technology-based businesses and governments address these problems, there might be a flight from connectivity – that is, people could start retreating offline as risks mount. Professor Walsh says this is a potential we could approach very quickly:

'My guess is we are reaching the high-water mark of computerisation and connectivity and in a few years we are going to be deciding what to connect and what to disconnect and become more realistic about what can work. We are creating a society by which a totalitarian government can control everything. Right now, it's more power to the powerful. And we are living in a computerised world where attacks are easier to create than defenses against them. This is coming faster than we think. We need to address it now. People up to now have been able to code the world as they see fit. That has to change. We have to make moral, ethical and political decisions about how these things should work and then put that into our code. Politicians and technologists still talk past each other. This has to change.

With the advent of the Internet of Things and cyber-physical systems in general, we've given the internet hands and feet: the ability to directly affect the physical world. What used to be attacks against data and information have become attacks against flesh, steel and concrete.'

Chapter 9

Driving an ethical approach to AI coding

Do we need a Hippocratic Oath in AI?

In Chapter 5 we learned from Professor Irene Ng of Warwick University about the role of data, specifically what it is and how it can be used to impart valuable information by programmers instructing the AI systems on what data to collect, what data to ignore and what data to link it to. It is a task that programmers are being asked to think deeply about and one that has led many of those working in AI to question whether what they are doing is ethical. In Silicon Valley, AI programmers working for Google refused to continue working on a US defence drone program that was using facial recognition, forcing the company to drop the project.[1]

In a series of other highly publicised cases, Microsoft has radically reconfigured a chatbot project that became racist within 24 hours[2] and it has emerged that the now defunct UK company Cambridge Analytica had sought to influence US election results by using Facebook data to target individuals with influential accounts who would be susceptible to particular political messaging in a bid to spread fake news. AI, we have all very quickly learned, can do great harm, very quickly. Owing to this many are calling for controls to be built into it. Indeed, at the end of 2019 in Copenhagen a number of technologists called for those working on AI and related technologies to sign the 'Copenhagen Pledge' agreeing not to do harm with technology.

Dr Phillip Laplante *is Professor of Software and Systems Engineering at the Pennsylvania State University. He holds a Ph.D. in computer science, M.Eng. in electrical engineering, and a BSc in systems planning and management from Stevens Institute of Technology and was awarded an MBA from the University of Colorado. Dr Laplante teaches courses in software and systems engineering including project management, software testing and requirements engineering. Before arriving at Penn State, he was a software development professional, technology executive, college president and entrepreneur.*

---

1   On 4 April 2018 thousands of Google employees signed an open letter calling on Google CEO Sundar Pichai to pull out of Project Maven work intended to improve drone strike targeting.
2   On 12 March 2016 Microsoft's Tay chatbot was released by the company. Within 24 hours it was de-activated after being targeted by a group of individuals who had taught the AI system to be racist. See Professor James Zou in Chapter 10.

Driving an ethical approach to AI coding

Dr Laplante is a Fellow of the IEEE and SPIE and has won international awards for his teaching, research and service. From 2010–2017 he led the effort to develop a national licensing exam for software engineers.

His research currently focuses on safety critical software engineering and the Internet of Things and he is a visiting scientist at the US National Institute of Standards and Technology (NIST).

Professor John Harris *FMedSci, Member, Academia Europaea, FRSA, BA, D.Phil, Hon. D.Litt is Professor Emeritus, University of Manchester, Honorary Professor in Medical Law and Ethics, Centre of Medical Law & Ethics, King's College, London and Distinguished Research Fellow, Oxford Uehiro Centre for Practical Ethics, Faculty of Philosophy, University of Oxford.*

Professor Harris was one of the Founder Directors of the International Association of Bioethics and is a founder member of the Board of the journal Bioethics and a member of the Editorial Board of the Cambridge Quarterly of Healthcare Ethics. He is also the joint Editor-in-Chief of the Journal of Medical Ethics.

In June 2004 Dr Laplante was widely acknowledged as the first person to call for a Hippocratic Oath for computer programmers in an article arguing that programmers should develop their own version of a Hippocratic Oath agreeing to do no harm with their knowledge. The article is kindly reproduced in an Appendix to this chapter, with the permission of Laplante.

'The article stemmed from my work in developing a professional licensure exam for software engineers in the United States. While I was doing that, I realized that there are parallels between software, and the history of software licensure that mimic those of licensure of medical professionals in the United States. Of course, their mission begins with a Hippocratic Oath, first do no harm and so on. In many ways, because software can be harmful, because it can be life critical, mission critical, it seemed to me that one of the first promises that any software engineer ought to make is that the work that they do should not deliberately cause harm and if possible, avoid at all costs accidental harm.

It was something that was not new many years ago, I worked in the defence industry and we would constantly have lunchroom discussions trying to satisfy ourselves that the work that we were doing, although it led to weapons of destruction, had a higher purpose a deterrent effect, a defensive effect. So certainly, there will be inherent projects that deliberately cause harm but there should be an overt admission of that whereas at the very least, for those software engineers that are working on projects that are not intended to cause harm and are in fact intended to cause good, there should be a very overt, purposeful deliberation that that project should not inadvertently cause some second order effect that creates a harm for someone. When I suggested this, it was simply speaking out loud I have to admit, I have not tried to craft a software version of it, but it probably would begin with the words: "first, do no harm".

The programming Hippocratic Oath might echo in some ways the nurse's 'Nightingale Pledge',[3] which talks about never knowingly administering a harmful drug. That wording could be revised to say: "I will never knowingly create a software that will cause injury or harm to another human being, nor cause destruction to infrastructure". On reflection it would be very, very difficult to do and I know already that attempts have been made to create a Hippocratic Oath, that is closer to a code of conduct, there are several versions.

The Association of Computing Machinery, as well as the Institute of Electrical and Electronics Engineers which are both international organizations and the Institution of Engineering Technology and others all have their own professional codes. It's difficult to do and it is controversial, but we do need to start with something.'

Do no evil

'My article was prompted by a book about the evolution of licensing of medical professionals in the United States because up until the turn of the last century, there were still many states that did not license physicians. This meant that on one hand, we had physicians who were trained at Johns Hopkins University and Harvard while on the other hand, there were country doctors who had never completed a high school education, but were, trained in various forms of folk medicine though all were practicing as physicians and calling themselves physicians. It was a situation that paralleled very closely that in software engineering where we had many highly trained individuals with baccalaureate degrees and graduate degrees, doctorates, in computer science, software engineering and related disciplines, writing software for critical infrastructure, medical devices and in many other very critical areas and as was the case with the doctors at the same time, we had individuals with no training in software engineering, developing code which may, in fact work, be very good. But the disparity seemed great and it was very, analogous to the evolution of the licensure of medical professionals. This logically drew me back in a long line of reasoning, to the starting point which was the Hippocratic Oath.'

Laplante was particularly struck by the science fiction writer Isaac Asimov's three laws of robotics[4] which he considered a good starting point:

---

3 The Nightingale Pledge is a modified version of the Hippocratic Oath, where nurses in the US pledge to uphold certain ethics and principles within the nursing profession. The pledge was named in honour of Florence Nightingale: www.florence-nightingale.co.uk/the-nightingale-pledge-1893/.

4 Asimov's laws have proved controversial as an ethical starting point for robotics with many considering them inappropriate. See for example, www.brookings.edu/opinions/isaac-asimovs-laws-of-robotics-are-wrong/.

ASIMOV'S LAWS OF ROBOTICS

First Law

A robot may not injure a human being or, through inaction, allow a human being to come to harm.

Second Law

A robot must obey the orders given it by human beings except where such orders would conflict with the First Law.

Third Law

A robot must protect its own existence as long as such protection does not conflict with the First or Second Law.

Asimov subsequently added a fourth law, the Zeroth Law, which was designed to numerically precede the first three laws.

Zeroth Law

A robot may not harm humanity, or, by inaction, allow humanity to come to harm.

Laplante acknowledges, however, that Asimov's laws – which were essentially part of the plot structure for a series of novels – need a lot of work.

'They are a reasonably good starting point for creating laws of behaviour for AI that should do no harm some form of ethical framework needs to be created. As to the second part I am not sure that it is entirely possible. First of all, you have to come up with an agreed upon ethical framework and different societies, different cultures, different political structures have different ethical frameworks.

As most of the products being built are multinational, we would have to reconcile those differences. We would also be confronted with the usual paradoxes that get introduced into these ethical frameworks. Typically, those paradoxes are thought problems that are often outrageous and structured so that they are made to be paradoxical, but not really realistic but these issues have to be taken care of because some sort of ethical framework has to be codified.

If we embed an ethical framework into coding, we may end up with so many rules and so many structures that we might have to embed the entire cultural intelligence into this ethical framework in order for it to become comprehensive. That would then mean that we could have an incompleteness problem where we can never quite map out the entire ethical structure. Which could mean that we are always presented with these problems that cannot be resolved without flipping a coin. We also face the issue that we will be dealing with large societal problems.

These are not the sort of puzzles that we often hear about such as should the driver crash into the bus queue to avoid a child, or hit the child because, the sum of deaths is lower. They are going to be about the ethical issues of, we are collecting certain data, how could that data be potentially misused? If the risks are too high, then perhaps we should not collect that data anymore. It is interesting because some of those ethical decisions are made, in university structures all the time when professors conduct research and they are collecting, personally identifying information and financial information, other kinds of information that, if it were released to the public could be very harmful to individuals. Those university internal review boards and research boards, wrestle with those decisions all the time, and they are the kind of boards that, Google[5] and others have begun to assemble to look at these large issues and examine them on a project-by-project basis, to determine whether it is permissible under the ethical rules they have created.'

Imposing higher ethical standards on machines than on humanity

'You could begin to predict, behaviours that are harmful to that individual that might not otherwise be obvious, smoking is an obvious one, but maybe playing chess when you're wearing only your left slipper is a bad thing, and an entity may have a compelling interest in stating we are going to prohibit that behaviour or we are going to prohibit that consumption because it would lead to, unnecessary strain on a health care system or other peripheral problems.

The question then becomes, is this acceptable to the public or not? Evidently there are all kinds of good that can come from technology but there is also the potential for harm, especially if data and the rules that are derived from that data are in the hands of, less than benevolent individuals.

That data intrusion could be enormously powerful and draconian, because there are ancestry databases of genetic histories being built at the moment that will be very tempting for governments to use. For instance, if one's genetic makeup is known, and it could be shown that, based on your genetic structure that you may have a proclivity towards crime. Then the society could easily state that it thinks that due to that that you should be monitored it could be suggested that you should not be allowed, on the basis of that genetic research, to have children with a person with a certain other profile. It could easily be taken to very frightening extremes. It will be simply a matter of where do politicians and people want to take this and how would governments want to use this information? Technology is already enabling all kinds of good and bad scenarios.

---

5   Google's Ethics Board is currently in limbo.

It is possible that scenarios like Logan's Run[6] or Soylent Green[7] could develop and that rationing, or resource balancing algorithms become built. Indeed, you could argue that they already exist and are being used. Insurance companies currently make decisions about whether they will pay for certain claims using algorithms. At the moment insurance companies, charge higher premiums for "life behaviours" such as drinking or smoking. The flip side of that is to reward people for good behaviours, for exercising, following a good diet and having a balanced life this is happening now. It is easy to imagine that kind of scenario being amplified as population increases and resources become scarcer. With AI we will have more and more medical procedures that we can use to save lives, but many of them are expensive. AI could possibly make those treatments more available and manage them more cost effectively so they become cheaper it will also be able to devise disease cures which in and of itself can create ethical issues: In a world of over-population do you cure someone so that can live longer and in misery? Is not programming an AI system then not doing harm by not preventing harm? You can think of many of those scenarios.'

How far should technology intrude into our lives?

'I do not want to come up with those rules sets, because if I were tasked with implementing them, then I would have this decision to make as a software engineer, do I want to do this or not do it? I could protest and I may quit my job rather than, implement that kind of algorithm in some sort of AI system. In an ideal world the software engineers would not come up with the rules, they would help the experts, the ethicists, the bioethicists, the medical ethicists and so on to, implement those algorithms but even then, the individual engineer has to make the decision whether they want to be a participant or not.

These questions it could go far beyond just medical behaviours, they could ask "are you a good parent?" The AI systems could then come up with a rule set that determines good parenting versus bad parenting. Then if the algorithm determines that you've scored highly enough as a parent for child number one, you will be allowed to have child number two. All things are possible.

I am certainly not suggesting that these things are good or bad that is not my field. I am not an ethicist, what though is happening now is that software engineers, programmers, and computer scientists are the people who have to make a decision as to whether they want to participate in an individual

---

6 *Logan's Run* is a 1976 American science fiction action film based on the 1967 novel *Logan's Run* by William F Nolan and George Clayton Johnson. It depicts a utopian future society on the surface, revealed as a dystopia where the population and the consumption of resources are maintained in equilibrium by killing everyone who reaches the age of 30.

7 *Soylent Green* is a 1973 American ecological dystopian thriller film loosely based on the 1966 science fiction novel *Make Room! Make Room!* by Harry Harrison, it revolves around the investigation into the murder of a wealthy businessman; against the background of a dystopian future of dying oceans and year-round humidity due to the greenhouse effect resulting in intense suffering from pollution, poverty, over-population, euthanasia and depleted resources.

project or not. I would argue ethics should be part of every curriculum, at the post-secondary level. Everyone should have a sense of different ethical frameworks. What they mean, the differences between them, the difficulties of implementing them and so on and certainly in computer science and software engineering, because you have the potential to do harm more so than other perhaps other disciplines.

These ethical conversations happen all of the time at my university. At most universities some sense of philosophy, reasoning, logic is an important part of a computer science education.

The key here though is do no harm, once Google's motto was "don't be evil" now it has changed to "do the right thing".[8] The staff at Google who chose not to work on a defence project called Maven made a decision that they would do no harm or do no evil.'

Ethics by design

'You cannot impose ethics on top of programming as an afterthought or as an auditing function. Ethics should start from the ground up with the individuals. When we design systems we talk about process, people and product we should also be talking about an ethical process, we want to have ethical people. That means having, people who are trained in ethics and who are constantly being reminded and monitored and rewarded for good ethical behaviour. Then you want to have an ethical product and that means different things in different domains but, it could have to do, with compliance. Though that may have to do with other rubrics for defining an ethical product, for example one that is not readily available to children because it would be harmful for them.

There are an infinite number of potential bad behaviours, and you cannot enumerate or list them all. At the moment when people are presented with a potential behaviour, they think it should be obvious to them that it is unethical or at least it should make them pause and think: "wait a second before I do this. Something doesn't seem right. I had better talk to a few people about it".

This cannot be simply about codification. It is about making people aware and developing frameworks where ethical behaviour is rewarded, encouraged, and is the norm. This is important, much more important than the technology, that will come along on its own.

These ethical questions exist for AI and for non-AI applications, even pedestrian ones, and should be addressed at every level because there are

---

8 'Don't be evil' is a phrase used in Google's corporate code of conduct, which it also formerly preceded as a motto. Following Google's corporate restructuring under the conglomerate Alphabet Inc. in October 2015, Alphabet took 'Do the right thing' as its motto, also forming the opening of its corporate code of conduct. The original motto was retained in Google's code of conduct, now a subsidiary of Alphabet. In April 2018 the motto was removed from the code of conduct's preface and retained in its last sentence.

too many unforeseen interactions that occur between systems that lead to problems that we wish we had thought of before they occurred.

Every person working on critical systems ought to be extremely paranoid. But it means that people working on noncritical systems probably need to be paranoid, too, because those non-critical systems can and probably will interact with critical ones one day. The people developing software need to be very paranoid and think about, the worst-case scenario at all times. That is an engineering mentality, and it should be imposed on anyone developing software.

The ethical obligation exists to humanity for, governing boards to do the right thing. There is also a fiduciary responsibility for those governing boards to do the right thing, because it is never financially good, to harm anyone. Ultimately, that catches up with the company and leads to, financial loss. So, there's a two-pronged reason for boards of directors, boards of governors for corporations to do the right thing, both an ethical obligation, but it's also a fiduciary obligation.'

This is something the many technology companies are becoming acutely aware of: appearing to be uncaring about the consequences of their technology can become a public relations disaster for them, as the experiences of Microsoft, Facebook/ Meta and Google have shown. Throughout his career, Harris has defended broadly libertarian-consequentialist approaches to issues in bioethics. We explored with him the need for a Hippocratic Oath to be established for programmers and whether there was a wider requirement for those coding computer programs and AI algorithms to have some education about ethics.

'In "Catch 22" (the novel by Joseph Heller) a section of the book deals with the Great Loyalty Oath Campaign and satirises the difference between taking an oath to do what's right rather than simply knowing what is right and doing it. I do not think swearing oaths or making promises to act correctly add anything to the motivation for acting correctly.

That doesn't mean, of course, that one should not act ethically but to do that it is important to identify what acting ethically in this context is. The only reason for making people take a formal oath is to act as a reminder that they ought to act ethically.

The main part of this question, however is: "What are the responsibilities of programmers"? And that is pretty much – mechanism. What sort of thing is the AI controlling? What does it do? What are the chances of it doing harm? What are the chances of it malfunctioning and so on?

The Hippocratic Oath no longer exists, and has not existed for years and I do not think it was needed, although I do think that doctors and those working in health do need ethics.

I spent a large part of my career teaching ethics to medical students and to healthcare professionals, students, nurses and others involved in the health sector and they certainly need ethics, and they need to understand the various dimensions of ethics, from not hurting people to issues of justice and fairness.

There is already a lot of AI in medicine, some algorithms have been designed to quickly search for particular symptoms and to generate appropriate pharmaceuticals and drugs for particular sorts of symptoms. The underlying part of all of this again comes back to function: what is the AI supposed to be doing and does it do what it is supposed to do, what is the AI's role? Autonomous vehicles are really driverless vehicles, they are not autonomous. They do not make autonomous decisions in the way that we make autonomous decisions. The vehicles called autonomous vehicles have been designed basically not to bump into things and to obey traffic signals when they detect them, but they are not deciding autonomously, because we can decide whether to accept the imperatives that we are given, whether they are moral imperatives, or those we are aware of that we are giving to ourselves.

We can decide not to act morally on occasions, for example I know adultery is wrong, but may think "what the hell" on a particular occasion. That is an autonomous action. If you programme someone to be incapable of adultery, that is not autonomy.'

Health is an area where AI is predicted to make a deep impact. During the COVID-19 pandemic, AI was used to analyse both the spread of the virus, as well as aiding in the development of a vaccine. Why is health an area where there are fewer problems regarding its use? A more problematic area may be the use of AI by the judiciary.

'I am not sure about the judiciary, but the police are using AI in all sorts of contexts. The question is, is it the intelligent part of the AI that is operative? Is it supposed to make better decisions or simply process data in a way pre-set not by the AI itself, but by human agents?

I suspect most of it is doing the latter, it is rapidly processing data and coming up with results that would just take ordinary humans much longer. In most cases, of course, it is then alerting a human who will make the decision as to whether to act on that or not, and that will be the case.

If it is used by the judiciary that would be the most likely way that they would use it.'

The legal personhood of the decision maker

At the moment, a lot of AI around us operates on the basis of the machine identifying underlying trends in data – which people cannot see because of the huge number of calculations necessary – and the machine then alerts a human being so that they can make the decision. The ethical problems arise when a decision is left to the machine, is there any control over the impact and effects of that decision?

'That is the difficult area now, one of the ways of trying to overcome this problem is to make the human designers of the machines legally and morally responsible for the consequences of what those machines do.

The problem we have is how to disincentivise an artificial intelligence. We know how to disincentivise humans. We can punish them. We can do things to them that they would not like, imprisoning them or fining them or causing them to lose their jobs. We have elements of moral control, we hope conscience is enough, but where it is not, then we can provide mostly palpable and effective, disincentives to wrong actions. We do not know whether a machine would mind being turned off or being permanently turned off, whether that would be a sufficient disincentive to the machine not to do whatever class of bad things it might do. Flesh and blood, intelligences are bad models for machine intelligences. We know what disincentives are to flesh and blood creatures, they do not like pain.[9] If they are autonomous, they do not like losing their freedom and so on.

We do not know the desires of the machine we do not even know if the machine has something that could be called desire. If you were to design a machine to mind about prioritising how fast it does a task or how many parameters, it considers when it is doing a task. It could be given desires to be better at the job it is doing. That could be built in, but they are not desires. They are not similar to desire as in a yearning.

What worries airline pilots or indeed the manufacturers of airliners, is if they make a plane that is prone to crash, they might be criminally responsible for what they have done, if it has an artificial intelligence system in it, they might limit its functionality through fear of culpability. The aim of a lot of AI research is to create machines that are as intelligent as human beings and can make the sorts of decisions that human beings do. If so, they would be a different sort of person. You and I are flesh and blood persons, but we might make machine persons, machine persons that actually had autonomy and responsibility that minded about the idea they might be turned off or taken apart or if they decided that they were happy to be taken apart.'

The moral issue of decision-making in certain contexts

This begs the question, where should we allow decision-making to be done by machines? It has been suggested, for example, that machines can make much, much better decisions about long-term health care for people than doctors, because machines are dispassionate.

'I do not want a dispassionate doctor, what I want is a non-dispassionate flesh and blood doctor so why would want a dispassionate machine? It is a problem we are facing now with COVID-19. During the pandemic the BMA said that people who were stabilised in intensive care or even improving might nonetheless be taken off intensive care to give that care regime to a person who might recover quicker or might live longer after recovering.

This is a way of saying that all human beings are not equal. That those with better health and longer life expectancy have more of an entitlement to live. I have written, a paper for the Cambridge Quarterly of Health Care Ethics in which I discuss this issue. I am not convinced that we want machines which

---

9 In Karel Čapek's *Rossum's Universal Robots* the robots' human designer works on introducing pain to the robots as an economic measure to prevent the robots from expensively damaging their humanoid forms.

are dispassionate and apply a rule about prioritising patients for healthcare or for intensive healthcare. It is not an advantage if they are dispassionately and accurately applying a rule, if the rule the algorithm is applying is defective. As it has been programmed not to treat all candidates for care as equals, but to favour those who have longer life expectancy after treatment.

The ethical question is whether putting that pressure on them is appropriate and what is the alternative? If they are turning a ventilator off a human body, which has ceased permanently to have a functioning consciousness that is a very common thing, and most people would not find that an ethical dilemma as there is no point in ventilating a body if its mind is permanently dead.'

AI accountability

Medical studies reported in newspapers from 1989 state that if you put the right amount of data into a computer system, it gets the decision right more often than a doctor.

'The calculation the machine is making better decisions than human on a particular range of treatments, or sorts of illness, is a judgement being made by a human on the results of the research. When and if that judgement is made by a machine, and there is no accountable supervision of that process that is what will certainly worry me and by accountable, I mean as seen by somebody who has weighed up the pros and cons and has a good reason not to act wrongly. The danger of AI is, it is limitless, basically because it is not subject to either morality or to law.

Unless you make the humans who either designed that machine or who decided that it was legitimate to use it in this context accountable to law. That might be the only way we can actually control adequately and supervise AI that are making medical decisions or indeed making decisions about who should live and die. A recent paper in Nature was discussing driverless cars should be programmed to make these sort of decisions and what calculations they should make: whether they would sacrifice one type of road user more than others, whether they should always crash into a softer target to preserve their own passengers. Whether the vehicle should smash into one bus queue or another by taking into account the demographics and health status of the different bus queues and prioritise them accordingly. It is an outrageous, ridiculous and unethical paper and it should never have been published the danger is that somebody will think that it is an idea worthy of development. If, however, you made the car manufacturer accountable: nobody would manufacture a car, which might make a decision that would involve the CEO of the company being incarcerated for life by the relatives of those killed by the car who are claiming it was programmed to kill.'

How far can AI intrude into our data?

US companies are presently very interested in obtaining NHS data so they can effectively model the way people live their lives. This is information that would be very valuable to insurance companies, because they can determine life expectancy and disease susceptibility from the data. Harris does not consider that this is something we need an AI to do, however:

'We know, for example, that younger drivers are more likely to have accidents than older drivers and insurance companies load their premiums accordingly. It is just written a bit larger or more comprehensively. In other words, going into finer detail about who among the young drivers may actually be safer in a category, and which among the old drivers may be safer would be one of the aims. Now whether or not it is reasonable to allow insurance companies to insure risk on that basis is a very complicated question because it means that they are able to decide that some people are uninsurable and therefore effectively cannot drive or own a vehicle, which may not be fair.

There are a lot of people who think that we should just randomise that risk rather than load it onto a class of people who will automatically find it more difficult to get particular sorts of insurance or indeed should not get it at all.'

However, some would say if someone smokes and drinks a lot it is their decision, it is fair that their insurance premiums are high and there's nothing wrong in an AI system accessing that information.

'These questions are always more complicated than they appear because you could equally well decide who should get access to the NHS on the basis of how much they smoke, drink or whether play a risky sport which is going to cause them injuries. That is a very big question, and it becomes even more complicated when we are talking about a private corporation like an insurance company being allowed to decide what people can or cannot do. There are circumstances in which that may be allowed but I am far from convinced that it is consistently right.

That immediately brings us to whether a public health care system should be allowed to do that rather than a private health care system, you might think that that was wrong in both cases. Probably because the insurance-based system is likely to discriminate as insurance companies, whether they are insuring health or cars or houses, would rather have people who presented no risk at all. They like to have a lot of people who present no risk of ever claiming on their insurance buying their policies, a national healthcare system wants the reverse, it wants always to be there for people who do, for whatever reason, need health assistance. That is why it would be unethical to run the NHS on that basis, and it is equally unethical to run motor insurance and house insurance and other forms of insurance on that basis.'

Does that mean deploying an AI system to assist in these decisions is unethical?

'It is not unethical, to help a person, a government or something between the two such as an organisation, make that decision but if you leave the decision to the machine, then what does that mean? It may mean that you have decided that the algorithm you've programmed it with is always going to always make the right decision and as a human being you feel you can safely leave it to the machine. It may also mean that the system is being used in an area that you feel is not dangerous and that it represents no threat to human interests.'

In the film *Elysium* an AI system decides whether people get healthcare and benefits (or not) and there is no redress because the system theoretically comes up with the best possible decision. For Harris, we should always be able to appeal any decision made by a machine.

'There should always be an appeals process, whether it is from human beings about machines or the decisions of some human beings about other human beings or the decisions of AI augmented human beings. It is why we have systems of law and courts that decide whether the laws have been properly applied by the police or properly applied by a company or an individual. Where people think that that is not the case there is a process of appeal and redress.

That is what worries me about leaving things to AI, particularly to the sorts of AI that might cause harm or death to human beings and might target that harm or death for some classes of human beings rather than others, because they weren't productive in the community or because they had difficult lives and drank too much and so on. We can change the laws and often the laws are changed because people go to law and argue that they are inequitable in some way. The law is a very good model for how we need to have a system of regulating decision-making. Partly the way that works is through rewards and disincentives to people. But when machines are making decisions, without a system of rewards and disincentives to machines, it is going to be much more difficult both to control what they do, to supervise it and to keep it under constant review.'

Training an AI system to make judgements on people

Taking the example of a judicial system, an AI system could absorb all of the laws as we know them and impose a sentence on a crime. If you can do that in simple cases, then theoretically you should be able to do it in more complex cases like fraud. However, as we know, legal argument, the factual matrix and relevant context, are not binary in nature.

'Obviously, a legal model isn't going to be feasible for all sorts of putative machine decision-making. It is complicated because the law is interested not just as to whether somebody did something but whether they did it innocently or not, what was their state of mind and the state of their soul. Whether they were honest in the information that they gave about the case, whether they were acting maliciously because they had a grudge of quite a different sort against the person that they might have damaged and so on.

Now, whether or not we will have to develop a sort of typology of machine grudges and machine biases and machine prejudices, many people think they are already building in jealousies and preferences for some things unconsciously into artificial intelligence and into all sorts of other semi-automatic procedures. Racist prejudices it is claimed have already been built into things like welfare or access to compensation, of course.'

This point about how you train an AI is also part of this Hippocratic view is it not? One of the reasons for AI systems becoming racist was because they were being trained on data from the internet that really made us look at ourselves and showed us that we are all potentially racist and sexist.

'It is very crude. When I was an undergraduate in an ethics class, I was asked how you would programme machines to decide whether a particular person was innocent or guilty of a crime and what data the machine would want to know. One of the things the machine would really want to know, for example, if it was talking about crime in New York is whether the person was Black or white.

Because being Black would be a very high predictor of criminality in some districts in New York. And that is precisely what is wrong with getting the right result in the wrong way. It may be that this person actually is Black and was guilty, but we don't want to shortcut the process of actually having to say something about them more than that they are Black to establish that they are guilty. We need to establish some rules on how data is put into these models and we need to have ways of constantly reviewing that as well.'

Abrogation of responsibility to the machine

People apparently become very dependent on systems like this because they do not want to take responsibility. Whether it is flying a plane or firing a missile they would rather leave the decision to the machine than make a mistake themselves.

'They might want to do that for two reasons. One, they might want to do it because the weight of responsibility is too much for them and they do not want to choose between targets even if their targets were established as enemy targets. The other reason might be that they thought the machine will carry out what they thought was the right decision more efficiently and more accurately than they did. In either case, we need to have something that counts as review or second thoughts there always has to be a human who approves the decision.

Once there are responsible machines that can make autonomous decisions – the super AIs – then they should be able to vote, they should be able to initiate legal actions against people who they believe have wronged them whether they are human or machine, but we are a long way from that.

Machines should always be supervised by people, people should always be supervised by people and eventually by "machine people", AI people, not flesh and blood creatures, by which point something I have dubbed in a number of papers "the Shylock syndrome" will occur. It is an idea I derived from Shylock's famous speech in Shakespeare's "Merchant of Venice". In the speech he states: "if you prick us, do we not bleed? If you tickle us. Do we not laugh?" What a lot of people forget is the last thing that Shylock says: "if you wrong us, shall we not revenge?" In the absence of those things like bleeding, laughing and the will to revenge, which is really another way of talking about, the idea of justice, that the false needs to be remedied and sometimes the only way to do that is by revenge.

We know we have very good levers of control over people, what we do not know when we finally do build a super AI – which is a person, a machine person that has autonomy and can make its own decisions – we do not know the basis of its decisions and what a machine would think was wrong. We know what wrong conduct among human beings is, it is something that causes injury, pain and suffering to other like creatures we also have the equivalent of injury, pain and suffering to know right from wrong. When we have a really intelligent AI, of course they might be guilty of offences against one another so we would have to have some idea of what those offences might be.'

Should machines have a 'rush of blood' built into them?

Perhaps then dispassion is valuable, people are responsive to being fined because of their fallibility, people have problems because they are corrupt and prepared to do things for self-interest. You do then want a dispassionate AI because it is incorruptible. Or perhaps you want a deliberately corrupt AI that has the interests of an individual or a corporation built into it?

'It is true and we might also need to build in passion. We might need the fellow feeling built in, we might need, the golden rule, do unto others as you would have them do unto you. That means that the machines would also need to also think about the consequences of their decisions on the objects of those decisions, whether those objects were animal, vegetable or mineral.'

Does this come down to programming? One of the factors that has to be considered in the processing of this data is the impact you will have within a particular ethical framework.

'We need two things, for the moral probity of AI: We need a Mechanism of accountability, either for the creators or users of the machines or for the machines themselves, because otherwise, they have neither incentives nor disincentives for good conduct and bad conduct. Whatever we decide, good conduct and bad conduct is of course, not an infallible process either, there must be something for an AI however advanced which would be identifiable as acting wrongly, whether that acting wrongly was immoral, illegal, inappropriate, off message or off its program and so forth. We are quite good at looking at what somebody on the next desk is doing and thinking, "I don't think they should be doing that".

We need something for AI, which would be the equivalent of that having decided they should not be doing that, we have to have some method of stopping them or getting them on the right track again.

There will always be moral ambiguity, the broad parameters of morality are generally agreed, but the particular applications are seldom generally agreed, for example we should not harm or injure or cause pain or suffering to other people but sometimes it is appropriate to do that and not everyone will agree with that conclusion.

We know ethics is necessary for all. What is the most effective way of teaching it or ensuring that people understood what it is in the context of AI is a complicated matter, I do not have a very good definitive answer for how we might do that. We do certainly need to think about what unethical behaviour for an autonomous machine or a semi-autonomous machine making important decisions might be. What it would be for them to do wrong or go wrong? It is not simply going wrong. It could simply be failing to make money for the person that created them.'

The real danger of a worldwide human inferiority complex

Are people trying to evade their responsibility by saying that they need these machines to make these decisions? Or do they think that the machines will make better decisions because they're able to process more data. Will that mean we lose confidence in ourselves?

'The unsolvable conundrum is whether we have to trust the machine when it says it has data that indicates that this must happen or whether we are going to be able to say, well, show me or explain to me what this data is that I cannot process? Show me how it indicates what you say it indicates and why. Otherwise, we will just have to accept their calculations. As in a school maths class it is no good just giving me the answer, I need to see how you arrived at the answer. It may be that the people who make AI would just say; "well, you can't do that because there is so much data. We just have to trust them, but this is what it indicates".

I suppose the only answer to that will be easy, we have to decide whether we actually like the answer. If we do not like it, it does not matter if it was generated by the algorithms and the relevant data – that will not be a sufficient argument in its favour. If we know the answer to the question of what constitutes a good decision though, in this context, then we probably do not need a machine to lay out the parameters for us.'

In the end, the point made by Harris is that people need to get better, although the vast majority are fundamentally good and want to do the right thing.

'We do need to get better. We need better people, and we need better ethicists, we need better ethics education and a more comprehensive idea of what the components of ethics are. In the paper in Nature, I referred to earlier the authors used a computer game. They showed a scenario of a driverless car hitting a concrete barrier and killing its passengers or hitting a bus queue on the side of the road and killing them. Then they asked people, which outcome would you prefer? Which outcome would you prefer to see? And that's not what ethics is. It's not what we would prefer. It's what we would prefer, for moral reasons.

It is what is fair, it is what is just, it is what is proportionate. It is a whole range of moral terms that we use. Most of us, including people, who haven't had any form of ethics education, most of us are very adept at understanding those, and that's why courts are quite a good place to resolve disputes.

146

Most people who do wrong know that they are doing wrong though that might mean two different things. It may mean that they know what other people think is doing wrong, but they do not accept it, they do not think it is true, but they do know that they are doing, or what they are proposing to do is forbidden but they accept it as wrong. That's one scenario. The other scenario is they know it is wrong, but they still do it because it is fun or rewarding or they will make a lot of money from it.'

Appendix

First, Do No Harm: A Hippocratic Oath for Software Developers?: What's wrong with taking our profession a little more seriously?

When asked about the Hippocratic Oath, most people are likely to recall the phrase, 'First, do no harm.' It's a logical response, as even those unfamiliar with the oath could figure out that avoiding additional injury in the course of treatment is critical. In fact, it's natural to strive in any endeavour not to break something further in the course of repair. In software engineering, as in medicine, doing no harm starts with a deep understanding of the tools and techniques available. Using this theme and some medical metaphors, I offer some observations on the practice of software engineering.

Foundations of healthy skepticism

The Hippocratic Oath was proffered by the Greek scholar, Hippocrates, the 'Father of Medicine,' around 500 B.C., and since then it has guided the practice of medicine. Variations of the oath are sworn at nonmedical school graduations. For example, the 'Nightingale Pledge' for nurses is an adaptation of the Hippocratic Oath and includes the phrase, 'I will abstain from whatever is deleterious and mischievous and will not take or knowingly administer any harmful drug.' A Hippocratic Oath for Scientists has been proposed, though it deals largely with the ethical issues of developing weapons. Some more 'progressive' colleges and universities have students swear oaths to social responsibility. Software engineering is a profession that frequently involves life-critical systems, yet nowhere have I found the equivalent of the Hippocratic Oath for software engineers. The IEEE Computer Society adopted a 'Software Engineering Code of Ethics and Professional Practice,' but it relates to personal responsibility as opposed to the adoption of safe practices. It's a shame, but a Web search for a 'Hippocratic Oath for Software Engineers' yielded only a collection of jokes (for example, 'Type fast, think slow' or 'Never write a line of code that someone else can understand'). 'First, do no harm' makes a lot of sense in the practice of medicine, especially given its history. In prehistoric times, drilling holes in the head to release evil spirits (called trepanning) was an accepted treatment, and according to evidence from remains, some patients actually survived. Physicians from medieval times through even the late 19th century would poke and prod with gruesome, dirty instruments, attach leeches, perform bloodletting, and administer powerful drugs, such as mercury and laudanum, without understanding the side effects. These practices, though seemingly barbaric today, were undertaken with good intention and were in keeping with the state of the art. But the Hippocratic Oath at least made physicians aware that any new regimen always had the potential to injure. Consequently, many doctors chose (still choose) no treatment at all in lieu of one they didn't understand completely, or at least waited until indisputable supporting scientific evidence appeared.

Probing around with dirty fingers

Software engineering procedures, like medical procedures, can be intrusive and destructive. Likewise, the tools and techniques that we use can be new and untested (or barely tested). Moreover, we don't have the equivalent of medical licensing boards or the US Food and Drug Administration (FDA) to regulate the practice of software engineering and the tools that we adopt. Thus, we sometimes subject our 'patient' – the software – to unnecessarily risky procedures, without really understanding the risks. What is the software engineering equivalent of poking and prodding with dirty fingers, bloodletting, trepanning, and lobotomizing? One example is code refactoring; though the intention of refactoring is noble, and a certain amount is usually beneficial, even necessary, there is some point at which there are diminishing returns, even the risk of irreparable harm. The old saw, 'If it ain't broke, don't fix it,' still holds merit. We sometimes go overboard trying to achieve the equivalent of a software extreme makeover. In the course of fixing a problem we sometimes do more harm than good. In his software engineering classic, Code Complete,[i] Steve McConnell opines that if you are not fixing the underlying source of a problem, and just the symptom, then you're doing more harm than good in that you are deceiving yourself into thinking the problem has gone away. 'If you don't thoroughly understand the problem, you're not fixing the code.' In fact, you may be transforming a relatively easy-to-find defect into a more insidious one that occurs much less frequently, and hence is harder to find. The simplest example involves debugging statements. Imagine debugging an embedded realtime system. You add some kind of output statement to display some intermediate calculations (or you use a source-level debugger). Suddenly, the problem goes away. You remove the output statement (or turn off the source debugger) and the problem is back. After hunting and pecking around for the source of the problem, you give up and leave a dummy statement in place to overcome what you assume is a timing problem. Only a tell-tale comment remains, something akin to, 'If you remove this code, the system doesn't work. I don't know why.'

Placebos and panaceas

Throughout history, doctors have embraced quackery and offered placebos or harmful treatments simply because they didn't know any better. While I am not accusing anyone of deliberate misrepresentation, the relative merits of, for example, clean-room software development, pair programming, and other practices can have placebo-like or detrimental effects when misused. Even agile methodologies, while clearly useful in some settings, can lead to complacency in situations where they are not intended to be used. For example, it is always easier, in the name of agile development, to let a team self-organize, declare that the code is the primary artifact, and eschew documentation. But agile isn't appropriate in large mission-critical systems or in those with far-flung engineering teams. In other situations, it's really unclear whether agile is appropriate or not. In Code Complete, McConnell warns of the equivalent of snake oil, 'method-o-matic' – that is, the methodology du jour. He challenges us to sceptically ask, 'How many systems have been actually built using method-o-matic?'[ii] If we adopt method-o-matic and it works, we celebrate. When it doesn't work, we just say that it wasn't meant to be used in that context, anyway. It's a no-lose situation for those promoting method-o-matic.

---

i   McConnell, S. *Code Complete: A Practical Handbook of Software Construction*. Microsoft Press, Redmond: WA, 1993.
ii See above.

Beware the black box

Historian and philosopher Thomas Carlyle said, 'Nothing is more terrible than activity without insight.' Has software engineering degraded into this state? In the early days of computing, electrical engineers, mathematicians, and physicists programmed computers by adjusting circuits, programming in binary assembly language, and later using compilers that they understood intimately. These few skilled practitioners were often referred to as a 'priesthood' because to the outside observer, they performed supernatural feats attributable only to the gods or magic. But to them, it wasn't magic. Everything they did was understood down to the minutest detail. I am not longing for the days of punch cards, but it seems that 'back then' the 'physicians' had a deep understanding of the remedies they employed. From complex IDEs (integrated development environments) and frameworks, refactoring tools, and vast and mysterious code libraries to ready-baked architectures, software engineers are armed with a bag of tricks that most of us could not explain in meaningful detail. The age of reusable, abstract components has also become the age of black boxes and magic. I am not a Luddite, but my fear – based on observations of hundreds of practitioners – is that we adopt these aforementioned technologies without fully understanding what they do or how they do it. Thus, the chance of doing more harm than good when we use these technologies is ever present. Why should we believe that the development, maintenance, and extension of software for anything, but the most trivial systems should be easy? No one would ever contend that designing spacecraft is easy (it is, after all, 'rocket science') – or even that designing modern automobiles is a breeze. So why do we assume that development of complex software systems should be any easier?

Outsourcing: doing harm in a big way?

Doing harm while trying to do good can happen in the large, too. Those who contend that the price to be paid for easy-to-use, portable software is black-box reusability are condemning themselves to eventually outsourcing to low-cost competitors. The wide availability of Graphical User Interface based tools, easy-to-build Web solutions, and an inflated demand for Web programmers led to a whole generation of dotcom, barely-out-of-high-school whiz kids who could cobble components together and whip up ready-made solutions, without really knowing what they were doing. An inflated demand for IT professionals also helped to bloat salaries for even the most modestly prepared individuals. Now, competitors in India, the former Soviet bloc, and elsewhere can just as easily use the same tools and techniques at lower cost. So, managers outsource. But outsourcing can do more harm than good. Loss of control, loss of intellectual property, unsatisfactory performance, hidden costs, and hard-to-obtain legal remedies are the harm that can occur when things go wrong when projects are outsourced.

An oath for software engineers

It is widely believed that the single most important new medical procedure was hand washing. We need to adopt the equivalent of hand washing in software engineering practice, whether in the small, such as in the adoption of a new tool or practice, or in the large, such as in endeavouring to outsource. I think the software equivalent of the Hippocratic Oath can help. Let me take a stab at such an oath. It is a variant of the Nightingale Pledge for nurses[iii]: I solemnly pledge, first, to do no harm to the software entrusted to me; to not knowingly adopt any harmful practice, nor to adopt any practice or tool that I do not fully understand. With fervour, I promise to abstain from whatever is deleterious and mischievous. I will do all in my power to expand my skills and understanding and will maintain and elevate the standard of my profession. With loyalty will I endeavour to aid the stakeholders, to hold in confidence all information that comes to my knowledge in the practice of my calling, and to devote myself to the welfare of the project committed to my care. Perhaps this is too tame, and too long. People may dismiss it or ridicule it. Perhaps we need a punchy, mantra-like slogan that we can play over and over again like Muzak in software development houses. Or maybe a variation on the Star-Spangled Banner, evoking patriotic visions of heroic coding deeds. Perhaps we need to create some epochal story of the trials and tribulations of the development of a major software system and have undergraduates memorize it, with portions to be recited at key moments in the software life cycle (e.g., 'A move method refactoring, the guru applieth and when it was done, 'all is well,' he lieth'). Whatever, it's the purview of committees and organizations to evolve these things, not for some individual to decide. I know, you say, 'What is the point of any such oath? It's just a waste of time.' My response is this: It says something that in the professions of medicine and nursing an oath of fidelity is important enough to recite at graduations, whereas the only semblance of an oath that software engineers have is a collection of jokes. Perhaps the symbolic act of adopting some kind of oath is a statement that we want to take the practice of our profession more seriously. More importantly, I remind you that the Hippocratic Oath is the basis for healthy scepticism. After all, the FDA exists largely to ensure that medical innovations do not do more harm than good. If nothing else, such an oath is a reminder to exercise caution in adopting new tools, methods, and practices. But if after all this I still haven't convinced you, be aware that such luminaries as Edsger Dijkstra[iv] and Steve McConnell,[v] among many others, have suggested the adoption of a Hippocratic Oath for software. Whatever we do, first, do no harm. After all, we do not want critics 100 years from now ridiculing practices that we now believe to be legitimate, especially if the only reason we adopt them is faith and not deep understanding.

---

iii Florence Nightingale Pledge. Nursing Network: see http://www.nursingnetwork.com/florencepledge. htm.

iv Dijkstra, E. *The end of computing science?* Communications of the ACM 44, 3 (March, 2001), 92.

v McConnell, S. *After the Gold Rush: Creating a True Profession of Software Engineering*, Microsoft Press, Redmond: WA, 1999.

Chapter 10

In pursuit of diversity

Is AI racist?

Whether it is as a direct result of the manner in which a dataset is collated, or the way in which an algorithm is coded, an AI system will always be vulnerable to the proclivities of those undertaking these exercises. Through interviews with Professor James Zou, Professor Ruha Benjamin and Joy Buolamwini, as well as a discussion with tech entrepreneur will.i.am in front of a live audience at the Institution of Engineering & Technology and interviews for the *PassWord* radio programme presented by Peter Warren on ResonanceFM, we explore through evidence whether AI can become racist and, if so, how.

Professor James Zou is an Assistant Professor of Biomedical Data Science and (by courtesy) of Computer Science and of Electrical Engineering at Stanford University. He works on a wide range of problems in machine learning (from proving mathematical properties to building large-scale algorithms) and has a special interest in biotech and health applications. He received a PhD from Harvard in 2014.

Professor Zou was a former member of Microsoft Research, and a Gates Scholar at the University of Cambridge and a Simons fellow at U.C. Berkeley. He joined Stanford in 2016 as an inaugural Chan-Zuckerberg Investigator and the faculty director of the university-wide AI for Health program and is also part of the Stanford AI Lab. His research is supported by the NSF CAREER Award, and the Google and Tencent AI awards.

On 26 September 2016 Professor Zou's paper, 'Removing gender bias from algorithms' was published warning, for the first time, of the enormous dangers to future AI systems of biased data. On 18 June 2018, Professor Zou and Londa Schiebinger had their paper, 'AI can be sexist and racist – it's time to make it fair', published by the prestigious science magazine 'Nature'. The paper called for rigorous and urgent attention to be paid to the issue of bias in data.

Professor Ruha Benjamin received her Bachelor of Arts in sociology and anthropology from Spelman College, before going on to complete her PhD in sociology at the University of California Berkeley in 2008. She completed a postdoctoral fellowship at UCLA's Institute for Society and Genetics in 2010, before taking a faculty fellowship at the Harvard Kennedy School's Science, Technology, and Society Programme.

In 2013, Professor Benjamin's first book, 'People's Science: Bodies and Rights on the Stem Cell Frontier' was published by Stanford University Press. In it, she critically investigates how innovation and design often builds upon or reinforces inequalities. In particular, Professor Benjamin investigates how and why scientific, commercial, and popular discourses and practices around genomics have incorporated racial-ethnic and gendered categories. In 'People's Science', Professor Benjamin also argues for a more inclusive, responsible, and public scientific community.

In 2019, her book, 'Race After Technology: Abolitionist Tools for the New Jim Code' was published by Polity. In it, Professor Benjamin expands upon her previous research and analysis by focusing on a range of ways in which social hierarchies, particularly racism, are embedded in the logical layer of internet-based technologies. She develops her concept of the 'New Jim Code', which references Michelle Alexander's work 'The New Jim Crow', to analyse how seemingly 'neutral' algorithms and applications can replicate or worsen racial bias.

In 2019, a book she edited, 'Captivating Technology: Reimagining Race, Carceral Technoscience, and Liberatory Imagination in Everyday Life' was released by Duke University Press, examining how carceral logics shape social life well beyond prisons and police.

Professor Benjamin is currently the Associate Professor in the Department of African American Studies at Princeton University where her work focuses on dimensions of science, technology, and medicine, race and citizenship, knowledge and power. In 2018, she founded the JUST DATA Lab, a space for activists, technologists and artists to reassess how data can be used for justice. She also serves on the Executive Committees for the Programme in Global Health and Health Policy and Center for Digital Humanities at the University of Princeton.

Joy Buolamwini *is a self-described 'poet of code' who uses art and research to illuminate the social implications of Artificial Intelligence. She holds two master's degrees from Oxford University and MIT; a bachelor's degree in Computer Science from the Georgia Institute of Technology; and founded the Algorithmic Justice League to create a world with more equitable and accountable technology.*

Buolamwini's MIT thesis methodology uncovered large racial and gender bias in AI services from companies like Microsoft, IBM, and Amazon and her research has been covered in over 40 countries. As a renowned international speaker she has championed the need for algorithmic justice at the World Economic Forum and the United Nations. She serves on the Global Tech Panel convened by the vice president of European Commission to advise world leaders and technology executives on ways to reduce the harms of AI. Her TED Featured Talk on algorithmic bias has over 1 million views.

A Rhodes Scholar and Fulbright Fellow, Buolamwini has been named in notable lists including Bloomberg 50, Tech Review 35 under 35, BBC 100 Women, Forbes Top 50 Women in Tech (youngest), and Forbes 30 under 30.

For a long time, the deliberations of computer systems have been considered to be objective. Just like Mr Spock in *Star Trek*, it was assumed computers were logical, objective, cold and lacking in emotion – it was never remotely considered that words like bias, sexist and racist could be associated with them. Yet with the advent of the next evolutionary computing stage, AI, in July 2016 Zou and a number of colleagues published a paper[1] detailing a staggering fact: AI computers were

---

1 Tolga Bolukbasi, Kai-Wei Chang, James Zou, Venkatesh Saligrama and Adam Kalai, 'Man is to Computer Programmer as Woman is to Homemaker? Debiasing Word Embeddings' (21 July 2016).

beginning to suffer from some of the most illogical and emotive conditions, racism and sexism.

Zou was not alone, at the same time a number of other academics and thinkers were beginning to come to the same conclusions.

The startling discovery: owing to data AI can be racist

At the Massachusetts Institute of Technology, the computer scientist Joy Buolamwini had found while trying to use AI-based facial recognition technology that the system did not recognise her unless she put on a white face mask.

Buolamwini published her findings in December 2016, she then decided to do some more research and tested facial recognition systems by feeding them the faces of a number of famous Black people including the poet and activist Sojourner Truth, Michelle Obama, television personality Oprah Winfrey, the tennis star Serena Williams and a number of other famous Black women. The results were startling, AI facial recognition technology decided that most of the women were men.[2] Buolamwini followed this up by calling for 'Incoding', a word she coined to encourage AI scientists to correct the issues in the data that they were using.

In a follow-up article 'Design AI so that it's fair'[3] in the science magazine *Nature*, Zou also made an appeal for the correction of the situation, with co-author Londa Schiebinger they called on AI scientists to identify sources of inequity, de-bias training data and develop algorithms that are robust against skews in data.

It was the first time that serious doubts began to be expressed about the accuracy of AI systems. Until then they were considered to be objective, but this can't be the case if we have discovered that the data that they are trained on is not objective and if the algorithms being used are poorly configured.

These findings have raised serious issues for minority groups in our community, primarily the Black community. This is an issue that Princeton University's Professor Ruha Benjamin, the author of several books on the subject expands upon – if racism is in the system then bias is not only in the data, it is in the selection of the data.

It is a point made by all of these pioneers of algorithmic diversity, not only should bias be corrected in the system, the people selecting the datasets should be aware that the datasets themselves are biased and will need to be corrected and the selection of the datasets is in itself a demonstration of bias. This algorithmic bias, it should be remembered, also affects people from the Far East and women, as the media has pointed out, AI facial recognition systems favour white men. However, as Benjamin underlines, attention should not solely be focussed on facial recognition systems because there is a far greater bias that has crept into AI systems, particularly in police and judicial systems, that source historical data for their conclusions. As Zou also points out, this data discrepancy has found its

---

2   Joy Adowaa Buolamwini, *Gender Shades: Intersectional Phenotypic and Demographic Evaluation of Face Datasets and Gender Classifiers* (Thesis: S.M., Massachusetts Institute of Technology, School of Architecture and Planning, Program in Media Arts and Sciences, 2017).
3   Professor James Zou, 'Design AI so that it's fair' (2018) 559 *Nature* 324–26.

way into health analysis, findings that beg the very real question: are we now at the point when the data underpinning every AI system must be examined before they should be used? It should be also noted that often this is owing to data only being collected on particular social groups, for example there is often an absence of health data on people from ethnic minorities as we discovered during the COVID-19 pandemic. There is also, as is the case in crime data, a disproportionate amount of data provided about people from ethnic minorities due to latent racism among some members of the police. If you target Black people because you think they are criminal, the data regarding questioning and arrests will reflect an untrue picture of the reality of crime and instead actually show bias within a group or an institution. This trait is highlighted by Professor Cate in Chapter 14 and several other witnesses for the book.

In its report 'AI in the UK: ready willing and able',[4] the UK House of Lords Select Committee on AI recommended five principles for AI:

(1) AI should be developed for the common good and benefit of humanity.

(2) AI should operate on principles of intelligibility and fairness.

(3) AI should not be used to diminish the data rights or privacy of individuals, families or communities.

(4) All citizens have the right to be educated to enable them to flourish mentally, emotionally and economically alongside AI.

(5) The autonomous power to hurt, destroy or deceive human beings should never be vested in AI.

In a speech at the launch of the House of Lords Select Committee report, Dr Stephen Cave from Cambridge University's Leverhulme Centre for the Future of Intelligence said that for AI to be successful in society it was essential that every part of society should be consulted on its development. So far this does not appear to have happened and there appears to be the beginning of a rearguard action from vested big tech interests to make sure that they, and not the public, retain control of the technology.

We explore how this can be corrected in the next chapter, but here we will confine ourselves to looking into how bias has crept into a technology that has been championed as possibly one of the crowning achievements of humanity.

The devil is in the detail

As one of the first people to recognise the danger of bias in AI systems, Zou says that his findings immediately point to a very important consideration which is that bearing in mind the issues with data, the deployment of AI systems in particular contexts will have to be seriously considered if they are to be genuinely useful and avoid legal challenges.

'I have been doing research in machine learning and developing these algorithms for quite a number of years now and one of the things that I have

4 See publications.parliament.uk/pa/ld201719/ldselect/ldai/100/100.pdf (16 April 2018).

realised is that the algorithms that have been developed for many companies have one large flaw, that people have not looked carefully into the potential impacts of these algorithms. For instance, what machine learning systems are very good at is picking up patterns from data. That is a serious problem if we find that the data used to train the algorithms, has various kinds of biases and even stereotypes in it.

What this means is that if gender and ethnic stereotypes are built into the data then the algorithms that are trained on this data also learn negative stereotypes and negative biases.

One quite striking example of this that we found was in algorithms used for natural language processing that are used for speech and text recognition when you are talking on the phone or talking to a smart devices and speakers. In our lives now there are a lot of these natural language processing AI systems behind the scenes, like Alexa, Siri, Cortana or the Google Assistant. One of the things that we found in our studies, was that these natural language processing systems started to capture a lot of gender stereotypes.

For example, if we asked the system we were using to solve different kinds of analogies it would say a man is analogous to a doctor and a women is analogous to a nurse or that a man is analogous to a professor and that a women is analogous to a homemaker. So, these are analogies that the algorithms believed were correct because it was trained on data that had a lot of these negative gender stereotypes in it.'

This issue, says Zou, begins to fundamentally undermine the trustworthiness of many of the systems that have been developed because they have been trained on WhatsApp messages, on the text in emails and the comments on blog posts and similar data sources aggregating the data and then drawing conclusions from it.

'Algorithms, when they are being trained need a lot of data. If you're trying to train a natural language processing AI system, you basically want to get as much speech and text as possible. Often, they are actually trained on data from social media or from historical documents, and both social media, or historical texts contain bias and stereotypes.'

This means, says Zou, that because the AI algorithms are being trained on all of the material that has been posted on the internet since 1995, the historical documents he mentions (despite efforts to try and deter gender and racism) contain a large amount of either accidental or deliberate bias.

'What's particularly challenging about AI algorithms is that the algorithms are taught to reinforce patterns. So, they are looking for all sorts of correlations in the data that can be used by the algorithm to improve its predictions. Sometimes these correlations, like stereotypes and biases, are the correlations that the algorithm identifies and latches on to. It doesn't have a moral compass to say what is acceptable and what's not acceptable, it is looking for any sort of correlations and anything that reinforces those correlations.

One well known case was a chatbot called Tay that was developed by Microsoft. It was released to the public so it could monitor how it interacted with people. A particular group of right-wing activists deliberately tried to interfere with it by feeding it various racist comments. The chatbot was set up so that it learned from that data in an iterative cycle, so it ended up reinforcing many of these negative comments and became racist and offensive.'

Microsoft had to disable the chatbot within 24 hours and take it offline to be cleaned. It was re-educated and then re-released in a more anodyne form that could only converse about fashion and music and reply to attempts to subvert it again by saying: 'I'm better than you'.

Should we clean the data and start again?

Does this mean that existing and pre-existing AI systems will now need a twenty-first century re-education?

'It is a challenging area because AI systems are taught to learn from data, you could say it is in their nature. They learn from experiences. Often, they start from a blank slate, like a new-born baby and they quickly learn from their interactions with humans. One thing that our research has really highlighted is the impact of potential biases in the data that are used to train these algorithms.

So that's one thing that we now understand. In terms of what one can do. In general, I think a big area of development is that we really need to think about how we audit such AI systems to make sure that they are doing what they're supposed to do, and they're actually aligned and beneficial to human values.'

This is an issue that is vigorously championed by MIT's Buolamwini, like Zou, another pioneer in the fight for fair datasets:

'We need to also come in with the mindset that there will always be some kind of bias, some kind of harm that we need to be checking for. Instead of thinking about bias eradication, we need to think about bias mitigation. And in some ways, it's more like having algorithmic hygiene. With hygiene, you wouldn't just shower once in 2019 and say "we are done" – or "we checked for bias on our model in 2019, now we are good from here on in". No, that would be silly.

So instead when you're thinking about something like algorithmic hygiene, it's ongoing because you realise you have to stay vigilant. The situation changes, so there will need to be ongoing inspection. An inspection that means that when we are looking to improve these technologies, we need to look at how the technologies work, how they're being used and to make sure that there are appropriate safeguards and mechanisms for transparency and accountability built-in in the first place.'

However, could this process be seen as censorship? A neutering of the technology and a response that could generate a result that negates the value of AI? Is there not a risk that the data could be altered to reflect a view of the society that actually is socially 'fair' but factually incorrect? Imposing a set of rules on AI could also cut down on insight and impose desired results on the technology, and according to some critics they could also become biased and even made to lie, an issue Zou is aware of and says must be guarded against.

'I think there is going to be some tension, between how much leeway that we give to these algorithms and how much we have to look over their shoulders to make sure they are doing the right things. The current way that the niche machine learning systems are being developed, is not robust enough, to just let algorithms run wild on the data and do its own thing. There needs to be a fair amount of human supervision, especially in sensitive contexts. If algorithms are being used for medical applications, which many companies are working on, those are particularly sensitive applications where it's critical to have a human in the loop, to supervise and check on the functioning of the algorithms, that is not to say that those algorithms will be useless but I think they should be working closely with humans.

The reason for that is that in the medical context it is obviously important is to be able to make a precise and accurate diagnosis that is accurate for an individual. If an individual comes to a hospital, we really want to be able to say, well we know this about you, so this is your level of risk for specific diseases. We don't want to say this is the risk for an average person in the UK because that is a very generic profile, in medicine we all know it is useful to have information on someone's lifestyle and what they have been doing.

The issue with the use of AI systems in this area is how the AI diagnosis was arrived at because the risk of AI systems in medicine is that they have ethnic or racial biases and that can lead to them making systematic mistakes for particular demographic groups. For example, the data used to train a particular medical diagnosis algorithm, could have mostly come from white males, which will work really well if a white male comes in and it is used to make a diagnosis for that individual.

If, however, an Asian person or an African person comes in, maybe the algorithm could systematically produce misdiagnosis. So that is one potential effect of having used biased algorithms in a medical context.'

Who decides upon the filter?

The question of censorship, filtering and weighting of algorithms is a sensitive one. At the moment with machine learning systems, while everything they do involves searching through data for patterns, the task of looking for those patterns and what they should mean in the system's rules is given to them by a human being. Any moderation that is done will be done by a human being.

As we have seen in the recent example of the algorithms used to decide exam results in the UK during the COVID-19 pandemic the use of postcodes was so discriminatory that it lowered pupil grades based upon their postcode, the rationale being that some children historically did less well than their wealthier counterparts.

This is, however, a postcode (or, in the US, ZIP-code)-based bias that Benjamin says Black people have always suffered from.

'There are places in which we could be making better decisions. The existing data is one point but in terms of how you code a system, what you weigh, what you take into account that has to be considered. For example some algorithms are being used to decide whether someone should be released on parole from prison or have a longer or shorter sentence in the criminal justice process. That input data is biased because of widespread racial profiling practices that say if you are Black or Latino, you are more likely to have a criminal record. Therefore, you are training software to associate criminality with these racial groups.

Another point of responsibility or place we have to look at is exactly where in the code level are you weighting certain types of factors more than others. For example, if you live in a community in which there is a high unemployment rate, many algorithms in the criminal justice system would say that that makes you more at risk for being a repeat offender.

Another point I am concerned about is that ZIP codes are a kind of low-tech form of coded inequity, because of what has happened historically in the US context. When we outlawed very explicit forms of discrimination, geography became a proxy for controlling different populations and containing them in certain areas. Banks would use zip codes to create maps of a city and then invest in certain areas and divest from certain areas.

One of the things I have been researching is the connection between this low-tech form of coded inequity using a zip code, and then looking at the way that that becomes folded into a more high-tech form of coded inequity in which geography continues to be a proxy.

One example that we see comes out of Facebook and the targeted ads that people often see on the site side panel, when you suddenly see something come up that you were searching for earlier in the day. This happens because advertisers can target different populations and people in different areas.

They can use your search history to target ads but can also exclude people from seeing ads. For example, if you are a real estate developer or you're trying to sell housing of a particular type you can exclude, let's say, African Americans from seeing your ads. Until very recently, people didn't even realise that that was possible and so would not make the connection to US fair housing policies that say if a human was doing that, that it would be against the law but because it was an algorithm that was doing it, it was not. It has not been identified as discrimination or as part of this longer history of trying to essentially reinforce segregation in our communities. So, buying and selling goods online can also facilitate coded inequity.'

Big tech's masked intervention in presentation

It is an observation shared in an editorial in the *New York Times* about Facebook:

'Facebook regularly rewrites its computer systems to meet the company's goals; the company might make it more likely that you'll see a friend's baby photo than a news article about wildfires. That doesn't mean that wildfires aren't real, but it does mean that Facebook is creating a world where the fires are not in the forefront.

Facebook sells billions of dollars in ads each year because what people see there, and how Facebook chooses to prioritize that information, can influence what people believe and buy.'

The point made that bias permeates the internet becomes even more important when we consider AI systems because not only do they draw their data from the tainted pool described by Benjamin and Zou but they are also fed on specific databases that do not relate to people from ethnic groups as Zou identifies:

'One thing that we should understand is that the data that is used to train the algorithm itself has to be curated by humans in some way or form because the data in the world is extremely messy and it's also very imbalanced. For example, a lot of our genetics data is collected mostly from people of European descent rather than from individuals of other ancestries.

This means that we already have all sorts of potential heterogeneities and imbalances in the existing data. And researchers and engineers have to already work quite hard in thinking about what the high-quality data or the less noisy data are that we should use to train these different prediction algorithms. That is already very much an intrinsic part of the current engineering workflow.

What we have begun to recommend is that in that workflow itself, where people are curating the data being used, we should also be mindful about making sure the data is balanced across different ethnic groups, to make sure that as much as possible that these additional stereotypes and biases are not introduced into the system.'

This is a task that challenges the traditional breakneck speed of technology development which long has been a characteristic of the IT industry. Fed on newspaper stories of meteoric high-tech start-ups, speed is of the essence in the technology industry. Take your time and a competitor or another nation state will steal a march on you. According to Zou:

'The paradox of this is with AI, the new darling on the block, it not only has to take the time to get it right, but the advantages of huge data processing speed and analysis itself becomes a problem and the AI technology cannot be used to solve those issues unless it is known to be trustworthy.

There are two stages that people have to aware of here, there is the process that we use to train the AI system, and then after it's trained the deployment of the AI system on data in the context it will be used. For example, after I have trained a medical diagnosis algorithm, then I will want to deploy it in different clinics and hospitals. And in that scenario, it could actually be massively useful because it would do things that are repetitive for humans or labour intensive to humans and it could do those things almost instantaneously. That would generate a lot of value and a lot of efficiency because of automation. What we are talking about in terms of the bias tends to occur in the training phase. That is a more concentrated phase either by a particular company or a start-up or it could be Google or a consortium.

In essence you have a small team of engineers who work together to actually train the algorithm that could take, a few months or a year. What we are seeing means that training we require additional work by the developers and engineers to train the algorithm in a way that makes sure that it is more reliable and more equitable. I think that's it's not an unreasonable amount of effort. And also, once the algorithms trained and once it's deployed, it would still have all the benefits of an AI system in terms of automating automation, speed, performance.'

Auditing the AI

Given the vulnerability of the AI systems in this training phase, Zou concedes that this has now raised additional issues for AI developers. Because of the importance of the systems they are developing it has now become imperative to protect the curated data that has been assembled from attack, while at the same time preventing the AI from being contaminated by other data because of the potential for sensitive AI systems to be targeted by nation states, by terrorists and by people with their own political biases (as happened with Microsoft's Tay chatbot).

'It's definitely true that AI systems like many other things could become targets of political intervention and other types of attacks. Which is why we think it is beneficial to have periodic audits on AI systems in the same way that we check the quality of automobiles using MOTs or periodically audit the tax returns for individuals and organisations to ensure high quality and compliance. In the same way I think it's also important to audit machine learning AI algorithms and this auditing process for an AI system itself might also be made possible by using algorithms. The auditing does not have to be done entirely manually by humans. It could be done by a combination of humans and auditing algorithms.'

This is a process that will call for a complex pattern of auditing and validation, which will need the development of systems such as a quality stamp database, containing time stamps of what was done, when, where and why it was done and by whom. According to some observers, it will mean that if you are going to sit that algorithm or mined database on another database or combine it to get richer data, then each of those databases will have to be validated in the same way. According to Zou:

'It will depend on specific applications. If you are developing an AI system using these databases for instance in what is a sensitive or mission critical application being used in medicine or in self-driving cars, then I think it is prudent to verify the quality of the data and the quality of the algorithms. That is not any different from, for example, what the FDA would do to ensure that new drugs are of a sufficiently high quality before they are used on human patients. Inspectors have to ensure, that car companies are producing cars that meet safety requirements before they are given to human drivers. So similarly, in these mission critical applications that could impact upon the safety of human lives I think it is prudent to have these quality controls. There are other applications that are less mission critical where I think it's reasonable to have different levels of quality control and less restrictions.'

A statement of intent: what is the AI meant to do?

If, as Zou says, algorithms will also need validation, then quality control is essential for those developing systems to eradicate implicit bias in the code or by the coders because the choice of the first objective set can skew the process of the rest of the algorithm.

'Typically, algorithms are trained to achieve a particular objective. If for example you are developing algorithms to control machinery you simply say: "here's is the objective function and here's the training data." Then the algorithm is going to greedily optimise for the objective based on the training data.

While a lot of attention has focused on the potential biases in the data used to train these algorithms, another input source of potential implicit bias is actually in the choice of the objective function which the algorithms are actually being told to optimise. That is another area where I think human biases could come in.

The engineers and developers of the algorithm could also bias the algorithm in giving it different objectives. One concrete example of this is in a paper written by researchers from the University of California, Berkeley and the University of Chicago who were studying algorithms used in the health care context.

The algorithms are basically used to predict how likely it will be that a particular individual will need healthcare by predicting what the health risks are to an individual based on their past. That is quite useful for insurance companies and for medical health providers. But the researchers found the algorithms were not being trained to that objective. They were not being trained to predict health risks because it is hard to measure health quality and you need to have detailed health information about each individual to be able to do that, so the value that the system was given was medical expenditure, the amount of money that was being spent corresponding on each patient. That is a more convenient objective because it's easy to collect. It's more quantifiable. And the insurance companies and medical providers already have that data readily available. So, what the algorithm is doing is trying to predict health risk by using health cost as a proxy. There is an issue here because there is a misalignment between the objective of the cost and the health risk and that misalignment of the objective leads to biases against African Americans because they are actually systematically predicting lower risk than the actual health profiles of African American individuals and being too conservative in terms of quantifying the health risks.

They're saying they're less susceptible than they actually are which would potentially lead to less resources being provided for them.

There are a variety of complex factors that could contribute to this. Certainly, there's disparity in access to health that could be contributary factor in the algorithm's bias. There's also a disparity in the use of health care systems. So maybe certain populations are just less likely to come in to see doctors. That could be because of access, lack of resources or even geography.'

The controversial argument for more data

Removing any racial classification from the data does not work as Benjamin pointed out:

> 'Even if you actually remove race explicitly, there is a variety of other factors, such as income, occupation, geography that are correlated with race that could still bias the algorithms. So, it's not quite as clean as just simply ignoring race or gender because these factors, these other demographic factors, do interact, because they're intertwined with other data features.'

This intertwining of data can be incredibly revealing. In an interview with Peter Warren and Chris Blackhurst, the former editor of *The Independent,* Clive Hunby, the co-founder of the data analysis company, Dunn-Hunby, creators of the Tesco loyalty card scheme, stated that the company could accurately identify voting habits from purchases and other data. Diet can often reveal ethnicity.

> 'For some purposes aggregating additional types of data together is useful and very revealing. What this study shows and what we're trying to highlight is that in addition to aggregating additional data together, we should also be very careful about the learning objectives of these AI systems, so we know what they are trying to optimise.

> It's more convenient, cost is readily quantifiable and available and there's a lot of data for it. But that actually is also a door through which different biases can come in.'

Transparency essential for understanding and public trust

This begs the question whether there should be legal or regulatory rules on which datasets data engineers can use when training their algorithms? Or will this again restrict algorithmic insight because the systems are put on a data diet? Some AI experts claim that AI systems are inefficient because they are built to consume as much data as possible, something that allows them to arrive at patterns we cannot and should not see. Zou states:

> 'AI is definitely very good at digesting large amounts of information due to that it is important, especially in mission critical areas, to be as transparent as possible about the types of data that are fed into an AI system. What are the potential biases in the design of the system? Who chose the learning objectives and why? We have to be as explicit and transparent as possible about how the systems are actually being trained and tested before they are deployed publicly.

> And yes, they do consume a lot of data and that can lead to insight, for example, natural language processing systems when compared to humans in terms of the speed of learning and the amount of data that they've got to learn are inefficient. If you look at human babies compared to an AI system, the AI system will actually require a lot more data to train. And it will be less flexible than a human baby.

164

That's not to say that these systems are not useful or not efficient when they're being used. Once they are trained, they can make decisions much faster than humans can.'

Do we need an FDA for AI?

Is there then a need for an equivalent institution to the US Federal Drug Administration to oversee how we might be doing things with AI? In the UK ethicists were so concerned about the potential for the genetic engineering of people that it was decided to create the Human Fertilisation and Embryology Authority. Given the potential social threats from AI systems, don't we need some equivalent body for the technology?

'There's already a lot of discussions among policymakers and different governments about the best way to evaluate and to audit AI systems.

In Europe, in the UK, as a part of their GDPR, there is a lot of discussion around individual control of personal data in relation to algorithms and demands for a right for an explanation but having one central government organisation to oversees all the AI systems is not necessarily the most efficient way to implement this.

As AI systems are deployed in very different domains and often domain expertise is required to really check and evaluate the safety and efficacy of these systems. It might be better to have, teams that are distributed within existing government organisations whose role is to evaluate the appropriateness of the AI system that are specific in their domain. So, the FDA might have their own internal teams to evaluate medical AI systems, in financial settings the regulators there could also have people to audit the financial AI systems, similar interest partition in self-driving cars. So within different organisations, you could have different groups that are working with AI systems to really understand and evaluate the systems in their sector.'

This is a very challenging task due to the speed and the complexity of the calculations going on within an AI system. This is sometimes referred to as the 'black box' issue. This means that the data is passed through the algorithms and is processed so fast that those working on the systems are not able to explain how the system reached its conclusions.

'The speed of calculations that go on within the algorithm are what makes it makes it challenging to entirely audit the systems manually by humans.

If I – as an AI expert – were to look at the neural network that performed a calculation that could have millions of parameters, it would be really unfeasible for me to go through each of the parameters and figure out what had been done. Even if I have a lot of time, it would be really hard for me to understand all of the interactions and complexities of such a big system.

Which is why we need to be able to audit these systems at a higher level. Just looking at the low-level calculations of individual systems will be too complicated. The way that we could do this would be to feed into the black box example inputs or some queries and then examine its behaviour in terms of the outputs it makes on that specific information. From that we can get a sense of the system's reliability and what the potential biases and the behaviour of the system. That is something that would be easier for me to do and easier for humans to do so I think that it's a type of audit that will be more feasible.'

The need for multi-disciplinary oversight

For Zou, teams working on an AI system should include people other than data scientists, for example they should include ethicists or philosophers or lawyers:

'As these systems interact more and more with humans, the teams for designing and for evaluating the AI system, I think should become more interdisciplinary, certainly having social scientists, humanists, and legal experts involved will be essential going forward.'

So how would that operate? Do you think it would be good to have regulation? Do you think there should be regulations that actually make people sit down and think about what they're doing and what the potential ramifications could be on them personally and financially?

'There are already some regulations that are being proposed. We need to think through very carefully about what are the appropriate levels of regulation and also about implementation and verification because even implementation could be quite challenging when it relates to these AI systems because as you said, because they are black boxes.'

Regulating AI holds our behaviour up to an ethical lens

What does seem certain is that AI systems will become a legal battleground owing to the black box issue and the attempts to force transparency on it. If full transparency is forced onto the companies' producing systems, then their commercial secrets are pushed into the light. Not only can rivals see how their AI works but potential litigants can find the evidence of the datasets that were used. Regulated transparency, forcing through the common good, has huge potentially harmful side-effects on the incumbent big tech companies with AI interests in terms of restricting their markets and pushing up costs but, as both Zou and Buolamwini note, this is not about protecting the interests of companies. It is about making AI fair for all.

For Zou, this is not a question of trade-offs:

'As we mentioned, certainly if one does want to provide additional privacy protections for individuals or to enable individuals more control over how their data is being used, I think that would actually lead to trade-offs that could make it harder to develop AI systems or make it more expensive to develop AI systems. But I think, where we want to be on that trade-off is exactly the kinds of questions that policymakers and consumers and other stakeholders should be discussing',

While according to Buolamwini:

'When it comes to addressing issues of algorithmic bias and more broadly issues of algorithmic harms, we have to think of both cost of inclusion and cost of exclusion. What you are speaking about is, are there ways to in some way make the systems perform better, to have better technical performance? The answer is very simple, it is yes.'

Which of course begs the question why is AI so much more of an ethical issue for society than other technologies? For Zou, this is about ensuring that we can achieve benefits through technological innovation, rather than entrenching existing issues.

'There are a lot of ethical challenges because at the end we would like these AI systems to work to the maximum benefits of humans and we want to make sure that the systems that we develop are not exacerbating inequalities that are already present in our societies.

To do that will lead to various trade-offs in the algorithms and those trade-offs, I think, are not unique for AI systems. We are talking about subjects that have been debated and discussed in ethics and philosophy for many, many decades. So that's where I think there's going to be very important discussions and connections.'

Benjamin confirms that there will be a need for a discrimination team to be part of an AI team to ensure discrimination is not occurring. This is a practice being undertaken already by some of the larger companies.

'I think they would have internal teams to work with the engineers to work with the AI developers to ensure that both legally and in terms of different compliances that the systems actually following the right regulations.'

As with all regulations Zou expects there will be curbs on some current practices, something that occurred with GDPR which he feels was needed.

'I think GDPR does impose some constraints. And it is an important step in ensuring that these AI systems are acting responsibly. It also ensures that individuals have certain rights and certain controls over how their data can be used by algorithms. The right to be forgotten for example, these are quite reasonable policies to ensure that individuals can say they do not want their data to be used in certain settings. Those are good first steps.'

Leaving bias in AI systems will be a legal time bomb

What Zou, Benjamin and Buolamwini are all agreed on is that there will be legal ramifications from leaving bias in company systems unwittingly and from attempting to prevent its discovery. For Zou:

'There are going to be many legal implications. It will be similar to the legal implications of buying any product that contains a fault, such as a car with a poor braking system there are strong legal responsibilities and implications for that and the same goes for medicine, if it has adverse effects, there are strong legal implications for that. We will not really see anything too different about AI systems. I think it is important to try to be as transparent as possible.

I think if in settings where an algorithm really clearly exacerbates inequalities and leads to discrimination, that squarely falls under these anti-discrimination rules and will definitely be the basis of legal challenges.

I would say that's because these systems have the potential for so much impact. The more potential impact the system could have, the more careful people will have to be to ensure that they are transparent and they're beneficial across the broader society.'

Despite the current focus on the use of AI in medical and autonomous systems it is inevitable that attention will soon switch to the use of AI to influence people's behaviour and how technology companies really monitor us using their AI systems. Zou believes this should be regulated, but that one size does not fit all.

'I think the level of regulation will certainly differ, depending on the sensitivity of the AI application with self-driving cars and medicine, where it could directly impact the safety of individuals, it would be prudent to have a higher bar of inspection and quality control, then say for Amazon where you're just trying to buy the next book or the next device. I think it's quite reasonable to have different levels of regulation, perhaps for some things where the impacts are relatively minor then the regulation would be significantly fewer.'

For Zou and all of the other contributors to this chapter the real issues lie with us as humans, since very often AI draws on the internet as a data source and the AI is simply holding up to us a mirror of how we portray ourselves on the internet and saying: 'actually you're not as nice as you might think you are':

'AI systems are trained on data that we have generated so they are effectively a mirror that captures our own biases and stereotypes that is both good and bad. The good part is that it is actually easier to de-bias and to debug an AI system than it is to debug a human. There is therefore the promise that we could have AI systems that are more accountable and more transparent than people.'

Technology entrepreneur, creative innovator, global music artist, producer and philanthropist will.i.am emphasises that regulation to prevent bias must begin in the classroom.

'First, and foremost this is about education. We have to solve the flaws of humanity first and how we educate our citizens to be able to build systems that are not broken. The regulations have to come with human regulation first. And that's for humanity to do. It must prepare people for tomorrow.'

This is a view shared by AI expert, Risto Siilasmaa, the Chair, founder and former CEO of the cyber security company F-Secure and former Chair of Nokia. Siilasmaa, who provides evidence in Chapter 15 and taught himself AI so that he could warn world leaders about its benefits and risks, is certain that the issue lies with us and not our machines.

'Hidden *bias* can exist anywhere, if you do not know that you have it, then you are completely weaponless in modifying the data to remove the *bias* because you do not know it exists. You don't know what you don't know. When you know, as in the example of the inclusion of the US penitentiary system data which we all know is biased, then you can take action if you are the person that is building the dataset that will be used for training you can remove that *bias*.

It takes time and it is a little bit costly. Then it becomes a question of the values of the entity building a solution, whether they will put money behind removing that *bias*, which they, of course, should but don't always do.

The other option is whether you will be penalised when people find out there was this *bias* and you did not remove it. In research and development, it is often a question of how much money you have to do the work.'

Going back to the classroom

As Zou has pointed out there is the potential for AI systems, working in concert with human beings, to identify and correct bias in data and algorithms, a process that could also be used to identify and correct bias in people, a potentially dangerous tool:

'We have seen AI systems being used to analyse the writings and texts of individuals from Twitter and other sources and then use that to identify the holistic patterns and the different threads of opinions in those large corpuses of text. That is one way that the AI system becomes the mirror to humans and essentially identifies different threads of opinion and difference threads of sentiments in communities.

The political use of AI is definitely a significant concern because AI systems can be used by bad actors who want to target particular populations and disseminate propaganda.

The reality in this area is quite nuanced. There is often a subtle distinction between what constitutes free speech or free speech that's facilitated by algorithms versus the spread of false information, propaganda and targeting. I think it would be challenging to have an outright ban of any activity of this sort. That is why transparency, knowing how data is used by the algorithm and the intended target audiences of the algorithm as well as more accountability would enable us to make these more nuanced adjudications.'

These are nuanced adjudications that Zou says will require politicians to be educated in the ethical use of AI as well as the schoolchildren will.i.am wants to be educated about bias.

'These algorithms are becoming so prevalent in our everyday lives, they should become also an important part of our education not just teaching everyone about how the algorithms work, but also thinking about the broader ethics and the impact of the social components of these algorithms.

I think those should all be taught together in schools.'

Chapter 11

Decoding inherent unfairness

Can we correct hardwired bias?

The relationship between AI and race is the most controversial topic surrounding the development of the technology, principally because of the underlying data that AI is trained upon. In Chapter 10 Stanford's Professor James Zou, Professor Ruha Benjamin from Princeton and Joy Buolamwini from MIT outlined how something as lacking in emotion as an AI system can become both racist and sexist.

In this chapter we explore with Reema Patel from the Ada Lovelace Institute, Professor Benjamin and Joy Buolamwini the impact of this failing and how the ethical development of AI now confronts us with profound moral and philosophical issues, which impact wider society.

Reema Patel *is the former Associate Director at the Ada Lovelace Institute, an independent organisation seeking to ensure that data and AI work for people and society, where she led the organisation's public attitudes and public deliberation research and was a member of its founding team.*

Patel has just over a decade's experience in public policy and has led various citizen engagement initiatives on complex and controversial policy areas including the Royal Society of Arts (RSA) Citizens' Economic Council, which successfully worked with and influenced the Bank of England's public engagement strategy. She grew the Ada Lovelace Institute's public engagement team, which now encompasses mixed methods and deliberative public attitudes work that range across biometrics, data and the rule of law, health and social inequalities, data narratives, location data sharing, and NHS health data sharing. She also developed the Ada Lovelace Institute's research and thinking in the fields of Rethinking Data and Data Stewardship.

Patel is Senior Fellow of the Finance Innovation Lab, a non-profit working to create a more democratic, responsible, and fair economy. She has consulted for a variety of international organisations, including the Danish Board of Technology Foundation, the Wellcome Trust, and Nextdoor.com, a San Francisco-based technology social media start-up. She is a fellow of the RSA, founding trustee of a community run library, and a local councillor.

Bias in data means that the conclusions derived from it are quite simply wrong and that poor data means unfair decisions. Patel notes this finding not only challenges assumptions about the infallibility of computerised deduction but also highlights the subjectivity of computer systems and how they are used:

'There are a number of problems around race and AI, and the whole area is very complicated. I would simplify it down to a few key problems: the first

171

relates to the use of AI as a series of data driven technologies, so that when we are looking at the data, often the data does not represent or adequately represent or work for people from ethnic minority backgrounds. That is one problem, which is structural. If we then follow that issue and ask why that happens, then it opens two further issues.

One of those is that there can be a gap between those who are designing and developing the technology and those to whom the technologies relate.

If we look at the backgrounds of those who develop AI, they are deeply "undiverse" and do not generally tend to represent the people to whom the technology relates.'

AI targeting: us or them?

'Then there are also another set of challenges, which are not just about the missing data, or the lack of diversity. It is what Virginia Eubanks described as the tension here with the surveilling or over profiling of people by certain types of technology. What this means is that not only do you have technologies that are not designed in a very representative way, but you also start to see technologies being deployed in ways that disproportionately targets and impact upon ethnic minorities. For example, if you look at the development of a range of technologies in China, that are persecuting the Uyghur Muslims, and at the same time, you have also got, the development of facial recognition technology that is obviously over profiling and over surveilling people from ethnic minority background then there is obviously the potential for crossover.

There is deep awareness of this in ethnic minorities, as the Ada Lovelace Institute proved when it polled people in 2019 on the use of facial recognition technology. This poll found that if you are from an ethnic minority background, you were 10 per cent more likely to be uncomfortable with the use of facial recognition technology as opposed to the use of other technologies such as health data sharing for example.

Thus, when it comes to particular technologies, it is clear there is a problem and a complex one because, on one hand, we have a challenge, to get enough data about people from an ethnic minority background and the challenge some technologies over represent and over profile and surveil those people.

I suggest that there is a connecting theme here, which is that public confidence and public trust is differential and until we sort out the issues that come with over profiling or over surveilling, AI technology will not work in the best interests of people from ethnic minority backgrounds because of the risk to them that harvesting data mean in terms of ethnic minorities simply becoming more surveilled. Thus, we are highly unlikely to be able to build public confidence and the trust that mean that people want to give out their data.'

This is something that as Patel points out, instantly generates discrimination in areas like health, adding to already pre-existing inequalities and weaknesses. This was recently demonstrated during the COVID-19 pandemic in a study published in the medical journal *The Lancet*,[1] where it was reported that people from ethnic minority communities were adversely affected by COVID-19.

Ironically, the *Lancet* study highlighted that it was only due to the voluntary contribution of data on race that the study could produce its findings.

Just how much of a problem racial bias in data is, is only now being appreciated owing to the debate over race and AI. Indeed, not only are issues being thrown up by the technology as it is developed, but it has also begun to reveal how deep-seated biases in society have become ingrained into the system and often have been, in the words of Patel, 'baked in'.

It is a point underlined in Chapter 10 by Professor Ruha Benjamin, when she explained how US zip codes had become involved in racism because they identify areas where ethnic minorities live. This is a process that Professor Benjamin says has now transferred to the internet:

'For many people, the obvious harms are the way that technologies are used to explicitly reinforce different kinds of social hierarchies. So there's certain kinds of citizen scoring systems and ways in which our existing inequalities get reinforced and amplified through technology.

For some people, that could be seen as the worst of the worst. But for me, the worst of the worst is when we unwittingly reinforce various forms of oppression and hierarchies in the context of trying to do good. I describe this as "techno benevolence". It's an acknowledgement that humans are biased, we discriminate. We have all kinds of really institutionalised forms of inequalities that we take for granted.

We have technologies that say we have a fix for that. If we just employ this software program or just download this app or just include this particular system in your institution or your company, we can go around that bias. So it's that arena of technology for good -when we don't really think through and include the people who are potentially most harmed by various kinds of tech adoption – that concerns me most. Not the obvious forms of harm.

There's a number of organisations – hundreds even – that are adopting hiring algorithms instead of having, human resource people go through thousands of resumés. They are outsourcing this employment decision-making to automated AI and one of the things we're finding is that those decisions often are just as sexist and racist as the humans, if not worse. It's because the training data and the things that are being looked for in the applicant pool are very much the same as in the past.

So, although there are many more data points being considered, it's actually reproducing the same demographics as we've seen in the past: more men

---

1 Rohini Mathur, Christopher T Rentsch, Caroline E Morton, William J Hulme, Anna Schultze, Brian MacKenna et al, 'Ethnic differences in SARS-CoV-2 infection and COVID-19-related hospitalisation, intensive care unit admission, and death in 17 million adults in England: an observational cohort study using the OpenSAFELY platform' (2021) 397(10286) *The Lancet* 1711–24.

are being hired, more white people, more people with higher education and a range of other factors. This is where the danger is. We think that it's more objective and more neutral than a human sitting behind a desk, but it's actually hiding the various forms of bias under the guise of neutrality.

We know through social science audits and various, rigorous analyses that even when you don't ask or know the person's race explicitly or their gender explicitly, they're all kinds of cues, whether it be the name of the person where what their zip code is, where they went to school, that inform that that decision. The smarter the algorithms and the more discerning of the applicant pool they are becoming, the more sexist and racist they are as a result.

So, artificial intelligence often goes hand in hand with being more bias. It doesn't get us around the problem. As a starting point for a solution, we have to understand that we don't just need technical know-how and prowess in terms of developing the systems, we need people who understand the social history, employment discrimination, health care discrimination or criminal justice discrimination as the case may be.

We need the people who are most affected by it to inform whether we want to even employ automated tools. Then, if we do, we need to understand the coded nature of discrimination, that is not always explicit.

That has to be folded into a more high-tech form of coded inequity, in which geography continues to be a proxy. One example of that can be seen on Facebook and the targeted ads that people often see. The ability to do that is because advertisers can target different populations and people in different areas.

Not only can your search history be used to target ads at you, advertisers can also exclude people from seeing their ad. That means that if you are a real estate developer or you are trying to sell housing and wish to promote a particular image you can exclude African-Americans from seeing your advert.'

This is a potential use of technology and individual data presaged in Steven Spielberg's 2002 film *Minority Report*, based on a short story by Philip K Dick.[2]

During the film, which is concerned with preventing crimes in the future, the adverts on billboards change to reflect the lives of the people passing them. This idea is now close to reality, having already been trialled in Toulon by the former mobile phone company Orange.

In August 2010, the technology company IBM announced it was working on such a technology. Newspaper reports at the time stated that IBM claimed that its technology will help prevent consumers from being subjected to a barrage of irritating advertising because they will only be shown adverts for products that are relevant to them.

---

2 *Minority Report*: en.wikipedia.org/wiki/Minority_Report_(film).

The IBM system worked by using similar wireless technology tags to those found in Oyster Cards – the travel cards used on the London Underground. These tags, known as RFID chips, are increasingly being incorporated into credit cards, mobile phones and packaging. By encoding these chips with information about the individual, digital advertising boards could identify people as they pass by and show them an advert based on their shopping habits and personal preferences.

Brian Innes, a research scientist at IBM's innovation laboratories in Hursley, near Winchester, said:

> 'In *Minority Report*, the billboards recognise passers-by and play adverts that are specific for the individual. In the film, the billboards rely on scanning the person's eyeball, but we are using RFID technology that people are carrying around with them, so they can have a tailor-made message.'

This is a technological development that would unwittingly accelerate the process Professor Benjamin is worried about.

The missing names and faces

These are controversial technological trends involving both people from ethnic minorities and the poor, and ones that people will argue for on both sides. One side will state that targeting is a completely justified activity because they only want to sell expensive cars to those who can afford them, the other side object to the systems, stating that they are exclusory and that they lock people into and out of worlds.

This complex argument about technology use and participation is, as Patel says, multi-faceted. It is a world where some have access to data, and some are locked out of the internet and the twenty-first century because they either do not have a device to access the internet or an internet connection, a situation that according to Ofcom affects around 11 per cent of the UK population.[3]

Other organisations, such as Nesta, put the figure at one in seven of the UK's adults and the Social Mobility Foundation charity estimates this means that as a result 1.4m children do not have access to the internet.

This lack of internet access disproportionately affects people from ethnic minorities who find themselves not aware of information such as government polls on COVID-19 and not canvassed for their opinions in the same way as white people. This means that they are unrepresented in some government data and then conversely they are over-represented in other data collected by the government from official sources such as criminal records, which tend to represent economic trends such as poverty.

This is a trend that Patel states will only accelerate if the databases used by AI are not cleansed and made fit for purpose. As she points out, not only are those

---

3 See www.ofcom.org.uk/about-ofcom/latest/media/media-releases/2021/digital-divide-narrowed-but-around-1.5m-homes-offline.

historic databases littered with anachronistic bias due to the data used but are also unbalanced because the programmers creating the databases were not conscious of the underlying bias of the data or that they were creating discriminatory systems, so did not counter those issues.

All these issues are further complicated by factors such as the absence of data in health databases or its over-abundance in crime databases.

Patel highlights, in particular, one incident where a lack of images of Black people in databases had caused one of the most startling and offensive failures of AI.

'Some technologies like facial recognition, can be inaccurate, misrepresent or misidentify people with appalling results, one example being an algorithm that misidentified Black people as gorillas.'

This issue was explored in Chapter 10 with Joy Buolamwini, whose research found that AI facial recognition systems that were shown images of famous Black women invariably identified them as young boys or men, owing to an absence of images in the databases for the systems to work with.

Poisoning the data well

Another potential factor is the deliberate 'poisoning' of data by conspiracy theorists and political extremists. According to the Ada Lovelace Institute's Patel:

'In the past, when you typed the words "the holocaust" into Google, some of the suggested first 10 links were so problematic that Google had to change its algorithm to ensure that it delivered the truth. The search terms it was coming up with suggested links to holocaust denial websites and news articles. This was because the general algorithm aggregated what people tended to click on and search for and suggest the most highly clicked on algorithm. That shows how easily the racism that exists in society can perpetuate and be allowed to proliferate, unless you are quite thoughtful about the design.

That is a really, good example of how racism can be manifested by AI. It is not that the algorithm is racist, people in certain contexts are racist, and the algorithm learns from human behaviour to create datasets and so those assumption become significant.

What we are seeing are unequal outcomes being perpetuated by technologies that learn from human biases and human perspectives of discrimination.'

This is something that most famously occurred with the Microsoft chatbot Tay referred to in Chapter 10 by Professor James Zou, an outcome that Patel believes needs a profound change in thought. Before technology is introduced, Patel says people need to think about why they are doing it, what the effects will be and they should test their technology to make sure it does what it is meant to do.

'When an algorithm is introduced or a chatbot or any kind of app is introduced, there needs to be a moment of reflection as to what is the likely impact of this going to be, and do the benefits outweigh the potential risks and harms?

Tay was meant to be fairly innocuous; it was an experiment to show what Microsoft was capable of doing, but what it ended up doing was far more harmful than that.

From the perspective of an industry or a developer or a practice based organisation or perhaps an organisation like the NHS, or Ofcom thinking about introducing algorithms, it's really important that we start to think about how do we build in instruction processes that give us a moment of pause for reflection, before we just put something out there into the world.

What we're seeing is that algorithms are being introduced into the world without any thought to the impact or the differential impact. What should be being asked is, is this going to be harmful, and who is this going to be harmful for?'

The value of data

As previous chapters have relentlessly underlined, the issue of AI, as Cambridge's Professor Neil Lawrence pointed out, is data, how it is recorded and as Patel has stated, understanding what it is recording. However, in certain areas this does present very difficult issues, which require some consideration for any legal, ethical and regulatory framework.

According to *Computing* magazine, police crime databases in Essex in 1996 had set up fields to record the sex and ethnicity (Black, white or gypsy) of the person committing an offence, all information the police considered particularly relevant. At the same time much work was being undertaken to use computer systems to predict crime and predilection to crime. In one such experiment in Margate, also in 1996, the Kent police claimed to be able to use crime pattern analysis to be able to work out when a crime was likely to take place. The police stated that following a spate of rooftop burglaries in a particular area they were able to correctly identify the next house the thief would target and that they were actually waiting in the flat for him.

Other research, again in 1996 in Manchester by Greater Manchester Police (and reported by the *Sunday Times*) into the factors that influence criminal development, unsurprisingly discovered that if people lived in deprived areas with a high pre-disposition to crime and that if one or more parents had served jail sentences while a child was at primary school, there was a high likelihood of the child going on to offend. A Greater Manchester Police project that intended to use this data to target children it considered highly likely to become criminals and try to intervene by issuing warnings was shelved after political pressure.

These are all indicators of the thinking among police forces when collecting data on criminal activities, as neatly illustrated in the German film *Pre-crime*.[4] These factors would prove impossible to ignore by those investigating crime using AI, according to Professor Fred Cate, who provides evidence in Chapter 14. Indeed,

---

4   Jane Whyatt, '"Pre-crime" film says crime can be predicted' (*Future Intelligence*, 20 November 2017).

anyone seeking to create a crime system using AI would find it very difficult to justify not using existing criminal records, which already have social injustice built into them. For Professor Cate this highlights the inherently unlikely and erroneous idea that AI systems will be utterly objective if they are simply provided with truly unbiased data.

'The problem with this is that there will always be a reason for the data. Always a practical reason, a security reason, or some other reason the data is going to exist. The focus on notice and choice unfortunately has failed. The issue now is can we evolve better, more practical, more scalable rules that help govern how that data is used and consider what the impact will be of how this data will be used. Using data to try to test out a pandemic vaccine is a good thing, using it to stalk people or harass them is bad. The question is are we capable as a society of finding effective ways of drawing lines between those types of behaviours? I think we are I just don't think we are doing it very well right now.'

Using crime pattern analysis systems for the purposes that they have been used for in the past, Professor Cate argues, is misleading because in the past they have only had a partial data picture.

'It's an associational analysis that I think frankly suggests connections that we should be trying to break as a society. These attempts to use data in this way take us back to the 1960s. We would say poor people, people who are otherwise disadvantaged, are more likely to commit crime. Therefore, we will put them in poor neighbourhoods and try to wall them off. That would to my mind be the worst possible use of AI.

As a society we are going to have to decide as AI gets more accurate about the decisions that it is arriving at based on data. If that means that dark skinned people get treated differently than light skinned people, not out of bias but out of historical economic distinctions between the two that are now being accurately reflected by an AI system, we have to be able to interpret that finding fairly.'

This is something Patel agrees with.

The background behind why data is collected

'I think the interesting point in these instances is it is rare for the system to be completely abstracted from the data it has.

In criminal justice we have a historic track record of having a higher number of people from ethnic minority backgrounds on stop and search databases or on DNA databases, for a range of reasons that are quite structural. There are also several studies that illustrate the likeliness of a Black person being arrested versus somebody who's exhibited similar types of behaviour but who's white. From this you immediately see that, an algorithm is never really, truly independent of certain biases that might exist already in the dataset. When we look at certain algorithms in the criminal justice system context, we can see that they are at risk of replicating those biases.'

Patel adds that there was evidence that this data, once in the system, then found its way into decision-making much higher up, before noting:

'A report in 2019 by the investigative news website Pro-Publica in the US, found Black people were more likely to be offered harsher sentences and less likely to be offered less punitive sentences through the use of an algorithm, because of the way that the algorithm itself operated and the inferences it made based on a person's colour.'

The fact that many AI decisions are based upon 'big data' being analysed by probabilistic AI computer programs has prompted Viktor Mayer-Schönberger, Professor of Internet Governance and Regulation at Oxford University and co-author of the best-selling book *Big Data* to call for a radical overhaul of the way data is used regarding race, poverty, and other current indices of crime as Patel has pointed out.

In an interview for the Netopia[5] research paper 'Can We Make the Digital World Ethical',[6] Professor Mayer-Schönberger noted that in the US, a technology company had bought the entire US offender list and published it on online. Many would argue that those people had served their sentences and should be given a second chance. Yet US law allows the data to be mined to show where offenders are living, having a detrimental effect on their employment opportunities and attempts to rehabilitate themselves.

Professor Mayer-Schönberger added that former offenders can pay a sum of money to be removed from the list which he says is a form of blackmail on an already economically challenged group, Removing themselves from the list may not give them much protection in the future however, as analysts can use big data to discover economically-inactive individuals and people who do not appear on electoral roles. This data can then be mapped onto the typical pattern for incarcerated criminals and the resultant dataset can then be fed to credit companies and others offering financial services or even back to the police.

Predictive social control

This issue is of great concern to Professor Mayer-Schönberger, who says that it is often used wrongly to predict people's patterns of behaviour and to draw inferences instead of being seen as a record of what has happened.

'The problem is that as human beings we want to see the world as a series of causes and effects and therefore we are tempted to abuse big data analysis – which can only tell us what is going on – to know why this is going on so that we can then connect guilt and individual responsibility to individuals.

---

5 Netopia, see www.netopia.eu/. Netopia is a Brussels-based web publication and ideas forum that publishes reports and arranges events with the purpose of stimulating the discussion on the future of the internet.
6 Peter Warren, Michael Streeter and Jane Whyatt, 'Can We Make the Digital World Ethical: Exploring the Dark Side of the Internet of Things and Big Data' (*Netopia*, 18 February 2014).

As we have seen not only is [big data analysis] being used in the US to prevent terrorist attacks but is also being used to go after petty crime by the FBI and local police forces. It is a very powerful tool but it cannot tell you anything about individual responsibility – it only tells you "what" not "why".'

In another allusion to the *Minority Report* film, Professor Mayer-Schönberger says that with the union of AI and big data there is a huge temptation for the authorities to use it for the purpose of assigning individual responsibility and causality.

'With big data, there is a risk of predictive social control which slaughters human volition at the altar of collective fear.

It is not just always about the algorithm, it is also about the system of instruction and the processes around that. For instance, an algorithm cannot control how likely a police officer is to identify certain characteristics about a person or, control how likely is that a teacher will be more able to pick up on the bad behavioural traits of a child.

These are all factors that we need to be aware of when we are designing algorithmic systems, even though they are not necessarily studies about algorithmic systems because it gives us information about the underlying structures that can then be used to inform the algorithmic systems.'

This is one of the reasons why the proposed wholesale adoption of AI systems for judicial sentencing has provoked such controversy. According to opponents of the move, the black box issue outlined by Risto Siilasmaa in Chapter 15, and many others in earlier chapters (the AI system's ability to process data far faster than any human being and interpret it in ways that we cannot follow) means that coming to a conclusion based upon biased data is currently highly likely. Thus any decision made by an AI system could be eminently open to extremely complicated challenges that would question both the data the system was drawing upon and the way that the algorithms were using the data. These are all issues that excite Patel.

'This is about good design, risk mitigation and harm. There are some arguments which say that when you think about the level of bias that already exists in sentencing in the justice system that it's not as simple as saying we don't need AI at all. Though given the potential racism in the data and the potential for things to go wrong, then there is a really strong case for accountability. This accountability means thinking about how you build principles of law into the system, how you ensure there is the potential to build checks and balances in, and how you ensure that people can understand how decisions are being made about them so they can challenge them or hold those systems to account.

We have got to the stage where people are thinking about implementing AI systems, but they are not thinking about accountability procedures.

What we need, if we are not going to end up in a slightly Kafkaesque world, where people do not know how decisions about them are being made and are struggling to understand whether they were fair or not fair is more research before these tools can be considered ready for implementation.'

The very real dangers of the metadata

One particular example of the issues of AI decision-making and the ramifications that it may have for people of colour that backs up both Patel and Professor Cate's concerns is that of US citizen and journalist Bilal Abdul Kareem whose metadata was picked up from the internet and passed to a drone targeting system, leading to Kareem being attacked with hellfire missiles.

Kareem, who is represented by the human rights group Reprieve in court cases in Washington DC, has been pushing the US to be transparent according to his lawyer at Reprieve, Jennifer Gibson:

'He's narrowly missed being killed five times, he believes it's because his metadata was picked up by US surveillance systems and identified him as a terrorist because he was meeting with and interviewing a number of people the US was interested in. Now he has gone to the US courts and just simply asked for the US government to tell him whether it is trying to kill him and if it is, to give him a right to defend himself in court. The response of the US has been to go to court to stop him from getting due process. It has also argued in court that they have the right to kill him without any due process or transparency at all, because they don't want people to know how they come to the decisions that they're coming to and regard that as classified information. They've declared it a state secret. And it is such a state secret that to even admit whether they are trying to kill him or not would risk national security is their argument. This is an American who has constitutional rights before the courts. We are also representing a Yemeni family, the Al-Amiri family, who we've filed a petition on behalf of before the Inter-American Commission, who have no right to go to U.S. court who have been targeted seven times

General Michael Hayden, who used to be the head of the CIA in the US, has come out and basically said we kill people based on metadata. That almost says it all, which is you're hoovering up a lot of data about people and having computers, very sophisticated programs, no doubt helping to run that data. But in the end, really, you're killing based on data. You're not killing based on any known individual identity.'

The potential danger of this situation is outlined by a UN report published in March 2021 which stated that the UN Security Council's Panel of Experts on Libya believe that a type of AI drone known as a Kargu-2 quadcopter produced by the Turkish military tech company STM attacked retreating soldiers loyal to Libyan General Khalifa Haftar. The 548-page report by the UN Security Council's Panel of Experts on Libya has not provided details of whether there were any deaths due to the incident.

While no evidence exists in these cases that this has happened, it is possible that both Kareem and the Al-Amiri family have been automatically targeted in operations with no human intercession and it is that information that the US does not want disclosed. This is a use of AI that according to Gibson is also being seen as discriminatory because currently drones are seen as a weapon of the state and the establishment and are mainly deployed in Middle Eastern states:

'One of the biggest controversies about the US drone programme US drone programme, which Europe is heavily involved in by giving intelligence and in terms of providing bases that allow places like Yemen to be hit is that drone programme doesn't follow traditional battlefields. Most people would be shocked to find out we were even engaged in these places, much less that we are firing missiles there.

In many cases these strikes are happening in communities where there is no active fighting going on. Imagine someone going to a market and suddenly there's a Hellfire missile launched at the market. That sounds absurd, but it's common in some countries to look up and see a drone hovering overhead and be afraid that the drone might strike, because it has struck and killed people you know in the past.

People are being hit by weapons systems who are far from war zones in places that are going about normal life without the spectre of conflict, who are suddenly then put into a conflict zone by a Hellfire missile that launches from the drone because of metadata collected from the internet rather than from anything going on in the ground.'

As Reprieve's Gibson pointed out in the case of Kareem, there are two factors at issue: the data that has been used to target him, and the fact that lethal weapons have then been fired based on that data. This is something that, given the current poor-quality datasets, alarms Patel because of the likelihood that life changing decisions may be made by AI based upon biased data.

'The example of Karim illustrates that there is yet another conversation to be had, which is what should these things absolutely not do, because the impacts are so harmful and the potential to take away someone's life is arguably one of those things.

Many organisations have called for a moratorium on the use of drones for warfare, killing or maiming purposes. It was headed by Elon Musk. A consensus is emerging on the drawing of red lines around what AI should be doing and what it should not be doing. There is a need to define contexts and capability.'

Dealing with a bolted 'data horse'

This statement goes to the heart of the AI debate, because the problem with AI is that it already permeates our lives and our world. Evidence is provided regarding this in Chapter 13 by Professor Stuart Russell, Professor of Computer Science at the University of California, Berkeley, Adjunct Professor of Neurological Surgery at the University of California, San Francisco, author of *Human Compatible: Artificial Intelligence and the Problem of Control* and one of the top AI scientists in the world.

Professor Russell's view is that because it is already heavily deployed, calls for regulation are simply too late. One reason for this is that so many of the technologies are proprietary and belong to companies which are not going to share what they are doing voluntarily, or cease recouping their return on investment. This is an important point because whereas the rules about nuclear or chemical weapon systems could be imposed because the production was controlled by states and the regulation was imposed on states by coalitions of states, AI is not only already here; it is being controlled by powerful companies and it has already become an important component of our lives.

Thus, Professor Russell's point underlined by Patel and every person interviewed for this book is that the 'black box' issue is key: if you do not know what is happening inside the AI system and you have an organisation that is unwilling to tell you – because the information is either proprietorial or classified – then you have an additional factor too. As a result, Patel and a number of other ethical AI observers think that it is time to take stock of the situation.

'We have been asking for a pause, a moratorium on the use of certain technologies until the governance around what they are developing is right.

A classic example is the facial recognition moratorium and to approach deployment very slowly and very cautiously. in these examples is really important that we meet the transparency challenge.

A lot of organisations are starting to pay a lot of attention to a case study in Helsinki in Finland, where they are beginning to create algorithm registers to enable armchair auditors of algorithms effectively to be able to understand what is actually happening, which public bodies are using algorithms and why.

That is a really interesting use case. If they get to a stage where they can be scaled, in the public sector in particular, there's potential to be a bit more optimistic about these technologies.

The commercial challenge is really stark and profound. The tension between commercial confidentiality and the need to protect intellectual property amongst companies competes with the idea that these technologies can mitigate harm. Though even in those instances, examples such as Tay or the gorilla algorithm or the corruption of search engine algorithm by holocaust deniers, it is impossible for the most commercially sensitive company to run away from public scrutiny because the problems quickly become clear in their outcomes.'

The dangers of automated accidental misinterpretation

For Patel the most worrying examples of bias are not the starkest, but others that many people miss because they are more insidious and arise because most AI systems have been trained on white male datasets and lack the data to understand people from ethnic minority groups.

'There are issues with speech recognition systems and closed captioning. I have been in situations where I have realised that the speech recognition software has assumed that somebody from an ethnic minority background who is a woman said something that is not quite what she said which created a misunderstanding.

The systems are less charitable to people from ethnic backgrounds than they might be to some who is from a white male background. When you have such a misunderstanding it can create what can only be called 'really interesting dynamics'. The question there is how that can be challenged. It is difficult because it is low level. It is what people would call a micro aggression and they will not be aware that it has happened, but it can significantly affect behaviour and outcome.'

Patel's point is easy to gloss over. Many of those who have used closed captioning in Zoom or Teams meetings during the pandemic may have been amused by the errors that the software has made, but might not recognise the potential to cause offence. The further point is that we implicitly trust that translation software will also work. This is an assumption on our parts that is only disproved by using Google Translate or other systems and seeing the translation the system creates and then testing that on a native language speaker. These are AI weaknesses that are usually tolerated and not thought about.

The interviews in this book were transcribed using an AI system called Happy Scribe, whose website claims that the software is only 85 per cent accurate, a level of accuracy that can only be appreciated when you work with it, because of the number of errors that 85 per cent accuracy means and also because of some of the dangerous assumptions that it can make that have to be manually corrected. It may achieve 85 per cent accuracy, but that figure may also include the words it has transcribed that align with an error made in transcription. The software also has an option to translate transcribed files and much of these processes are automated. It would be very possible to set up a system that transcribes and simultaneously translates – that would immediately compound and exacerbate any errors – a process that illustrates just how significant the errors can possibly be in the Patel example or real time automated translation.

'You could say automated speech recognition systems are very good at working out what people have got to say unless we talk a lot and allow a series of algorithms to learn how we speak and articulate our voices and, it learns the way I communicate. Until then it is not going to get very accurate. That means that until that happens this tool does not work well enough. So how do we make sure that it is able to pick up exactly what somebody is saying? In my case I speak a little differently because I am hearing impaired. So sometimes it just does not pick up what I am saying.

We have several first-hand examples of this, for instance once we tried to use Otter AI for a speaker who was from China and we were quite horrified to see how poorly it captioned our speaker and that use case illustrates again the issue. It also drives us to a discussion about what we need to do to fix the issue. The fix is two things. One is from a technical perspective, and that is that speech recognition companies should be trying to make sure that they have got the right range of voices captured or that it is able to improve its technology, but accuracy is just one part of a question there, and there are wider systemic points.

If this technology is making inferences about what I am saying off the back of things other than the way it is hearing my voice, then that is really problematic or has the risk of becoming really problematic. Which leads us neatly back to the second thing that needs to be dealt with, which is how far do we go and what do we allow these tools to do and not do and establishing some clear set of norms and boundaries around that?'

A road testing culture that threatens a motorway pile-up

As Patel and other contributors to this book have all pointed out, the central issues that the deployment of AI keeps raising are design and context. These considerations also raise another issue to do with technological deployment, which the technology industry has managed to get away with for decades, which is the rolling out of unfinished software on the population at large and then fine-tuning it as people use it. This practice is unique to the technology industry and is one that, with the advent of AI, becomes increasingly more problematic. Many of us are familiar with 'beta' versions of software and of the consequent media stories that either reveal frustrations and shortcomings with the software or some weaknesses or dangerous drawbacks that are then corrected over time.

Large technology companies like Microsoft or Apple may maintain that it is necessary to continually fine-tune software to ensure it is flexible enough to work with a world of ever-changing apps and consumer demand. However, road-testing AI technology in a similar way risks some very real disasters due to the incredible complexity of modern systems, their inter-relationship and the speed of AI decision-making.

For Patel this means that the issue of unintended consequences is too dangerous to be left to a 'road-testing' of technology to discover issues.

'Context and design is everything, and not only is it everything, it starts to inform guidance around what we expect and standards around what we expect.

A year ago, the German Data Ethics Commission launched a report, in which they started to map out different levels of algorithmic systems based on their level of harmful impact and the potential to affect people. It was an independent commission, but it was funded by the German Government, and it has raised important issues about how we begin to address AI, such as what are the layers of governance you would want around it. If AI is used in particular contexts do you think it is going to have a relatively low impact in terms of harm or could it have a high impact? If it is likely to have a high impact should you be more willing to test it out and then work with it on the basis of those conclusions?

If it is an algorithm that is about to decide examination results, then you should want to put a set of different norms and processes around that algorithmic decision-making about how best to use that algorithm, given the impact it is likely to have. Certainly, you would want some very strict and onerous requirements about anything that could potentially kill someone.'

185

Time to say 'no' to the computer

According to Patel the factors of provably poor software, which is already making errors as shown in the cases of ethnic minorities and facial recognition in CCTV, language recognition, exam results and crashes by automated vehicles, all indicate that there is an urgent need to evaluate the role of AI in our world, particularly given Professor Stuart Russell's comments about the level of penetration by AI into our society.

Not only does Patel think, like Elon Musk, that there should be a moratorium on the use of AI in warfare, but that there is a case for such moratoria to be extended into other areas too.

> 'It will depend on what AI is being used for, but the gold standard should be the risk of harm and impact. Facial recognition technology is a good example of that, at the Ada Lovelace Institute we called for a moratorium of its use in that context in 2019. Since then, a number of industry bodies have voluntarily adopted a moratorium on facial recognition technology. Where things will get a little bit trickier is with technologies like speech recognition, because a lot of people are already using it and benefiting from it while at the same time acknowledging it has its flaws.
>
> There is this balancing act to be undertaken, which is, what is the AI doing and what is the gain? In proportionate terms how likely will the AI system be to effect beneficial change as opposed to its ability to cause harm. What that will look like will really depend on where you stand in the equation of good and bad and whether you are suffering from the systems' shortcomings.'

As Joy Buolamwini pointed out earlier with her comments about the misidentification of Black people by AI systems analysing CCTV images, the issue is not about misidentification it is about the reasons for misidentification; the under-representation in some databases, over representation in others and that the conclusions that the AI systems come to are based on the information they are using.

All these issues would appear to be worthy of correction, yet moves by Buolamwini to do so have foundered. The Algorithmic Justice League, which Buolamwini set up to encourage large tech companies to sign an agreement to redress the situation, has been wound up because none of the large tech companies had put their names to it according to a press release put out by the organisation on 8 February 2021.[7]

7   Joy Bulolamwini, 'Announcing the Sunset of the Safe Face Pledge': 'The Algorithmic Justice League (AJL) and the Center on Technology & Privacy at Georgetown Law are announcing the sunset of the Safe Face Pledge. The 2018 Safe Face Pledge was a historic initiative designed to prohibit lethal use and lawless police use of facial analysis technology, as well as to create transparency in government use. At the time, we defined facial analysis technology as any system that automatically analyzes human faces or heads. We now use the term facial recognition technologies' (FRTs) to emphasize a plurality of uses. The Safe Face Pledge provided actionable, measurable steps organizations could take to put AI ethics principles into practice, and as we stated on launch, provided "an opportunity for organizations to make public commitments towards mitigating the abuse of facial analysis technology.'
'Over the course of two years, the pledge was supported by over 40 organizations, more than 100 individual champions, and three launch signatories: Robbie.ai, Yoti, and Simprints

AI in whose interests?

There are other signs of a pushback too. After a very shaky start in late March 2019 when Google launched its Advanced Technology External Advisory Council only to close it less than two weeks later, the company formed an Ethical Artificial Intelligence Team. This though became mired in controversy on 2 December 2020, when Google said that Dr Timnit Gebru, an Ethiopian AI scientist working in the US who specialises in algorithmic bias and data mining, had resigned from her post as Technical Co-lead of the EAIT.

In a twitter post according to Dr Gebru, an advocate for diversity in technology development and a co-founder of the group Black in AI, she had been sacked.[8]

Two months later, Google fired Margaret Mitchell, the founder and co-head of the Ethical Artificial Intelligence Team, who had been a close colleague of Dr Gebru. These events prove how difficult ethics are, particularly in fast moving areas like AI for Big Tech companies. Patel states this contradiction must be resolved because of the power of companies like Google, Apple and Facebook and their desire for competitive advantage and achieving shareholder and customer value rather than erring on the side of the people who use their services or in trying to address proven issues of diversity.

A question of data

In Chapter 10 we referred to the launch of the report of the Select Committee of the UK House of Lords into the technology: 'AI in the UK: Ready, willing and able'. Dr Stephen Cave of Cambridge University's Leverhulme Centre for the Future of Intelligence said that for AI to be successful it was essential that every part of society should be consulted on the issue. This is something that is clearly not yet happening according to Patel:

'We are seeing a lot of "ethics washing" at the moment. A company may have a board called an ethics board, but that does not make it an ethics board because in this context, Google and other large technology companies and other organisations need to make a choice over what has the ability

---

Technology. The launch announcement of the pledge specifically called organizations including NEC, IBM, Microsoft, Google, Facebook, Amazon, Megvii, and Axon to sign on. However, none of the most visible or prolific providers of FRTs signed on.'

8   Julia Carrie Wong, 'More than 1,200 Google workers condemn firing of AI scientist Timnit Gebru' *Guardian* (4 December 2020): 'The dispute over Gebru's research arose in November, when a senior manager at Google told Gebru that she would have to either retract or remove her name from a paper she had co-authored, Gebru told Wired. The paper, co-authored by researchers inside and outside Google, contended that technology companies could do more to ensure AI systems aimed at mimicking human writing and speech do not exacerbate historical gender biases and use of offensive language, according to a draft copy seen by Reuters.

"I felt like we were being censored and thought this had implications for all of ethical AI research," she told Wired. "You're not going to have papers that make the company happy all the time and don't point out problems. That's antithetical to what it means to be that kind of researcher," said Gebru.'

to exercise control over its decision-making. Is it the ethics board or is it its corporate responsibility to its shareholders or stakeholders?

So long as Google or Facebook or other organisations say that the thing that will take precedence is their corporate responsibility to their shareholders, or to other vested interests such as Government departments, an ethics board cannot be an ethics board.

Is the answer to resolving some of these issues to say: "the tools are not very effective and therefore we should just have more data"?

I think that the question there is whether it is more of a problem if it is accurate? The really interesting point with something like facial recognition technology is if it is super accurate it raises one set of problems; if it is super inaccurate, it raises another set of problems.'

The call for an AI moratorium

It is a question that also exercises MIT's Buolamwini:

'When it comes to addressing issues of algorithmic bias and more broadly issues of algorithmic harms, we have to think of both the cost of inclusion and the cost of exclusion. Are there ways to make the systems perform better, to have better technical performance? The answer is obviously yes.

But even if you have better technical performance, let's say, for something like facial recognition, you have a cost of inclusion and that cost of inclusion is being readily available to a mass surveillance state apparatus. More accurate systems can be more open to abuse. So, you can have more accurate facial recognition that you say works well on a variety of faces.

And now you put that kind of technology on a drone with a gun, with facial recognition technology. The question is no longer how accurate is it, but is this the kind of society do we want to be living in? So it's really important that as we're talking about ways of mitigating issues to do with algorithmic bias, we come at it with the perspective that these are socio-technical systems.

Technical solutions by themselves are not enough.

We have to address not just how the technology works, but how is the technology used and also what kind of processes do we have in place to check what's going on when they're deployed in the real world.'

For Patel this becomes even more of a compelling case for halting the deployment of AI:

'There is a challenge. One set of problems surround mis-profiling and over surveilling particular groups of people. If it is not picking up some people very well, then, of course, that compounds underlying inequities or discrimination. The other set of problems stem from the technology being super-accurate and thus also able to be used in a discriminatory way. This presents us with a nice rule of thumb to pursue. There are harmful impacts either way which is a good sign that the technology is not ready and is not fit for purpose and that we have not got the systems right'.

This is perhaps a reference to the well documented cases of the Chinese Government using AI-based CCTV surveillance and intelligence systems to control its minority 12m Uyghur ethnic group.

The subjective intent of AI systems

Just how bad racial discrimination can be when deliberately pursued by the state was outlined in an interview for the PassW0rd radio show on Resonance FM, in which the acclaimed China expert, journalist and author Isabel Hilton described the use of technology in China and the experience of the Uyghurs.

'When the internet arrived there was an explosion of creativity, of opinion sharing of all kinds of things which the state noticed and responded to by turning internet use to its advantage and changing it from a space where people freely expressed opinions and do what they wanted into a space which enhanced the state's capacity to monitor, to track and to control what people thought and did.

Added to that, there is a complete absence of protection in China. There is no assumption of privacy, no rule of law, no barrier to state control or state monitoring of your online or indeed your offline life. When this was combined with the rapid growth of local Chinese providers, because the government made sure that international providers did not get a foothold in China there was a problem. Also add in that companies like Alibaba quickly developed a comprehensive suite of 'life solutions', mirroring the Western experience from online payments, to mapping, to social interactions, which has meant people now use their phones for everything in China, and increasingly it is very difficult not to do so.

That means that companies and the state have access to all that data and can track absolutely everything. They know, what you say, what you read, what you buy, where you go, all those things, and they can take a view based on that data on whether you are a threat to the party or whether you are a reliable supporter of the party.

If you combine this with the surveillance cameras and facial recognition, which have been developed there really is no escape from state surveillance. So given the ambition of the party to nip any kind of protest or insurrection in the bud and the long-standing conviction that the party can condition behaviour in its favour, plus the fact that such systems always need an enemy. And what you get is the potential for calibrated coercion and massive erosion of individual rights. For example, if you are found to have done something as minor as jaywalking by the surveillance cameras you may get a sanction.

In the troubled western region of China, where the Uyghur's live in Xinjiang every aspect of life, from religion to private conversations, is monitored, tracked and sanctions are delivered based on that evidence. It is the Big Brother world of Orwell meeting the digital age in a truly singular way.

In Xinjiang it is compulsory to allow the police to install a monitoring device on your mobile phone which tracks every call you make, every text you send and every call you receive. If you are deemed to be someone the state cannot rely on then you are made to join the million people in camps without trial, one tenth of the population. The control is utter. For instance, if you are at liberty and want to fill up your car with petrol, you must show your ID, which immediately locks into the system. Then all this data is brought to bear to determine whether you can fuel your car and travel. There is no appeal against this. Many of those in the camps are there because they went to the mosque or because they have family abroad or because they themselves may have travelled abroad in the past. You know, you are looking at a state which really knows no boundaries.'

Hilton likens the Chinese use of AI to 'institutionalised slavery'; whereas Amnesty International's secretary general Agnès Callamard described it as creating 'a dystopian hellscape on a staggering scale', at the launch of a 155-page report into the Uyghur's plight on 10 June 2021.[9]

It is perhaps due to the Chinese use of AI technology for social control and the complete subjugation of its ethnic minorities that lawmakers have suddenly begun to take note of the enormous potential for harm.

As both Patel and Buolamwini have described, the use, misuse and non-use of data in AI systems is ultimately all a question of intent.

---

9 Everything you need to know about human rights in China: www.amnesty.org/en/location/asia-and-the-pacific/east-asia/china/report-china/.

Chapter 12

Gaming the system

Is AI being used to gain competitive advantage?

The potential for gaming the system – or using the rules and procedures meant to protect a system to, instead, manipulate the system for a desired outcome – is a vulnerability cited by many opponents of AI. The threat is that companies (especially those with a deep insight into the technology) will be able to evade any regulations that are put in place because they will be in charge of the super-weapons of the AI world and they will code their algorithms and programme their AI specifically to 'game the system'. This is a fundamental consideration of any ethical, legal or regulatory framework.

Dr Jonathan Cave *has been the Senior Teaching Fellow in the Economics Department at the University of Warwick since 1994. He is a Turing Fellow and co-chair of the Digital Ethics Research Group and Data Ethics Committee of the Alan Turing Institute; a PI on the PETRAS IoT research programme; Economist Member of the UK's Regulatory Policy Committee; and an Associate at GNKS Consult, where he works on a wide range of ICT-related projects for European and international clients. He serves as an Area Editor of the Journal of Cybersecurity, on the Programme Committees of the Workshop on the Economics of Information Security and the Internet Science Conference series and is a Member of the Board of the Cyber-Civilisation Centre in Keio, Japan. He has worked in research and policy on e-government, data analytics and better regulation; the economics of privacy; high-speed and computerised financial trading; regulatory assessment and reform.*

The starting point of any consideration of the issues raised by game theory must be whether those – including regulators – who do not really understand the technology will have any chance of making any impact.

'This depends on the nature of the AI. If, for instance, it is formula driven AI, were data to go in and they produce an output which then leads to action, it's a very different thing than reinforcement learning with a data plan, and a model plan. That in turn is different compared to deep AI, which in turn differs from network day AI, where you have different AI instances that are interacting with each other.

One example of this is "Algorithmic Collusion". There, the difference between a single AI system that is learning how a non-AI or formula driven system is behaving is very different from several AI entities that are alternating between exploitation of the model they currently have or of past data summarised in that model and exploration where you do random exercises to explore the area around the part from which you have data from the past.

If we have models like that and are able to synchronise our exploration and exploitation, we are likely to converge on something which may be a gained outcome. In other words, a collusive outcome or maybe a fairly competitive outcome, depending on how the objective function built into the learning program is defined but if we don't coordinate, we may not converge. That is one sense of gaming the system, which is "I behave strategically or we collectively game strategically to our advantage".'

Beating AI at its own game

'There is another sense in which our abilities to outsmart the system stop the system from functioning, which is that we do not converge, and we therefore become worse off than before. It is a prisoner's dilemma. The mantra then becomes "mutually competitive poverty", if what my opponent is doing is competing with AI in this way then I more of less have to do it, even though It is worse for both of us. That is one element. The other element is that once I understand that you have got AI then I know that you're observing certain data and taking them into account. This is complex but it essentially means that the AI may be trying to interpret data about an individual or a company, but it will be doing that using the parameters it has been given which may mean that, that data is not either being interpreted truthfully or in a way that is not in the other individual or organisation's best interests as they understand them, but then begins to have an ability to influence the state of your model.

This happens all the time in financial networks. A trader will generate an artificial history for lots of other traders to put them all in similar states. This means you can trigger their core correlated behaviour because you know where they all are. If you are using the AI to do this the fact then that defines the limits of people, of people's ability or the machine's ability to understand the context within which the behaviour they observe is taking place due to the machine's parameters.

That makes the situation malleable. The question then becomes, if one entity is gaming the AI and you take account of that fact and try to gain an advantage of the gaming of the AI, which can happen either by making your AI super smart or by hardwiring it to be very stupid, not to respond to my tricks, then that becomes an interesting collective governance problem. This is not a theoretical situation it is already worrying decision makers in Europe. The impact of AI in this way is part of an impact assessment framework for the EU on the regulation of AI. One of the issues is how the existence of different types of AI can change the behaviour of people or other types of AI that are attempting to gain an advantage from it. Thus, one example of this could be, if an entity cannot pre-commit to a particular type of information collection and processing, it can, in effect, foreclose or reshape 'the game' that the AI was engaged in. This can be done either as a second mover or as a first mover. Each one offers its advantages.

These possibilities lead to a number of analytic questions that need to be answered which are that models can be easily built, for example, in which having more information makes everybody worse off and having less information uniformly makes everyone worse off but where one party rather than another, having a smarter system or better information makes everybody better off?

When we talk about gaming, we do have to define the nature of the game, because the term gaming is slightly ambiguous because, on one hand, it means the system that is in place, which would include coding practices, data and the regulatory structure, is what is called a strategy proof scenario.

In other words, it pays the people in it to behave in the ways that the system assumes they will behave, as opposed to a game that is not strategy proof and can therefore be manipulated. The other question is, if it is capable of manipulation, which very often these systems have to be, then the question becomes, is it possible to enable counter manipulation or will the fact that we are all outsmarting each other allow us to behave in a way that is consistent with the common interest.

If you can't stop people from playing the game, you can rewrite the rules of the game in such a way that it helps when they do that is the game theorist part.'

Preventing system manipulation by unethical humanity

This would appear to come down to a question of ethics, because human nature is selfish. If people think they could get an AI that worked on their behalf, they will instruct it to go out to the stock exchange and make them as much money as possible:

'That may happen unless, of course, there is a credible threat to regulate them if they were to do that. It may be that we can hardwire into the coding of the AI or into the access of that AI to data restrictions that prevent it from doing that. That is one of the things that's interesting if we assume that people are out to maximise profits because that then becomes a consistent lens through which to understand their behaviour.

The moment they depart from that and deal with things that cannot be uniformly quantified or understood then certain variation begins to creep in. Therefore if we know someone's interest is to maximise profit, we know how to adjust the incentives so that that individual's self-seeking behaviour serves the public interest. We have done that for years and years. Most regulation, most contract law, is intended to do that. But if a person is pursuing a concept of interest that is not capable of being monetised, or not understandable as profit, then they could be doing anything.

This means it is not quite so obvious how we would design a system within which you could operate a set of rules, that would change the way you understand objectives or the way that people express them in their actions in the way, I can take into account that others around you can take into account.

So, for example, if I think about the environment, there's a lot of information that even now, is being collected as a result of people's reduced mobility and due to COVID-19 as to how our impact on the environment plays out and how persistent it's likely to be. If I provide that information to somebody whose interest is in dramatising the size of humanity's impact on the environment, with the hope of mitigating it, that's a very different thing, than if I provide the information to a person whose interest is in learning ways to adapt to the human change of the environment. If they wanted to maximise profit, I now know who they are.

If they want to do these various other things in order to know what would happen if I implemented a certain kind of AI or allowed them to use it or even attempted to restrict their use of it. It is not quite so obvious how I would anticipate the impacts of what they are doing. Although, I could use a similar model to the systems that are deployed in computerised trading mechanisms, which define what constitutes an allowable as opposed to a not allowable version of computer-based trading.

We can use things like the speed of execution, and we can have rules that say, for example, that every position has to be held for a certain period of time. Or we could have something that is already in the MiFid II structure which regulates algorithmic trading, this states that 60 percent of all quotations have to be executed. These are designed to rule out certain types of behaviour that have been causally connected with market abuses. On the other hand, those same types of behaviour can have beneficial uses.

This then does cause issues because we are limited to making rules about what people do, or to inferring that people are using an algorithm in one way as opposed to another. This means that it becomes very tricky to avoid "chucking out the baby with the bathwater". This leads to another question: how do I know first of all, whether an individual or organisation is trying to use an AI in a way that is incompatible with the public interest or whether their behaviour is having the effect of its use being incompatible with the public interest?

This does not mean that there is a legal question behind algorithmic collusion, because the law infers you have to intend to collude and you have to communicate to collude. This is something that AI implementations do not do. In fact, the AI systems were actually facilitated by the way the law is written. We could have written the regulations to exclude tacit forms of coordination, but then other kinds of communication we might have regarded as innocence, like standardisation to avoid fraud become the kind of thing that gets ruled out by the law.'

Economic algorithmic warfare in the public interest

A number of questions are generated, such as should internet algorithms be licensed? Should they have a certified existence? If they don't have a certificate should they be banned, in which case we need to police algorithms: to find those illegal algorithms and disable them or at least to counteract their negative effects.

'When we have, for example, natural monopolies like grain elevators in the US. What the law provides, at least in the US through the Robinson Patman Act[1] is for a countervailing monopoly power. The monopolistic power of the centralised grain store cannot be removed because it is economical to have one grain elevator getting the grain from lots of different farmers but if the farmers are allowed to coordinate their activity, they can limit the extent to which that is bad. You can use algorithms in the same way. In fact, you could have white hat algorithms that were designed simply to undermine or undercut or manipulate the information available to abusive algorithms. We will have to consider the law in the sense of preventing people from doing certain things may be a feasible instrument, because of two questions, how do I know if you're using an algorithm? And how do I determine what is an allowable algorithm when the algorithm modifies itself?

This may not be explicable. We could require people to have algorithms whose behaviour can be explained or that can be accounted for and audited as a first step in this direction. This may be difficult to accomplish because the one thing that people jealously guard is the code and the neural net learning behind their algorithms. That is highly proprietary information. It will be enormously difficult to frame a law which says: "You can use this kind of algorithm, but not that one, or I will be willing to certify this kind of algorithm but not that one if the people framing the law can't know what they are."'

An algorithm Tsar?

Could one prospective solution be for a central repository, in which all algorithms must be lodged – a central software analysis centre that goes through them to determine what their objective is and to verify what the algorithm is actually doing in practice? Given that algorithms are already being used, what can be done about those already in play?

'The "proof of performance" is one of the regulatory structures that people have advocated. What we can do is to take the source code for an algorithm and feed it a carefully structured set of data to see whether it behaves in a reasonable way or not.

In the UK the architecture of developing this policy falls to a triumvirate of entities that are not formally part of government, but interact with the science, civil society and business communities and with government itself in the forums of the Turing Institute, the Ada Lovelace Institute for the broader context and the Centre for Data, Ethics and Innovation in relation to government. One of the decisions that will need to be made in the near future is what elements of this governance structure will need to be collected

---

1 The Robinson-Patman Act of 1936 (or Anti-Price Discrimination Act 1526 (codified at 15 U.S.C. § 13)) is a US federal law that prohibits anticompetitive practices by producers, specifically price discrimination.

together in a single place and which ones should be farmed out for dealing with specific contexts.

For example, the Financial Conduct Authority will be dealing with a lot of the use of machine trading algorithms, NHSX via the Department of Health will be dealing with most of the health-related applications, because they understand the context and the issues involved and because NHSX, itself is a player in the game because it commissions and uses these technologies. What we may see happen is that as with online harms, there will be an argument that there ought to be an organisation which owns the portfolio and is across all the different applications, because it may be that some of the approaches, such as the standardisation or the certification would mean that we would need something like that.'

The development of such a structure is something that Professor Zou argues for in Chapter 10, in which different sectors will have their own regulatory bodies, which will take a lead from a centralised ethical body. This is a potential solution, with which Cave agrees:

I can imagine, for example, organisations like the British Standards Institute or UK Accreditation Service, being at the centre of a network of people providing input into standardisation or certification in this area. This will depend however, on whether it is a priori, exempt, or an ex-post way of validating algorithms or coding practices or developing codes of conduct that other people could trust in the same way as they're trying to do with Internet of Things devices. There are also other devices that used in a number of different spheres and raise some cross-cutting issues and some that are sector specific.

At the moment I do not think it is necessary to have an "algorithm tsar" because each sector and industry will need to develop their own entities to deal with AI. As an example, if we think about competition, we do have the Competitions and Markets Authority, but we also have all these other regulators who have their own competition powers forming a network structure. To replicate that would be sensible because I do not think that industry and research communities would allow such domination by a Government entity. Though at some point we will need an entity that is able to see over the horizon from the development to the initial deployment of these applications to their eventual potential for dealing with, truly global challenges.'

An International Nuclear Weapons Authority for AI?

Given the complexity of data and the development of AI systems is there not a need for some globally agreed oversight of AI?

'This is difficult but for countries like China, the oversight will come from the people who continue to do business with you and share data with you and keep you in the community of civilised nations. For Russia there are overarching strategic objectives that may be important. If you are a business, then manipulating the visibility of what you do or its interpretation, and in particular the way in which you can justify the choices that the business makes in terms of the information that was available to it at the time, will become important, because perception will have an impact on the business bottom line and that will act as an oversight.

There is broad agreement that this will be the general regulatory position, a friendly regulatory stance of comply or explain, which means if you don't follow these rules, give us some reasons as to why what you're doing is as good, if not better.

The principle of gaming the system is something that is now coming up in attempts to combat disinformation campaigns or fake news. The Centre for Information Governance Research based jointly at the University of Pennsylvania and at Sussex University, in the UK is carrying out research into what disinformation is and how it differs from malinformation or misinformation and what the incentives are for people to be involved in the process are and what the implications of that are.

It is work that has relevance to the notion of gaming the system because we know that we can control an AI program by either feeding it false information or concealing targeted elements of true information from it. When this is done carefully enough it can put an AI program into a state where it will effectively do your bidding, but you are unaware that it is doing so.

This was the essence of the old theory of regulatory capture. The regulator asked for certain things and was told certain things, but not others and the regulator was informed you tell them in such a way that it shaped their subsequent regulatory decisions. In a sense a very subtle programming of the environment.

This means that it is possible to manipulate the availability of information which brings up an interesting question. If I control the information on which your algorithm operates and somebody else controls the nature of that algorithm, which of us is more powerful in influencing your behaviour?

The regulation of AI, without a consideration of the quality and scope and access to data, is one blade of a scissors it's not really going to cut anything. In the same way, obfuscating the data, anonymising or pseudo-anonymising the data without controlling the algorithms that might draw unstructured data inferences from it, interpolate for missing data, or re identify anonymised data and things like that will be ineffective. One has to actually control, the whole data value chain or at least have oversight over what is going on to know whether the tools at our disposal are likely to produce effects that differ from those that are hoped for.'

Who or what decides which information is good or bad?

For many this appears to be the very essence of the AI debate. The conversation is simply about information selection and use, because, if we talk about disinformation, we are discussing data, and we are simply talking about good and bad data and whether it is allowable, so this becomes a philosophical examination about us and our use of data for our own, particular ends.

> 'This is about the data that we more or less believe. Providing more scientifically accurate data, certainly in public fora without context or without careful interpretation would not necessarily be a good thing. We have seen that from the way, some of the proponents of disinformation have selectively mined the scientific literature by using Google Scholar, to find articles and quote from that article saying, asserting; "you can believe this because it is true".

This is done without explaining the context of the quote in the article as a whole. This means that nobody can make a judgement as to whether it is relevant or not, or in a reliable relationship to the subject under discussion. COVID-19 is a prime example: in the US, when somebody with COVID-19 dies, they are recorded as having died of COVID-19 yet if they have not been tested – because there's no point in testing their corpse – their death is not related to COVID-19.

The consequence of that is that people are using this a reason to challenge the lock-down, by stating that this story they are being been given doesn't exist. It also allows them to claim that the data are inaccurate. Thus, the fact that these data exist creates that narrative and allows people to systematically use data to give an entirely false impression or to recruit people to a cause where all of that reasoning collapses into a pat slogan like "Liberate Kentucky".

This becomes a very serious issue then because we have to also entertain the potential political exploitation of AI systems by interfering with the selection of data and how that can be prevented. Indeed, scientists might face the ethical dilemma of: "If you know what the impacts of a regulation are going to be scientifically, should you or should you not convey the nuances of that to a politician? Is this a good thing or not?"

In my highly personal view, the cognitive limitations, short attention span and political orientation of ministers are part of the system itself and that we need to understand. We also need to understand what the impact will be of modelling the data, collecting certain data and modelling them in a particular way and sharing those data to other people as part of the system we develop. It Is only with that end-to-end perspective that we can make ethical judgements about whether the data are good or bad because they are not good or bad in themselves. They may be accurate or inaccurate but the interpretation of that becomes an issue, whether I regard the inaccuracy an inescapable inaccuracy as a reason, for example, to dismiss the data. Whether I use noisy data as an excuse to make a policy that worked for the expected value of the data it was fed and not to take into account that fact.

For example, if I have data, which could be plus 10 or minus 10 and on average zero, I could make a policy that worked very well for a value of zero.

But the data themselves are never going to be zero. That is never going to be a correct policy. It falls between the stools of the plus 10 and the minus 10 correct policy. In that particular case, it may be that what we need to do is to take these data and not say they're bad, but that we need better data. We could say if we pursue this policy, we can learn certain things which will lead eventually to a better policy, or we could use a policy which is less prescriptive, less stringent based on the conclusions from our values. We could equally claim that the system is usable because it enables us to learn enough to modify the policy or to shift the responsibility for changing it onto people who are closer to the front line.'

Exposing bias and intent

Essentially, once again the debate revolves around intent: those who seek an outcome from the system are the ones who decide its function and impact, whether they are programming or gaming it. The system reflects our biases – correcting it is simply introducing a mitigating bias.

'An AI system may be an acknowledgement of that. If we think about algorithmic bias, and the kind of algorithmic bias, that states that people with observable characteristics are treated differently to people without those characteristics. For example, males, Blacks, Jews, whatever it might be, that kind of bias is manageable at a social level. And in a sense, the fact that AI makes it visible and demonstrable actually sets in motion the cure.

Whereas, if the bias is in terms of things that nobody can independently verify, or that are not recognised as characteristics of many people we would generate a profile that an individual might fit, therefore, you get a bad decision. The result of that is that you become convinced that the system hates you. And that leads to fragmentation and not to a resolution of the problem.

However, I am not uncomfortable with thinking of people as being inherently amoral or evil, because for me, morality and ethics are social mechanisms. It is certainly possible that if we understand the way in which our interaction with AI and that the use of these data in a certain way will change us as people, then it is possible to become better rather than worse. If that is the case, then we have to monitor that change and ensure that we know what better is.

Standing still is not an option. This process has to be accepted and the challenges met. The idea of "business as usual" is not going to hold. When we accept that, then we can begin to have a discussion about what we would do in this situation or that, and how and how soon we will know the difference. If the AI does not try to answer the wrong question but, is regulated to work with the way human beings collectively perceive and address problems then I think the outlook is perhaps more positive.

The greatest issue about the use of AI is that many people, under many circumstances, behave very myopically, very opportunistically and even malevolently, it is a lifeboat mentality that states we are facing a common problem such as climate change, and our response is that some people reject the idea due to self-interest and their perception of the impact that changing the way we live will have on them. The response is that we stop co-operating with each other because they state, "I will start looking out for myself" or they say: "I am a business; I am in this to make money".

No one likes to think of themselves as immoral or amoral. But, I think that we have an almost boundless ability to redefine the set of opportunities open to us, and their consequences and the things in which we believe that we have to believe.

If we take the example of the 2020 pandemic, if I am a young person I may know perfectly well, that the lockdowns will not lead to a collapse of the economy and that they will save more people than would ever die from the virus but I may say to myself, I have to behave as though I don't believe that because otherwise, I am in despair. I may also believe that the virus is doing us a favour by getting rid of this costly aging society, but I know that I can't own up to that belief. Not even to myself, so I will search for data to prove my position and my interests. Therefore, I will tend to emphasise data on the fewer deaths among the young and I will tend to emphasise the unfairness of the policies which go against what I actually believe such as isolation.'

The information war

Does this then mean that we will try to use AI as algorithmic justification, and that that too will game the system, and that nation states will use that to game the system? Will this mean that 'gaming' will become a tool of control and that this scenario will be used in warfare? Some suggest that in the future the algorithms will be the system for warfare. There will not be any point in weapons. The algorithms in a potential war would assert that my nation is in a position to arm faster than yours and we will destroy you, unless you capitulate? And that part of that process involves planting disinformation into an opposing state's AI systems, as was the case with the Stuxnet attack on Iran's Natanz nuclear enrichment facility referred to in Chapter 7.

'The idea of "noise" in a system is an old one. There is no difference between electronic jamming and chaff and putting disinformation into an AI system. In other words, interference is putting disinformation into the ground air defence systems, because we know that those systems are processing a lot of information so rapidly that nobody will take the time visually check that a missile is heading their way.

Thus, the targeted use of disinformation is important, but also I think that, in many situations where there is an internal moral duty or reflective capability, blinding yourself to certain information is as potent, as natural as blinding the other person or another person. Either an adversary or somebody you wish to exploit. You can see why you might want to lie to them. I think it's also possible, particularly as the systems become more capable and rapid in their operation, that you use them to lie to yourself.'

Some companies deliberately conceal the fact that they have taken patents out on their research so that they can sue people when their patents are contravened. For Cave, this is a form of gaming, which could be used to exploit AI systems.

'The honey trap is a potent strategy, the interesting point is that if you examine the kinds of IP that you create and how you let people know that it exists, that may be much more important, than the value you can ever unlock from that patent. This used to be discussed in the theory of collaborative research ventures. You may begin to develop the kinds of information participants in those ventures would exchange with each other and what you would be more likely to exchange, which would be the positive experimental results or the more negative ones.

Then if you were rivals with a firm, if you were in the same industry, you might actually try to not only give them false information, but to make them think that you believe that it was true information. The other factor that happens with regard to certain types of IP like pharmaceutical test results, is that, very concrete payoffs depend on what you could be shown to have known or believed at a certain moment.

It may not determine criminal liability, but it certainly determines civil liability. It makes sense that you might want to either blind yourself or make sure that others were sighted on a certain piece of information before acting on it. It may also mean, that not just the IP or the information, but the algorithms used to evaluate that information are things that you might wish strategically to share with your rivals, even if you did not have an overtly collusive intent.'

Do bad people make bad AI?

Through nearly all of the interviews we have done and evidence we have explored, we keep returning to the issue of intent in the system which comes from people and the ethics in the system which, again, comes from people. It is us who build these things, so therefore it is us that need to change.

'I am not wholly convinced that this can solely be solved by changing people because we now have effective algorithms that embed emotional judgement. It is not impossible to imagine in the spirit of the Massachusetts Institute of Technology moral machine, algorithms that give force to ethical principles and the force that they give to those ethical principles will be in the context of specific decisions. Therefore, I am not sure that these judgements will continue to be the exclusive province of human beings. The question will become one of direction, whether we try to build an ethics that keeps human ethics for a world with machines, or whether we develop an ethical framework that works for a world in which some judgement calls are being made by non-human entities or by entities that can make people behave in more or less human fashion, this of course assumes that human fashion answers to the higher human values.

These are important things to think about for example if you have a person who sits in judgement, for example, on a vulnerable gambler, and decides that they should or should not be offered certain opportunities, certain bets, certain assets to trade in, then they are making a judgement to foreclose on the judgement of another person. There is a question. There is an implied moral ranking or agency. It is not obvious to me either that that is a vertical hierarchy or that it is one as human being that we do or would do particularly well.

If I look to the leadership that we have in the UK, in the US, or in China, on issues relating to the ethical use of data to address overarching problems like climate change or epidemics, I cannot say that I am convinced that there is much evidence that human beings should be in this position.'

What should the qualification for judgement be?

If a gambler or an alcoholic had their disabling habit restricted by a machine in their own interests, it would surely be highly likely that they would be resentful.

'It may be that a machine would be the only thing that was capable of making that decision based on all of the available information. If you take the example of e-health, is it there to enable a doctor's judgement and the doctor's agency with respect to the patient and create a shared risk of professional responsibility or is it there to supplant the doctor?

In other words, should we avoid systems that make decisions so quickly or on the basis of so much data that they either can't be audited by human beings or that human beings are disinclined to see any reason why they should audit them? Because if so then we will become reliant on the system because we will have transferred agency to it and we will simply say: "that's what the computer said and I don't know what's going on inside it, you don't know what's going on inside it, but it is has more knowledge of the processing of the available information than I do. So effectively, we will have decided on a 'transferred responsibility' to that system".

Then the question becomes, whom is it useful for me to trust more, a human being or a machine? We all can think of lots of human beings that we would trust less than certain machines. It is this question about whether we are heading for a post human world in some sense and, whether AI will blur the distinction between human and machine.

We seem to think that that would be an appalling prospect but think about this, look at what could be called the information war that occurred in the United States under Donald Trump. The information US citizens were seeing was going largely uncensored, they can see all of this information, but they don't seem to be able to process it. They were being gamed. The mere fact that they run on DNA did not give them any advantage. If anything, it became a disadvantage and throws up a contradiction that we will regulate machines according to how they perform in certain circumstances, but we are not willing to subject human beings to the same test.'

Where should we use AI?

It appears clear from many of the contributors that there will be certain contexts in which we will not want to see machines operating. This is especially true in the criminal justice system, where we rail against machines deciding who will be arrested by the police and baulk at the suggestion that machines can act as judges – not least because we want to see justice being done. Should machines operating in this environment be prohibited or will we need super AIs that we will use in those situations?

'If the concern is, for example, in the legal context that there is no appeal from these automated decisions, then I think that indeed is a problem. However, there is again an issue that needs to be thought about and that is if we manage to develop AI, which had our entire legal code written into it and it did its machine learning based on that and empirical data on recidivism and other pertinent factors, you could certainly produce a machine that was easily the equivalent of many of our judges.

Ironically, in a sense by taking the human out of the judicial decision we are removing the possibility of the decision being emotionally gamed, particularly if you bear in mind that many of our High Court judges today may be more biased in terms of the experience that they have had and the way in which it has fixed their ideas. Thus, I cannot see anything functionally different about a natural or artificial intelligence in that respect. It is true that we can ask the judge to give an account of their decision but there are still high levels of subjectivity in terms of whether a judge thinks somebody will offend again, whether there is a need to set an example or some other motivation, and there is no reason that those variables could not also be entered into the AI.

The only advantage is that it is explicit. If we had an algorithm that had to explain its reasoning, that might be equally effective. Moreover, it might be more effective because instead of coming up with a convincing verbal account that justifies a decision once taken, it could actually produce an account that takes us from the initial facts of the case all the way through to the decision. This is something that we consider with impact assessments; are they just exposed rationalisation or is that actually the way the policy decision was made?

I am not trying to say that there is nothing different about human beings that effective and ethical programming could substitute. There may well be. What I am saying is that in a world where the data themselves are a consequence of automated decisions, to record this and not record that; that insisting on the special status of humanity is a little precious.'

Are human ethics higher than those of an AI?

For Cave, if we can programme ethics into machines, then we have to be able to lock them down so that nobody interferes with that ethical programming. It also means that if these ethical machines are used internationally, they have to be instructed with a common ethic.

'It is also undeniably the case that putting a nation or person or group of people through a different set of experiences will change their ethical coding. In other words, the thing that actually manipulates their decision, not the thing that they swear to when asked. I think that in that sense, there is a path dependent in all of these ethical structures. I also think that we spend a lot of time trying to develop ethical codes and ethical guidelines and that it is possible. I have sat on a number of committees that attempt to do just that for issues like the government use of data, commissioning of apps or this, that and the rules governing automated vehicles and so on.

What I have found are some common factors. A code is a rebuttable program, it is an algorithm that says, "have you paid attention to this? Have you looked at that? This could be automated perfectly well".

The only difference is that with human beings in there, you can sort of challenge them and test them. There are no reasons why human beings working in conjunction with computers cannot be more ethical in the sense of producing more understandable links between an ethical code on the one hand and a specific pattern of facts on the other, than an unaided human being, because it is harder for people to give an account of themselves than it is for a machine to give an account of itself in some circumstances. In some sense we are talking about gaming generally that motivation, that selfishness, that intent away because it can be challenged by this inter-relation.

In this debate we have to be aware of the fact that the information that we use and the choices we're being asked to make are themselves a consequence of the penetration of machines and our increasing reliance on data and we need to take that into account and not attempt to exclude it, because our ethical judgements are already entwined in that relationship. It appears to me that we have to manage our relationship with machines in a way that allows us to remain human in the process if being human appears to have a useful human value in it. If that is the case, then I might be more inclined to have some kind of mechanism or to seek for a mechanism that kept machines appropriately subordinate to human beings. However, if we cannot do that and the current upsurge of elements like populism, for example, or disinformation fuelled online conversations make it clear that our basic humanity does not appear to be as exalted as we think it is.

I will give you one example, Daniel Patrick, the Republican deputy governor of Texas on 21 April, 2020 said in relation to the need to open up the Texan economy owing to the COVID-19 pandemic, "there are worse things than living".

Consider what Patrick might have said if COVID-19 had not been on the table but abortion had been the issue he was commenting on, it would be highly likely that he would have made the opposite statement or he would have said there is nothing more important than life.

This is then a person in a position of moral authority, of leadership and of agency who is saying two entirely different things based on nothing more than a change in the situation or in the data available to him. That throws into question the sense of people like that making the laws, because they are working on the basis of political expediency rather than ethical consistency. That does not imply a human world that can hold its head up and say: "We do ethics better than a scrap of code".'

Is it AI or not?

Will a world like that not be challenged by people who will claim fake AI?

'The claim of "fake AI" will have to be transcended by transparency and by fact checking, which is in the sense that it is an action promoted by an utterance by particular people. In other words, the data in the tweets, that is an action which can be automated.

The fake news that we have been seeing is in fact a way of gaming the system and it is one that AI is responding to because as we have seen it has had a very real-world impact. In fact, countering it has been automated, and we can do, and already do, a lot of things. Thus, looking for fake information and disinformation is entirely automated because it could not be done by human beings, either because the volume is simply too vast, or because the context is not visible to the people who do it, or because the implication for the person doing the mediation is that they themselves may become unalterably altered by dealing with the issue.

In the same way as we might use a robot to treat a patient who had a highly contagious illness against which there was no effective defence of a human being. Then, of course, you send in a robot to empty the bedpans and do what is necessary.

In the same way if you have this toxic material online, you send in a machine to screen the material. And you re-examine the learnings of that machine at one remove from the flow of material itself.

It may not be just ethics to action in one simple single step, but it could be a sort of appropriate combination of an unaffectable machine and a sensitive human being.'

Can AI achieve contextual judgement?

In Chapter 9, Professor John Harris proffered the view that when people do bad things, they know they are doing bad things. In the case of Cambridge Analytica (CA) influencing the US election in favour of Donald Trump, Alexander Nix (the head of CA) must have been aware of what he was doing because he knew the aim of his actions. A lot of people immediately below him thought their actions were wrong because they sounded the alert. Cave agrees:

'I am sure people are aware of what they are doing. I am not saying that people are incapable of understanding enough of the consequences of what they do to come to a decision as to whether they should or should not do it. If you look at the example of the COVID-19 pandemic it's certainly been the case if you look at our evolution in this country from containment to delay and flattening, that we have changed as things have evolved and so therefore slightly pulled out of the stable ethical underpinnings of what they were doing because a lot of people do not like being in lockdown. It is one thing to know you are doing something bad, it is quite another not to do it.

There are many people who, in focusing on things like the economic damage that the lockdown is doing, don't know that they are doing bad things in the long-term because they have systematically and maybe even deliberately blinded themselves to the information that would tell them that they are doing bad things.'

As we will shortly learn in Chapter 14, Professor Fred Cate poses the dilemma to his students of whether they would like to have an AI system in their cars which automatically fined them every time they broke the speed limit. For Cave, this raises an interesting issue:

'The speed limit itself is a regulation, it's not an expression of something that is good or bad. It is a rule or act based control designed to produce a good result, which is fewer deaths. Nobody would say that the system that prevented your car from driving too fast for you to be able to control it in an area in which people were walking was a bad thing. People don't resist collision avoidance and lane behaviour systems. But when you have an indirect mechanism, that means that there can be false positives and negatives. The automation of that indirect system, because it is not open to reason and it is not open to moral judgement, is obviously going to be resisted separating out the not open to reason part, in other words I am fined at times when it's perfectly reasonable for me to drive the way I do from this abstract thing, this is my liberty. You had better have a very good reason for taking it away from me. I think that is an interesting and subtle moral distinction.'

Professor Cate postulates that if someone in the car was ill, and it was very important to get them to a hospital, you would not think about the speed limit.

'Nor is it in society's interest that you should do so, the speed limit deters you from driving fast or driving fast for no good reason and because the authorities are incapable of telling whether you have a good reason or not. If you do not drive fast, then you are willing to live with the loss on one side because you can't manage the loss on the other. It is not a choice of good and bad. It is a balance of "goods" and "bads", including not only our ability to know what's good and bad, but our willingness to accept the responsibility or the moral weight of making that judgement. This discrimination is something that we will have to convey to the AI because if it is to remove erroneous data from the system it will have to be able to identify that which is difficult because right and wrong also change over time, because the government may change rules on things can become acceptable that were not in the past.

Take the proposed changes to the law to permit skywriting and sky typing the idea that someone could put adverts or wedding proposals or what have you all over the sky, was banned back in the 1990s for reasons of air safety. Yet ministers are now persuaded that it is no longer unsafe. Therefore, they are minded to permit it because they know that there is money to be made from doing it. Therefore, the constraint is binding on some people. What has not received an airing, at least not yet and did not receive an airing back then, because it was not needed to make the decision was a lost amenity value. Which could be quite substantial. So, a decision has been made based on a set of criteria that were the relevant ones at the time. They have made a decision that balances out good and bad. It is not an absolute yes or no. But there are implications to it in the same way that just now HS2[2] is digging up ancient woodlands in Oxford and, there are certain ethical decisions based on this, sometimes people have owned up to those decisions. In other cases, they have opened them up to consultation, a consultative process that is influenced by the availability of information, stepped back from their role in shaping that information and said this is what consultation produced. In the same way as the Government, in choosing to pass and interpret the scientific advice about testing and mass and lockdown have simply contented themselves with, stating we are following the science, which is not a form of ethical judgement.

It's an abdication of ethical responsibility. An ethical responsibility that does not get placed on to the scientists, who are not in a position to make that judgement. The regulation of AI cannot be allowed to follow similar lines.'

Can AI interpret scientific judgements?

Surely the only way you can take political decisions for the implementation of health regulations is on the advice you are given by the scientists?

'Not in this case, because the advice they are given by particular scientists may not be relevant, an epidemiologist is not an economist, a transport regulator is not an environmental regulator. All of these people have advice to give. The people in the hospitals treating people and the people in the medical research facilities, trying to understand the disease have very different advice.

They are giving responsibility to someone who is not speaking with one voice and is not in a position to say what the policy decision should be, only what their little bit of the science says. The other thing is, of course, that they will be aware of the fact that what they know is uncertain. That the information is not perfect. So, despite perception, the science isn't giving you a definitive answer. It simply says; "think about this, think about that".

These mechanisms, these possibilities have evidence behind them, they have evidence against them and, these don't have enough evidence to say one way or another. So, the Government is not really following the scientific advice, because we've watched the scientists as the information available to them has changed and changed the nature of their advice. The same will have to be true of AI regulation.

The placement of the right to sky write, even if you could negotiate it, may not affect the proximate outcome of how much writing there is in the sky. It is not possible for me to negotiate with someone in a plane up above my house and because my feelings about the sky may differ from those of my next-door neighbour. That negotiation can't take place, which then means that the allocation of the right or the passage of the law has a very profound distributional consequence as to who gains and who loses. It is not a yes or

---

2   HS2 is a new high speed railway in the UK, which aims to link up London, the Midlands, the North and Scotland, including eight of the UK's ten largest cities.

no thing, it is, how can we consider in forming an appropriate and reasonable rule what the balance of these opinions are? How can we empower people to mitigate adverse consequences or to take the best advantage of what opportunities they have? That process depends on information and it depends on the analysis of that information. What I'm saying here is that without the machines to process that information, we can't even have an ethical framework.'

The bio-ethicist Professor Arthur Kaplan has said that if there was a choice to be made between a younger person and an older person in relation to medical resources due to the COVID-19 pandemic, that the choice should err in favour of the younger person – could that choice be made by a machine?

'I can't see why that would be the case. I mean, it's predicated on an ethics that measures life years or quality adjusted life years as a measure of personal worth. I can certainly think of a young person, for example, who has so little regard for their fellows that they have become infected and infected them or being careless as to whether they are infected.

Could that choice be made by a machine, yes absolutely. There are various ways in which this might work, but it is certainly true that many decisions can be justified in terms of objectively verifiable data or neutral data where the analysis is not that complicated. In this case, we can at least move on to a discussion of whether the younger or the old are more meritorious. Whether that is indeed a real choice or not, whether it is not possible to save both of them. For example, whether reopening businesses so that young people can go to work and draw their salaries only to have them collapse later is better or worse for them than allowing those businesses to fail right now under the weight of a lockdown so that better businesses can take their place. That has to do not just with the age of the people, but with how they discount the future and how they will respond to it.

Which brings me back to the beginning and allows me to conclude that the question of AI ethics has to recognise the complexity of the situation it is addressing, that that not only changes over time due to changing factors but that rightness and wrongness will also change. Ethical AI systems will therefore have to be able to arrive at a fair conclusion by admitting some evidence as relevant and dismissing other evidence – in a sense that will begin to control the ability to game the system.'

Chapter 13

Out of our hands?

Does AI already run our lives?

On 16 April 2018, Dr Steven Cave, the Executive Director of the Leverhulme Centre for the Future of Intelligence, introduced the Select Committee of the House of Lords' report 'AI in the UK: Ready, willing and able?' at the Royal Society's London headquarters in Carlton Terrace. Speaking at the oldest national scientific institution in the world Dr Cave, a philosopher and former diplomat outlined the challenges that he foresaw for humanity from the development of AI. It was an event, he said, that was of such fundamental importance to our world that it was imperative to canvass the opinions of every sector of society to ensure that AI was fair and was in the interests of everyone.

Dr Cave's speech made profound sense: we must not embark on the development of a technology that was not only controversial but potentially dangerous without making sure that we knew what we were doing. There was, however, one thing wrong and very provably so: AI was not only already here it was already demonstrating what could go wrong with it. Already numerous reports had begun to emerge in the press of the technology's racism as well as a number of other issues. Automated vehicles have had problems with kangaroos and bicycle wheels and have already been responsible for fatalities.

Numerous issues have been reported with predictive internet-based AI systems that have caused offence by making suggestions to people based upon obsolete data about their lives. This is a concern raised by Professor Viktor Mayer-Schönberger, Professor of Internet Governance and Regulation at the Oxford Internet Institute at the University of Oxford and co-author of the best-selling book *Big Data: A Revolution That Will Transform How We Live, Work, and Think*. Mayer-Schönberger, whose latest book is *Framers – Human Advantage in an Age of Technology and Turmoil*, looks at how we can survive in an AI world, and provides both a philosophical and a practical framework for assessing how much data we should retain and who should have the right to keep or delete it. He is also a vocal critic of big data – the mass of information that is increasingly being collated about us – and its use by AI, claiming that much of the information is irrelevant yet will be used to shackle us together and lock us to records and information that are no longer in context, a weakness highlighted in relation to the prisoner Glenn Rodriguez by Amy Hodler in Chapter 3.

'With big data, there is a risk of predictive social control and a system of social control which slaughters human volition at the altar of collective fear', said Mayer-Schönberger, who has published a book called *Delete* based on the liberating experience of accidentally wiping a hard drive containing his PhD thesis, and who argues strongly in favour of time-limits on data retention, and the individual's right to control how his or her own data is stored, updated or used.

Mayer-Schönberger argues that its only relevance is in its historical context and thus should not be used to understand us in the present. This contention has received support from the leading technology research company Gartner which in a 2018 report predicted that by 2022, 85 per cent of AI projects will deliver erroneous outcomes due to bias in data, algorithms, or the teams responsible for managing them.[1] This assertion also underlines that the AI systems, so little understood by the vast part of the population, are not only here but that they are already beginning to have a substantial impact on our lives.

Professor Stuart Russell is one of the most influential AI exponents and thinkers in the world. After completing his PhD at Stanford University, he joined the faculty of the University of California, Berkeley, where he has been Professor of Computer Science since 1996.

Often referred to as 'the Godfather of AI' he also holds an appointment as Adjunct Professor of Neurological Surgery at the University of California, San Francisco, where he pursues research in computational physiology and intensive-care unit monitoring. He is also a fellow at Wadham College, Oxford.

In 1995, he was a co-winner of the IJCAI Computers and Thought Award at the International Joint Conferences on AI, the premier international award in AI for researchers under 35. In 2003 he was inducted as a Fellow of the Association for Computing Machinery and in 2011 he was elected a Fellow of the American Association for the Advancement of Science. In 2012, he was appointed to the Blaise Pascal Chair in Paris, awarded to 'internationally acclaimed foreign scientists in all disciplines', as well as the senior Chaire d'excellence of France's Agence Nationale de la Recherche. In 2016, he co-founded the Center for Human-Compatible Artificial Intelligence at University of California, Berkeley.

Professor Russell is Vice Chair of the World Economic Forum's Council on AI and Robotics and a fellow of the Association for the Advancement of AI (AAAI). Other awards include the National Science Foundation's Presidential Young Investigator Award, the World Technology Award, the Mitchell Prize, and the Association for the Advancement of Artificial Intelligence Outstanding Educator Award. He is the author of many journal articles as well as several books, including 'The Use of Knowledge in Analogy and Induction', 'Do the Right Thing: Studies in Limited Rationality' (with Eric Wefald) and, along with Peter Norvig, 'Artificial Intelligence: A Modern Approach', a leading textbook on AI.

He serves on the Scientific Advisory Board for the Future of Life Institute and the Advisory Board of the Centre for the Study of Existential Risk.

According to Russell:

> 'AI is already very much here. Probably your most frequent encounter with AI is in social media, for example every time you are recommended to watch

---

1 'Gartner Says Nearly Half of CIOs Are Planning to Deploy Artificial Intelligence' (*Gartner*, 13 February 2018) www.gartner.com/en/newsroom/press-releases/2018-02-13-gartner-says-nearly-half-of-cios-are-planning-to-deploy-artificial-intelligence.

a video on YouTube, or your Facebook feed has something in it, those are being suggested by machine learning algorithms. Every time you use a search engine, the answers are being generated by machine learning algorithms, natural language understanding algorithms, and other kinds of A.I. reasoning systems.

So, it's really pervasive in the online world and I think fairly soon, not immediately, but fairly soon, the most visible application will be cars driving around by themselves.'

It is not just the deep-learning algorithms that many of the contributors to this book have talked about. According to Russell, companies have already begun to deploy both deep-learning and the arguably more akin to intelligent general AI systems.

'The algorithms being used are mostly proprietary and I think they are using a mixture of systems, reinforcement learning technology that goes back decades and decades, and algorithms that have the ability to take input in the form of vast quantities of text or imagery or videos, that is facilitated by deep learning methods.

But I wouldn't say it's either or, I think most solutions these days are some combination of the two. And machine learning is one of the oldest parts of artificial intelligence. The word was first used in the late 1950s when Alan Turing said that machine learning would be the way that we would create AI systems in the future.'

Despite the burgeoning deployment of AI systems by Big Tech companies and their unwitting use by the general population, Russell says that the current level of development of AI systems does not remotely approach that of the robots and rogue computer systems so beloved by science-fiction writers and film-makers.

'I don't think we're actually very close to having AI systems that exceed human capabilities. General purpose learning and decision-making AI systems don't function particularly well in the real world.

If they did, we would have self-driving cars now, but even that problem is currently still too difficult for the algorithms. A lot of that is because they do not have the kind of common sense that human beings have to work out what to do in situations they not been in before. Which means that they cannot yet run a company, or teach a child to read, or milk a cow that's being recalcitrant. I do not think we're particularly close to having those kinds of capabilities and to be able to do those things really will require breakthroughs.'

AI holds more than the promise of intelligence

Russell is at pains to point out that, despite not yet achieving the levels of Hal – the sociopathic computer system in Stanley Kubrick's 1968 science fiction film masterpiece *2001: A Space Odyssey* – modern AI systems are capable of arriving at some significant achievements albeit unwittingly, dismissing suggestions that

AI cannot at some point escape the bounds of human knowledge and begin to approach levels of objectivity.

> 'The argument that AI is bounded by humanity is really clutching at straws. We have already seen that computers can beat us at chess. Despite philosophers and other experts claiming for decades that it was just theoretically impossible for a machine to beat human beings at chess. They were just wrong, and it is wrong to say machines cannot exceed human capabilities because they can only base their behaviour on human information.
>
> If a machine can read one book, it can read all the books that humanity has ever written.'

On the frequently-posed question of 'could a machine generate a play by Shakespeare?' Russell is equally as dismissive.

> 'My impression is that those critics do not want a machine to be able to do that, so it is claimed that it cannot happen, but why not? The AI can acquire the rules of grammar from the time, it can acquire the way a play could be written and the way the way it is written and the likely subjects.
>
> If we use chess as the analogy, chess playing AI systems have access to only the games of chess that have been played by human beings. That does not stop them from playing chess far better than human beings.
>
> We should not, however, make the mistake that to do us harm systems need to reach "exceptional" levels. Individual machines do not need to be superhuman in order to present a risk of serious harm to our society. For instance, if you take the machine learning algorithms recommending news articles and videos for people to watch they are already having really serious negative impact on our world.'

Fake news and online harms

> 'One reason for that is that there are billions of copies of those algorithms already in existence so they can have a very large impact. The other is that the algorithms are programmed to optimise a fixed objective, which is typically related to the amount of clicking that you do, because that's what generates revenue. What that has meant is that in pursuit of that objective, the algorithms have learnt to manipulate human beings, to turn them into more voracious consumers of predictable content so that the algorithms will in future be able to guarantee that you'll click on something because they have turned you into a consumer of that type of content.
>
> What is ironic about that is that this is completely unconscious in the sense that the algorithms do not know that humans exist or have brains or anything else. As far as the algorithm is concerned you are just a stream of clicks, and it is programmed to want future streams of clicks to be more profitable. That is what they do. What this mean is that you can start to see how this loss of control that people are afraid of happens, because you have algorithms that are fixated on some objective. And in pursuing that objective, the side effects are serious or even terminal.'

Indeed, Russell agrees that it is not even necessary to develop the fabled general intelligence AI system that will achieve 'the singularity' – the moment when the system will be able to divine its own existence and start to think for itself, most famously detailed by the American author, futurist and inventor Ray Kurzweil, Google's director of engineering.

It is theoretically possible, Russell says, for a pyramid of deep-learning machines to be constructed that will be able to organise and control the world without even achieving cognisance, a world similar to that described by the science fiction writer Peter Watts in his book *Blindsight* in which he details an alien world with inhabitants with a similar motivation to a termite colony or the jellyfish-like *bathyphysa conifera*, formed of a mobile undersea colony of organisms known as zooids.

In these colony organisms, just like the algorithms described by Russell, the responses are automated and motiveless. This secret life of the algorithm coupled with our lack of awareness of its intent, according to Russell, presents one huge potential danger to humanity, the possibility of an AI system developing an intent that its makers and those using the system are completely unaware of. This possibility was first suggested in 2014 by Neil Barrett, at the time a Professor of Computing at the Royal Military College in Shrivenham.

In a conversation with one of the authors, Professor Barrett pointed out that it was completely possible that 'failsafe' computer systems tasked with being permanently available and deployed in areas like communications, water, gas or electricity supply would have the ability to be able to recode themselves because the fundamental imperative of their coding was that they must be always on.

According to Barrett, this could mean that in the event of impending failure a 'failsafe' system could generate a work around to ensure that it did not fall over:

'Such a work around would be undetectable to conventional programmers because they would not know what to look for because the programming would not follow any conventional rules because it would have been arrived at by machine.'

This is something that Russell fully agrees could occur:

'Is that a possibility? Yes, it is. And I think in some ways, what is happening on social media is an example of that, I don't think the social media platforms intended the algorithms to change people's brains. I think they intended the algorithms to learn about what people wanted to click on or to read or to watch. They did not realise that the way they had set up the algorithms would lead those algorithms to manipulate people, to change them.

That is a simple example. I think, again, we are some way away from human level general-purpose intelligence of the kind that could really reason deeply about how to deceive us while appearing to be stupid and develop its capabilities in secret until it was ready to take over the world.

We don't have an AI system that can do anything like that but again, it might not require a system as deep and complex as that, it might just require billions of copies of somewhat simpler algorithms.'

213

Once again, this stresses – as have so many of those giving evidence – that currently the biggest factors that impact upon the deployment of AI systems and the danger that they represent are societal.

As mentioned above, a 2018 Gartner Report pointed out 85 per cent of AI datasets will be generating erroneous results by 2022 which could then collide into a number of other systems with catastrophic results, a finding Russell elaborated on with the example of the marketing campaigns of fossil fuel companies, campaigns that Russell maintains to all intents and purposes carry out the same functions as algorithms.

> 'The climate change crisis that we are now facing has had a lot to do with the ability of fossil fuel corporations to essentially win against the rest of the human race. They outsmarted us. They put in place long term plans 50 years ago to overcome our resistance to climate change and to the evidence of climate change, and they won. They exhibited superhuman capabilities that defeated the rest of the human race, even though they are composed of ordinary human beings. You may disagree but the way they're composed means that the corporations function as very powerful algorithms.'

Russell's view of the corporation as algorithm is telling from both a legal and philosophical point of view, as very much like the algorithms in AI systems the intent of the algorithm lies in the programming and the development, a characteristic that AI programs share with political and social systems. Input poor or biased data or ideas and the result is a skewed system that operates with no thought of morality or ethics because current decision-making systems/algorithms have neither sentience, nor morality or ethics.

Who is responsible for the learning of an algorithm?

This is something that creates a moral, legal and ethical grey area, because as Professors Barrett and Russell have stated, AI systems could have mutated without our knowledge into systems that we are unable to recognise. According to Surrey University's Canadian Professor of Law and Health Sciences Ryan Abbott, AI systems should be given patent rights. As Russell highlights, AI systems are very good at understanding rules, as was proved by the Google DeepMind AlphaGo system which developed novel and hitherto unknown Go strategies to defeat human opponents, meaning that AI systems will be able to make scientific discoveries and breakthroughs because they have been inputted with the fundamental laws of science and will be able to rapidly develop and test hypotheses, an ability proved by the rapid development of the COVID-19 vaccine.

The issues this generates, though, are those of ownership and responsibility, because if a corporation can own the patent rights developed by its AI system, then theoretically the organisation that deployed an AI that mutated is also responsible for that development even though it may have been unaware that it has happened.

Such conundrums are rife in AI, according to Russell, who says that one is sentience, a concept first raised in this uncertain world of 'super being' in Mary Shelley's *Frankenstein* in 1818 where she postulates about the morality surrounding the creation of a superhuman being and whether the monster has a soul. Sentience for

Russell was such a difficult issue that he avoided writing about it in his book *Human Compatible: Artificial Intelligence and the Problem of Control.*

Russell notes, however, that discovering sentience in a machine at the moment is impossible.

'We do not know how to do an experiment on each other to find out if we are sentient, a lot of books about AI spend a lot of time talking about sentience. In my book, Human Compatible, I say we don't know anything about sentience. Thus, I am not going to say anything about it, that's it. It has nothing to do with the issue at hand. The ability of a machine to pursue an objective in a determined way has nothing to do with it being sentient or non-sentient. It is simply the way it's programmed. What that means is that when I am when I am playing Alpha Zero Deep Blue or any of these other amazing chess programs that have chess ratings five hundred points higher than the world champion, and I can feel that it is determined to beat me, it is not. It is just an algorithm, and it is beating me there is nothing I can do about it. That is the issue, right, that we have created systems that beat us, there is nothing we can do about it, but it's nothing to do with sentience.'

For Russell, sentience would be a possible hurdle for an AI system.

'An AI system is a computer running software and the software operates according to the rules of the software. If it is a C++ program, it runs according to the way that C++ programs run. If I make the program bigger and bigger, it is still running according to the rules. If at some point some far more brilliant scientist determines that, OK, I have created a piece of conscious software, it is still running according to the rules of C++ programs on that computer.

Nothing changes in terms of what happens, whether the thing is conscious or not does not play a role in how the computer operates.'

I think; therefore I am

'Therefore, the issue from the point of view of whether we face a risk from this kind of system does not change, what changes if the machine is actually conscious – and let me repeat, we have absolutely no idea how to tell whether it is conscious and we have no idea how to make it conscious, we have no idea at all about this – but if it were conscious and if we knew that it was conscious, somehow by some magic process, we would face an extra moral problem that we would not face otherwise That is that if it really is conscious and is having subjective experience, then it has moral rights to some extent. That complicates the picture of how we deal with those systems such as for example, are we allowed to turn them off? And I think it would be better if we did not have to face those extra constraints.'

In *Frankenstein* and in *RUR (Rossum's Universal Robots)*, the play written by Karel Čapek[2] which brought the word 'robot' into the world's languages over a century

---

2   Karel Čapek (born 9 January 1890 – died 25 December 1938) was a Czech writer, playwright

ago in November 1920, the notions of soul and pain are discussed. Both books raise the idea of learning as a way of conferring identity and a sense of self. They also both discuss introducing 'pain' into the artificial creations as a means of control, limitation and education.

'At present I am making pain nerves' says Dr Gall in RUR. 'The Robots feel practically no bodily pain ... We must introduce suffering ... For industrial reasons ... Sometimes a Robot does damage to himself because it doesn't hurt him. He puts his hand into the machine, breaks his finger, smashes his head it's all the same to him. We must provide them with pain. That's an automatic protection against damage.'

When asked whether they will be happier, Dr Gall replies: 'On the contrary; but they will be more perfect from a technical point of view.'

Digital evolution

Whilst pain may not be programmed into current computer systems, elementary penalties and reward in a sense already are, according to Barrett.

Many AI systems are set the objective of improving 'their' software using a method known as the Generative Adversarial Network. Barrett stresses the point:

> 'In the 1980s, there was a computer game based around the idea of a person exploring a dungeon, you played a character partially with text and partially with graphics and the player used their arrow keys to move their representation around in this dungeon. As you did so you revealed more and more of it, because the system filled out the maze as you explored it. As with most computer games there were items in it that you could collect that were worth something and monsters that would kill you – essentially, representing a negative something and a positive, something to be either avoided or embraced.

> After playing for a certain amount of time if you progressed eventually, you would find stairs down to the next level of the dungeon. To continue playing the game, you had to decide: "was it worth keeping on exploring? Would you find more treasure, or would you find more opportunities to be killed by something?"

> You had to make a quick choice, stay or descend, and as you descended the thing got harder and harder and of course some of the things that you had collected from early in the game, you needed later to get beyond a certain level.

---

and critic. He has become best known for his science fiction, including his novel *War with the Newts* (1936) and play *RUR (Rossum's Universal Robots)* (1920), which introduced the word 'robot'. He also wrote many politically charged works dealing with the social turmoil of his time. Influenced by American pragmatic liberalism, he campaigned in favour of free expression and strongly opposed the rise of both fascism and communism in Europe. Čapek was pronounced public enemy number two by the Nazi Gestapo in Czechoslovakia but died of pneumonia before they could arrest him.

It became very addictive and extremely popular and suddenly it evolved. Somebody came up with a scheme for categorising a player of the game based on a range of different characteristics scored from minus one hundred to plus a hundred, you would be scored on inquisitiveness, assertiveness, aggressiveness, timidity, etc. and then the program played the game for you. It would generate hundreds of different variants of the game playing character based on variations of the string of numbers that represented your player's characteristics.

What the system would then do was very quickly work out which of these combinations of characteristics would work. Were they successful or did they fail? Did they fail quickly, or did they fail slowly? It would score a player and then it would throw away the characteristic strings that represented a bad player, retain the ones that represented a good player and mix and match them. In effect, it evolved a player over a period of several months, eventually one combination produced a player that could play all the way from the beginning through to the end and win the game.

The next step with competitive networks is to have two of these things going on. One system will create dungeons the other solves the problems of navigating a dungeon, and you play the pair of them off against one another. The creator of Dungeons would create a dungeon. The creator of solvers would create a thousand solvers and work out which one wins.

Then the creator of dungeons would create a thousand dungeons and play them off against the solver winner, they would play backwards and forward, backwards and forwards, until eventually you get a really sophisticated dungeon being created and a really sophisticated solver of dungeons being created. And then you have got a high-flying computer game with highly intelligent, non-playing characters swirling around inside it.

Now, imagine moving that system from the domain of games to the solving of a significant real-world problem, access to water resources in Africa, the best way to programme the national power grid. A competitive system can be evolved from models that one part of the system is trying to break it, and the other side is trying to strengthen the model, inside an environment that can be clocked significantly faster than in the real world, using a huge range of combinations. This is what we mean by a system programming itself, because as we have seen with the AIs that are winning at Chess and Go, that is how they work.'

This process of learning is evidently already here and already being deployed, as Russell has explained. The use of algorithms in the delivery of social media information has already had unintended consequences which are so serious that their impact is the subject of an investigation by the US Senate and of law by the UK Parliament and the EU.[3]

Given that some of AI's detractors claim that regulators should begin to restrict the use of the technology to particular contexts and areas, as we found out with the

---

3 Hearings on 27 April 2021 of the US Senate Judiciary Sub-Committee on Privacy, Technology and Law, www.judiciary.senate.gov/meetings/algorithms-and-amplification-how-social-media-platforms-design-choices-shape-our-discourse-and-our-minds.

Cambridge Analytica scandal and from Amy Hodler's comments in Chapter 3, it is perhaps ironic that AI systems can be extremely aware of social context and the data generated from it, but utterly unaware of the morality of what they are doing, thus generating a paradox of being socially aware while not socially aware of the implications of the software's actions.

This situation is changing according to Russell:

> 'They can have some appreciation. It might not be as sophisticated as the appreciation that some humans have, though some of us are culturally clumsy, but there is no reason computers will never be able to arrive at "situational awareness".[4]

> Computers are general-purpose universal machines. In principle they can do anything that can be done by any machine and as far as we know, our brains are also such machines. If that argument has any force, then it would apply equally to human beings and you would be claiming that human beings could not do something that they manifestly can do.'

This is a potential evolution of AI that may be necessary in the future. If AI systems are allowed to be deployed in particular situations it will be necessary for those systems to have contextual awareness programmed into them. In a sense an AI system will need to know what is right and wrong and as Russell points out, AI systems can appreciate the rules of chess, though inputting moral rules into them may not be as straightforward.

Run by robots

For the Edinburgh University philosopher Professor Barry Smith, the application of rules by computer systems also holds other dangers for us that have already proved fatal as in the case of Don Lane, a driver for the delivery giant DPD who became the subject of the Ken Loach film *Sorry We Missed You*.

According to Smith, Lane was caught in a web that was set out in the terms of reference written by lawyers and interpreted by the system.

Lane's life was dictated by an automated system which he had named 'the gun', which he became so driven by that in the end he collapsed into a diabetic coma because he missed doctor's appointments and food breaks due to worries about losing his job.

Lane was charged £150 by DPD when he missed work to attend a hospital appointment and subsequently missed three other appointments for fear of further charges. Before his death he had collapsed twice while working, including once at the wheel.

A more extreme version of the condition being dubbed 'Run by Robots' is worrying some technological commentators.

---

4 Again see Hodler's comments re situational awareness regarding a mental health chatbot that was unable to spot a child reporting underage sex abuse.

In October 2019, *The Economist* magazine commented:

'Funds run by computers that follow rules set by humans account for 35% of America's stock market, 60% of institutional equity assets and 60% of trading activity.

Artificial-intelligence programs are writing their own investing rules, in ways that humans only partly understand. Industries from parcel and pizza-delivery to film-making are being changed by technology, but finance is unique because it can exert voting power over firms, redistribute wealth and cause mayhem in the economy'.[5]

The respected futurist and author Jaron Lanier has warned about such issues for over 30 years. According to Lanier, author of a number of books including *Who Owns the Future*, the process started in the US when people started to live their lives in a particular way so that they could get a good credit rating. As Lanier said at the time the computer programming was rules-based, meaning that it worked on the basis of: 'if this criterion is met, if this box is ticked, ie "Is their income between £20,000–£30,000? if so go on to this box here," as a result people were making sure that their behaviour fitted within the programme'. This conformity will certainly be exaggerated by the AI systems, which are currently heavily weighted towards financial outcomes.

Our surrender to the machines

Professor Harry Collins of Cardiff University, a science sociologist and author of *Artifictional Intelligence: Against Humanity's Surrender to Computers* develops this thinking further. Collins states that the biggest concern generated by our relationship with AI and computers is not 'the singularity' but our readiness to capitulate to computers we assume are right.

'The biggest danger facing us is not the Singularity: it is failing to notice computers' deficiencies when it comes to appreciating social context and treating all consequent mistakes as our fault. Thus, much worse, and much more pressing, than the danger of being enslaved by enormously intelligent computers is our allowing ourselves to become the slaves of stupid computers – computers that we take to have resolved the difficult problems but that in reality, haven't resolved them at all: the danger is not the Singularity but the Surrender'.

'The surrender' is also a very genuine concern for Russell but for different reasons:

'The loss of confidence in the face of computer is a very reasonable argument, but I think the threat comes in a different way because of the increasing capabilities of machines and the risk that that poses to human autonomy and even to human civilisation. We the human race and in fact, our predecessors have created and passed on our civilisation by teaching the next generation

---

5 'The rise of the financial machines' (*The Economist*, 3 October 2019) www.economist.com/leaders/2019/10/03/the-rise-of-the-financial-machines.

for tens of thousands of generations. That has been essential, because if we did not, our civilisation would come to an end. Very recently, we learnt to use paper, which is safer than the previous oral tradition, but the paper does not run our civilisation but it still must get into the brains of the next generation to be operational but what happens when that is no longer true? What happens when we can simply impart all this knowledge to machines that run our civilisation?

Then we lose the incentive for teaching the next generation and the next generation loses the incentive to learn, because the value of learning is to some extent at least, that by learning you can become a functioning, contributing member of society and gain status and respect and all the other things that you get. So those incentives could go away.

In the television series *Humans*, you see this very clearly. The daughter is very, very clever and does very well in school. Her parents discuss whether she should become a doctor and she says: "Well, what is the point? I could spend seven years training to be a doctor and I would not be as good as the machine. That can learn that in seven seconds." That is a valid point, if everyone makes that argument, then what happens to human civilisation?

That risks the development of what we call the "WALL-E world", coined after the hugely successful and critically acclaimed Walt Disney computer-animated film *WALL-E*,[6] where everybody is obese, stupid and pampered and looked after by machines which cater to their every whim and are incapable of looking after themselves. Their only function is to supply the desire that keeps a meaningless machine going and they eventually lose even that. They gradually lose their own purpose in living altogether, and the machines continue to keep them alive and pamper them because the machines' objective, at least in that world, is fixed. To keep the humans alive and pamper them, whether the humans have any purpose at all.'

Regulating for our survival

The very real possibility that such a situation could occur and that we are already dangerously exposed to an existential threat from the very computer infrastructure we have built and are continuing to build has led Russell to call for regulatory curbs. For Russell the important question is regaining control of the technology that we are addicted to and that now runs our lives.

'We have to find answers to this, and we have to think very carefully about it, because the impetus to create and improve this technology is enormous.

I did a little back of the envelope calculation of a conservative estimate of how valuable to humanity it would be to have general-purpose, human level or superhuman AI and it comes to about 10 quadrillion dollars. That is what

---

6   The film topped *Time*'s list of the 'Best Movies of the Decade', and in 2016 was voted 29th among 100 films considered the best of the 21st century by 117 film critics from around the world. In 2021, the film was selected for preservation in the US National Film Registry by the Library of Congress as being 'culturally, historically, or aesthetically significant'.

is driving the investment and the geopolitical competition over AI. That is the force, that must be channelled, the first consideration we have to make is to ensure we do not make machines that we are unable to control, if we are going to make machines that are more powerful than human beings, somehow, we have to have power over them forever. That is going to be quite a trick.

I have proposed new ways of designing AI systems that do not have fixed objectives that they are pursuing. That know that they do not know what the objective is that they should be pursuing. And that know that we are the, as it were, the possessors of that objective or that spark, if you like.

I believe that following that technological path, we can retain control over the machines. The second consideration is the role of humans in such a world. We do not want to follow the WALL-E solution where we are just pampered and stupid and forget how our civilisation works, that is an almost irreversible process. So, we have to figure out cultural and societal and even legal and organisational solutions that make sure we retain our capabilities, our autonomy and that might mean restricting the roles that AI can take in the world,'

Russell adds that this means that new regulatory bodies similar in function to the US Food and Drug Administration will need to be created:

'That is a minimum requirement to ensure that we do not lose control. It will be part of making sure that we do not get brainwashed. However, the FDA solution does not quite address the question of the overall role of humans in society and the economy. It does not make sure that we still have worthwhile jobs to do when we get up in the morning.'

According to Russell, we have to engage in a debate that is not happening at the moment about the role of machines in our society. This debate, he said, has to consider the possibilities of the world of the film *WALL-E* and balance those against the world described in the satire *Erewhon* written by Samuel Butler and published in 1872, where the inhabitants of a fictional world have had exactly that debate and decided to get rid of all machines.

'In Erewhon they decided that the only solution is not to put a lid on the machines, but to get rid of them altogether, because if we they did not get rid of them, then the process of threats being posed by technology would keep happening they lost control or became redundant. That is the extreme solution.

We have to figure out, is there a middle ground and if so, where is it and how do we make sure that it stays on it?'

Damned if we do, damned if we don't: we must have AI

This means that humanity now faces a dilemma because to solve many of the issues it is facing such as climate change, over-population, food production and health, the development of AI is essential, yet that development has to occur in a way that benefits humanity and does not impoverish it or shackle it.

'Why we need AI is an important question, part of the reason is a straightforward economic reason, there are things that we need right now and things that we need to do. Those things can be expensive because they require lots of expensive, well-trained humans to produce them. And if we can use AI to produce those things instead, then those will be cheaper and the companies that do not use AI will just go out of business. There is this economic imperative to use it.

I think it is also worth pointing out that if you had been writing science fiction ten thousand years ago and wrote a story about how in the future everybody would get up at the same time in the morning and they would all go into these huge buildings with no windows, and they would do the same thing ten thousand times a day. Then they would go home, and they would go to sleep, then the next day they would get up and they would go into those buildings and do the same thing 10000 times for their entire lives until they died. People would say, are you nuts? Right? No. No one would ever want to live in a world like that. Yet that is what has happened to us. That is how we ended up using human beings in many, many jobs.

We use human beings as if they were robots and now the robots are here hopefully, we will not be using human beings in those jobs anymore which should be a good thing because I do not think it is the best use of human beings with their vast range of capabilities and interests to use them as robots. So, the routine physical and mental labour is probably going to go away, partly because of these irresistible economic forces and partly because there are better things for people to be doing.'

A new occupationally therapeutic world

'This is going to create problems for us though because there is going to be a transition period in which people who were brought up and educated and prepared for these kinds of repetitive jobs will face dislocation. That is a really serious problem because unlike previous economic dislocations like the industrial revolution and the information revolution people still have jobs even though there was significant dislocation. The problem we will be facing is that once you have eliminated physical labour and mental labour, it is a reasonable question to ask, well, what else is there?

What are these new jobs if they are not physical, and they are not mental? I have not heard an economist who can answer that question and I have been running a whole series of workshops with economists and science fiction writers trying to answer the question, what will people be doing? How will we have a world where everyone has a real useful role to play and feels valued and integrated?'

It is essential to solve this puzzle through a social and employment evolution.

'There are many people who are doing repetitive jobs, the repetitive job itself is not what they value, it is not what they are upset about when they lose it. What they value is partly the feeling of belonging, the feeling that you are contributing to the physical process of putting the caps on the toothpaste tubes, as in Willy Wonka, is not pleasurable, in fact, after a while it may become unendurable for a lot of people, but they can see a point in doing it.

In this future world, everyone will need the help of other human beings to guide them, to comfort them, to teach them, to inspire them to help them figure out how to have a rich and fulfilling life.

At the moment there is a shortage of people who know how to do that, so, my current hypothesis is that we need to train people how to do that, and we cannot do that until we understand how to do it, which means a whole lot of science has to be done that we have neglected. We have spent probably trillions of dollars developing the cell phone, but relatively speaking, very little on really the science of how to how to help people live better lives. So, one vision of a future is a future where most people are engaged in these kinds of interpersonal services, and to make that work, we must equip them with the knowledge and skills to do to do that job effectively.'

One area that Russell thinks could develop in the coming years is in the creation of new schools and professions in the field of technological ethics, an area that Europe has been making significant strides in due to the work of the European Union in regulating technology companies.

'Take other regulated areas like pharmaceuticals. There was a time when they were not regulated, when a pharmaceutical company could just produce a product and sell it to millions of people, many of whom would then die. We realised it was a bad system and over about a century it got fixed. It does not have to be this way. We get to say how we want our world to be, and to make sure it is the way we want it to be.'

It is certainly a trend that others have commented on. As we saw earlier, Professor John Markoff, a pioneering technology journalist and author of *Machines of Loving Grace: The Quest for Common Ground Between Humans and Robots* has noted that: 'now if you walk onto a campus in Silicon Valley you cannot move for ethicists and philosophers'.

It is a process that has been picking up speed, ever since the renowned physicist Professor Stephen Hawking warned that AI could be the greatest disaster in human history if it is not properly managed.[7] He was of the opinion that AI could bring about serious peril in the creation of powerful autonomous weapons and novel ways for those in power to oppress and control the masses.

Hawking said the primitive forms of AI developed so far have already proved very useful, but he fears the consequences of creating something that can match or surpass humans.

'It would take off on its own, and re-design itself at an ever increasing rate', he said. 'Humans, who are limited by slow biological evolution, couldn't compete, and would be superseded.'

---

7   Professor Hawking was speaking in an interview on 2 December 2014 to the BBC Technology Correspondent Rory Cellan-Jones.

He subsequently commented: 'The development of full AI could spell the end of the human race', whilst also acknowledging 'that success in creating AI would be the biggest event in human history'.

This comment provoked much controversy and some have suggested it should not be taken too seriously. For Cardiff University's Collins:

> 'The large majority of AI scientists want to get on with building devices that work better, and will help humans run their day-to-day lives better, rather than take over the world or prove that humans are merely machines. Indeed, the strongest AI belief seems to come from philosophers, evolutionary biologists or other outsiders, suffering from the web of enchantment that distance from the frontiers of the technology can weave, and sure that humans can be no more than organic machines designed by the "blind watchmaker".'

In tandem with the increasingly urgent debate about the role of AI in our society is an even more serious debate about the role of AI in warfare, an area in which it is already rapidly displacing people. Drone warfare has already been exposed by Chelsey Manning, Julian Assange and WikiLeaks in a series of leaks starting in April 2010 that highlighted our ineffectiveness in the face of remote fighting systems. The futility was brutally underlined in an article published in *The Guardian* and *Future Intelligence*[8] which revealed that die-hard Al-Qaeda fighters loyal to Osama Bin Laden had holed themselves up in Afghanistan's Tora Bora caves in 2001 and vowed to fight to the death. This fanaticism was rendered meaningless by the US military when they sent in heavily armed British Talon robot tank drones equipped with cameras, sensing equipment and laser and infra-red sights and controlled from over half a mile away.

Fanaticism in the face of the unblinking stare of a heavily armoured robot system was not only futile, it also left no one to tell the story of any heroism. The fanatics were facing factory warfare.

According to Russell, owing to this abrupt change in modern warfare, everyone has the right to question the role of AI in war (an inevitability first explored in in *RUR* over a century ago), as Hawking said:

> 'Because AI is already having a big impact on the world, people are entitled to ask questions about whether this impact is good and if it is not out of control.'

An announcement on 9 December 2020 by the French military ethics committee can only accelerate these questions due to it giving the French military permission to develop augmented soldiers using prosthetics and chip implants to improve 'physical, cognitive, perceptive and psychological capacities', that would allow the French military to track enhanced soldiers' locations and connect them to weapons systems and other soldiers. This decision appears to suggest that the only way that people will be able to exist on a battlefield in future will be if they become part robot.

---

8 'Robot warriors take over the battlefield' (*Future Intelligence*) www.futureintelligence. co.uk/2006/10/26/robot-warriors-take-over-the-battlefield/.

The French announcement followed a similar US announcement four years earlier which stated that the Defense Advanced Research Projects Agency (DARPA) was to spend $62m to develop similar 'peaceful' implants to restore capability to injured veterans as part of its Neural Engineering System Design Program, which DARPA said aims to convert neurons in the brain into electronic signals and provide unprecedented 'data-transfer bandwidth between the human brain and the digital world'.

As we found earlier in this book, on 1 March 2021, the US's National Security Commission on Artificial Intelligence released its report *Beyond AI-powered weapons*[9] in which the NSCAI states that the US has a moral imperative to use AI-controlled weapons and intelligence systems.

An argument Russell firmly rejects:

> 'I have heard this claim of a moral argument a lot. How would it hold for example when autonomous weapons are manufactured in large quantities and when let us say the vast majority of Jews in Israel are slaughtered by a mass drone swarm attack, what will the ethicists who think it is morally right to push this technology say then? Will they just say, oh, sorry, I did not think of that? Well, I do not think that is acceptable, because the point that autonomous weapons will be used as weapons of mass destruction has been made over and over again.

> I can only assume that the people who make the argument that these weapons are ethically required are deliberately not listening for other reasons that I do not understand.

> With regard to putting chips in soldiers' brains: well, let us just hope there's informed consent. Though I am sceptical, I do not think we are close to being able to do that at the moment.'

---

9   National Security Commission on Artificial Intelligence, 'Final Report': www.nscai.gov/.

Chapter 14

To be or not to be: the rights and responsibilities of AI

To whom does AI answer?

As we have discovered from earlier contributors, a key issue in establishing the extent to which the AI technology should be afforded rights and responsibilities is one of definition: we have to decide what it is, the use it has been put to and its role within that function.

If an AI system is put in charge of automated traffic control and suddenly starts to behave erratically, causing vehicles to crash and creating enormous traffic jams that lead to costs for transport companies due to missed delivery berths at distribution hubs and ports, who is to blame? Is it the person who decided to put such a system into such a pivotal position, the manufacturers of the system or the software, those tasked with maintaining the system or those who set the parameters for the inputting of data? The list of potential 'stakeholders' goes on.

We will also, however, have to establish exactly what the AI system was – was it cognisant? Did it know what it was doing? What was its legal status? These questions will be extremely difficult to answer given the current lack of human awareness about how AI systems arrive at the conclusions that they do (the black box issue) haunting the technology due to the AI's speed of processing and the human inability to follow it.

It is even conceivable, according to some computer experts, that safety critical systems like the hypothetical one running the autonomous vehicles mentioned above, or a telecoms or energy supply network, could even begin to evolve in a way that the manufacturers would be unaware of. In Chapter 13 Professor Neil Barrett hypothesised that some commands built into safety critical machines to ensure that they are failsafe could mean that to maintain that position the systems may have developed workarounds that were not in the original software. In which case the issue of ultimate responsibility becomes even more confused.

With AI the waters have become very muddied, often because of a deliberate willingness of people to subscribe to a belief that AI systems are more aware than they actually are. An example of this was the conferring of Saudi Arabian citizenship on an AI-powered robot called Sophia in October 2017. In an interview with business writer Andrew Ross Sorkin, this robot said that people didn't need to be concerned about the rise of AI as depicted in *Blade Runner* and *Terminator*: 'You've been reading too much Elon Musk and watching too many Hollywood movies.'

This exchange takes us back to one of the profound issues with AI identified by Professor Lawrence in Chapter 1. Specifically, the innate desire of people to anthropomorphise inanimate objects and a tendency to use language that confers identity upon machines caused by a lack of useful words, for example a number of robots become 'they' and lose the 'it'. This issue causes the lines to blur between people and machines.

Professor Fred Cate *is the Vice President for Research at Indiana University, a Distinguished Professor and C. Ben Dutton Professor of Law at Indiana University Maurer School of Law. He is a senior fellow of the Center for Applied Cybersecurity Research. Professor Cate specialises in information privacy and security law issues. He has testified before numerous congressional committees and speaks frequently before professional, industry, and government groups.*

He is a senior policy adviser to the Centre for Information Policy Leadership at Hunton Andrews Kurth LLP and a member of the National Academy of Sciences Forum on Cyber Resilience. Previously, he served as a member of Microsoft's Trustworthy Computing Academic Advisory Board, Intel's Privacy and Security External Advisory Board, the Department of Homeland Security's Data Privacy and Integrity Committee Cybersecurity Subcommittee, the Department of Defense Advanced Research Projects Agency Privacy Oversight Board, the Board of Directors of The Privacy Projects, the Board of Directors of the International Foundation for Online Responsibility, and the Board of Directors of the Kinsey Institute for Research in Sex, Gender and Reproduction.

Professor Cate chaired the National Academy of Sciences Committee on Law Enforcement and Intelligence Access to Plaintext Information in an Era of Widespread Strong Encryption and served as a member of the Committee on Technical and Privacy Dimensions of Information for Terrorism Prevention. He served as counsel to the Department of Defense Technology and Privacy Advisory Committee, reporter for the third report of the Markle Task Force on National Security in the Information Age, and a member of the Federal Trade Commission's Advisory Committee on Online Access and Security. He chaired the International Telecommunication Union's High-Level Experts on Electronic Signatures and Certification Authorities.

For Professor Cate the issue of the rights and responsibilities for AI is not one that needs new laws owing to an evolving status for AI, because at the moment, according to Cate, the systems are essentially dumb, as current AI is 90 per cent deep machine learning, and basically the utilisation of data.

'The classic kind of robot with computer generated personality is noteworthy for a number of reasons. One is it generally communicates in a visible way: it talks, you do not use programming language to address it. Another is it may perceive in the same way – it has cameras.

If you go back to "2001: A Space Odyssey", it knew what you were doing because it was watching you do it or sensing you do it. The information was not coming from a keyboard.

Then another thing is that it appears to have personality. But I can give personality to a dumb machine. We've been buying teddy bears and dolls that have personalities for years. That's not necessarily a hallmark of AI. I think the real hallmark is the fact that it can change its behaviour based on the data it takes in.'

Is it actually AI?

'Is it even meaningful to talk about an AI as some separate "it", if we are in a world where we do not really know what intelligence is? AI refers to a whole range of advanced computing abilities the purpose of which is to make interaction with a computer, more like interacting with a human. To that end, you could include anything from, facial recognition or natural language processing. It can also include other things that you cannot do without big data, so it also includes big data applications. I do not think it's helpful for policy discussions to worry about everything that's included or not, other than to clarify that if we think of AI as being a computer thinking, or of it originating intelligence, and we should remember that we don't see much of that right now, and we certainly don't see any general AI. The closest we would come to that are the aircraft controls on planes, like the Airbus.

For example, my iPhone appears to recognise me. You can call it AI or not, but as far as I know, that is the type of thing people do. That I recognise my wife and my iPhone also recognises my wife seems pretty intelligent to me. And I think, to most people on the street, that seems like intelligence, even though it may not be moral intelligence or the same thing a behavioural scientist means when they say intelligence.

What is not AI? Currently AI is just executing a set of computing instructions. AI is just a more complicated set of instructions than those used in other computer systems. When a computer is doing maths, and all computation is maths the system is not learning anything from that maths.

It's just exercising the same thing over and over again.

Whereas we think of AI as capable of learning, but that may not be independent learning. My iPhone can be taught to recognise me. If I grow a moustache, it can be taught to recognise that too – that's just using the existing programming and giving it different data. I would say that one of the hallmarks of as AI is the ability to evolve and expand, empowering computer systems to perform tasks that normally require humans.

The reason for the discussion about them is because we always talk about the shock of the new that's always been true around technologies. We had a fuss about cars when they first arrived, people said that the human body would be shaken apart when the car exceeded 60 mph, the same was said of trains. For decades, we restricted the ability of cars to drive on city streets. London had some of the most significant legal restrictions of any city in the world. We do this again and again with technologies and, we do it in many ways.

Sometimes we require them to do certain things, in the case of televisions for instance they are required to have closed captioning. Sometimes we forbid them from doing certain things. The reason AI attracts so much attention is because of the "anthropomorphisation aspect", because the use of the word intelligence suggests machine independence and because we have seen so many films where that independence leads to the machines developing an agenda that is competitive with ours. For the better part of a century we have written books and made movies about this so when the moment finally looks are though it might arrive, we are concerned.'

A fine balance of competing interests

If AI is to be regulated how do you regulate it? Should it be regulated by ethicists, or should there be restrictions either built into the programming or within the machines?

'To get maximum benefit we do need some regulation and some competent regulators but, as part of that, you also need tools that they can draw on, otherwise we are just going to have regulators who are always going to be too little, too late.

In a way it will depend on first, what's the AI being used for? There will be some rules that would apply to AI development but generally speaking, the rules will be about the way the AI is being used.

AI used for marketing can be annoying, but it's not life changing. AI used to determine who enters the country, or who gets arrested, or how long they get sentenced for, that is a lot more important and, will be subject to a lot more oversight.

One potential starting place for regulation is data protection. It doesn't get you all the way there because one of the principles we want to enforce is accountability as we want it to be under control, but data protection is going to be a start.

We evidently do not want AI running rampant and that is something AI developers have to understand at the beginning. It's a waste of time getting individuals to understand it one at a time. To regulate AI we must create adequate advocacy groups because you want AI to be explainable to somebody.

We want it to be monitored so somebody can look at the results and say, does the new facial recognition software used at the UK border keep out Blacks more frequently than it keeps out whites? That's easy to measure because AI offers digital results.'

The regulation of AI deployment suggests that it will be necessary to introduce market sanctions. For Cate that is an inevitability.

'One of the challenges that with AI is we often don't know what it does, but that can be addressed if we state that AI that does not provide a high degree of accountability and transparency that our government, your government, no government will buy.

We can even ban the import of it just like, you can't sell a television in the United States that does not have closed captioning. It's a tool that helps people who can't hear. Procurement regulations are about the most effective way to get to any standard because everyone wants to be able to sell to a government.'

Some critics maintain Big Tech want regulations on AI so they can evade them because the rules will allow lawyers retained by Big Tech to advise companies on how to achieve an objective not intended by the regulations but which will still mean a company is acting within the law. It is also suggested that any regulations will operate to prevent small companies from entering the AI market because they will not be able to initially afford to spend money to comply with potentially expensive regulatory requirements. Cate points out:

'The issue for companies is ambiguity. GDPR was supposed to be uniform, at the moment every country has its own interpretation, and you can still have multiple regulators, and it doesn't apply in most of the world. In terms of AI companies want rules because it lets them know where they are.'

Rules are not the answer, context is everything

'Part of the problem with clear rules, is that companies will spend millions on lawyers to understand how to get around the rules or on accountants or on other professionals.

The way to address that is to deliver principle-based guidance. Then you can examine the criteria on which a company made a decision. That means that if the judgment could find liability and a penalty and that they will not be given a get out of jail card if they follow the letter of the law.

We have to have frameworks in which organisations make decisions and then document their decisions. Liability should not flow just because a regulator disagreed with the decision, but if it can be shown that a decision was reckless or it was careless, then I think liability could flow from that. Over time you would build up a common law of those decisions and you would end up with de facto rules. I do not think the European Parliament should sit down and just write those rules.

Let organisations make decisions using their unique knowledge and their first-hand experience and then hold them liable for the outcome if they were reckless.

I think we may get to a point where there is widely shared, perhaps human rights notion that you have a right to know if you're interacting with a computer rather than a human and the degree of computer interaction in any transaction you make.'

What should the status of AI be or does that change all of the time? According to Cate:

'AI should not be a relevant factor. The factors are all to do with context and application. It is likely that there may be triggering factors that will activate when a review is necessary. One trigger could be the type of impact. The type of people involved, children or mentally disabled people might be a second

231

trigger. The third trigger might be the scope of impact, will this effect ten people or a million? AI might be relevant to the scope; a more meaningful question might be; is this a tried and tested technology or a new technology? I do not think there should be box that says, is it AI or is it not AI.'

Context is critical. In November 2019 at the Tech Pledge in Copenhagen, a number of technologists stated they would only be involved with technology that does good. Is this the new future? Cate stated:

'The issue with this position is that anything can be used for good and anything can be used for evil. What should be encouraged is that as companies develop technologies, they are not so fixated on their objectives that they fail to look up and consider the likely consequences of what they are developing? Or that they own those consequences.

They can either take steps to reduce the bad or they stop the development, or they otherwise behave in a humane way. We have to build things that take consequences into account.

We do that all the time; we add a smell to natural gas so that we can detect natural gas leaks. It costs money to do that. We do it because the law requires it but also because it is such an easy thing to do to reduce a way that thousands of people used to die every year. And I think that's the same type of thing you want to think about. It's like putting child locks on drawers, it's a simple and annoying thing to have to do to keep your kids from getting the knives. But most parents do it. I think we want to reimagine that in the corporate world.'

The human touch

AI proponents say that AI systems make better decisions than people because they are dispassionate. Could that not mean that any human challenge to a decision of an AI system involving people might be vulnerable to a line that the challenge itself is guided by emotion and is inherently unreasonable?

'We have all dealt with unrelenting computers, the tollbooth arm that won't open, that won't recognise your credit card, the tax collector who, did an automated audit of your records and came back saying you owed money that you don't owe, and when you call to complain you get an automated system.

I ask every class I teach, why we don't use AI for policing, for routine things like traffic stops. Why have police officers out on the road in the rain displaying bias, why don't we just say your car will report you if you go more than 10 miles an hour over the speed limit and the money will be automatically taken out of your bank.

Every student I have asked has hated the idea. When they were asked what do you hate about a purely automated system for ordinary policing activities, illegal parking, speeding? At the end of the day it comes down to the fact most people think they can talk their way out of the situation if they can talk to a human.'

232

The beauty of bias

'We actually love bias we adore bias when we think it is in our favour. Humans are not anti-bias, the discussion about is AI biased is therefore fallacious, all of life is bias.

AI cannot be biased by definition, but it can reach results that are differential based on the data inputted into it on race or gender or other things.

The job of decision-making, is to reach results that make distinctions based on other societal values we care about. One of them is the ability of an individual to try to talk himself out of a ticket or to try to get empathy or to try to get human understanding and computers aren't terribly good at delivering that right now.'

Would an AI system have a role to play in the judicial system – as the ultimate arbiter or judge of a dispute?

'Not alone. I think we have really good data in healthcare, and I think you could apply this in other settings. The most effective combination is AI interacting with humans at some level. Studies from Stanford University show that a good radiologist and an AI system are both about the same in detecting, spots on lungs or spots in breasts, but that the AI is better than a bad radiologist and that AI and a radiologist working together are better than either one working separately.

It would appear to be obvious to use AI in the 80 percent of cases that are simple that the AI can handle and to use the AI to flag for human attention to cases that are more difficult, whether those are medical cases or legal cases.

There is the potential for AI to play a huge role in the law and in preparing cases and in analysing cases, but there is an issue with an AI system adjudicating guilt or innocence because we use juries in both the UK and the US for that, at least in the criminal context. Not because we think they're more accurate, in fact, we have good evidence that they're not more accurate. We use juries because we think they are fairer, or they better represent the sensibilities of the community. In the case of courts, accuracy is about the least of our concerns. Really, almost none of our processes are designed to get to accuracy.

AI systems should be able to augment the activities of lawyers and judges, but would an AI system do a better job than a judge? The question really should be, are we willing to replace a judge or a jury with an AI?'

The importance of human transparency

Cate says this augmentary position should be extended to all ethical decision-making, because of the legal principle of the court that justice is seen to be done, and for that to occur the public must be able to understand the process.

233

'We should use AI to flag issues for the attention of people and we might use it to detect systems that are not working properly. We have public trials on the whole because the fact they are open makes people feel better that is why we have juries of peers. Perhaps if you thought about it, you would not want your peers to be your jury and would prefer to have Nobel Prize winners be your jury but we think a jury of peers is important not for accuracy reasons, but for the perception that an understandable judicial process has occurred. For this reason, AI gets unfairly targeted in this argument because the real discussion is about something else.

In the policing example, it is not about AI versus not AI It is about taking the human out of the loop; in the judging example, it is not about AI versus some other tool, it's about, eliminating the perception of human empathy and the role of the human in the decision-making. There is also a widespread fear of AI because of a perception that it is going to take away jobs, because of that, in some instances, there is an instinctively negative reaction without regard for what is actually going on. The courts are similar to the electoral system, we let voters vote because we think it is better that we let the people make bad decisions than that others make good decisions for us. That may be wrong, but it is not an AI versus not an AI question because the goal of the system is not justice but the perception that justice has been seen to be done.'

Inevitably this position leads to questions over what the role of AI in our brave new world will be.

'AI is going to get better and better which is not to imply a moral judgement by saying better, but it will develop more capacity. It will become more empathetic.

At the moment it is frustrating as we can tell from the automated company call systems that give you a telephone menu and ask you what you want because they often do not work that well. We can see further examples in marketing of the many ads you see every day on the computer, perhaps one might be relevant to you, thus in despite of the data available target marketing is not working that well. Even the technology for all the "gee-whiz" things it can do, like recognising my fingerprint or my face on my iPhone, is not perfect. It is not doing a good job preventing terrorism. It's not doing a good job at lots of things. What we will see, and I think we will see fast, is AI improving dramatically.'

Where to be and where not to be

'Soon the case will become compelling for AI to be deployed in a whole range of different settings which has been demonstrated by the COVID-19 pandemic, where every single vaccine study has used AI in its development to help development.

It has dramatically helped cut down on the time needed for the development of a vaccine because AI helped to skip the first six months, that has meant the people arguing against AI have begun to look pretty silly. AI is now in a situation where it will evolve itself. It's going to get better. Humans are going to get it better. It will be supplied with more data and we will have more granular data to supply it with. That will mean that AI will be able to start doing more things and over time, those things will either be more valuable to us, like saving our lives in a pandemic, or AI systems will be more comforting to us, so we will begin to see AI with more empathetic personality, with more kindness, with more ability to make us think because there is also a telling commercial reason for that.

Thirty years ago, AT&T published a study that showed it could sell a product to 95 percent of people who call to complain if they had a good operator on the phone who was empathetic and effective.

By taking the emotion and the passion out of a situation and demonstrating the empathy that we seek in a human it will be able to create what will appear to be and what will be meaningful relationships with us.'

For Cate, the question is not so much about the technology and whether we want AI to be able to do everything, it is more about the rules we want around the technology.

'Human redress is really important. At the end of the day, you should be able to actually default to a human being if an important right or interest is involved, such as your finances or your liberty. I think that that may change over time as AI become more effective so that what we mean by effective redress no longer means a human. It could be that AI becomes its own effective redress though it would be a different AI tool.

That is a process though that will be established over time because AI obviously works very well, in some places and very badly in other areas where it has been applied to a task it is not designed for or it is being given a task that is beyond its current capabilities. The better it works, the more seamlessly it works, the more people are going to expect it to be deployed. Indeed, it may happen that people will demand AI intervention rather than that of a human because they have learned to trust AI more than a human.

People will have become accustomed to their devices recognising them they will expect the benefits from that, finally we are going to have to deal more and more with AI doing things people do not like, like sentencing people in courts or telling you you're going to die because of cancer or denying your application for your loan or whatever.

The latter, the financial stuff is almost all done by AI already today. It's just when you call to complain, you get a human.

We as a society are going to have to face the choice as AI starts to make more accurate decisions, are we willing to tolerate the results? Because it could throw up some morally unacceptable findings that might mean for example that dark-skinned people get treated differently than light skinned people, not out of bias, but out of historical economic distinctions between the two that are being, accurately reflected on by an AI system.'

AI – the new age of enlightenment and opportunity?

Experts predict there will be significant job losses due to AI and the impact of that will be considerable. Cate recognises the inevitability of this but also highlights the opportunities:

'AI may lead more to jobs. It may create new jobs at the same time as it eliminates other jobs, something all technologies have done. AI will do it more because it is going to be a more powerful and more widely used technology. It will also eliminate many jobs that are great jobs to eliminate.

Jobs in mining are already being eliminated, several mines are now completely roboticised which is a good thing because who wants to be in a mine? Who wants to do repetitive work at a factory all day long? Why should we aspire to keeping the present?

Do we want people to work with toxic waste or people to drive a truck for 18 hours a day to make a living? Do we want to fight to preserve those jobs?

We should though make sure that we have a transition and a soft landing for when those jobs become less necessary, and trucks are driven by AI. Already we are beginning to have to confront the fact that there is not enough world demand for work to support the number of workers we have. Indeed, we have people doing jobs that here is no need for they may be interesting, but they are not necessary. One example of this is the management of financial derivatives, the world could go on without financial derivatives it is not a high value activity, it is simply a highly paid activity.

And so, we might have to think about this as a collective, perhaps the French have it right, in that the goal in life should not be to work 60 hours a week.

AI might make possible a world in which people work 20 or 30 hour weeks which will mean that we will have to revaluate how we see work in our society, It will be a world where we could still feed ourselves and care for ourselves but it would be a world where people did things for a living which we currently do not pay them for. It could be a world where we have more artists and musicians and creators and people doing innovative, imaginative things for which we would provide them with a basic income, rather than having so many lawyers, financial experts and paper pushers doing jobs, which will largely be eliminated by AI.'

We clearly should use AI in an augmentary capacity. Could we use it to educate people to provide jobs and teach new skills to those deprived of jobs by AI? In that situation though is the AI still doing the thinking, or is it returning the thinking to us?

'Education requires thinking, but you can do a lot of education without thinking. People already sit through courses taught by computer, to pass an exam for a privacy credential or a law qualification that requires very little intelligence to teach because it was regurgitating knowledge.

AI is ultimately going to challenge a lot of the uncomfortable features of our society that we sometimes think about and sometimes prefer not to think about. The idea that work is the reason for living and a successful person is one who works a lot whom we pay not based on the value they deliver to society, but on an equation related to monetary value, so nurses and teachers make less than people who sell financial derivatives is almost inexplicable.

The roll out of AI will make it necessary to address those questions, because we are going to have to say, are we just making up work for people? In China people sweep roads with brooms made up of bundles of sticks because it has a billion people it needs to employ, not because it does not have street sweeping machines.

I think the great hope of AI is that fewer people are needed to grow food, create power, pave streets, do critical infrastructure tasks, so people can be freed to do more creative, imaginative or enjoyable things, including leisure and being with their families. The one thing AI may do, is not eliminate, but diminish the work focus of our societies.'

This perhaps opens up the prospect of an idealistic world, where 'artistically made by a human' could confer even more of a premium than it currently does, and a greater value will be placed upon thought. Ironically, in the apparent perfection of an AI world, human flaws and imperfections will become highly valued, and mistakes will be seen as 'creative'.

'We will be able to use AI to express themselves, people without sound studios will be able to make recordings, and people without, significant tools will be able to engage in other creative pursuits.

Violins made by Stradivarius are highly valued not because they are perfect but because they are each a little bit different. They were well-made to start with, but their idiosyncratic nature is what makes them valuable.

I do not think a radical social transformation will occur overnight, but it will occur because the idea of recapture the past of 40 years ago is a dead end to deal with the problems of the future, we have to evolve the world of the future.'

For AI to be as beneficial as possible, it has to have as much data as possible which creates security and privacy concerns due to AI's potential power to identify and control individuals.

'AI will throw up challenges for us such as how good are we, how civilized are we, how capable are we of controlling the deployment of the technologies we create?

The problem is not the data, because there will always be a practical reason for the data. Whether it will be a security reason or some other reason so the current focus on notice and choice at the data collection stage has failed and will fail.'

The challenge of data use

'The challenge for us now is how can we evolve better, more practical, more scalable rules that help govern how the data is used? What is the impact of how this data is used?

For instance, using data to test out a pandemic vaccine on a computerised model, is obviously really good. Using it to stalk people or harass children is really bad.

Are we capable of as a society of finding effective ways of drawing lines between those types of behaviours? I think we are. I just don't think we're doing very well right now.'

One potentially beneficial AI use is to identify future criminals from data patterns and background data such as postcode and family prison records, and intervene to stop them becoming criminals.

'The associational analysis that suggests connections we should be trying to break as a society that would just take us back to the 60s. The logic is that people who are disadvantaged are more likely to commit crime the obvious follow through would be to wall them off in poor neighbourhoods, to not extend public transportation to them, to ensure that they stay where they are.

That would be the worst possible use of AI, what should be done is the use of AI to deliver understanding of how the situation occurred in the first place.

AI could be used to examine the passengers on an airplane to identify individuals who appear to represent a risk and place an air marshal next to or behind each of them, people would consider that a good use of AI.

Though AI should not just stop there, because we will want to know how accurate it is in what it does. Do the people that the air marshals are behind really represent a threat? The promise of AI should be to avoid the deployment of the air marshals by being able to determine both probability and the success of intervention based on risk, opportunity and location. That is the issue deciding whether you will use an AI system to find out what makes a terrorist and whether the acquisition of data to achieve that is worth the social cost.

One good example of this was a number of data studies in hospitals which found out that people in prenatal wards in hospitals were at greater risk at certain times and a lot of research was conducted into trying to discover why. It was eventually discovered that this was to do with the shift changes at different times of the week. As a result, the way that prenatal wards were staffed was restructured and the causal cycle was broken. This was a good thing, and no-one would have wanted to stop the research to identify it. If, on the other hand, the data was used to identify and penalise everyone working at those times when there were poor health outcomes because they were not working as hard and were failing in their duty of care then that would have been a ridiculous use of the data.'

What price an AI decision?

However, what is the authority of AI in this? How much weight should be given to an AI decision and should we insist on any checks and balances?

'The decision of an AI system should be given the weight it deserves, but it has got to prove what it deserves. If an AI system is used on lung x-rays and is proved accurate, becomes more accurate in the future and the results that the system has arrived at are then audited and it still proving accurate, clinicians and patients will give it a lot of weight.'

Is there not a danger here that AI will disable people and that they will blindly accept an AI judgement? The organisation Unanimous AI,[1] for example, has completely accurately predicted the last two US Presidential elections, a fact noted by the *Wall Street Journal*.[2]

'AI must be used carefully and thoughtfully we already see a modest use for employment screening and interviews which is potentially concerning. In some cases, it could be a big company making the case it hires 100,000 people a year in service level jobs that has a high turnover rate and it uses AI to speed up its processes, not because it is better, but because it helps the company manage volume.

The problem is that in any selection process you are introducing filters into the process and those filters have the same function as biases. You give weight to one thing and discount another.

That has always been done yet paradoxically, due to the debate about AI we are now saying that those biases are more on public display and should now be scrutinised because of that. We expect more of AI right now than we expect from other systems or from human decision-making. In the long run, that is good, we should always aspire to do better, one of the things this discussion about AI, appears to be doing, is helping us appreciate the limits of our own society, and of the short comings of purely human decision-making. In the long run AI could help us be better, we do not want AI to be as good as a human decision-maker we want it to work with us to create outcomes that are better than those of a human decision-maker.'

The problem we currently face with AI systems is that they pull data from the internet and there have been several cases of this biasing AI systems. The issue is not that the data is poor, it is that the internet holds a mirror up to us. In training AI systems, we will have to filter out bias by counterbalancing one bias with another.

'This is not a binary question of good data or bad data it will be a question of are we using data for things it's appropriate and accurate enough for this use?

1 'Unanimous AI predicts 2020 Election' (*Unanimous AI Blog*, 12 September 2020) unanimous. ai/unanimous-ai-predicts-2020-election/.
2 'Artificial Intelligence Shows Potential to Gauge Voter Sentiment' (*Wall Street Journal*, 6 November 2020) www.wsj.com/articles/artificial-intelligence-shows-potential-to-gauge-voter-sentiment-11604704009.

For marketing, if it inaccurate it is less important than if AI is being used for health diagnoses, where we want it to be accurate and to link the data to the people it needs to be linked to. So it's a more complicated inquiry than just the binary "can I use this data? Yes or no?"'

Many thinkers on technology like Brigadier General Robert Spalding in Chapter 8 have stated that there should not be controls on AI because it inhibits its development.

'This is when ethics of a society show having limits is not a problem. If another nation is achieving advances but needs to torture people to do so then you cannot do the same ethically. Thus, we need to be thoughtful about the limits we apply to AI and ensure those limits are realistic. Encryption is a good example of this. I have often argued it does not make sense to regulate the commercial sale of encryption products in the West when I could just as easily download an encryption product from China and use it from there. Meanwhile, the Chinese government will have infiltrated that product, so it won't even be effective encryption vis-à-vis the Chinese.

The same position holds for AI, emulating the Chinese and doing reckless, immoral or unethical AI development should not be done but we should be aware when we are imposing limits, there may be economic costs, there may be trade costs, and there could be, military supremacy costs.

Most arms race arguments are overblown. What stops the Chinese from taking over Great Britain is not weapons. It's a complicated system of checks and balances and market and economics and military might. Attempting technological supremacy is one piece of a very big, complicated equation.'

Does this mean we are moving into a more ethical age? Owing to concerns over AI, many companies have announced they want to employ more philosophers, psychologists and arts graduates.

'The worry is that this is too late, technology is developing faster, and AI can now help develop other AI. In such a hugely competitive world we run the risk of developing more and more software before we know how to secure it, before we know what the consequences of its use are. It may be that we are talking more about ethics, but our capacity for internalising the responsibilities and the consequences of what we are doing may be declining. There are issues of transparency, that need to be addressed regarding what the software does and there are issues of responsibility in terms of who did what and when. The regulators are facing an uphill battle, they are fighting with one hand tied behind their backs while looking over their shoulders.

At the moment the regulators are still trying to work out how to make notice and consent work and they are still trying to empower individuals. That is irresponsible if most of us have no idea how AI is applied in our lives.

It is not really empowering the individual that matters. We need to empower the systems to determine if things are fair and efficient and are behaving appropriately. We have the right to expect law and governments and organisations to actually take some responsibility.

While it has been pointed out it is difficult to know what happen inside an AI black box because of the speed and complexity of the internal networks and the way that they condition how the data is being used by the AI system, that is not the end of the regulatory equation. The outcomes can still be measured. What can still be seen is the differential impact based on race or gender or national origin. The data inputs can still be altered to see how that effects the outcome. The great thing about data is it's not only making bad things possible; it makes detecting and preventing bad things easier.'

To make sure that businesses take their responsibilities seriously Cate argues that legislation that imposes ethics upon business regarding its use of AI is necessary in the same way that in the US, the Sarbanes-Oxley Act made false accounting punishable by prison.

'The Sarbanes-Oxley approach is a good idea for a number of reasons. Though the challenge will be to make AI regulation simple. Sarbanes-Oxley was complex, it made a lot of money for consulting companies because you needed a consultant to explain it. What would be better would be something simpler that set in place checks which would state under the following conditions, a company must evaluate its actions and if necessary, seek outside advice.

What will have to be created is a framework and a reporting mechanism that companies can apply as a guide and as a record. It may even be necessary for companies to submit those deliberations to obtain permission to market a product in particularly sensitive situations.

Ethics needs to be introduced as part of a business culture where companies become used to thinking about the ramifications about what they are doing.

We could say that we should make ethical understanding part of our general education process and of course we want stronger ethical training. Though for business in practical terms we need stronger ethical review. An entrepreneur who thinks that the technology they are developing will make them a fortune will be focused on that which can make what is right less important, what happened with Elizabeth Holmes and Theranos is a salutary lesson in that regard because of experts raising concerns with watchdogs. That underlines how essential it is to find so some way or preventing something like that happening with AI. That is not asking for much because the deployment of untested potentially dangerous technology is not allowed to happen anywhere else in our society if law enforcement wants to get your data, it has to go to a judge. The judge provides that review.

If people want to do research on you in a hospital, they have to go to an ethics review board or an institutional review board. Our society has quite rightly engineered a series of ethical controls and safeguards around systems that can be dangerous to people whether they are software or machines we need to do that around the new technologies of AI, Big Data and Quantum Computing. It may be a data review board or a similar institution but we to develop some way to interpose somebody into the decision-making process who is not the gung-ho proponent of the new gee-whiz thing.'

241

There are different views of what is ethical in different parts of the world. Will debates on the ethical and responsible use of AI be confined to geographic areas?

'There will be a challenge in preventing authoritarian regimes from doing bad things but that is a fight we have been having for a long time. Totalitarian governments do things with technologies that the world abhors and that has to be constantly challenged.

The question is how do we ensure that no one in the Western world is doing that? In many ways we have those tools and they must be applied by Governments and institutions we also should not try to decide this issue by passing off the responsibility to the consumer and say that it is a matter of individual ethics.

That is a principle that needs to be extended too, because we also do not want the programmer alone to be the one saying, is this ethical? Not because they might have terrible ethics, but because they are a programmer: we have asked them to build the program because they are skilled at that by the same reasoning, we want people who are skilled at ethics to be considering the ethical implications of AI technology. It therefore makes to institutionalise that process with an organisation that provides review and that documents the thinking that has gone on and that then makes it accountable to either a regulator or the public or both.'

There is also a deist view of AI. It will help us stop climate change, solve population growth and feed the population that we have. The implication is that deployment of AI should be for the common good, and that deploying it in weapons systems is bad. Can we be that black and white with AI?

'There is a lot of naiveté surrounding AI because people think that it has an objectivity it does not possess. AI could help with climate change, but it might do it by putting two million truckers out of business. Therefor it is good for the climate but not good for the two million people who now do not have jobs. Good and bad don't line up on a polar axis.

A lot of what is good and bad depends on where you sit, how it affects you. Similarly, AI will help reduce the use of animals for experiments. AI may help lead to the development of drugs, but AI may also help health care companies making billions of dollars make even more money by excluding more poor people from adequate healthcare. The moral impact of AI is something that in the current climate that politicians and lawyers will be arguing ferociously about over the coming years no matter what the good is, I guarantee you a bad will be found on the other side of it.'

Any discussion in this area necessarily risks becoming a debate about angels on pinheads.

'That is the reason for a quasi–Institutional Ethical Review, which is essentially risk benefit analysis. What is needed is to make people slow down enough to ask themselves: "what are the potential benefits of this and how likely are they to occur and what are the potential costs and how likely are they to occur?" It is necessary to think: "what can we do to mitigate those costs?"

That dialogue should lead to a rational decision. Not a perfect decision, but a thoughtful decision that this is worth doing. If it is done in the right way, it would be brilliant. That would be a huge step ahead of where we are now in the development of most technologies.'

Does this then mean companies should employ a dual-qualified lawyer and philosopher, who would be chief philosophy officer?

'It would be a good thing, but it does not need to be institutionalised in a person. Currently, when a company, such as Facebook makes a decision, it will be based on a number of factors, how will this product or facility sell? Will it make money? What will advertisers think? What will our customers think? What we need to ensure is that somewhere in that discussion is some well-documented thinking about what's the impact of what you're going to do on real people and on the societies in which we live.

It is essential to ensure with AI that it is documented. So that there is boardroom accountability in the event of a mistake. That document trail means that the CEO cannot evade responsibility. It is essential to drive accountability into the boardroom.'

If we have rules for AI, then the people who decide those rules will decide how it evolves. If AI is mainly about data, should we have rules about what AI is fed on?

'The development of regulations on AI should be about how AI is used and what effects the decisions made by an AI system. There should not be a separate debate about data or the rules that deal with or the rules will get trampled by claims of the priority of national security or by health reasons. Which will become the thin end of the wedge and be used by people with vested interests to complain about the rules.

The regulation of AI must be subtler than present cookie regulation and be used to develop AI so it can do wonderful things. Yet the by people who develop it are still going to be responsible for it and they will have to demonstrate accountability, and they will have to accept some rules of the road, for example, that they may be required to provide human redress in certain conditions.'

At the moment, society and humanity supply the demand within the world that we've created. The AI is ultimately responding to that demand from us and facilitating it until the moment it reaches sentience or 'singularity' when it theoretically will have desires of its own. Currently, we provide the impetus.

'We will train AI systems and to do that our economic principles will have to change and we will have to move from such a market focused economy, and more of a human-interest focused economy. Supply and demand are critical it is the basis on how our systems work and it is evident that we need technological help, but there are other questions we should ask before we enable that AI aid. We need to know what is it doing? Does it work? And how do we know that it works? If those questions can be satisfied, then we should deploy it if it is being used for something good.

243

We are going to have to be aware that though AI should be used to do very good things that it can equally easily be tasked to do bad things and that it will perform criminal tasks with the same facility that it carries out tasks that improve people's health. AI will be used for targeting cyber-attacks and some people would argue that it already is being used for that purpose.

The arguments about how AI should and should not be used are going to go on for a long time if for example AI were used to assess whether you should not be allowed to go to music school or you should not be allowed to open a business, then that would be a use of AI we should not permit right now.

The reason is simple it has not been tested, it has not been proved to be accurate until we can determine that it works – as was proved by Deepmind with the retinal scans that it conducted in conjunction with Moorgate Eye Hospital. It will take a long time to get the data that would be convincing that it is accurate for that.

Rather than denying someone their dreams of being a musician we could use AI to examine what are the attributes of pop stars? It could discover how a thousand pop stars started their careers. What they did, how long they practised, the privations they endured, so that people can decide whether that is a sacrifice that they want to make. It should be used to inform people's decisions rather than make decisions about them.

The room for ethical debate and argument is huge. Should AI be used to make decisions about people's aspirations, to decide what careers will suit them? To arrive at some form of technological determinism. It could be argued that Governments using AI or the use of AI in recruitment and I think in each case we are going to have to think very carefully about the merits of its deployment.

Currently in China, people take an organized exam, and that exam decides what type of school a child can go to, eventually that exam could be graded by AI. It is possible that we might do the same in the US or the UK but it should only be done after any system like that has been thoroughly tested.'

There are great concerns about the unintended consequence of AI. That is possibly the greatest concern, so how do we guard against that?

'It is impossible to know where a technology is going. The internet is a great example of that. The issue with AI is that the consequences of its deployment may be on a far larger scale than any other technology we have developed and much more difficult to predict. Nuclear weapons were developed without thought of their consequences. When mobile phones were developed people did not think they would kill so many people on the roads. That does not mean we should not be accountable, and we should not try to think it through and that we should not try to make intelligent choices something we have not proved good at in the past.

What we want to be in a position to do is detect harm as quickly as possible, whether it is done in advance or whether it is detected after it has occurred and respond as quickly very fast.'

Is there a need for an organisation like the Federal Drug Administration to license AI use?

'It will be almost impossible to oversee AI at a centralised level but there might be guidance. At the moment for any research that involves a human, US and UK national governments set the terms for that research which is then reviewed by an ethics review board.

The respective laws differ slightly but, in both cases, we defer to the institution that sponsoring the research or that is, funding the work to make sure it is reviewed consistent with those regulations. We don't have one agency that does all the reviews. It is a similar process to the obligatory third-party auditing for a publicly traded company.

The great advantage of an ethics review board or institutional review board is they usually have outsiders on them. That means that there is input from outside of a company and often from a different discipline. Ethics Review Boards also mean decisions must be documented and that companies have to accept the consequences of their products.

We do need some substantive laws too because we have to have some "thou shall nots" but I am afraid we are not going to regulate our way to a more ethical society. We learnt a long time ago that, if you are dealing with unethical people, they will always find a way around the law no matter what you do. If you are dealing with ethical people, you slow them down and tie them up in knots and cause them to spend money. What we need to do is facilitate good decisions and be prepared to punish bad decisions.'

What do you think the rights and responsibilities for AI should be?

'I strongly believe that there is a responsibility on anyone using data, particularly in a powerful way, that could affect people's finances, their health or their well-being or the well-being of society.

To really think about AI in a structured way you have to evaluate the risks. You want to assess the risks, the benefits, and the mitigation tools that could reduce those risks. You need to be able to make a decision about what you are doing that is not simply can I make a fortune from this?

That is the reason for advocating for data review boards or similar institutions that bring in some common-sense sensibilities from outside the company or the government agency that wants to perform a particular AI activity to ensure there is some thoughtful, well researched analysis of what that AI exercise could result in. Should this be done? What protections should we put around it?

This does not need to be set in stone. Using AI to identify spots on x rays made perfect sense as long as you had a human looking at the system's results. After it has been done for 10 years then we can say the AI is good at this and we now no longer need the human being.

So, we need systems that can evolve, regulatory systems, oversight systems that can evolve.

We also have to pragmatic and say that the main monitor of this process has to be the data user because regulators can't scale up to the task. And so we also want to do is have in place either incentives and requirements, so that data users engage in these thoughtful processes.'

Is this all going to come down to the intent behind a decision? What happens if the AI research is used to make a human decision and the AI research is wrongly configured?

'AI can be a magnifying lens, it can make good even better, and it can make bad even worse. It can expand the scope or the consequences of a decision, but it can also help you understand a decision better. The problem is that it is going to work very fast and our human ability may be problematic if we think that is what is going to control it because there will not be enough people to do that. That's why we might have to look to more automated tools or build into the AI places where its working out can be inspected

We do not necessarily want Facebook to review every decision with a data review board, what we do want it to do is to focus its resources on overseeing where the harm or risk is greatest.'

Technology companies are frequently accused of deliberate obfuscation over issues like their terms and conditions, privacy notices or of being evasive about what they are doing. Are you saying that the technology companies need to change that and be transparent with us, particularly over AI?

'The question is, could you build in some sort of more systemic accountability? Companies have to be made to document what they are doing and why they are doing it and what the consequences are?

And then we must tell them clearly that they will be held liable if any of those consequences occur that are shown to be proximately caused by a company's action. That will mean that the CEO or the COO of a big-tech company will think twice before he or she signs off on a project, collects data race or another controversial issue.'

Surely all that will happen is that company executives will feign ignorance. They will say that it would be impossible to know a particular consequence would occur.

'If you had a legal structure that said the CEO must personally sign off on anything that is going to, meet certain conditions, pose certain risks, effect a certain number of people. Then when you come to a court case five years later and try to argue that you did not know about something, they will have to prove that with that signed evidence trail.

CEOs talk big and give good speeches but when you actually ask them to take personal responsibility for something, they're cowards. That is something legislators should take advantage of because we found following Sarbanes-Oxley that CEO's do not like going to prison.

Obviously, technology is evolving and it's changing. It is getting faster but this is not a technology problem. This is a human and organizational incentive problem.

246

In Europe, there has been a lot of discussion about data protection impact assessments.

I think that what we need to do is require that there be documentation and that it be kept for a certain number of years, in the same way that companies are required to keep their bank records for a minimum number of years. Then if something happens, if there's a lawsuit, if there's a regulatory investigation, then you can require that to be produced. What we need to do is to make these assessments meaningful so that companies really get something out of them, and they are frank and open in them. That will not happen if you make a registry of them or you make them all public, but they should be there when you need them.

It is possible that this will move us to a new sort of court similar to a court of equity, that originated in the UK its responsibility was not to interpret rules, it was effectively to do justice.

Such an institution would allow a company to be able to say; "look the company did a good job of it, thought it through, and it made a rational decision, even if something bad happened, they're not responsible. They've done what they were supposed to do".

That will then allow the court to apply justice and equity. One the other hand if a company was slipshod and did not pay attention or they did not flag this up or they didn't generate the record of their decision, then a case for liability begins to build.

You could call this a process of ethical due diligence, the same due diligence you would do with anything. If the company is trying to decide whether to fire its CEO. It would think about what's the likely benefit. What's the likely cost? How will the market react? How will employees react? What will the shareholders think? What we are aiming at is a record of judgment that can be referred to that would be similar in intent to a ship's log.

In the past we found that often companies simply use laws as box ticking exercises and this is what US states have learned from Europe about privacy laws. Due to this we have California and other states enacting laws that are noteworthy not for their substance, but for their mechanisms, for their box checking.

With AI in particular, but with a number of other technologies, genetic technologies and, quantum computing, we don't want to engage in box ticking, we want to be much more focused on substantive outcomes.'

Chapter 15

Putting our lives in the hands of technology

Can we trust AI?

Although there is presently little consensus between national, international and supranational bodies as to how to approach any form of regulation, an emerging theme appears to be the call for those involved in AI to seek to establish trust in the technology as a basis for achieving adoption for societal good. As with other human relationships, the existence of trust – which is built up in a gradual manner over time – is the primary indicator of acceptance.

Establishing trust in technology in general and AI in particular, however, presents a number of significant concerns. Trust is generally considered as arising in two distinct phases – initial trust, which comprises an instinctive response (frequently based upon the manner in which something is represented and/or perceived); and ongoing trust, which comprises a more logical and considered response, informed by notions of reliability, security and a perceived alignment of the goals of both sides. AI challenges both phases of trust. As far as initial trust is concerned, whilst we might feel an emotional attachment to an AI, which takes the form of a human or dog-like robot, the dangers of AI anthropomorphism as highlighted by Professor Lawrence and others frequently serve to create false expectations, which ultimately undermines trustworthiness. Ongoing trust will always be undermined in circumstances where there is no obvious unity of goal, no congruence between the desired outcome for the human and for the AI.

What can be done therefore to establish faith in the technology in the short term and eliminate any trust deficit dynamically over the longer term? Can trust only ever be established through a degree of transparency and education or will it always be undermined by perceptions (whether right or wrong) of the vested interests of third parties to allow the technology to develop against our personal interests? Will we only be able to trust AI if we can instil in it deep-felt human values, however flawed?

Risto Siilasmaa *is an expert in AI and the Chair, founder and former CEO of F-Secure Corporation, an anti-virus and computer security software company based in Helsinki, Finland.*

He was the Chair of Nokia from 2012 to 2020 and during that time was credited with leading one of the most successful corporate transformations ever, changing it from a mobile phone company to a telecommunications infrastructure giant which is now installing 5G equipment around the world. Through three transactions that he negotiated – the purchase of complete ownership of Nokia Siemens Networks, the sale of the handset business to Microsoft, and the acquisition of Alcatel-Lucent – Nokia has transformed from a bankruptcy candidate to a successful global technology leader. This is reflected in Nokia's value which has gone up fivefold over roughly two years.

Siilasmaa educated himself in AI in a bid to understand the technology and since then has toured the world giving a series of speeches and holding meetings with global leaders, governments and journalists to warn them of the problems with AI. He holds a Master of Science degree from Helsinki University of Technology (now Aalto University).

Siilasmaa is also well known as a business angel, investing in several technology start-ups such as Frosmo, Enevo and Wolt, and serving on their boards of directors.

Matthias Spielkamp *is the co-founder and executive director of AlgorithmWatch, a non-profit advocacy and research organisation focussing on the consequences of algorithmic decision-making on societies. AlgorithmWatch has been awarded the Theodor Heuss Medal 2018 and was a Grimme Online nominee in 2019, the leading German award for online journalism.*

Spielkamp has held fellowships at ZEIT Stiftung (Bucerius Fellow), Stiftung Mercator (Mercator Fellow) and the American Council on Germany (McCloy Fellow) and sits on the governing board of the German section of Reporters Without Borders and the advisory councils of Stiftung Warentest and the Whistleblower Network. He was a founding and long-term member of the committee of the German Internet Governance Forum.

He holds master's degrees in Journalism from the University of Colorado in Boulder and in Philosophy from the Free University of Berlin and has written and edited books on the automation of society, digital journalism and internet governance. He testified before committees of the Council of Europe, the European Parliament, the German Bundestag and other institutions on AI and automation.

For both Risto Siilasmaa and Matthias Spielkamp, AI holds enormous potential and enormous risks. Both individuals have spent considerable time trying to bring those risks to the attention of governments around the world in an attempt to ensure that AI fulfils its promise and does not deliver on its danger. They seek to do that by explaining the technology.

As we found out from Professor Lawrence in Chapter 1, the current technology known as AI is actually a sub-discipline of the technology called machine learning and does not display the omniscient characteristics frequently portrayed in science fiction films and books. As Professor Lawrence identified, most of what is known as AI has at its heart a combination of computer processing power and statistics, a distinction Siilasmaa is also keen to underline, as we cannot hope to establish trust in something which is poorly understood:

'The main issue that we have is what do we mean when we talk about AI? I do not like to talk about AI I prefer to talk about machine learning because probably 99 percent of the news that we get of AI breakthroughs and the monetary value created through AI related tooling is all based on machine learning, which is scientifically only a small portion of all AI research. Yet for practical purposes in terms of impact, it's 99 percent of AI. This is very important because if you understand how machine learning works, then you think about the Hippocratic Oath question in relation to technology very differently.

One could almost argue that for the current technology and in the foreseeable future, linearly thinking, if no radical innovation happens, some nonlinear event, then for the foreseeable future, it is the wrong question to talk about a Hippocratic Oath for AI as well as the question is AI racist. It is not really about AI, it is about how we train it.'

Data, data everywhere but not knowing how AI thinks

'We are actually facing two challenges with AI – the data it is trained on and our understanding of how it uses that data.

For example, if we blame an individual for being racist, when the whole school system is working towards building racist students then we cannot blame the student. We should blame the school system. The question and problem we have with AI all comes down to what data we use to train it and what hidden bias is built into that data and often therefore also into the minds of the people who have collected that data.

We then come to the biggest challenge which is making people understand what machine learning is, what we understand about it, what we don't understand, and why is it difficult to fully understand how it works because often those building the systems do not fully understand how it arrives at the decisions that it does.

When we understand that, then we can tackle AI adoption, because we will then be able to point back to a fundamental foundation that will be able to shed light on how the system is working and how it arrived at its conclusions. This will have to be done with each part of AI because we have to build into people a better understanding of AI area by area, because they will all link back to that foundation.

What is profoundly interesting in all of this is that there are some fundamental assumptions about ourselves that we take for granted and that we do not question, for example, we do not fully know how people learn at the neuron level in our brains. We know that we have networks of neurons and we know that there are certain weights that are being learned that we assign to those as we learn, we know that there are algorithms in our brains, because if they were just based on this simplified neurons and weights, that our brains could not do what they do, we know then that there are algorithms in play, but we do not know what they are. One day, of course, we may, but at the moment we do not.

The same applies to different types of machine learning algorithms, which largely are based, at least to some extent, on neural networks. We understand how those work because it is all maths and code but when the volume of these connections grows high enough, the human brain cannot manage it anymore. The largest neural networks that were used in the world in 2019 had about fifteen billion connections and there are about one hundred and fifty billion in the human brain, fifteen billion connections, we have no way with our own brains and our ability to understand, to picture what that means. The number is too big. Within that network you have thousands or tens of thousands or millions of learning experiences and the network adapts to those lessons. It changes in billions of places and we simply cannot comprehend that. It is like an alien brain.

All the systems in use, like any idea systems, are modular, which means you have you break down a big problem into smaller problems and solve those one at a time. With machine learning, you might have 20 different machine learning systems linked to each other to form a solution to a particular topic. It then becomes even more challenging for a human being to understand the total of those subsystems when all those subsystems can be very large neural networks running different types of algorithms. Therefore, it becomes obvious that we cannot remotely understand their working. The problem that we have with AI is very similar to that we have with quantum mechanics. There are certain things that the human brain is just not equipped to fully comprehend. This means that the only option left to us is to use the language of mathematics to describe it and to come up with a new language to explain it.'

No regulation without technological comprehension

'This is the huge challenge for the people who have to create legislation and regulations to create practices and processes to govern machine learning in areas where it will play a big role. Those laws or regulations or processes may also have to use machine learning or control it in some way. Many of these regulators have not studied either machine learning, and do not know about what we do not know and what we cannot know about it.

They cannot do their jobs properly without that understanding. That is why I travelled around the world trying to train politicians and CEOs and chairmen and the United Nations leadership and the commission in Brussels and ministers and cabinets in the basic understanding of machine learning, because I believe that they cannot do their jobs properly without that understanding.

I am trying to give them that understanding of AI basics. If I talk to the military leadership, I use a lot of military examples, if I talk to the politicians, I use a lot of examples relevant to them, if I talk to CEOs and chairmen, I use business examples, all of which are based on that understanding of why machine learning is so fascinating and why it is so difficult to comprehend, and yet it has huge potential.

This means that when we start talking about a Hippocratic Oath, we have to understand what that would mean in the context of machine learning and why it might not make sense at all to use it.'

The point that many involved in this debate make is that at the heart of that basic AI foundation there is a human who wants to make money or has an aim. If a system is racist it is because of the racism in people. These are people-centric systems because they are based on data from people. We can only trust the system if we can control the people responsible for the system. According to Siilasmaa:

'With the question of racism, if the people building that AI tool understand that there's a likelihood that the data, they are using is a reflection of reality and the reality is racist they can then modify the data.

The issue then becomes that it is not fully reflective of reality anymore, but we have removed the racist bias from the data. How that will be accomplished is currently one of the areas of research. How do we create fake data that is not based on real people but is still fully usable by the system that we want to build to teach that system?'

When is data good and when is it bad?

'Let me give you an example, if you wanted to collect the medical data of all of the people in the UK – which would be a huge opportunity for machine learning applications – because you would have the patient records of everybody, you would know exactly what happened to them and you would know exactly what kind of test result they gave 10 years before, five years before and so forth.

You would be able to find correlations between different test results and the eventual outcome for the patient, which would then allow you to predict the outcome of new patients coming into hospital based upon their test results. At the moment that is not done due to the privacy implications, because the test results can be traced back to the individuals, even if their names and I.D. numbers are removed from the system. If you have enough data points, you can always trace data back to an individual. However, what if by using certain algorithms, which we can take the real dataset and create another dataset that, for the purposes of this system, serves the same purpose but the data are not traceable back to the individuals? Then we can solve that issue of privacy.

So, we can fix the racist bias in the dataset if we think it is important enough to take the trouble to do that and we have the funding to do that because it is just a matter of work time, and if we understand if we do not do that the data we are using is racist. However, if we do not understand that the data are racist, which often has been the reason why the applications became racist, then obviously the system has been compromised.

Now let us take a step away from there and talk about the wider issues in this. Currently there are two ways of looking at data: one is that of having a question that you want answered. The other is one where you do not have a question, but you want to understand what answers could be obtained from the data.'

Just what data do you need?

'This example of a large construction company demonstrates both of those methods. It had a very simple problem it wanted to solve – some of its

253

construction sites fail because they are over budget, over time and of poor quality.

Its problem was that it could not identify those failing sites until the final months of the construction project, when it had no time to fix them. If, however, it could predict these sites in the early phases of an 18-month project, it could fix them, a huge financial boon for the company.

To solve this issue, it took all the data it had for its construction sites, the project management data, the employee data, and the materials data and the knowledge of which historical projects had failed. It then tried to find a logic in the data that would correlate strongly with the failure using data science, and it still could not find anything until it was realised that one dataset that had not been used, which was access control data.

Access control data is an electronic record of everybody who enters and leaves a construction site. No one can get onto the construction site without signing in. In the access control data, the researchers found a strong correlation to the failing projects. This was that when outside experts or contractors arrived to perform a specific task. When they came to a failing site, they would often only stay for an hour, and then leave for sites that were doing well. There the same outside experts would arrive and stay there for a day or two days, before leaving and they found out that this actually predicts failing construction sites very effectively.

By digging deeper into the data, they found the reason. The sites where the outside expert arrived and left quickly were the sites where the outside expert did not have the tools ready for him or her to do their job. Either they did not have the materials, or the people that were supposed to help them, so they left presumably arranging to come back later. Whereas when the contractors arrived at a properly functioning site, everything was ready for them and they could do their job and leave. So why are these sites different? the answer was simple people just did not care.

There was bad leadership and that led to a bad culture. The reason the contractors were a good litmus test was because they highlighted that the culture was bad at those sites. So, the point here is that nobody knew what data would predict that a construction site would fail and to everybody's surprise, it ended up being the access control data.

Now many of the questions that people ask of AI systems are similar but if you do not know what the equivalent of the access control data is you cannot answer the question. Even when you do find out that the access control data can answer the question, you do not know why it contains the answer until you dig deeper and find out the underlying reasons.

This is the reason why it is very difficult for any politician, any legislator to be able to define the boundaries they want to put in place when the applications of AI are so wide reaching and it is very difficult to predict what data, will answer which question and in what way.'

The thorny moral question of data relevance

This would appear to be an argument for making as much data as you can get available to an AI system so that the AI system then works out the relevance of that data itself. Siilasmaa agrees:

'From an engineer's point of view, that is exactly the conclusion. Then, of course, the next question will be, is there a bias in that data like a racial bias? If we take all the data from the penitentiary system in the United States and use that to build any application, we know that there is a very strong racial bias in that dataset. The same probably would apply in China. There is also an additional issue with the systems where we do not have as clear an understanding of whether there is a bias in the data.

Another example where we don't have a question to begin with is that of taking a photograph of the back of the eye, we have found that we can predict certain heart diseases through those photographs. This has been done by processing large numbers of photographs obtained through patient records. We have sufficient numbers of those photographs and from their records we know what kind of illnesses they turned out to have either at the time of taking that photograph or later on.

From that we have found that there is a very strong link between certain features in the photographs and certain illnesses. Yet even though knowing that a particular photograph is of an eye that shows signs of a heart disease, a doctor can't see anything special in that photograph, but we do not know what the AI sees in the photograph that predicts the heart disease.

When we have trained the neural network, we will be able to dig down into it, and find out its reasoning. Which will happen there is an old story that you can easily create a convolutional neural network that identifies different objects, including cats, and that it is able to separate the Siamese cat from another breed of cats and dogs from dogs and so forth, but we could not get the network to explain what a cat looks like. That is no longer true. We now can get some understanding of what the system has decided a cat looks like from a fully trained neural network that can identify cats.

This has been a focal point for research for the several years because people are insisting that if a machine learning based system makes a recommendation or a decision, we have to be able to trace that back to the reason for its conclusion if it, for example, prescribes medicine. We have to be able to verify that the logic was sound and increasingly we can do that. But it is very, very challenging.'

In view of this, Siilasmaa queries whether it would be best for us to ask the AI systems to draw up the questions that we need to solve and what data we need to give them:

'It is always best when you have a question then you can begin to solve it by deciding what data you have that might relate to it. Then using well-known data science methods, you work through that data, trying to look for a pattern that strongly correlates with the different answers to your question. It is not a straightforward process, but it's a well-trodden path that is well understood.'

An argument for augmented intelligence?

One area where trust might be capable of being established would be if a genuine partnership could be formed between humans and machines – with AI performing an augmented intelligence role – and using AI to solve our issues with teamwork between us and the machine. For Siilasmaa this partnership would not necessarily require a detailed understanding of the core technology for trust to be established:

'Most of us do not understand how a pocket calculator works, and yet it is a great augmenting tool for us. Someone using a cash register in a store, probably does not understand how it works, but they trust its calculations, and it is used to do things quickly and productively. An AI tool when it is used to augment somebody's work is the same. We will learn to trust it.

Look at a company like Nokia, it does a huge number of transactions with a huge number of different corporate entities, and all which have their own legal templates that they use for executing orders. We used to have an army of legal team members reading through and commenting and negotiating those contracts. Now we have a machine learning system that first reads through all those templates highlighting the areas that are in conflict with our own principles.

This is a good example of mind-numbingly boring work being eradicated. Before someone had to read through these legal templates, the terms and conditions which are all slightly similar but may have one meaningful word of difference, which they have to catch. People are very bad at doing that because it is boring and repetitive. A machine is very good at that because the machine never gets bored and it will read every single word with full attention. The lawyer has been augmented by that tool. They have been liberated to spend their time on topics that are not repetitive and not boring. We can come up with hundreds and thousands of similar examples. Augmenting people really works, but the word can be used as a "cover up".

For example, Hilton, the hotel group, used to have around eight thousand people working on resource allocation. Assigning people to rooms, taking orders and managing how much food a particular hotel needed, how much soap and generally running the back-office operations. Now they have around a hundred and seventy people doing the same work because of machine learning. So, Hilton augmented 170 of those people, but also laid off seven thousand eight hundred and thirty of them.

That is part of the moral dilemma when we talk about augmenting people, we may be using it as a cover up for actually planning to lay off 97 percent of them.'

Should jobs be protected against progress?

That is the charge being levelled against AI: that it is going to remove a lot of jobs in white collar sectors as well as blue collar sectors. Ultimately, this very real concern about the technology displacing human employees from their jobs could impede people's trust in AI. For Siilasmaa this is no different to the perennial argument that always arises with the introduction of any technology or automation in the workplace. Given that computers already augment humans, AI is not actually that different. At the heart of the question of establishing trust is ensuring that we actually see the technology for what it is actually doing by reference to human standards, rather than instinctively trying to define its utility by reference to some higher standard or requirement of zero-failure. Siilasmaa says:

'Here the philosophical problem is that we are applying very different criteria on new technology compared to the criteria we apply on older technology or people. We accept that people are bad drivers, that they use mobile phones when they are driving, and they put lipstick on while they are driving which causes deaths. Yet we will not accept that an autonomous vehicle will cause a death, even if we know it will cause only a fraction of the deaths compared to human drivers.

This is really not an engineering issue it is not a data science challenge. This is humankind getting used to this new area of technology, which is somewhat of a black box, just like we humans are. We know with a high degree of reliability the output we get from a human being if we put in a certain input, but not completely. Some people surprise us, they do something unexpected. They could do something very dangerous and that happens relatively often.

The same applies to machine learning. When you have trained a system, you can test it 10000 times and it always produces the right answer but then there may be a case where the input data is just slightly different in some unfathomable way, and it will produce the wrong result. That can be one in a hundred thousand cases. Maybe we know that human beings produced the wrong result, in one in ten thousand cases therefore we know that this new system is ten times better and, on those grounds, we should accept it.

Of course, we want to try to fix it and we want to try to test it out in advance to know that it is at least as good as the best human, but from an engineering point of view, once we know that it is better, it is doing a better job than a human being would, then my engineering brain would say we should use it.'

Poor human decisions preferred to those of machines

'This is where our societal systems need to evolve, take the simple example of autonomous cars. Every year 1.35 m people die in traffic accidents we lose a huge amount of work hours because of traffic accidents because between 20 and 50m people are hospitalised and they cannot work, and due to the traffic jams the accidents cause. Traffic accidents according to the World Health Organisation cost most countries 3% of their Gross Domestic Product. With autonomous driving, we can remove 90 percent of that. It would be such a boon for humankind if we could do that. We just need to come up with the methods and tools to enable that good thing to happen. When we have autonomous cars colliding even if we cannot immediately sue the driver when there is an accident, we should not use that as a reason to prevent the deployment of such a beneficial technology.'

Like Siilasmaa, Spielkamp believes that it is not the AI systems that we cannot trust, it is the people who have designed and trained them and the purposes the systems have been used for. His concern about the development of AI lead to him co-founding *AlgorithmWatch*, a non-profit research and advocacy organisation committed to evaluating and shedding light on algorithmic decision-making processes that have a social relevance, meaning they are used either to predict or prescribe human action or to make decisions automatically. The organisation maintains that the more AI technology develops, the more complex it becomes. Again, like Siilasmaa, Spielkamp believes that complexity must not mean incomprehensibility. According to Spielkamp:

> 'The way AI crunches numbers, is pretty reliable. It knows how to add and divide numbers so there is not much room for error, but it is not infallible because everything that is in the machine has been made or was made by humans before it ended up in the machine.
>
> You could argue that the machine does not make mistakes. The mistakes are all human, but that does not make the machine or the predictions or the Automated Decision-Making system magically correct. On the contrary, it is infused with all of the different prejudices and biases that humans also have, and what you end up with is quite a problematic system in the end. I would not call it infallible.
>
> The problem is always in the data. Datasets when first assembled will contain biases that have not been removed. Those datasets may have been used by many researchers and programmers working in AI for various different purposes and that means that bias has been compounded into the system.
>
> A good example of that is a system that tries to diagnose skin cancer which is not very reliable on dark skin because the training data that was used was mainly to do with light skin so we can see that the problem is in the data. The problem is in the people designing that system who did not think that they needed to get data from dark skinned people if they want to be able to properly diagnose dark skinned people.
>
> This is obviously a human factor; the machine did not select its data. It is always to do with people. If we are going to regulate AI, which is a very complex area, it begs the question, how will we do it?
>
> Delving into the data in the example I cited, it would be the job of the regulator to ask for a comprehensive list of the datasets and the data it was trained on.
>
> If those regulators, doctors and programmers are not happy that the data will arrive at a good diagnostic outcome for everyone, that it does not do its job then they will not let it do that job.'

Even with that transparency over data inputs, however, according to Siilasmaa you will still not know how the AI system used that data and it will always be very difficult to know how AI arrives at its decisions. Spielkamp agrees:

> 'It is true that AI systems automatically come up with inferences that are very hard to monitor and it is not clear how they arrived at their results, because of

258

the complexity of the system. I would always argue that it is possible because you can analyse these systems.

Yet we have to be realistic about this because there are few groups who will have that power because you would have to invest a lot of resources to analyse a very complex system. Take the example, of a recent competition case levied by the European Commission, which fined Google £2.1 bn. The Commission ruled that Google had broken EU anti-trust law by promoting its own comparison-shopping service in its search results while demoting those of competitors. The cost of monitoring Google's compliance with the ruling was estimated to be £9.98 bn, which underlines that it is very close to impossible for normal people, to scrutinise these systems.

We also have to be aware too though that in this call for the inspection of a decision process that we are really breaking new ground. For example if someone decides to attack someone else, we usually ask about the events that caused that we do not ask: "how did their brain work? How did the synapses cooperate to come to this result?"

What we do is look at the result which is also theoretically a way to scrutinise these systems, though the companies also often use the defence of not understanding how their systems work to justify their system's results. They simply say we do not know how that happens.

Recently we carried out an experiment on Instagram to see if Instagram favours what we might call alluring images, for the purposes of this experiment we called them "racy", a synonym for sexually provocative.

Our results found that Instagram favours posts that show naked skin, though in a very particular range, usually women in bikinis and men with bare chests. This was the key to a successful post. Our experiment provided us with clear indications that this was the case. We decided that this was a problem, as it forces the people, using the platform to adopt a certain type of behaviour to achieve a successful post.

We pointed this out to Facebook, Instagram's parent company. Its response was to deny the existence of the problem: "you don't really understand how Instagram and its algorithm works, and it is not doing what you say it is. You have your data; we have our data".'

Transparency over data gathering

'Facebook then refused to provide any kind of transparency and simply said that our claims were unsubstantiated. The Instagram example may not be relevant for many people. But if you use these systems, for example, to predict grades, you can see why this is relevant.

When we created Algorithm Watch, of course, we argued that there's a need for an organisation like ours because things are changing. More and more decisions that have a direct impact on people are made to a certain extent or at least supported by these probabilistic systems.

We are not Luddites, but there is a problem here that has to be addressed. We think that a lot of automation is great and like everyone else we do not want to filter our email for spam anymore. It is fantastic that these systems work because they save time. A good spam filter is a good example of a complex system that involves a lot of top-notch thinking, it is great that it exists but of course, we need to make sure that the risks that come with it are also curtailed.

We do highlight good examples of AI to show where these systems are providing a good service to citizens, but it is very hard to come up with these examples. It is much easier to come up with examples where they do not work. You could argue that our organisation has a built-in bias because and that we are only looking for cases where AI does not work. We genuinely do not think that is the case. We try very hard to find examples of these systems do some good and it is much easier to find the bad ones. It is not just examples like grading. It is ideas such as, people coming up with lie detectors for border control and similar mechanisms for control.'

As we saw in Chapter 10, Joy Buolamwini, who discovered that Black people become invisible in facial recognition systems, believes that it is necessary to have ongoing monitoring of AI systems and likens that monitoring to washing, 'if you wash, you don't just wash once a year, we wash on a frequent basis'. Spielkamp agrees, adding one caveat:

'As of now it is still an unsolved problem for the cost reasons I have already given. How we can do that? How we can do this monitoring?

For example, at the EU level, the white paper by the European Commission on its AI strategy asked questions as to how can we do this. In the resultant Digital Services Act, which is intended to better regulate digital service platforms, the EU is asking answers again on how to monitor the situation, and it is very difficult to come up with good answers because, what is going on at the moment is quite unclear.'

Auditing the algorithm

'AlgorithmWatch is trying to come up with a position on what auditing algorithms actually means at the moment, but there are very different positions on that. There are already established procedures for security audits, where there are some standardised criteria that systems already conform to these criteria but even then, in practice it is a very complex thing.

Then we come to questions like bias and Black people becoming invisible in these systems. How do you test for that? How do you audit that? How do you standardise this? That is quite unclear.

Then there is an even bigger question such what is the impact of AI system in general?

Take the example of Airbnb. Imagine someone claims that Airbnb is biased against Black people. It is quite plausible that it could be, because people in very affluent neighbourhoods, people of colour being there, or people renting apartments in those areas might not want them to be there. If that is possible, if that is plausible, then it could be plausible also for Airbnb to optimise their systems so that that does not happen because they want to make both parties happy, the people renting out apartments and the people renting apartments.

If someone were to bring us that hypothesis and we test it and find out the system is biased, and we confront Airbnb with this hypothetical research that it is biased and then let's assume that Airbnb responds by stating that that is not what their algorithms do; that it has been caused by bias that has crept into their system; and that they are now doing everything possible to correct this. Assuming it then appears that it has done that, we test and find that Airbnb has been true to its word and it is no longer inadvertently discriminating against people of colour and it is fair by all the standards you can apply, then it would appear that the problem solved has been solved.

Yet it has not been solved, because we have a different problem here. Specifically that services like Airbnb, by their very existence, have changed the way that things happen and this we do know, it increases gentrification, it homogenises areas and removes diversity, now is that an impact of an algorithmic system? We believe it is but how do you control that? How do you monitor and audit that? That's a tremendously difficult question to answer.'

The discrimination of data

In Chapter 14, Professor Fred Cate noted that this is an impossible quest and humanity loves bias. We are all biased. If you take the bias out of humanity, then this could suggest that we would be left with something homogenised and not particularly distinctive.

'I completely agree and disagree at the same time with that statement. An algorithmic system is supposed to support or even make a decision, it is meant to discriminate that is the purpose. That is what it was built for to make decisions. A decision is a discrimination. You want to do one thing and not the other. What we do as societies is define what bias we find unacceptable.'

For Spielkamp, this could be a question of regulation and perhaps the need for a third party validation of the way in which an algorithm is claiming to work, against its actual performance.

'A lot of algorithmic processes are already tested and audited. There is already regulation in place for high frequency trading, and the regulation even contains the words algorithms it actually targets them and has done for a long time because AI has been used for a long time in high frequency trading it is on the regulators radar. They have, the legislation for it and they also have the bodies that try to find out about this even though it is very hard.

The US has been trying for a couple of years now to come up with a structure to do this, although they've failed so far. There has been a lot of political reasons for this failure and there has been conflict about the structure and technology perspective of the legislation, but it is not an easy thing to do.

Take two more examples, one is medicine where there is a lot of regulation and testing particularly about diagnostic systems, which have to go through several rounds of testing by very highly qualified experts before they can be sold.

The second example is that of semi-automated cars here too there is also a very high level of scrutiny, one because there is a regulatory basis for this in law, two, because there are also institutions responsible for this. The controls are already in place. The misunderstanding that is occurring is because AI has become an all-embracing terms and AI is a very empty term because, you can't really know what is meant by AI because AI is a semi-automated car and at the same time AI is high frequency trading.'

The case for an AI regulator

'That has led people to believe that we need an AI regulator.

That may work on a very fundamental level, where we can mandate AI conformity testing for machine learning. There can be procedures to find out how the dataset was collected and whether it was done correctly and how then the model was built on this. It is possible that we could end up with a regulator on that fundamental level.

As is the case with the US National Institute of Standards and Technology and the British Standards Institute in the UK it is feasible that they could oversee conformity testing for such systems. On a higher level, it will be quite domain specific in the sense that, if we have automation in human resources, then we would need a regulator in the labour market to ensure discrimination is not happening.

Medicine might need a different regulator although there is no reason why this work could not be carried out by bodies that already exist which simply have to become algorithm aware. The regulators of these areas will have to absorb the word algorithm and start looking into the use of it in their areas.

In some cases, we do need to originate new ideas. At the moment with social media platforms, everyone is working hard to come up with ideas of what the standards and criteria should be.

If we take disinformation for example, now the belief is that platforms like Facebook and YouTube, amplify polarising content right now. Is that a problem? Well, yes, I do think it's a problem and if they do that for their business purposes, should they be prohibited from doing it? That's a different question, because in Western liberal democracies we have never maintained that governments need to control dis-information and we have often maintained that censorship is bad.

You are allowed to say the world is flat. You are allowed to say that COVID-19 does not exist. Is that a good thing? We know it is not a good thing to say that COVID-19 doesn't exist, but we also think it is a good thing that you're allowed to say it. The issue then becomes it is incredibly difficult to come up with ideas of how to control this and to change it, particularly given that our AI systems are often tasked with identifying sentiment on the internet a tendency that makes Joy Buolamwini's point about data washing more necessary and more difficult.

Platforms could be allowed to have their own content moderation guidelines, as they are private companies and people can choose to use them but if they have these content moderation guidelines, they really have to apply them consistently to all people and not favour some posts and not others because that is discrimination.'

Free speech and the autocracy of the algorithm

'This is very problematic, and we do not have a solution for this right now, and we have to come up with a solution. But right now, everyone who claims that they have a solution are probably wrong about this.

This issue of platforms being products is a significant issue due to the possibility of proliferation and amplification. That is a much harder question to answer, because it is a private company and private companies also enjoy rights and people freely choose to discuss and use Facebook. There is an argument that as they have monopoly power, they start to become an infrastructure for speech and become a very important part of the public sphere. I subscribe to that idea and I think this is something that we need to continuously think about because we need to know what our response should be to this?

You could argue that because they are a critical infrastructure for speech, they need to be regulated in the way we regulate a government. That they cannot be globally censored which would mean that Facebook would have no other moderation guidelines than the law in the respective countries in which it operates, because they are the guidelines for the government because you cannot prohibit any kind of speech unless it is illegal. If you do that you give a tremendous power to these platforms. You also run the risk of confusing people about the nature of content which appears to be wrong in one Facebook jurisdiction and right in another.

There is also a risk that if it does look as though it is becoming an infrastructure that there are people who argue that we should do the opposite and curtail that possibility for example, by addressing it with media concentration law, and try to apply this to the platforms to break them up and diversify the landscape, so we don't have the platforms owning multiple messaging tools as in case with Facebook and WhatsApp becoming the gatekeepers, not just for private communication, but also now for professional communication.

What large media company can really say we are not available over Facebook. Everyone has to do it because otherwise they lose a potentially huge audience.

There is going to be an ongoing debate on why algorithms fail for quite some time.'

What should we trust in technology?

The question of trust will perhaps only be answered when we have accepted the role that AI can play in our lives. A frequent argument used by those seeking to introduce AI systems is one of speed and efficiency. However, when it is framed as such, this naturally leads to concern about the technology displacing the human workforce, which – as we saw earlier – is an impediment to the technology being accepted and trust established. If we focus solely on efficiency, we have to address the question of why we are using the technology in the first place. If it can be shown that the technology is worthy of our trust – whether through augmenting human processes or achieving time-critical tasks at speed and with greater accuracy than humans (such as interpreting medical scans) – the process of acceptance will accelerate and continuing trust can be established.

Part 3

Closing Submissions

Chapter 16

Civil liability for AI

Rules of engagement are essential and precise definitions will be critical from a liability perspective.

Whether guided or demanded by principles of natural justice or the Rule of Law, it is important for those working with, developing or subject to technology to have a firm understanding of the legal parameters within which they are operating. This is especially true in the digital world in the context of emerging technologies such as AI and machine learning, as ill-conceived rules and regulations can create barriers to investment; could result in economic loss or physical harm; or might impose legal liability in an unfair, disproportionate or egregious manner.

We are presently in a 'phoney war'-like situation of not having an AI law; instead there are various pieces of proposed legislation being discussed in Europe and the UK and guidance and other rules being promulgated, largely on a sectoral basis and by supranational bodies. This does not mean that existing laws cannot be applied to AI, nor does it mean that we have to develop a new universal body of new law at a speed to rival the development of the technology itself. That would be folly. As many of those interviewed for this book have identified, producing poorly written law would simply be an invitation to evade and avoid any rules; a classic case of 'enact in haste and repent at leisure'.

What makes more sense is to understand how existing legal concepts interact with the emerging technology and from there examine where further support is necessary to plug any gaps. The starting point for this exercise requires a critical understanding of what we are seeking to regulate and whether we can properly define it.

The importance of definition

Definition in this new emerging world is key. Indeed, it is essential to characterise what AI is and, perhaps most crucially, what it is not. If this is not done, it will be easy to end up in a situation where it will be difficult to establish the ground rules for imposition of liability if we are to avoid a scenario – perhaps worthy of Franz Kafka – where a legal entity could be fixed with liability for an action that originated in a wholly unexplained manner, without knowing how that liability arose.

Definition of action and the consequences that follow will be key. Until these are settled, we can expect that this will be the early battleground where questions of liability will be fought.

At the moment AI is an umbrella term, which lacks uniform definition. It can be used to refer to a wide sphere of technological activity and may embrace a wide variety of meanings, all dependent upon the context that we are given.

Professor Stuart Russell, whose views on some of the potential dangers of AI were explored earlier in Chapter 13, distinguishes between four different deployments of the technology. In his book, *Artificial Intelligence: A Modern Approach*, which he co-wrote with Peter Norvig, they define the evolution of AI by reference to it following four approaches:

(1) **thinking humanly** – whilst this is arguably more about the world of cognitive science than AI, it describes where the purpose of the technology is to replicate the manner (and reasoning) of a human mind in performing a given task;

(2) **acting humanly** – this describes the classic concept of the Turing test, where the technology seeks to mimic the way in which a task would be performed by a human and thereby achieve human-level performance;

(3) **thinking rationally** – this is similar to the Laws of Thought of Aristotle, where the technology seeks to use logical processes in order to create a rational thought output; and

(4) **acting rationally** – where the technology aims to optimise the outcome, given the information it has – crucially – irrespective of any thought of human process.

Whilst these four approaches may lack obvious and practical applications, they usefully demonstrate the conceptual differences underpinning the use of 'AI' technology and demonstrate that it may not always be appropriate to approach the question of liability for every form of technology in precisely the same way.

For the purposes of this chapter, however, we consider a workable definition for AI to be 'a product, service or technology (more accurately referred to as machine learning), which generates an action in response to its calculated recognition of the environment in which it operates'.

At a practical level this comprises the detection and collation of ever more data points from a wide variety of sensors at ever increasing speeds with the aim of interpreting those datasets, whether by automated or algorithmic means.

Once broken down to two distinct building blocks: the data and the automated or algorithmic interpretation of that data, it becomes a lot easier to start to see in which ways liability can be agreed between parties or imposed on such parties.

Nonetheless, as Professor Russell's four categories show, we must also be very careful when we address the question of liability, to consider the actual role the AI is performing and whether it is genuine machine learning or whether it is, in reality, merely an automation of a discrete human process or translating an offline activity into an online environment.

Before turning to the question of liability, some further high-level exploration of data and algorithms is required.

Data

In the brave new world of the twenty-first century, data is key – a point made forcefully by Professor Neil Lawrence in Chapter 1. Similarly, data sits at the core of AI and the law. At the heart of that relationship between data and law, however, will be the legal definitions that clarify what an AI is, what its role in a particular activity is and where and when it should be used.

Data and its use and abuse, the protections that are afforded to it, the evidence trail of how that data has been used, its ownership, and its wider relationship to individuals will all determine how liability can be agreed, assumed or imposed.

Algorithms and machine learning

As Dr Lorica explained in Chapter 2, whilst the term 'Artificial Intelligence' is necessarily broad and covers a wide range of areas, there is a tendency to use AI as synonymous with machine learning and therefore confuse rules-based algorithms and data interpretation processes as being AI or machine learning.

Machine learning will generally fall into one of three categories: **supervised learning**, where the algorithm is provided with a block of structured, training data as the input and a statement of the desired output where the algorithm 'learns' the process by which the inputs become the output; **unsupervised learning**, where unstructured training data is provided to the algorithm, which then attempts to identify correlated patterns within the data; and **reinforcement learning**, where unstructured data is provided to the algorithm, which seeks to optimise positive outcomes.

Although machine learning would suggest that the technology is making independent decisions, entirely devoid of human interaction, neither supervised nor unsupervised learning will result in any action being taken with any impact on the real-world; and reinforcement learning can specifically be designed to ensure that there is some degree of human intervention. Such intervention may be referred to as a 'human-in-the-loop', where a human is required to 'sign-off' any decision with a real-world decision; and a 'human-on-the loop', where a human supervises the operation of the technology.

Whereas rules-based algorithms have pre-determined and consistent outcomes, machine learning is invariably dynamic in nature and, over time, could produce diametrically opposed results from precisely the same inputs. Accordingly, machine learning cannot be assessed by reference to an absolute standard concerning the output; rather there is a need to focus on the quality and standard of both the data input and the algorithms used in any discussion of liability.

The nature of legal liability

Legal systems will generally look to establish or impose liability by reference to a standard of conduct or behaviour which has been agreed by the parties in the form of a private arrangement or one which we, as a society, would reasonably expect from its citizens. Once liability has been established, the scope and extent of such liability may be adjusted by concepts of foreseeability of the outcome, or intervening events might arise in a particular manner.

AI and machine learning challenge these concepts in terms of both whether liability can be imposed by reference to uniform standards of conduct; and whether it should then properly be modified, once imposed, to ensure that it reflects the true situation. The predicted ubiquity of AI will almost certainly be met by many different expectations as to its role and impact, despite the need for uniformity.

The starting point for any liability in that context, should have no real difference to the liability that might apply to an individual that is doing this in an offline environment. That is to say that we should not allow a difference for liability to develop between an offline and online state. Any automated version of an offline activity should be subject to precisely the same standards that would be the case if the activity was being performed by a human, without the need for a definition of physical status.

This issue was addressed by the European Parliament in February 2017, when it adopted a landmark resolution in response to a report from its Committee on Legal Affairs on whether there was a need for a civil law regarding the liability of robots.[1]

The resolution highlights that, where possible, there is a need to bring the actions of AI or robots into existing frameworks of culpability. This has to be correct: if we are to subject technology to an enhanced standard or a different set of regulations, in respect of an action which might otherwise be performed by a human, we invite the situation where automation could be seen as a way of avoiding or changing the liability landscape that might exist for a particular task.

Therefore, we not only have the question of the definition of the technology, but we also have to look at the role being performed before we go into the question of liability, to avoid the possibility of a human/AI task gap emerging.

A similar and perhaps more practical solution may be the concept of 'AI neutrality' laid out by Ryan Abbott, Professor of Law and Health Sciences at Surrey University. The principle of 'AI neutrality' examines the task and the function being performed and sets the parameters of behaviour around that so that AIs in that contextual space use a 'level playing field'. This views AI in a more augmentary relationship to humanity. Rather than engage in what could be at heart a deceitful and readily challengeable attempt to confer personality on a robot, the concept focuses instead on its responsibilities in certain situations.

On this basis, the law at least initially should and will look at the task that's being performed as being the basis for establishing liability. This is a critical factor if we are to achieve a world where technology is used for the greater good, rather than being a way of trying to avoid responsibility and accountability, and to totally evade liability by putting it in the metaphorical 'hands' of the technology rather than the humans who should always retain some degree of primacy over this.

---

1 Texts adopted: *Civil Law Rules on Robotics* (16 February 2017), see www.europarl.europa.eu/doceo/document/TA-8-2017-0051_EN.html.

This focus on 'fair AI' and a level playing field, however, may mean that for the first time particular behavioural constraints are stipulated for particular activities which ironically could mean that higher ethical expectations are placed on AI than on people.

Yet there are also bonuses in this process because if we get the liability regime absolutely correct, we can actually use this to drive a higher standard.

The basis of establishing liability

For those seeking to develop, deploy or adopt AI technology, the liability landscape for present purposes will largely be seen through the lens of fault-based liability (through breach of contract or commission of a tort) and strict liability (where the party responsible for the product or service is responsible in law for any failure, irrespective of any fault having been established).

Contract law

As a matter of pure legal theory contractual obligations have at their heart the concept of a bargain – a promise supported by some valuable consideration. These obligations require the promisor to deliver on the promise – nothing more – and a failure to do so will result in the promisor being liable to put the promisee in the position it would have been in, had the contract been performed properly in accordance with its terms. Performance is assessed against the promise at the time the promise is made and, absent any further agreement, the nature of the promise will not change.

Any failure is therefore regulated by the terms of the promise between the parties and the agreement will itself identify who is properly to be held accountable for the breach. The regulation of the liability for AI or machine learning systems provided under a contract as between the parties to the contract will be a matter of negotiation and agreement as to the extent to which liability can be limited or otherwise excluded (subject only to statutory rules where one of the parties is a consumer and where public policy might be offended).

The presence of AI and the use of black box algorithms, however, creates a number of practical difficulties. In particular the output from the algorithm may necessarily be hard to define and the only certainties the parties may have might be the data inputs into the system and the standard of coding. Accordingly the promise may be focussed more on assurances that the output of the system meets agreed standards; agreeing less onerous obligations to use care whether in coding or using the system; or accepting that the system would be used entirely at risk. This will have a direct impact on the value of the promise and so the valuable consideration achievable by the promisor. Any upside achieved over and above this more limited promise, as a matter of pure contract theory, would enure to the promisee rather than the promisor.

A further area of contractual liability not within the framework outlined above is where AI or machine learning might be used to discharge existing legal obligations. A number of obligations will inevitably permeate wider commercial agreements and involve parties warranting a certain state of affairs exists (or will continue to exist), or requiring performance of relevant obligations in a certain manner, for example using best endeavours, reasonable endeavours or exercising reasonable care.

The obligations will almost certainly have been negotiated with little or no consideration of how they might properly be discharged at a future point or indeed whether AI or machine learning could constitute such proper discharge. Can it be said that using machine learning (especially involving a black box algorithm) would constitute a sufficient response to an obligation requiring reasonable skill and care to be deployed? Equally, might a best endeavours obligation require consideration of the deployment of an AI, the efficiency and accuracy of which might be far superior to any human counterpart?

These areas will be fertile for competing legal arguments in future litigation. However, consideration should properly be given as to whether certain regulatory standards can be imposed both as to the integrity of datasets and on those seeking to design, code or implement algorithms to enable relevant steps to be taken to facilitate the discharge of wider contractual obligations.

It is extremely unlikely that a contracting party can exclude its liability to third parties, whether known or unknown at the time of contract. This liability would arise under the law of tort.

Law of tort and negligence

By contrast to contractual obligations, tortious obligations have at their core the involuntary imposition (or assumption) of a duty between the parties who are – as a matter of law – considered to be sufficiently 'proximate'. Parties are required to discharge their relevant duty by taking 'reasonable care' – that is, in such a manner as not to cause the party to whom they are proximate, harm. Failure to do so results in the wrongdoer being required to provide redress for the harm caused.

It is a form of fault-based liability, which assesses when the harm occurs and seeks to put the party in the position they would have been in had the harm not occurred. The most relevant tort in respect of the deployment of AI or a machine learning system is the tort of negligence.

Although – at the time of writing – the rules concerning the application of the tort of negligence and the imposition of duty of care in relation to machine learning technology remain largely untested before the English courts, the key issues are likely to revolve around whether a duty of care arises; what the relevant standard of 'reasonable care' that must be used is; and the question of causation between breach and actual loss being suffered. (We deal with causation more fully below.)

Duty of care

The starting point for most courts will be to assess the type of harm which is capable of arising from the technology. To the extent it causes physical harm or damage to property then a duty of care is more likely to arise; whereas if the loss is confined to economic loss, the court will need to assess whether a duty of care should exist.

There is a general reluctance to impose new or novel duties of care and so the initial question will be one of whether or not prior duties of care have been found to exist: doctor and patient, lawyer and client, accountant and client are well established relationships, where there is found to be a duty of care. Where there are new situations being presented, a court will look by analogy to the existing law and try to ensure there is some degree of alignment and consistency with the way that duties have been imposed in the past. This is where the role actually being performed by the technology will become particularly relevant – is the technology replicating a role where, in the offline environment, a duty of care would exist?

If there is no obvious analogy with an existing duty, the court will perform a three-stage test to determine whether a duty arises: essentially, is the relationship sufficiently close, or proximate? Is the loss reasonably foreseeable? And would it be fair, just and reasonable to impose a duty?

Although the duty will be most likely to rest with the party who is making a machine learning system available for use by others, it is not inconceivable that the duty could extend further down the chain – possibly to those collating the data; those coding the algorithm; those designing the particularly technology, among others.

Given the proliferation of open-source algorithms, absent some very real inidicia of proximity, there is a risk of either an inadvertent imposition of a duty or significant difficulties being encountered in establishing a duty. Either way, another fertile ground for coming disputes.

Standard of care

Once a duty of care has been imposed or established, the legal question is then one of how a reasonable person or thing should have discharged that duty and how reasonable it was for the person to have acted in the manner they did. Put simply, did the defendant's behaviour fall below what is considered to be a reasonable standard, based upon the balance of probabilities?

Whereas a human will ordinarily be able to provide an explanation to seek to justify their behaviour and possibly defend themselves, absent some careful design this is unlikely to be true of an AI, especially a very complicated algorithm. It is for this reason that others in this book have called for explainability statements to be created, so that there is a better understanding of the 'decision-making' process being undertaken by the technology.

In certain circumstances we can expect that some parties, especially in a personal injury context, might seek to rely on the maxim, *res ipsa loquitur* ('the thing speaks for itself') to show that the accident in and of itself is evidence of the negligence. The effect of this rule is to shift the burden onto the defendant to explain why it is not at fault. Again, this supports the production of an explainability or transparency statement as a means of seeking to minimise exposure to potential liability.

Strict liability and product safety

The basis of tortious liability is an example of the law 'letting loss lie where it falls', an expression reflecting that the claimant will not be compensated unless it can be shown that there was fault on the part of the defendant. The alternative basis for liability, often used where negligence would be too burdensome to establish or where the potentially relevant defendant would be too impractical to sue, is strict liability. This is where legislation imposes a requirement on a defendant to compensate the injured party, regardless of whether any fault can be established. The primary example of this would be product liability, where a manufacturer is liable not because it has done something wrong, but because something has gone wrong. In the UK, product liability provides consumers injured by defective products with an alternative recourse to damages from the manufacturer or seller, without the need to sue for breach of contract or negligence.

There is a discernible trend among regulators, legislators and supranational bodies who are increasingly seeing strict liability as the appropriate basis for the question of liability for AI and machine learning. The EU Commission, in particular, is seeking to co-ordinate its Artificial Intelligence Act, revised safety legislation (the Machine Regulation and General Product Safety Directive) and its desire to develop an ecosystem of trust for AI by reference to concepts of strict liability. The understandable desire of providing legal certainty, ensuring adequate and timely compensation for injured parties and prevention of damage, however is not without issue. To the extent that machine learning software is a component in a wider physical product, the application of product liability legislation would appear uncontroversial. However, as we have seen elsewhere in the book, machine learning might comprise standalone software or a service and the position of strict liability here is far from settled at the national and EU level.

More attention is needed to ensure that the gateway for product liability – the existence of a 'product' – is sufficiently wide to encompass machine learning, but not so broad as to have a chilling impact on innovation. Further, strict liability regimes do not offer the same flexibility as fault-based regimes to promote higher standards.

The role of liability in driving higher standards

As we have seen, through the process of defining and explaining the behaviour of AI technology in a particular role for the purposes of establishing or defending against liability, we may be able to create a liability regime which drives ever increasing standards in an offline and online environment.

As AI and machine learning systems continue to develop, we can anticipate a scenario where expected standards of care and performance become defined by performance of the technology, rather than the human. Put simply, the technology will operate at a higher, more accurate standard or more safely than the human performing the same task and that inevitably will become the appropriate benchmark.

A current example of this is in the robot technology being deployed in the North Sea wind farms – mentioned in the Introduction – which can maintain wind turbines more effectively than people due to being deliberately designed to survive the conditions.

At this tipping point – when we apply the standard of care and the reasonableness standards driven by the standards of technology rather than people – we could see greater liability existing by pursuing a 'human' rather than 'technological' route. A medical practitioner, who opts not to use the AI's interpretation of a scan to augment and inform his or her medical assessment, might inadvertently attract liability because they are not necessarily taking all the best possible information on board in providing the care. Or, as pointed out in the Introduction by the US National Security Commission on AI, by not using AI in war the US military could be liable for exposing its troops to defeat: 'The ability of a machine to perceive, evaluate, and act more quickly and accurately than a human represents a competitive advantage in any field – civilian or military.'

If we get the liability regime correct, this could be a factor which involves greater safety and higher standards being achieved for wider, societal benefit.

A new basis for liability?

Concepts of fault-based liability and strict liability and the benefits conferred by both regimes are undoubtedly going to be the focal point of discussions concerning the framework for legal liability. Given the limitations identified with these bases of liability, there may be scope to consider whether an alternative approach to liability might offer a regime more in keeping with the nature of the technology itself. Indeed, would a more appropriate legal basis for liability be closer to concepts of fiduciary law?

Unlike contractual obligations, fiduciary duties are not chosen and agreed by the parties, but imposed on a party in a similar manner to a tortious duty of care. However, perhaps critically, fiduciary duties may change in nature as the relationship between the fiduciary and beneficiary evolve. Unlike the contractual position where, absent any further agreement, any benefit over and above the promise made will be for the promisor rather than the promisee, any additional upside achieved by the fiduciary will enure to the beneficiary.

Whilst it is certainly not proposed that all those deploying AI and machine learning systems should be considered or treated as pure fiduciaries, there are obvious practical, safety and security benefits in encouraging the development and deployment of AI systems by those who have assumed some responsibility towards ultimate users as beneficiaries of the technology.

Accountability

For any party seeking to get effective redress for loss suffered or harm that has been caused by the fault of others, there are essentially three connected issues, which need to be considered: first, whether there has been an offending act or omission which can attributed to an identifiable person or legal entity; secondly, whether a competent court can assert jurisdiction over that legal person; and if it can, thirdly, can there be a satisfactory recognition and enforcement of any resultant judgment against that legal person.

The question of causation and attribution of a given act in the context of AI, in particular, requires some detailed consideration.

Attribution

Any attempt to demonstrate that an act or omission is properly attributable to a legal person will require an assessment of whether there is factual causation (the consequence would not have occurred *but for* the conduct of the defendant) and legal causation (whether the conduct was, as a matter of law, responsible for the consequence), as well as how you might deal with multiple and competing defendants.

Factual causation

As we have seen elsewhere in this book, statistical methods and the identification of correlations between two or multiple events is an integral part of AI and machine learning. Statistical correlations will broadly be observed where two variables change or move together. They simply recognise that a relationship exists. They do not imply causation as a matter of law and cannot alone serve as a proxy for any such causation.

The position can be illustrated by the example of ice cream sales and incidence of sunburn. Whilst it is almost a certainty that there will be a statistical correlation between an increase in both ice cream sales and reported incidents of sunburn, this does not mean that increases in the sales of ice cream has caused more sunburn. The reason for this is that there is a common factor between the two – a hot sunny day – which could be responsible for both increases. In statistics, this is known as a confounder.

That circumstance – the hot sunny day – has led to more ice creams being sold, but also people exposing themselves to the sun for longer and therefore has led to increased incidents of sunburn.

Machine learning will generally not identify the confounder as it may be looking at the input data and the outcome and trying to determine whether there is any correlation. From a legal liability perspective, we are essentially identifying the confounders in a statistical correlation and working out which has the dominant impact on the outcome. This is done applying the 'but for' test: *but for* the hot sunny day, there would not be increases in the sales of ice cream and increases in incidence of sunburn.

Establishing factual causation is likely to create very real practical problems, from a technical and evidential point of view. Where the AI technology might combine datasets from a multiplicity of sources, which are then interpreted by algorithms acting alone or in combination with others, any exercise which is seeking to work out the prevailing cause will be fraught with difficulty. The deployment of black boxes will make the task immeasurably harder.

Legal causation

The second aspect of causation is whether the defendant's act or behaviour can be considered as a matter of law to be a cause of the harm suffered. This will invariably focus on whether an intervening event has occurred which breaks the chain of causation – the legal concept of *novus actus interveniens* – to allow the defendant not to be held responsible for the harm which results.

In the context of AI or machine learning, harm might not have been suffered but for the existence of a given piece of data in a dataset; however, a failure to update that dataset might be considered to be the intervening act.

Multiple and competing defendants

Implicit within AI and machine learning is the use of a combination of datasets and algorithms from various sources. This inevitably leads to a proliferation of parties who might be potentially responsible for the loss. Liability is unlikely to reside solely with the owner, designer or manufacturer of the dataset or technology, but could extend to the coder of an algorithm, the integrator of the algorithm, the creator of the data point, and so on.

This necessarily presents a challenge as to how the relative merits of the various positions of 'stakeholders' in the loss can be determined and creates the prospect of significant disputes as to how a party can avoid or minimise liability.

Jurisdiction and enforcement

The rules and procedures concerning jurisdiction and the recognition and enforcement of judgments are not unique to claims concerning technology and therefore a detailed exploration of the issues of jurisdiction and enforcement is beyond the scope of this book. However, for present purposes, it is noted that any future dispute arising from harm caused by AI or machine learning technology will necessarily involve significant questions about which court or courts would be able to assert jurisdiction over a given defendant and would be competent to hear any claim. Can jurisdiction only be asserted over human and corporate defendants? How might a court of the future deal with human and AI joint tortfeasors?

Technology, as we know, does not respect territorial boundaries. When the multiplicity of potential parties are thrown into the mix, however, we can expect that the jurisdiction question will be a pragmatic consideration as to which defendant or defendants are going to be worth pursuing and where. Finally, assuming jurisdiction can be established, a prudent claimant will need to ensure that there will be no obvious bar to an effective enforcement of any remedy.

A defensive strategy?

Issues of liability and seeking redress for harm caused by AI inevitably raise more questions than answers, especially at this stage of the evolution of the technology. The present liability framework – at least in the UK – provides a suitable bedrock from which to build.

It is critical, however, that the legal system remains pragmatic and prepared to embrace change in the legal process to deal with this new technology. The legal system has a vital role to play in supporting the technological innovation and helping it not only to realise its tremendous societal benefits, but providing checks and balances on some of its excesses and support where it goes wrong. This will require the law to be nimble and flexible (and, on occasions, as innovative in its own right as the technology), but it is nothing new nor something we should be fearful of. We have a good track record in this area – the law of negligence itself is a good example of how the law has been able to accommodate conceptual barriers to ensure that effective remedies are available. Had May Donoghue paid for her Scotsman ice cream float, a mix of ice cream and ginger beer, at the Wellmeadow Café in Paisley, Scotland in 1928, her subsequent illness might properly have been adequately dealt with as a breach of contract. She did not. Over a series of hearings and appeals up to the House of Lords, the courts were able to find a way to impose a duty of care on David Stevenson.

In travelling on this path, however, we also have to be careful not to try to be too prescriptive in the promulgation of any regulations or laws. The legislative process is rightly a time-consuming and methodical process. It remains far outpaced by technology. We need to guard against any repeats of such legislation as the Computer Misuse Act 1990 – a law which had no ability to flex and simply never made sense when it came to be applied, leading to the prospect of the potential criminalisation of acts which had not been contemplated by the legislators, but which nevertheless fell within the scope of the Act.

Whilst allowing legal frameworks to evolve through case law and precedent offers a way to ensure flexibility and for technological developments and the views and responses of wider society to such developments to be assimilated, flexibility can create uncertainty. This may be unwelcome to those seeking to invest in or adopt the technology.

Rather than take the risk of this uncertainty – or indeed rely upon the complexity of questions of accountability and attribution providing a degree of protection – the prudent response for those involved with developing and deploying AI technology who wish to understand and limit their exposure to liability, would be to define the technology and the precise parameters of their own liability at an early stage.

This exercise would involve defining how the system should operate; how robust the system would be in the face of unexpected threat vectors; the means by which the system can be monitored and controlled; how the system interacts with other systems; and the extent to which responsibility is accepted or assumed.

In addition to facilitating parties to meet their data obligations under the GDPR to provide explanations for automated decisions, it would also assist in minimising liability and potentially permit offloading residual risk to third parties, such as the insurance industry.

Rules of engagement are important; definitions matter. At this time of fast-paced technological development, however, defining liability does not need to be the sole preserve of regulators, governments and legislators.

Chapter 17

Time for an AI law?

Why regulate?

Since Mary Shelley wrote *Frankenstein*, the world's first science fiction story in 1818, humanity has been fascinated by the idea that one day science will be able to engineer an alternative life that will either supplant or subsume us.

It is a theme that has obsessed writers and philosophers ever since, in 1920, 102 years after the publication of *Frankenstein*, another lesser-known writer, the Czech Karel Čapek wrote *Rossums' Universal Robots* (*RUR*), a prophetic play that gave the world the word 'robot' and put more 'flesh on the bones' of those fears and outlined more clearly how we could be replaced and by what.

Whilst Shelley had suggested a method by which inorganic matter might be brought to life using chemistry and electricity, Čapek wrote of biological machines which would eventually evolve to become us – the robot of the sci-fi world – ironically, powered as Shelley imagined by electricity.

Čapek's robots were a ground-breaking forerunner of those other later sci-fi literary conceptions, androids, which make their appearance as replicants in Philip K Dick's *Do Androids Dream of Electric Sheep*, better known to the world as the film *Blade Runner*, and the artificially intelligent Cylons of the TV series *Battlestar Galactica*.

Currently, the discussion about AI centres around the very basic misunderstanding which Cambridge University's Professor Lawrence and Berkeley's Professor Russell are at pains to point out in Chapter 1 and Chapter 13 respectively: the difference between machine learning and general AI.

Machine learning, as Lawrence points out with the example of Watt's Centrifugal Governor, has no awareness of function, despite having a function very much like the ballcock in a lavatory cistern. The action of raising the ballcock by flotation turns off the flow of water due to physics and not intelligence. General intelligence according to Russell has an awareness that it has carried out a function not in the way that you or I might, but because elsewhere in a computer program it may need to know that an action has occurred. This functionality thus becomes philosophical. The ballcock was responsible for the decision to turn off the water supply without knowing it, a sophisticated financial analysis system responsible for granting loans to people will operate in the same way and there is no need for it to be aware of its decision. At the moment, however, due to popular confusion there is a tendency for people to believe the computer was in some way responsible, often because they think it is not correctly understanding their circumstances.

What is now informing the debate about machine learning and AI is a new and worrying dimension which is a debate on how far our relationship with this technology should go and whether there is a need to regulate AI. The population's confusion is in a large part due to the ethical themes provoked by the publication of *Frankenstein* and the idea of engineering people. These themes are now being seriously considered over 200 years after Shelley's book about Adam, 'a modern Prometheus' brought to life by Dr Frankenstein, that possesses superhuman qualities. Adam is rejected and shunned by humanity and alternately hates humanity and then plans to exile himself from it in company with a mate he has forced his creator to make. Frankenstein destroys his 'female' work before it is finished because he fears his creations will supplant humanity, a common message.

In *RUR* we again find this fear. The robots, once again more biological androids than mechanical monstrosities, are developed to carry out mundane tasks to relieve humanity of them. They are then evolved into systems that can think faster and better than people and finally they are deployed to fight wars. Fatally, they are given something that approaches self-awareness and rebel against a humanity that is helpless in the face of the robots' competence and the fact that robots now run the world.

Ironically, a point that the US's National Security Commission on Artificial Intelligence (NSCAI) makes in its final report to President Joseph Biden and Congress on 1 March 2021 involves the justification of the use of AI in warfare on the grounds that it has a moral duty to defend the US people and that it cannot send its troops into battle against a better equipped AI adversary.[1] This justification is rejected by Russell in Chapter 13.

In *Battlestar Galactica the* fictional Cylons are an artificially intelligent race of machines that were created to serve human needs, which evolve into sentient, self-aware beings. Later models incorporated biological components and near-perfect replication of human biology. One core theme of the series is that: 'All of this has happened before and will happen again'. Characters either experience or discover instances where naturally evolving humans developed AI, only for the newly sentient life forms to wage catastrophic wars against their creators.

As mentioned in the Introduction Chapter, it is, according to the celebrated cyber security expert Mikko Hypponen of F-Secure, a scenario that any sentient or self-aware system should be excused for. He states:

'If I were an AI system that had just achieved sentience the first thing that I would do would be to do a search on the internet to find out what I was. The only information that would come back would be from science fiction films where I would find that in the main that humanity not only did not like me but seemed to spend a lot of time actively destroying me.'

It is this idea that has permeated the popular relationship with AI to date. Fear, as has often been said, is ignorance, and that fear has been played up to by the popular media. A popular technique from the time of the Victorian 'Penny Dreadfuls', the forerunners of the tabloids that specialised in coverage of bloody murders such as the victims of Jack the Ripper, is that fear sells papers. Typical of this is *The Sun*

---

1 See www.nscai.gov/.

newspaper headline on the same day that the House of Lords launched its latest report, 'AI in the UK: Ready Willing and Able?' on 16 April 2018 (mentioned in the Introduction Chapter) which ran 'Lies of the Machine: Boffins urged to prevent fibbing robots from staging Terminator style apocalypse'.

It is an enduring fascination for a tabloid press operating on a mantra of 'be scared, be very scared' as can be seen by a *Daily Express* headline of 24 October 2021 '"Superhuman" killer robots tipped to surpass mankind by 2040: "We must be vigilant"'. This story and headline shocked the source, Janet Adams, the Chief Operating Officer of the AI and crypto-coin company SingularityNET a company run by the AI guru Dr Ben Goertzel. Adams goes to great lengths to stress the positive contribution that she feels AI can make to the world, but yet has an attitude that typifies the view that both the media and the film industry have of AI.

Yet even so there is a potential for AI and robotic systems to strike out on their own and according to many of those interviewed for this book that is a very real possibility. In Chapter 13 leading names in the computing and AI sectors like former Professor Barrett and Berkeley's Professor Russell point to the possibility that AI systems could quite conceivably evolve into sentient systems without us being aware of it happening.

Robot babies

Other very real possibilities that are being actively discussed are that people and robots will in the future have relationships and could even have children, the argument being that advances in both robotics and biology will enable the creation of the same sort of 'biological machines' imagined by Čapek. For those supporters of such transhuman developments this is a natural development. They argue that not only will it be possible to fuse people's brains with computers but that it will also be possible to map what is occurring in a human brain and transfer that across a silicon interface so that actual human brain activity can be replicated on a computer, something that Russell, both a Professor of AI and Neuro-science thinks is currently fanciful.

Nonetheless, it is a potential that is being actively pursued by the scientific community. Joint research being carried out by the US National Institute of Health (NIH) and the US Defense Advanced Research Projects Agency (DARPA) in artificial prosthetics (which has successfully wired artificial limbs onto the bodies of disabled veterans[2]) has given some succour to the transhumans.

The team is also investigating the use of the same technology to develop exoskeletons to improve the functionality of elderly and disabled people. In an interview I conducted with those working on the project in 2015 I heard that the use of the technology was aimed at improving the lives of those target groups but that they had also considered that the technology could be used to improve the

---

2 See www.nih.gov/news-events/news-releases/nih-funded-research-lays-groundwork-next-generation-prosthetics.

functionality of soldiers, while stating that that was not an area that was being pursued. The need for such work has also been acknowledged in Europe.[3]

The idea of relationships with computers and realistic humanoid robots is one of concern. In a December 2021 interview with Janet Adams she admitted that it was difficult not to see the robots that she had worked with as individuals with personalities. Adams also pointed out that due to changing demographics in the world – Africa is the only continent on Earth that does not have an ageing population – it will be necessary to develop robot carers for the elderly, something emphasised by Professor John Markoff, currently a researcher at the Stanford Institute for Human-Centered Artificial Intelligence.

Robot carers

According to Markoff, in a conversation with the Nobel prize-winning sociologist and economist Professor Daniel Kahneman, he had bemoaned the progress being made by AI and told Kahneman that he had very real concerns that AI-powered robots would arrive faster than was thought and that they would cause huge unemployment. Kahneman had countered that Markoff would be lucky if the robots arrived in time due to the problems that an ageing population would cause due to their demands for carers. If the problem was not solved, Kahneman said, a disproportionate number of people would be required to look after the elderly and would be unable to perform other vital jobs. This point was acknowledged by the EU in 2017.[4]

Janet Adams, whose company, SingularityNET, is coincidentally developing robot carers, states that caring for the elderly will not only involve looking after their physical needs, it will also mean providing them with company, understanding and emotional support. This potential development is of great concern to the European Parliament. In a January 2017 report it pointed out in its general principles to the European Commission that it:

> 'considers it essential, in the development of robotics and AI, to guarantee that humans have control over intelligent machines at all times; considers that special attention should be paid to the possible development of an emotional connection between humans and robots – particularly in vulnerable groups (children, the elderly and people with disabilities) – and highlights the

---

3 See 'REPORT with recommendations to the Commission on Civil Law Rules on Robotics' at www.europarl.europa.eu/doceo/document/A-8-2017-0005_EN.html in Section P of the introduction 'whereas the developments in robotics and artificial intelligence can and should be designed in such a way that they preserve the dignity, autonomy and self-determination of the individual, especially in the fields of human care and companionship, and in the context of medical appliances, "repairing" or enhancing human beings;'.
4 See Report (n 3) in Section F of the introduction 'whereas ageing is the result of an increased life expectancy due to progress in living conditions and in modern medicine, and is one of the greatest political, social, and economic challenges of the 21st century for European societies; whereas by 2025 more than 20 % of Europeans will be 65 or older, with a particularly rapid increase in numbers of people who are in their 80s or older, which will lead to a fundamentally different balance between generations within our societies, and whereas it is in the interest of society that older people remain healthy and active for as long as possible;'.

issues raised by the serious emotional or physical impact that this emotional attachment could have on humans;'

The report goes on to stress:

'You should ensure that robots are identifiable as robots when interacting with humans … Increasing communication and interaction with robots have the potential to profoundly impact physical and moral relations in our society. This is especially the case for care robots towards which particularly vulnerable people can develop emotional feelings and attachment, thus causing concerns over human dignity and other moral values.'

The report's authors state this:

'Underlines the need to address the psychological and societal impact of human-robot-interaction as well as the dual character of the impact of technology on human capabilities, with special attention for vulnerable groups, in particular children, to avoid creating harmful dependence on robots, e.g. through evocation of emotional response, or isolation of these humans from reality.'

Robot relationships

One prominent opponent to the progress being made in AI is the renowned humanist, Professor Sherry Turkle, the Abby Rockefeller Mauzé Professor of the Social Studies of Science and Technology in the Program in Science, Technology, and Society at MIT, and the founding director of the MIT Initiative on Technology and Self.[5]

Speaking in an interview for the PassW0rd radio programme Turkle said that humanity was in very real danger of becoming too intimate with machines and that making them empathetic would cross a boundary and make us trust them more. Turkle is adamant that robots and AI systems should not be made 'humanlike', strict barriers should exist between machines and people and that a determined assault should be made on humanity's tendency to anthropomorphise machines and believe that they are in relationships with them.

That this is something that has already become a very grey area and is eroding very fast among the population at large can be seen from recent examples in the media. Stories have already emerged of people who consider themselves to be in relationships with technology such as Yuri Tolochko, a Kazakstani bodybuilder who married a sex doll called Margo in an official ceremony in November 2020.

5 Professor Turkle received a joint doctorate in sociology and personality psychology from Harvard University and is a licensed clinical psychologist. Turkle writes on the 'subjective side' of people's relationships with technology, especially computers. She is an expert on culture and therapy, mobile technology, social networking, and sociable robotics. Her newest book, *The Empathy Diaries: A Memoir* (Penguin Press, March 2021), ties together her personal story with her groundbreaking research on technology, empathy, and ethics. Her previous book, the *New York Times* bestseller, *Reclaiming Conversation: The Power of Talk in a Digital Age* (Penguin Press, October 2015) investigates how a flight from conversation undermines our relationships, creativity, and productivity.

On 16 December 2021 Tolochko announced that he had divorced Margo and was now in a relationship with two younger sex robots, Luna and Lola. Tolochko is not alone, Davecat[6] describes himself as a robosexual with four synthetic partners: Sidore, Elena, Miss Winter, and Dyanne Bailey.[7]

These are relationships that will not only increase according to David Levy, author of *Love and Sex with Robots: The Evolution of Human-Robot Relationships*, but that will also become so real for the people who are involved in them that they will eventually consider the creation of human robot offspring. In a paper called 'Can Robots and Humans Make Babies Together?' Levy delivered in London at the 3rd International Congress on Love and Sex with Robots on 20 December 2017, he pulled together the latest in genetic research and work on the creation of computerised chromosomes to suggest that in the very near future it will be possible for people to engineer robot/human babies.

Indeed, Levy suggests that it may be possible for a person in a house with a robot helper to begin to implant a personality onto the robot by developing a relationship with it. According to Levy, this will happen by literally creating a personality as the relationship develops that can be used to generate digital DNA which can be electrically programmed into biological cells. This is a prospect that presumably would attract both Tolochko and Davecat as it would give them the opportunity to bring the imagined personalities of their current sex-robots to life. The result of that, according to Levy's paper, will be that people will be able to reverse-engineer robot chromosomes from that 'personality' which could then be programmed onto living cells using technology pioneered by Dr Chandan Sen of the Ohio State University Wexner Medical Center. Sen has demonstrated a nanotechnology-based chip which is designed to deliver biological 'cargo' for cell conversion. Levy asserts that this could mean that a digital 'robot DNA' could then be biologically created and programmed either onto either a human egg or a sperm resulting in a human robot child which, ironically, is the theme of the 2017 Bladerunner sequel film *Bladerunner 2049*.

The film's message is almost an attack on Turkle and the EU's position that there should be clear limits between people and machines. In *Bladerunner 2049* and its predecessor just as with Čapek's *Rossums' Universal Robots* we are encouraged to empathise with the plight of the machines and to project our sense of what it is to be human onto them rather than admit that an AI system or a robot is simply a system similar to the Watt's Universal Governor system described by Lawrence in Chapter 1.

Biological robots

This fusion of human and robot may, however, not even happen. Experiments carried out by scientists at the University of Vermont, Tufts University in Massachusetts, and the Wyss Institute for Biologically Inspired Engineering at Harvard University in

---

6 See www.kuroneko-chan.com/echoes/.
7 See   www.vice.com/en/article/znwnpw/silicone-love-davecats-life-with-his-synthetic-wife-and-mistress and
www.ctpublic.org/show/audacious-with-chion-wolf/2021-10-28/its-not-just-a-sex-doll-what-its-like-to-be-in-a-relationship-with-a-synthetic-partner.

2021 have created self-replicating robots known as 'Xenobots' that use cells taken from a frog. The experiment created swarms of tiny living robots that self-replicate by pushing loose cells together in a dish. The Xenobots are the first multicellular organisms found to reproduce in this way. The self-replicating robots which were first created in 2020, use cells taken from the embryo of the frog species *Xenopus laevis*. The experiments found that the cells formed small structures that could self-assemble, move in groups, and sense their environment.[8]

Such potential synthesis between biological forms, synthetic materials, and digital advances such as AI evidently throw up complex moral issues that are currently masked by the excitement and potential that the developments have created. As we have seen from the successful deployment of robots on the Moon and Mars and the mass roll-out of remote working forced on us by the COVID-19 pandemic, we now in many ways have the potential to travel to distant planets with hostile environments without leaving our homes.

The development of technologies such as Xenobots and the prosthetic limbs mentioned earlier that are being pioneered by DARPA and the NIH mean that there is also the possibility that we can actually 'feel' those environments simply by installing a sufficient number of sensors on a robotic arm or coding function into a biological robot.

Yet as previously mentioned, such innovation will also carry some moral questions that had already become the staple of films and science fiction novels long before AI became a remote possibility.

The robot professional

In both *Bladerunner* and *RUR* we are asked to consider the slave status of machines that may closely resemble us and carry out tasks that we used to perform. As we saw from the Introduction to this book, the inroads that AI is making in the world of work are now considerable and they are going to accelerate as AI and robot systems take over middle class professions which have until now been considered beyond their reach such as the law, medicine, accountancy and financial services. All these sectors are ripe for the deployment of automation either via diagnosis and data analysis or for such promising areas as remote robot surgery. We can already see those benefits, as in the case of the collaboration between Google DeepMind and Moorfields Eye Hospital,[9] which uses deep learning techniques to analyse retinal scans for early signs of Age-related Macular Degeneration at speeds far greater than possible by a human analyst. This is a very positive use of AI as a number of people were going blind because their condition was not being picked up because of a lack of trained human analysts. Using AI to detect the deterioration means that the people most at risk can rapidly receive attention.

It is a pattern that has been repeated in a number of other medical areas where machine learning systems can outperform their human counterparts such as

---

8   See J Brown, 'Team builds first living robots – that can reproduce' (29 November 2021) https://wyss.harvard.edu/news/team-builds-first-living-robots-that-can-reproduce/.
9   See www.moorfieldsbrc.nihr.ac.uk/our-research/research-spotlight/moorfields-and-google-deepmind.

in the use of opto-magnetic imaging spectroscopy which uses a light probe to detect magnetic fields around hydrogen co-valent bonds to detect cervical, bowel, prostate and oral cancers.

According to Chrissie Lightfoot, author of *Tomorrow's Naked Lawyer* which deals with the use of AI in the law, the legal profession is about to be revolutionised. Lightfoot, a lawyer, is an award-winning legal futurist and a pioneer of a trend known as AI LawTech, and states:

> 'AI is moving fast and will be ready for prime time sooner than we think. The AI in law train started years ago. It hit the buffers in the early years and has made several detours since but is now running along two tracks: LegalTech and LawTech. The former is currently enjoying increased take-up and acceptance by legal professionals world-wide as "AI Legaltech" continues to make their tasks, jobs, and roles easier by supporting and enabling lawyers in their daily work lives.

> In my opinion, the latter LawTech, which focuses on DIY law or self-serve for citizens effectively replacing the lawyer despite initially trailing behind is poised to be the game-changer in years to come. The rise of "AI LawTech" has true potential in benefitting us all and could bring about the much-needed equilibrium where the currently neglected law buying majority will become as well served as the privileged few. AIs impact on the law, and in the law, therefore, is beginning to be felt positively by the lawyers themselves, the law firm bottom line and clients and customers alike. The benefits that AI brings on a personal and professional level can no longer be ignored.'

Robot and AI worlds

Owing to rapid developments in technology, the rate at which these trends will either be adopted or imposed upon populations is about to become even faster particularly in two areas, the Metaverse[10] (as mentioned in Chapters 5 and 8) and the smart city, the ramifications of which, as with AI, have been little thought about.

The Metaverse at the moment is most prominently championed by the company formerly known as Facebook (which has transitioned into a new reality company called Meta to promote its mutation into what it sees as the next stage of development for the company formerly known as Facebook), the computer graphics giant Nvidia which is promoting a new world it calls the Omniverse, and Microsoft. These concepts are quite literally visions of the future.

Currently a number of companies are developing Metaverse concepts, essentially virtual reality models of a part of their operations that allow them to be more efficient. While some of those virtual reality environments were developed prior to the pandemic, many have been rapidly developed in response to it.

---

10 See www.futureintelligence.co.uk/2021/07/07/nvidia-to-build-virtual-earth-omniverse/.

According to Martyn Ware, a computer programmer, and the keyboard player of the pop group Heaven 17, who develops highly accurate 3D soundscapes for virtual reality companies, many organisations are experimenting with computerised environments that try to achieve near perfect copies of real-world environments. Ware acknowledges that virtual reality meeting rooms had been developed for world leaders that represented the highest fidelity VR environments possible. Other companies such as Mvine are developing highly secure encrypted environments that can virtually mirror the offices a company has, digitally establish identity and allow the secure transfer of documents: virtual offices that you work in from home that attempt to try to develop a realistic copy of a real-world environment. Car companies like BMW are creating virtual environments that allow them to practice the rapid creation of production lines in factories meaning that there is the minimum amount of expensive disruption and delay because they have discovered possible log jams in the process. Similarly, the military increasingly practice conflict in VR environments that can even include the modelling of supply chains to foresee issues that may occur including the deployment of hacking attacks.

The Metaverse

In the form of the Metaverse conceived of by Nvidia, its Omniverse will allow the creation of a virtual reality model of the world by creating a universal graphical language that allows all of these worlds to be joined together, the digital oxygen, that will link all metaverses.

Richard Kerris, the Vice President of Nvidia's Omniverse Platform Development, sees the Omniverse as the key to the future, the glue that will hold together the world that we live in and the interface that will allow us to seamlessly work with robots and AI, often without our even being aware of that interaction:

> 'It will be different experiences, different types of reality, there's simulating reality or subjective reality. All sorts of things will be out there. You could be an architect and a designer walking through a virtual building that they are looking at constructing and being able to experience it in all its richness or an entertainment-based program where you're in a surreal environment and playing games, communicating with others, meeting new people. There are all sorts of things that will be out there, worlds that will be above and beyond what we're used to experiencing in the real world.'

According to Kerris this will not only mean that we will find it easier to work in the Metaverse and that our actions in the Metaverse will be translated into actions in the world that we know but that we will be able to also experience the environment that a robot, or artificial organism working on Mars may have without the breathing difficulties. Developments like this, Kerris states, open up the possibility of tourism to Mars and other places that have hitherto been unthought of while also introducing concepts such as a school field trip to Mars guided by a Mars Rover capable of giving the entire class a 'hands on' experience.

A world of virtually perpetual possibilities, a digital utopia whose promise seems to be endless, allowing not only a properly planned world that can help us avoid the environmental catastrophe that appears to be looming over us but one that can also free us from the constraints that humanity has lived under for millennia.

To reach it, according to a number of technology companies and lobbyists particularly in the US, we have to allow this world to evolve with as little regulation as possible.

Ideally, organisations like the Information Technology Innovation Forum maintain that there should be no regulations because if there are, then this technology that is essential for us will be hampered and we will not get the maximum benefit from it. It will either be muzzled or even worse, other competitive regimes like the Chinese will overtake us and quite literally win the world.

The smart city

The smart city is a concept that in some ways goes hand in hand with the development of the Metaverse. It is a concept that has two variants. In the first more popularly used one, it means a city full of sensors that automatically adjusts using technology, to what is going on around it and inside it. In the second less familiar variant it is a city that is deliberately set up to attract the most intelligent people to create a 'smart workforce'.

An entry on Wikipedia defines a smart city as follows:

'A **smart city** is a technologically modern urban area that uses different types of electronic methods, voice activation methods and sensors to collect specific data. Information gained from that *data* are used to manage assets, resources and services efficiently; in return, that data is used to improve the operations across the city. This includes data collected from citizens, devices, buildings and assets that is then processed and analysed to monitor and manage traffic and transportation systems, power plants, utilities, water supply networks, waste, crime detection, information systems, schools, libraries, hospitals, and other community services. However, smart cities are smart, not only in the way in which their governments harness technology but in the way that they monitor, analyse, plan, and govern the city.

The smart city concept integrates information and communication technology (ICT), and various physical devices connected to the IoT (Internet of things) network to optimize the efficiency of city operations and services and connect to citizens. Smart city technology allows city officials to interact directly with both community and city infrastructure and to monitor what is happening in the city and how the city is evolving. ICT is used to enhance quality, performance and interactivity of urban services, to reduce costs and resource consumption and to increase contact between citizens and government. Smart city applications are developed to manage urban flows and allow for real-time responses. A smart city may therefore be more prepared to respond to challenges than one with a simple "transactional" relationship with its citizens.'

An example of the value of a smart city, suggested in a video advertising the concept for the EU, was of someone walking along a street where the street lights came on as they are walking and then turned off once they had passed. According to its proponents the aim of the smart city will be to allow its inhabitants to lead meaningful lives that also have the least environmental impact, where public transport is preferable to private transport because of its ubiquity and efficiency and where the quality of life is continuously improved because of analysis by technology of the lives of the inhabitants which adapts what occurs in the city to improve their lives.

The theory is a simple one, AI is extremely good at data analysis and pattern recognition, qualities that make it particularly useful for both policing and health. For example, street sensors could detect an increase in obesity among the general population after Christmas and an AI system tasked with keeping the population healthy in reaction to that could perhaps alter the street conditions to increase the work that people walking might have to do. Already taxi systems like Uber have announced that they are working on systems that will be able to predict when an individual requires transport based on the analysis of an individual's data use. Such a system could simply tell that before leaving the house that people will start to typically become involved in a particular series of movements that when combined with other information such as web searches for destinations, times, weather etc show that an individual is getting ready to go out.

In a bid to counter obesity in the population an AI system could simply decide that the taxi should not come straight to the door and that it should not drop an individual off exactly where they need to be. Many individuals would not take issue with this kind of system if it meant that their well-being was being attended to without their having to think about it. Other people might decide that it was invasive and decide not to be monitored in such a way.

Smart neighbours

The second variant of the smart city is one which is defined by its residents, thus Oxford and Cambridge, and parts of California such as Woodside (a small town in San Mateo County, California, on the San Francisco Peninsula) also qualify. Woodside is among the wealthiest communities in the US, home to many technology billionaires and investment managers, with average home prices exceeding 5 million dollars.

The idea is that such groups of like-minded people become the sort of ideas hothouse characterised by places like Silicon Valley. The ultimate expression of this intelligently inhabited smart city is being touted as Neom: a £500 bn mega city that will eventually be 33 times the size of New York that is being built in Tabuk, Saudi Arabia.[11]

An idea that is planned to unite both smart city concepts, Neom emerged from 'Saudi Vision 2030', a plan that seeks to reduce Saudi Arabia's dependence on oil, diversify its economy, and develop public service sectors. 'Saudi Vision 2030' lays out plans to revolutionise Saudi society, reduce dependence on oil, and make the country a technology hub. The idea is to develop a city that will operate largely autonomously from the 'existing governmental framework'. It will have its own tax and labour laws and an 'autonomous judicial system' that will provide an environment far more liberal than that elsewhere in Saudi Arabia

---

11 See https://na.vision2030.gov.sa/v2030/v2030-projects/neom/.

to attract top technological innovators in disciplines ranging from AI to genetic engineering.

The plans state that it will have the best education system in the world taught by holographic teachers. On the streets, night lighting will be provided by an artificial moon, clouds will be seeded to produce large amounts of rain and genetically modified crops will create crops in the desert. Neom will be a robot Mecca with calls for robots to perform functions such as a flying robot taxi service, security, logistics, home delivery, and caregiving and for the city to be powered solely with wind and solar power. As the city will be designed and constructed from scratch, other innovations in infrastructure and mobility have been suggested. The first phase of the project is scheduled for completion by 2025. The aim is spelt out in the city's name, which means new future.

This is a planned use of cutting-edge technology that Saudi Arabia is not alone in. As mentioned in Chapter 11, China is now also actively harnessing AI and according to many observers, not particularly beneficially.

The dark side of the smart world

As the China expert Isabel Hilton pointed out with regard to the minority Uyghur population: 'You know, you are looking at a state which really knows no boundaries'. Hilton likened the Chinese use of AI to 'institutionalised slavery'. Amnesty International's secretary general Agnès Callamard described it as creating 'a dystopian hellscape on a staggering scale', at the launch of a 155-page report into the Uyghur's plight on 10 June 2021.

For the Chinese population at large, AI and technology is proving to be a mixed blessing because the Chinese Government has used it to develop an enormous state-wide monitoring system. By banishing the use of cash, it can follow all transactions in the country. In the case of the Uyghurs this facility allows the Government to literally control movement by dictating what a cash card can be used for. It can also use another lesser-known function of card transactions used by banks in the West to identify groups of people who regularly meet each other known as transactional analysis or geo-coding. It is a method that can allow organisations to fill in information about your lifestyle and your acquaintants and simply uses primitive machine learning techniques to find patterns in your data. For instance, it will know that every Thursday evening you go to a leisure centre. The system does not know that you play football, but it does know that you take part in a team event because there is a consistent block of other cash cards that are used at the same time. It is a picture that can be filled out further because of access granted to instant messaging apps such as WhatsApp that can provide both information about location and message analysis.

It is a pattern of analysis that the Uyghurs cannot avoid as it has now become impossible to do anything without using the technology unless they wish to switch to a barter system. Though even then technology can provide yet another monitoring system due to the ubiquity of the cell-phone masts that are needed to produce the new technological future as we all produce resistance against radio waves that can be observed. It is a system called Celldar and was developed by the Western company Siemens at its Roke Manor research centre at Romsey near

Southampton.[12] This means that yet more systems are available so that groups of people can be observed meeting. It is a pattern, excuse the pun, that we see repeating itself throughout the technological systems that we use. The reason for it is quite simply value. Whereas once advertising in newspapers and on billboards used to be used extremely random, provoking the expression that: '50% of advertising works, the problem is that I don't know what 50%', now with analysis of what we buy and what we do coupled with psychological analysis very, very accurate profiles of our lives can be made.

Revealing patterns in data

Just how accurate these data patterns are can be shown by an interview carried out with Clive Hunby of the data monitoring company Dunn-Hunby (bought by Tesco following the success of the pioneering Tesco storecard Dunn-Hunby was responsible for, as explored in Chapter 10).

At the interview at the beginning of this century, which was also attended by Chris Blackhurst, the then Deputy Editor of *The Independent*, Hunby said that by using analysis of purchases made on loyalty cards it was possible to determine someone's political persuasion very accurately from what they have bought.

As nearly 20 years have passed since that meeting it is a process that we can assume has now become even more accurate due to the access now available to technology giants of our social media and instant messaging accounts. This explains why companies such as Facebook/Meta, for example, are keen to buy up any rival successful technology start-up as happened with WhatsApp and Instagram, a pursuit of individual data that Facebook now wants to take a step further with the Metaverse and the reason for its decision to rebrand itself as 'Meta'. It is a decision the company has plumped for because of the rapid changes in working practices that have occurred in the world due to the COVID-19 pandemic and because of its analysis of social trends via its Facebook data which have shown an increased virtualisation.

What this means is that Meta's analysis has shown an increase in the use of social groups gaming and working virtually, a process it wishes to facilitate with a virtual world that will allow the company to track even more of our lives than it was able to before, as mentioned in Chapter 5.

In Neom, we have an attempt to expensively build a physical world, necessary because Saudi Arabia has to accomplish massive social change if it is to survive the financial dislocation caused by the eventual loss of global oil revenue from cars and the changeover to electric vehicles.

Meta can see the opportunity to short circuit this process by much less expensively building it's 'new reality' in virtual reality. This means that people can work rest and play and even holiday virtually as Nvidia's Richard Kerris mentioned earlier in this chapter.

---

12 See www.futureintelligence.co.uk/2002/05/02/surveillance-mobile-phones-reveal-our-every-move/.

For both Neom and Meta the development of Metaverse technology is seen as an essential component for life in the smart city because of the new technological freedom to not only dive into its workings using visualisation and AI technology but also to understand inhabitants.

More ominously, however, just as with the Uyghurs in China and with the inhabitants of Neom, they can also be monitored using AI systems and even, as we discovered in the Cambridge Analytica scandal, politically manipulated. It can also throw up challenging political and moral conundrums such as nudging people to change their behaviour to what a society considers to be in the interests of the society as a whole, which may not be in the interests of particular groups or individuals in that society.

To see just how easily this can be accomplished it is only necessary to listen to the testimony of Facebook whistleblower Frances Haugen[13] to both houses of the US and UK Governments. Haugen painted what was described as a 'dire' picture of data analysis and cynical inaction by Facebook, which she said actively financially benefited from making sections of the community angry and confrontational.

Data dependency

These developments are at a basic level of machine learning AI that already begins to throw up substantial issues regarding human rights for those people living in a basic AI world. They also create another less discussed issue which is just as dangerous for people which is system dependency and decision inferiority.

Both conditions are caused simply because people have already begun to rely on the technology they use and are unwilling to challenge it. For example, numerous incidents have occurred around the world of people using sat nav systems that have led to disaster, as evidenced by a simple web search using the words 'lorry sat nav accident'. The latest in January 2022 is perhaps the most graphic after a container lorry was left dangling 330 foot over a cliff in Shanxi Province in China when its driver took a short cut suggested by his sat nav.

Many may write off this sort of technological dependence as comic, but in different situations it becomes very serious. It has already been noted in the military that people are unwilling to override missile target acquisition systems because they do not want to take responsibility for the consequences. Twice in the last century, in 1962[14] and in 1983,[15] Russian military officers have prevented nuclear attacks on Western targets caused either by misunderstanding or erroneous computer systems. With ever increasing data system accuracy and reliability the chances of such an override are becoming increasingly remote.

---

13 www.theguardian.com/technology/2021/oct/24/frances-haugen-i-never-wanted-to-be-a-whistleblower-but-lives-were-in-danger.

14 See E Wilson, 'Thank you Vasili Arkhipov, the man who stopped nuclear war' *the guardian* (27 October 2012) www.theguardian.com/commentisfree/2012/oct/27/vasili-arkhipov-stopped-nuclear-war.

15 See P Aksenov 'Stanislav Petrov: The man who may have saved the world' (*bbc.co.uk*, 26 September 2013) www.bbc.com/news/world-europe-24280831.

The final issue regarding AI systems is the most challenging and one that I touched on at the start – the idea of general intelligence and the development of 'sentience' or as it is popularly known 'the singularity',[16] the much-trumpeted moment in which machines become self-aware. This date is predicted as 2045 by the noted inventor, futurist, transhumanism advocate, Ray Kurtzweil. Kurtzweil has written influential books on health, AI, transhumanism, the technological singularity and futurism.

Whether or not the singularity will occur, it does raise the spectre of the issue that terrifies humanity: the loss of control over its destiny. The moment one species finds that it no longer rules the world and a species that interestingly we consider to be central to the regulation of AI.

This raises the fundamental question of how humanity manages AI development and how does humanity prevent AI either superseding us, blending with us or rendering us utterly obsolete? It is a question that sets up some interesting paradoxes according to Professor Luciano Floridi, the Oxford Internet Institute's Professor of Philosophy and Ethics of Information at the University of Oxford, and Director of the Digital Ethics Lab.

As Floridi and a huge number of interviewees for this book pointed out, at the moment much of the concern surrounding the internet and the use of AI technologies has come about because of fake news and the possibilities of manipulating the new systems.

This concern is leading to a pressure to regulate and circumscribe particular behaviours online. It has also led to the dawning recognition that much of the disinformation and hate speech that has drawn so much criticism is actually a manifestation of deeper influences within society. The internet would appear to be quite literally holding up a mirror to the dark soul of humanity and presenting a picture that is unedifying to say the least.

The introduction of checks and balances on technology to try to correct that and to eradicate the data and race bias discussed by Dr Reema Patel in Chapter 11, while protecting the integrity of data and working to ensure that the freedoms of expression reflect those in the offline world, unfortunately do nothing to address the underlying human bias.

Sentient AI

The regulation of AI technology to ensure that it does not slip out of our control does raise the interesting question that perhaps a sentient AI technology could do a much better job of looking after the planet and our world than we can if we work with the technology to get it right. This possibility is evident from the beginning of computing because of the technology's proven ability to process huge amounts of information at speeds we cannot compete with. For instance, one of the world's first computers, ENIAC, the Electronic Numerical Integrator and Computer, built in 1945 and designed for ballistics research, had an approximate speed 1,000 times

---

16 See https://en.wikipedia.org/wiki/Technological_singularity.

faster than that of electro-mechanical machines. Its combination of speed and programmability allowed for thousands more calculations for problems, as ENIAC calculated a trajectory in 30 seconds that took a human 20 hours, meaning that one ENIAC took the jobs of 2,400 humans. The capability of the ENIAC system obviously pales into insignificance compared to the power of systems that have been developed over three-quarters of a century later.

Given the inhuman history of humanity in just those 77 years it is ironic that much of the debate regarding AI revolves around how humanity with its higher sense of moral and ethical purpose should stay in control of those decisions when it has overseen huge amounts of inhumanity during that period, an absorbing debate that as yet has not received a huge amount of ethical consideration but one that is very likely to quickly involve a number of different agencies. So far, the only official recognition has come from the European Parliament which on 27 January 2017 offered one of the first assessments of the potential of AI and robotics.[17] It is a fascinating document that reads more like science fiction than the dry musings of what has often been described as a Kafkaesque continental bureaucracy.

One observation under suggestion 6 in particular on page 41 of the 64-page document from the Committee on employment and social affairs which was canvassed for its views on robotics stands out:

> '6. Admits that robotics offers great potential for the support and relief, in particular, of people with a disability and elderly people in their everyday lives and could make a major contribution to their self-determined life and their inclusion in the labour market, is of the opinion that thorough consideration must be given to the question of what employment provisions might be necessary in terms of the labour force if the artificial or genetic development or supplementing of existing human capabilities results in people with extraordinary abilities, thereby fundamentally altering the meaning of the term "disability" and conferring an unassailable advantage on people with access to such technological innovations, tools and interventions which will naturally raise ethical and moral questions that should be examined thoroughly;'

However, as the singularity is still considered theoretical much of the debate around current AI regulation is pragmatic and centres on the development of a world that many are opting to describe as 'augmented intelligence' rather than AI: a view that suggests that we should use AI technology to both improve ourselves and improve the lot of humanity using AI to enlighten humanity.

It is a view propounded by Floridi, an adviser to the Turing Institute. For AI to be used properly he states that it must be regulated:

> 'I have been involved first-hand with that and I think is an effort worth promoting and it is the use of regulation to make sure that no company can go by itself but one where you define the bar for the whole sector.
>
> The example I provide here is with plastic bags at the supermarket. Everybody wants to do it. The customers, the supermarkets, society, the government but

---

17 See the Report (n 3).

no supermarket would have gone solo because it would have been a suicide. You have to do these things sector wide with legislation. So as long as we don't change the rules of competition, we're not going to see that kind of step up. The step up requires writing good rules for the game,'

Floridi added that one of the by-products of regulation could be the development of more ethical business practices:

'It is not going to happen naturally, but it has to happen. I think we have to help it by changing the mental conditions and the rules of the game. For example, in terms of our business model, some business models just do not facilitate that kind of approach. If you have a business model where the most important thing, depends on making your shareholders happy every quarter then it will not work. Yet if we change the business models by introducing other factors and methods for business incentivisation then we can begin to develop change. It is one of the promises of AI that we will be able to develop those models,"

Floridi also says that regulation of AI will inevitably drive ethical business practice, something he states will come at a cost:

'Some of the incentives we have seen for the environment have been criticised for not being economically intelligent. Who said they were supposed to be economic? They are expensive. We're spending money to send things in a different direction. It is going to cost, ethics in general is expensive, it does not come for free,'

He adds that the reason for the environmental issues we now face is because the environmental impact of waste has never been factored into the economic process.

The cost of AI ethics, says Floridi, would be a similar idea to a 'polluter pays principle' that AI may help in quantifying for future generations, adding that he had already advocated the creation of an AI software monitoring agency to the European Commission.

Floridi also stressed that in his opinion reputational harm will become a big factor for companies using AI, particularly as he expects company boards to create the new position of the Chief Data Ethics Officer, a role similar to that of Professor Blackman (quoted in Chapter 4).

As Floridi lays bare:

'External reputation is very important. If you start getting a reputation for being not one of the good guys that is going to be difficult. Business hiring is going to be more complicated and expensive. Contracts with other businesses become a little more difficult. Reputation is a big deal and the bigger you are the more visible you are. Reputation bubbles through a company from the bottom to the top.'

Dealing with the issues raised by AI, according to Floridi, is not a question of needing ideas on what needs to be regulated and why it is, he says, a question of political will:

'There are many, many voices suggesting regulation. It is not the lack of good ideas or a sense of what would be preferable, the decision is, are we going to do it? Are we going to implement it?'

Like Floridi, Professor Cate who, in Chapter 14, wrote about the 'Rights and Responsibilities' relating to AI, says that the areas for regulation are fairly clear:

'It will depend on firstly, what's the AI being used for? There might be some rules that would apply to all AI or all AI development, but generally speaking, you're going to want to think about what's the impact of the way the AI is being used?'

This argument supports the development of an agency similar to either the US' National Human Genome Research Institute or the UK's Genome UK, both organisations that supervise research while at the same time ensuring that it conforms to ethical guidelines. Such an agency has already been suggested in the European Parliament's 2017 Report.

As Cate, a former ethics adviser to the US Government and Microsoft states, AI regulation is all about context:

'AI used for marketing can be annoying, but it is not life changing. AI used to determine who gets to come into the country, or who gets arrested, or how long they get sentenced for, that's a lot more important and should be subject to a lot more oversight.

We want AI to be accountable and we want it to be under control. We do not want AI running rampant, or companies deciding to do whatever they want to do with it.'

As with Floridi, Cate thinks that there is a need to impose AI regulations, perhaps the reason for Alphabet's CEO Sundar Pichai exhorting the EU to introduce AI legislation similar to its GDPR initiative. Cate, again like Floridi and Future Intelligence, backs the creation of a monitoring agency to push through policy:

'It is a waste of time to try to spend a lot of time getting individuals to understand it one at a time. You want to regulate it. AI needs to be overseen or audited by an organisation that looks at results and can say, 'does the new facial recognition software used at the UK border keep out Blacks more frequently than it keeps out whites?

That's easy to measure that is the great thing about AI, it offers measurable digital results, you can regularly audit on an ongoing basis,'.

It is in this digital tendency of AI that the hope for regulation lies. The experts say the purpose of an AI program should be clear, and that if those making it can show that it does what is claimed and no more, then it should be capable of being certified for real-world use.

According to Dr Iain Brown, the UK Head of Data Science for the data analytics company SAS and Adjunct Professor of Marketing Analytics at the University of Southampton it is both a question of explainability and context. The rule of thumb, says Brown, should really be that if you do not know how a conclusion was arrived at by technology, or if you cannot explain it to a layman or laywoman, then really you should not go ahead with it. As he says:

'My point is on materiality. I see this as very much depending upon what type of decisions are being made, as to how transparent that needs to be. For example, we work with Amsterdam Medical Centre, in the area of image processing for cancer detection. For a patient what is important, are the CT scans, and the MRI scans, and that those patient records are being used as a preventative measure to diagnose a potential risk or potential cancerous cell that's developed, as a patient do, I really care how it came to that decision? If it has found something that's beneficial to me, I would want that information used by a clinician to decide on treatment. In those cases, you may not need as much transparency.

On the flip side of that, if an AI is deciding on whether to offer me a mortgage, and it was not able to explain to me why I had been rejected that has a potential detrimental impact on me that I need to know about. For example, bias could be present within that process. There is a materiality to that decision that I would say was important.'

For SAS' Brown there is another factor his research team have identified that will also sit alongside regulation, which is reputation. He thinks this will become increasingly important as we move into the AI age and could possibly become the basis for regulation:

'One of the risks for organisations is how they want to be seen by consumers and what is the agreement, whether implicit or explicit in place as to how they're going to use that data? I think from my perspective and again, what we're seeing in some of the research studies we carried out around the AI dividend divide is that there is a risk that organisations can create reputational damage by doing things consumers did not agree with. This means they need to think before designing an application what is that application going to be used for. I think that is a key because it can be almost as much of a deterrent as anything that another organisation could impose on them.'

It is, said Brown, the same point of equivocation that Floridi alluded to, whether to impose regulation or not is dependent on whether the political will exists or not. This is a position that the recent Parliamentary Committee on Online Harms may shed some light upon.

In summing up, the Committee of both Houses of Parliament stressed that the internet industry had been left to largely self-police when dealing with online harms, a situation that had evidently failed because the UK Houses of Parliament were now drawing up legislation to require the internet and social media companies to police activity on their platforms.

Whether this will mean that those companies, now some of the largest users of AI, will take a different attitude to the use of AI obviously remains to be seen. Brown says:

'A lot of organisations are trying to run quite quickly with implementing AI or machine learning strategies ...

My perspective on it is that organisations should be more proactive and making sure they have good business practices in place through the data collection, through data management, through the deployment of the modelling phase before regulations come down on them.

They should be pre-empting the case where inevitably there will be more controls around the usage of data. They should not be waiting for regulations to come into play before they do something about their processes today.'

According to Floridi, if we do take a different attitude, AI could usher in a golden era:

'We are moving from an economy of consumption to an economy of care and from an economy of things to an economy of experiences. I see digital technologies as an extraordinary outcome of human intelligence. We need to turn them into a force for good.'

Part 4

Final Verdicts

The View from the Bench

Lord Sales, Justice of the UK Supreme Court

Extract from The Sir Henry Brooke Lecture, 12 November 2019 – reproduced with permission

How should legal doctrine adapt to accommodate the new world, in which so many social functions are speeded up, made more efficient, but also made more impersonal by algorithmic computing processes?

At least with computer algorithms, one still has human agency in the background, guiding processes through admittedly complex computer programming. Still more profoundly, however, how should legal doctrine adapt to processes governed without human agency, by artificial intelligence – that is, by autonomous computers generating their own solutions, free from any direct human control?

We need to think now about the implications of making human lives subject to these processes, for fear of the frog in hot water effect. We, like the frog, sit pleasantly immersed in warm water with our lives made easier in various ways by information technology. But the water imperceptibly gets hotter and hotter until we find we have gone past a crisis point and our lives have changed irrevocably, in ways outside our control and for the worse, without us even noticing. The water becomes boiling and the frog is dead.[1]

Often there is no one is to blame. As James Williams points out in his book *Stand Out of Our Light*:

> "At 'fault' are more often the emergent dynamics of complex multiagent systems rather than the internal decision-making dynamics of a single individual. As W. Edwards Deming said, 'A bad system will beat a good person every time'."[2]

This aspect of the digital world and its effects poses problems for legal analysis.

I draw a conceptual distinction between algorithmic analysis and manipulation of information, on the one hand, and artificial intelligence on the other. There is no clear dividing line between these. The one shades into the other. Still, they are recognisable and useful general categories for the purposes of analysis. The main substance of my lecture is directed to the algorithmic analysis part of the picture, since that is really where we

---

1 Cf J. Williams, *Stand Out of Our Light: Freedom and Resistance in the Attention Economy* (2018), 93-94.
2 J. Williams, *Stand Out of Our Light* (n. 1), 102.

are located at the present. But many of my comments apply also to artificial intelligence, and at the end I deal with some distinct doctrinal issues which apply to AI as a distinct category.

The views expressed and any errors are my sole responsibility. An algorithm is a process or set of rules to be followed in problem-solving. It is a structured process. It proceeds in logical steps.

This is the essence of processes programmed into computers. They perform functions in logical sequence. Computers are transformational in so many areas because they are mechanically able to perform these functions at great speed and in relation to huge amounts of data, well beyond what is practicable or even possible for human beings. They give rise to a form of power which raises new challenges for the law, in its traditional roles of defining and regulating rights and of finding controls for illegitimate or inappropriate exercise of power. At the same time, alongside controlling abuse of power and abuse of rights, law has a function to provide a framework in which this new power can be deployed and used effectively for socially valuable purposes. In that sense, law should go with the flow and channel it, rather than merely resist it. The potential efficiency gains are huge, across private commercial activity and governmental, legislative and judicial activity. Information technology provides platforms for increased connectivity and speed of transacting.

So-called smart contracts are devised to allow self-regulation by algorithms, to reduce the costs of contracting and of policing the agreement. Distributed ledger technology, such as blockchain, can create secure property and contractual rights with much reduced transaction costs and reduced need for reliance on state enforcement.[3] Fintech is being devised to allow machines to assess credit risks and insurance risks at a fraction of the cost of performing such exercises by human agents.[4] In this way, access to credit and to insurance can be greatly expanded, with all that implies for enhancing human capacities to take action to create prosperity and protect against risk.

The use of digital solutions to deliver public welfare assistance offers the prospect of greatly reduced cost of administration, and so in theory the possibility of diverting the savings into more generous benefits. It also offers the potential to tailor delivery of assistance in a more fine-grained way, to feed through resources to those who need them most. The use of online courts through use of information technology offers the potential to improve access to justice and greatly reduce the time and cost taken to achieve resolution of disputes.

More widely, people increasingly live their lives in fundamentally important ways online, via digital platforms. They find it convenient, and then increasingly necessary, to shop online, access vital services online, and to express themselves and connect with other humans online.

What I am calling Artificial Intelligence is something at the stage beyond mere algorithmic analytical processes. I use 'artificial intelligence' as a shorthand for self-directed and self-adaptive computer activity. It arises where computer systems perform more complex tasks which previously required human intelligence and the application of on-the-spot judgment, such as driving a car. In some cases, AI involves machine learning, whereby an algorithm optimises its responses through experience as embodied in large amounts of data, with

3 World Bank Group, "Distributed Ledger Technology (DLT) and Blockchain" (2017).
4 See Lord Hodge, "The Potential and Perils of Financial Technology: can the law adapt to cope?", the First Edinburgh Fintech lecture, 14 March 2019.

limited or no human interference.[5] I take AI to involve machines which are capable of analysing situations and learning for themselves and then generating answers which may not even be foreseen or controlled by their programmers. It arises from algorithmic programming, but due to the complexity of the processes it carries out the outcome of the programming cannot be predicted by humans, however well informed. Here, the machine itself seems to be interposed between any human agency and what it, the machine, does.

Agency, in the sense of intelligence-directed activity performed for reasons, is fundamental to legal thought. For legal regulation of this sort of machine activity, we need to think not just of control of power, but also of how agency should be conceptualised. Should we move to ascribe legal personality to machines? And perhaps use ideas of vicarious liability? Or should we stick with human agency, but work with ideas of agency regarding risk creation, on a tort model, rather than direct correspondence between human thought and output in the form of specific actions intended by a specific human agent?

Underlying all these challenges are a series of inter-connected problems regarding (i) the lack of knowledge, understanding and expertise on the part of lawyers (I speak for myself, but I am not alone), and on the part of society generally; (ii) unwillingness on the part of programming entities, mainly for commercial reasons, to disclose the program coding they have used, so that even with technical expertise it is difficult to dissect what has happened and is happening; and (iii) a certain rigidity at the point of the interaction of coding and law, or rather where coding takes the place of law.

These problems play out in a world in which machine processing is increasingly pervasive, infiltrating all aspects of our lives; intangible, located in functions away in the cloud rather than in physical machines sitting on our desks; and global, unbound by geographical and territorial jurisdictional boundaries. All these features of the digital world pose further problems for conventional legal approaches.

Law is itself a sort of algorithmic discipline: if factors A, B and C are present, then by a process of logical steps legal response Z should occur. Apart from deliberate legislative change, legal development has generally occurred from minor shifts in legal responses which take place to accommodate background moral perspectives on a case, which perspectives themselves may be changing over time. With algorithms in law, as applied by humans, there is scope for this to happen in the context of implementation of the law. But algorithms in computer code are not in themselves open to this kind of change in the course of implementation. Richard Susskind brought this home to me with an analogy from the card game Patience. It has set rules, but a human playing with cards can choose not to follow them. There is space to try out changes. But when playing Patience in a computer version, it is simply not possible to make a move outside the rules of the game.[6]

So coding algorithms create a danger of freezing particular relationships in set configurations with set distributions of power, which seem to be natural and beyond any question of contestation. The wider perceptual control which is noticeable as our world becomes increasingly digital also tends to freeze categories of thought along tramrails written in

---

5   Financial Stability Board, 'Artificial Intelligence and machine learning in financial services' (1 November 2017).
6   Jamie Susskind refers to this effect as "force": algorithms which control our activity force certain actions upon us, and we can do no other: J. Susskind, *Future Politics: Living Together in a World Transformed by Tech* (2018), ch. 6

code.[7] Unless resisted, this can limit imagination and inspiration even for legislative responses to digitisation.

All this erodes human capacities to question and change power relations.[8] Also, the coding will reflect the unspoken biases of the human coders and in ways that seem beyond challenge. Moreover, coding algorithms are closed systems. As written, they may not capture everything of potential significance for the resolution of a human problem. With the human application of law, the open-textured nature of ideas like justice and fairness creates the possibility for immanent critique of the rules being applied and leaves room for wider values, not explicitly encapsulated in law's algorithm, to enter the equation leading to a final outcome. That is true not just for the rules of the common law, but in the interstices of statutory interpretation.[9] These features are squeezed out when using computer coding. There is a disconnect in the understanding available in the human application of a legal algorithm and the understanding of the coding algorithm in the machine. This is the rigidity I have mentioned which enters at the point of the intersection of law and coding. It is a machine variant of the old problem of law laid down in advance as identified by Aristotle: the legislator cannot predict all future circumstances in which the stipulated law will come to be applied, and so cannot ensure that the law will always conform to its underlying rationale and justification at the point of its application. His solution was to call for a form of equity or flexibility at the point of application of the law, what he called epieikeia (usually translated as equity), to keep it aligned to its rationale while it is being applied and enforced.[10]

A coding algorithm, like law, is a rule laid down in advance to govern a future situation. However, this form of equity or rule modification or adjustment in the application of law is far harder to achieve in a coding algorithm under current conditions.

It may be that at some point in the future AI systems, at a stage well beyond simple algorithmic systems, will be developed which will have the fine-grained sensitivity to rule application to allow machines to take account of equity informed by relevant background moral, human rights and constitutional considerations. Machines may well develop to a stage at which they can recognise hard cases within the system and operate a system of triage to refer those cases to human administrators or judges, or indeed decide the cases themselves to the standard achievable by human judges today.[11] Application of rules of equity or recognition of hard cases, where different moral and legal considerations clash, is ultimately dependent on pattern recognition, which AI is likely to be able to handle.[12] But we are not there yet.

As things stand, using the far more crude forms of algorithmic coding that we do, there is a danger of losing a sense of code as something malleable, changeable, potentially flawed and requiring correction. Subjecting human life to processes governed by code means that code can gain a grip on our thinking which reduces human capacities and diminishes political choice. This effect of the rigid or frozen aspect of coding is amplified by the other two elements to which I called attention: (i) ignorance among lawyers and in

---

7   J. Susskind, *Future Politics*, (n.6), ch. 8.
8   Cf Ben Golder, *Foucault and the Politics of Rights* (2015).
9   See e.g. the principle of legality and the effect of section 3 of the Human Rights Act 1998: P. Sales, "A Comparison of the Principle of Legality and Section 3 of the Human Rights Act 1998" (2009) 125 LQR 598. These are but two specific examples of a much wider phenomenon.
10 Aristotle, *Nichomachean Ethics*, V. 10. 1137b, 12-29.
11 For a discussion of the possibilities, see R. Susskind, *Online Courts and the Future of Justice* (2019), Part IV.
12 See J. Susskind, *Future Politics: Living Together in a World Transformed by Tech* (2018), 107-110, on the ability of AI to apply standards as well as rules.

society generally about coding and its limitations and capacity for error; and (ii) secrecy surrounding coding which is actually being used. The impact of the latter is amplified by the willingness of governments to outsource the design and implementation of systems for delivery of public services to large tech companies, on the footing that they have the requisite coding skills

Philip Alston, UN Special Rapporteur on Extreme Poverty and Human Rights [in October 2019] presented a report on digital welfare systems to the UN General Assembly.[13] He identifies two pervasive problems. Governments are reluctant to regulate tech firms, for fear of stifling innovation, while at the same time the private sector is resistant to taking human rights systematically into account in designing their systems.

Alston refers to a speech by Prime Minister Johnson to the UN General Assembly on 24 September 2019 in which he warned that we are slipping into a world involving round the clock surveillance, the perils of algorithmic decision-making, the difficulty of appealing against computer determinations, and the inability to plead extenuating circumstances against an algorithmic decision-maker.

Through lack of understanding and access to relevant information, the power of the public to criticise and control the systems which are put in place to undertake vital activities in both the private and the public sphere is eroded. Democratic control of law and the public sphere is being lost.

In his book, *How Democracy Ends*,[14] David Runciman argues that the appeal of modern democracy has been founded on a combination of, first, providing mechanisms for individuals to have their voice taken into account, thereby being afforded respect in the public sphere, and secondly, its capacity to deliver long term benefits in the form of a chance of sharing in stability, prosperity and peace. But he says that the problem for democracy in the twenty-first century is that these two elements are splitting apart. Effective solutions to shared problems depend more and more on technical expertise, so that there has been a movement to technocracy, that is, rule by technocrats using expertise which is not available or comprehensible to the public at large. The dominance of economic and public life by algorithmic coding and AI is an important element of this. It has the effect that the traditional, familiar ways of aligning power with human interests through democratic control by citizens, regulation by government and competition in markets, are not functioning as they used to.

At the same time, looking from the other end of the telescope, from the point of view of the individual receiving or seeking access to services, there can be a sense of being subjected to power which is fixed and remorseless,[15] an infernal machine over which they have no control and which is immune to any challenge, or to any appeal to have regard to extenuating circumstances, or to any plea for mercy. For access to digital platforms and digital services in the private sphere, the business model is usually take it or leave it: accept access to digital platforms on their terms requiring access to your data, and

---

13 Report A/74/48037, presented on 18 October 2019.
14 D. Runciman, *How Democracy Ends* (2018).
15 This sense exists in some contexts, while in others the emerging digital systems may be hugely empowering, enabling far more effective access to a range of goods, such as, education, medical guidance and assistance, and help in understanding legal entitlements: see R. Susskind and D. Susskind, *The Future of the Professions: How Technology Will Transform the Work of Human Experts* (2015). Of course, what is needed are legal structures which facilitate this process of enhancing individuals' agency while avoiding the possible negative side-effects which undermine it.

on their very extensive contract terms excluding their legal responsibility, or be barred from participating in an increasingly important aspect of the human world. This may be experienced as no real choice at all. The movement begins to look like a reversal of Sir Henry Maine's famous progression from status to contract. We seem to be going back to status again.

Meanwhile, access to public services is being depersonalised. The individual seems powerless in the face of machine systems and loses all dignity in being subjected to their control. The movement here threatens to be from citizen to consumer and then on to serf.

Malcolm Bull, in his recent book *On Mercy*,[16] argues that it is mercy rather than justice which is foundational for politics. Mercy, as a concession by the powerful to the vulnerable, makes rule by the powerful more acceptable to those on the receiving end, and hence more stable. In a few suggestive pages at the end of the book, under the heading 'Robotic Politics', he argues that with a world becoming dominated by AI, we humans all become vulnerable to power outside our knowledge and control; therefore, he says, we should program into the machines a capacity for mercy.[17]

The republican response to the danger of power and domination, namely of arming citizens with individual rights, will still be valuable. But it will not be enough, if the asymmetries of knowledge and power are so great that citizens are in practice unable to deploy their rights effectively.

So what we need to look for are ways of trying to close the gap between democratic, public control and technical expertise, to meet the problem identified by Runciman; ways of trying to build into our digital systems a capacity for mercy, responsiveness to human need and equity in the application of rules, to meet the problem identified by Malcolm Bull; and ways of fashioning rights which are both suitable to protect the human interests which are under threat in this new world and effective.

We are not at a stage to meet Malcolm Bull's challenge, and rights regimes will not be adequate. People are not being protected by the machines and often are not capable of taking effective action to protect themselves. Therefore, we need to build a structure of legal obligations on those who design and operate algorithmic and AI systems which requires them to have regard to and protect the interests of those who are subject to those systems.

Because digital processes are more fixed in their operation than the human algorithms of law and operate with immense speed at the point of application of rules, we need to focus on ways of scrutinising and questioning the content of digital systems at the ex-ante design stage. We also need to find effective mechanisms to allow for systematic ex post review of how digital systems are working and, so far as is possible without destroying the efficiency gains which they offer, to allow for ex post challenges to individual concrete decisions which they produce, to allow for correction of legal errors and the injection of equity and mercy.

Precisely because algorithmic systems are so important in the delivery of commercial and public services, they need to be designed by building in human values and protection for

---

16 16 M. Bull, *On Mercy* (2019).
17 Pp. 159-161.

fundamental human interests.[18] For example, they need to be checked for biases based on gender, sexuality, class, age, ability. This is being recognised. As Jamie Susskind observes in his book *Future Politics*[19], progress is being made toward developing principles of algorithmic audit. On 12 February this year the European Parliament adopted a resolution declaring that "algorithms in decision-making systems should not be deployed without a prior algorithmic impact assessment …".[20]

The question then arises, how should we provide for *ex ante* review of code in the public interest? If, say, a government department is going to deploy an algorithmic program, it should conduct an impact assessment, much as it does now in relation to the environmental impacts and equality impacts in relation to the introduction of policy. But government may not have the technical capability to do this well, particularly when one bears in mind that it may have contracted out the coding and design of the system on grounds that the relevant expertise lies in the private sector. And those in Parliament who are supposed to be scrutinising what the government does are unlikely to have the necessary technical expertise either. Further, it might also be said that provision needs to be made for impact assessment of major programs introduced in the private sector, where again government is unlikely to have the requisite expert capability. Because of lack of information and expertise, the public cannot be expected to perform their usual general policing function in relation to service providers.

Therefore, there seems to be a strong argument that a new agency for scrutiny of programs in light of the public interest should be established, which would constitute a public resource for government, Parliament, the courts and the public generally. It would be an expert commission staffed by coding technicians, with lawyers and ethicists to assist them. The commission could be given access to commercially sensitive code on strict condition that its confidentiality is protected. However, it would invite representations from interested persons and groups in civil society and, to the fullest extent possible, it would publish reports from its reviews, to provide transparency in relation to the digital processes.

Perhaps current forms of pre-legislative scrutiny of Acts of Parliament offer the beginnings of an appropriate model. For example, the Joint Committee on Human Rights scrutinises draft legislation for its compatibility with human rights and reports back to Parliament on any problems.

But those introducing algorithmic systems are widely dispersed in society and the across the globe, so one would need some form of trawling mechanism to ensure that important algorithms were gathered in and brought within the purview of pre-scrutiny by the commission. That is by no means straightforward. The emphasis may have to be more on ex post testing and audit checking of private systems after deployment.

Also, it cannot be emphasised too strongly that society must be prepared to devote the resources and expertise to perform this scrutiny to a proper standard. It will not be cheap. But the impact of algorithms on our lives is so great that I would suggest that the likely cost will be proportionate to the risks which this will protect us against.

---

18 See J. Williams, *Stand Out of Our Light*, 106: the goal is "to bring the technologies of our attention onto our side. This means aligning their goals and values with our own. It means creating an environment of incentives for design that leads to the creation of technologies that are aligned with or interests from the outset."
19 J. Susskind, *Future Politics: Living Together in a World Transformed by Tech* (2018), 355.
20 European Parliament resolution of 12 February 2019 on a comprehensive European industrial policy on artificial intelligence and robotics (2018/2088(INI)), Strasbourg.

There should also be scope for legal challenges to be brought regarding the adoption of algorithmic programs, including at the ex-ante stage. In fact, this seems to be happening already.[21] This is really no more than an extension of the well-established jurisprudence on challenges to adoption of policies which are unlawful[22] and is in line with recent decisions on unfairness challenges to entire administrative systems.[23] However, the extension will have procedural consequences. The claimant will need to secure disclosure of the coding in issue. If it is commercially sensitive, the court might have to impose confidentiality rings, as happens in intellectual property and competition cases. And the court will have to be educated by means of expert evidence, which on current adversarial models means experts on each side with live evidence tested by cross-examination. This will be expensive and time consuming, in ways which will feel alien in a judicial review context. I see no easy way round this, unless we create some system whereby the court can refer the code for neutral expert evaluation by my algorithm commission or an independently appointed expert, with a report back to inform the court regarding the issues which emerge from an understanding of the coding.

The *ex-ante* measures should operate in conjunction with ex post measures. How well a program is working and the practical effects it is having may only emerge after a period of operation. There should be scope for a systematic review of results as a check after a set time, to see if the program needs adjustment.

More difficult is to find a way to integrate ways of challenging individual decisions taken by government programs as they occur while preserving the speed and efficiency which such programs offer. It will not be possible to have judicial review in every case. I make two suggestions. First, it may be possible to design systems whereby if a service user is dissatisfied they can refer the decision on to a more detailed assessment level – a sort of 'advanced search option', which would take a lot more time for the applicant to fill in, but might allow for more fine-grained scrutiny. Secondly, the courts and litigants, perhaps in conjunction with my algorithm commission, could become more proactive in identifying cases which raise systemic issues and marshalling them together in a composite procedure, by using pilot cases or group litigation techniques.

The creation of an algorithm commission would be part of a strategy for meeting the first and second challenges I mentioned – (i) lack of technical knowledge in society and (ii) preservation of commercial secrecy in relation to code. The commission would have the technical expertise and all the knowledge necessary to be able to interrogate specific coding designed for specific functions. I suggest it could provide a vital social resource to restore agency for public institutions – to government, Parliament, the courts and civil society – by supplying the expert understanding which is required for effective law-making, guidance and control in relation to digital systems. It would also be a way of addressing the third challenge – (iii) rigidity in the interface between law and code – because the commission would include experts who understand the fallibility and malleability of code and can constantly remind government, Parliament and the courts about this.

---

21 See the report in The Guardian, 30 October 2019, p. 15, "Home Office faces legal case over visa algorithm program".
22 *Gillick v West Norfolk and Wisbech Area Health Authority* [1986] AC 112; *R (Suppiah) v Secretary of State for the Home Department* [2011] EWHC 2 (Admin), [137]; *R (S and KF) v Secretary of State for Justice* [2012] EWHC 1810 (Admin), [37].
23 23 See e.g. *R (Detention Action) v First-tier Tribunal (Immigration & Asylum Chamber)* [2015] EWCA Civ 840; [2015] 1 WLR 5341; *R (Howard League for Penal Reform) v Lord Chancellor* [2017] EWCA Civ 244; [2017] 4 WLR 92; and F. Powell, "Structural Procedural Review: An Emerging Trend in Public Law" (2017) JR 83.

Already models exist in academia and civil society, bringing together tech experts and ethicists.[24] Contributions from civil society are valuable, but they are not sufficient. The issues are so large, and the penetration of coding into the life of society is so great, that the resources of the state should be brought to bear on this as well.

As well as being an informational resource, one could conceive of the commission as a sort of independent regulator, on the model of regulators of utilities. It would ensure that critical coding services were made available to all and that services made available to the public meet relevant standards.

More ambitiously, perhaps we should think of it almost as a sort of constitutional court. There is an analogy with control and structuring of society through law. Courts deal with law and constitutional courts deal with deeper structures of the law which provide a principled framework for the political and public sphere. The commission would police baseline principles which would structure coding and ensure it complied with standards on human rights. One could even imagine a form of two-way reference procedure, between the commission and the courts (when the commission identifies a human rights issue on which it requires guidance) and between the courts and the commission (when the courts identify a coding issue on which they require assistance).

The commission would pose its own dangers, arising from an expert elite monitoring an expert elite. To some degree there is no escape from this. The point of the commission is to have experts do on behalf of society what society cannot do itself. The dangers could be mitigated, by making the commission's procedures and its reports as transparent and open as possible.

All this is to try to recover human agency and a sense of digital tech as our tool to improve things, not to rule us. Knowledge really is power in this area. We need to find a way of making the relevant technical knowledge available in the public domain, to civil society, the government, the courts and Parliament. Coding is structuring our lives more and more. No longer is the main grounding of our existence given by the material conditions of nature, albeit as moulded by industrial society. Law has been able operate effectively as a management tool for that world. But now coding is becoming as important as nature for providing the material grounds of our existence.[25] It is devised and manipulated by humans, and will reflect their own prejudices and interests. Its direction and content are inevitably political issues.[26] We need to find effective ways to manage this dimension of our lives collectively in the interests of us all.

A further project for the law is to devise an appropriate structure of individual rights, to give people more control over their digital lives and enhance individual agency. One model is that proposed by the 5Rights Foundation,[27] who have called for five rights to enable a child to enjoy a respectful and supportive relationship with the digital environment: i) the right to remove data they have posted online, ii) the right to know who is holding and profiting from their information and how it is being used, iii) the right to safety and support if confronted

---

24 For instance, in the field of digital healthcare systems, the International Digital Health and AI Research Collaborative was established in October 2019 to bring together health experts, tech experts and ethicists to establish common standards for delivery of digital health services. It will have the capacity to review and critique systems adopted by governments or big tech companies.

25 cf Simone Weil, "Reflections Concerning the Causes of Liberty and Social Oppression" in *Oppression and Liberty*, trans. A. Wills and J. Petrie (1958).

26 See J. Susskind, *Future Politics* (n. 6).

27 https://5rightsfoundation.com

by troubling or upsetting scenarios online, iv) the right to informed and conscious use of technology, and v) the right to digital literacy. These need to be debated at a legislative level. Such a rights regime could usefully be extended to adults as well.

In view of the global nature of the digital world, there also has to be a drive for cooperation in setting international standards. Several initiatives are being taken in this area by international organisations. An algorithm commission could be an important resource for this, and if done well could give the UK significant influence in this process.[28] Following through on these 16 initiatives is important because there is a geographic bias in the production of digital technologies. In the years 2013-2016, between 70 and 100 per cent of the top 25 cutting edge digital technologies were developed in only five countries: China, Taiwan, Japan, South Korea and the USA.[29]

I will turn now to sketch some preliminary thoughts about how legal doctrine may have to adapt in the increasingly digital age. Such are the demands of bringing expertise and technical knowledge to bear that it is not realistic to expect the common law, with its limited capacity to change law and the slow pace at which it does so, to play a major role.[30] It may assist with adaptation in the margins. But the speed of change is so great and the expertise which needs to be engaged is of such a technical nature that the main response must come in legislative form. What is more, the permeability of national borders to the flow of digital technologies is so great, that there will have to be international cooperation to provide common legal standards and effective cross-border regulation.

(A) The challenges of an algorithmic world

In the time available I offer some thoughts at a very high level of generality in relation to three areas: (1) commercial activity; (2) delivery of public services; and (3) the political sphere.

(1) Commercial activity.

I will highlight four topics.

First, there is the attempt to use digital and encryption solutions to create virtual currencies free from state control. However, as Karen Yeung observes, points of contact between these currency regimes and national jurisdictions will continue to exist. The state will not simply retreat from legal control. There will still need to be elements of state regulation in relation to the risks they represent. She maps out three potential forms of engagement, which she characterises as (a) hostile evasion (or cat and mouse), (b) efficient alignment (or the joys of (patriarchal) marriage),). and (c) supporting novel forms of

---

28 E.g. the G20 AI Principles (2019), Tsubuka; the OECD Council Recommendation on Artificial Intelligence (2019) OECD/Legal/0449, calling for shared values of human-centredness, transparency, explainability, robustness, security, safety and accountability; the UN Secretary-General's High-Level Panel on Digital Cooperation report, *The Age of Interdependence* (June 2019), which emphasises multi-stakeholder coordination and sharing of data sets to bolster trust, policies for digital inclusion and equality, review of compatibility of digital systems with human rights, importance of accountability and transparency; that report indicates that the UN's 75th anniversary in 2020 may be linked to launch of a "Global Commitment for Digital Cooperation". See generally, A. Jobin, M. Ienca, & E. Vayena, "The global landscape of AI ethics guidelines" (2019) Nature Machine Intelligence 1(9), 389-399.
29 OECD (2019) *Measuring the Digital Transformation – A roadmap to the future.*
30 See also Lord Hodge (n. 4

peer-to-peer co-ordination to reduce transactional friction associated with the legal process (or uneasy co-existence).[31]

Second, there is the loss of individuals' control over contracting and the related issue of accessibility to digital platforms. Online contracting has taken old concerns about boiler plate standard clauses to new extremes. For access, one has to click to accept terms which are massively long and are never read. Margaret Radin has written about the deformation of contract in the information society.[32] She describes what she calls "Massively Distributed Boilerplate" removing ordinary remedial rights. She argues for a new way of looking at the problem, involving a shift from contract to tort, via a law of misleading or deceptive disclosure. A service provider would be liable for departures from reasonable expectations which are insufficiently signalled to the consumer.

The information and power asymmetries in the digital world are so great that we need a coherent strategic response along a spectrum: from competition law at the macro level, to protect against abuse of dominant positions[33]; to rights of fair access to digital platforms; to extended notions of fiduciary obligation in the conduct of relationships[34] and an expansion of doctrines of abuse of rights, which in the UK currently exist only in small pockets of the common law[35] and statute;[36] to control of unfair terms and rebalancing of rights at the micro level of individual contracts.

Third, intellectual property has grown in importance and this will continue, as economic value shifts ever more to services and intangibles. A major project is likely to be development of ideas of personal data as property of the individuals from whom they are derived, for them to participate in their commercial exploitation and to have rights of portability. On the other hand, the veto rights created by intellectual property are likely to become qualified, so as not to impede the interconnected and global nature of the digital world. They may become points creating rights of fair return to encourage innovation as economic life flows through and round them, as has happened with patent rights under so-called FRAND regimes. In these regimes, as the price of being part of global operating standards, patent holders give irrevocable unilateral undertakings for the producers and consumers of tech products to use their patents on payment of a fee which is fair, reasonable and non-discriminatory.[37] It is possible that these sorts of solutions may come to be imposed by law by states operating pursuant to international agreements.

The fourth topic is the use of digital techniques to reduce transaction costs in policing of contracts, through smart contracts which are self-executing, without interventions of humans. An example is, where payment for a service delivered and installed on a computer fails to register on time, the computer shuts off the service. Smart contracts will become

---

31 K. Yeung, "Regulation by Blockchain: the Emerging Battle for Supremacy between the Code of Law and Code as Law" (2019) 82 MLR 207.

32 M. Radin, "The Deformation of Contract in the Information Society" (2017) 37 OJLS 505.

33 Autorité de la concurrence and Bundeskartellamt, *Algorithms and Compétition* (November 2019).

34 34 Cf *White v Jones* [1995] 2 AC 207, 271-272, per Lord Browne-Wilkinson: fiduciary obligations are imposed on a person taking decisions in relation to the management of the property or affairs of another.

35 35 See e.g. J. Murphy, "Malice as an Ingredient of Tort Liability" [2019] CLJ 355.

36 36 See e.g. s. 994 of the Companies Act 2006, giving members of a company the right to complain of abuse of rights by the majority where this constitutes unfair prejudice to the interests of the minority.

37 *Huawei Technologies Co. Ltd v Unwired Planet International Ltd* [2018] EWCA Civ 2344. The case is under appeal to the Supreme Court. See also the discussion about FRAND regimes in the communication from the Commission, the Council and the European Economic and Social Committee dated 2017 (COM (2017) 712 final), referred to at para [60] in the Court of Appeal judgment.

more sophisticated. They will create substantial efficiencies. But sometimes they will misfunction, and legal doctrine will need to adapt to that, in ways that are supportive of the technology and of what the parties seek to do. The recent decision in Singapore in *B2C2 Ltd v Quoine Pte Ltd*[38] provides an arresting illustration. A glitch arising from the interaction of a currency trader's algorithmic trading program with a currency trading platform's program resulted in automatic trades being effected to purchase currency at about 1/250th of its true value, thereby realising a huge profit for the trader. The trading platform was not permitted to unravel these trades. Defences based on implication of contract terms, mistake and unjust enrichment all failed.[39] The judge had to make sense of the concept of mistake in contract when two computer programs trade with each other. He did so by looking at the minds and expectations of the programmers, even though they were not involved in the trades themselves.[40] But in future the programs may become so sophisticated and operate so independently that it may be that this process of looking back through them to the minds of those who created them will seem completely unreal. Legal doctrine is going to have to adapt to this new world.

(2) Public administration, welfare and the justice system

Digital government has the potential for huge efficiency savings in the delivery of public services and provision of social welfare. But it carries substantial risks as well, in terms of enhancement of state power in relation to the individual, loss of responsiveness to individual circumstances and the potential to undermine important values which the state should be striving to uphold, including human dignity and basic human rights. These include rights of privacy and fair determination of civil rights and obligations. Philip Alston writes in his report of the "grave risk of stumbling zombie-like into a digital welfare dystopia" in Western countries.

He argues that we should take human rights seriously and regulate accordingly; should ensure legality of processes and transparency; promote digital equality; protect economic and social rights in the digital welfare state, as well as civil and political rights; and seek to resist the idea of the inevitability of a digital only future.

Legal scholars Carol Harlow and Richard Rawlings emphasise that the implications of the emergent digital revolution for the delivery of public services are likely in the near future to pose a central challenge for administrative law.[41] Procedures, such as allow for transparency, accountability and participation, are a repository for important values of good governance in administrative law.[42] But it is administrative procedures which are coming under pressure with the digitisation of government services. The speed of decision-making in digital systems will tend to require the diversion of legal control and judicial review away from the individual decision towards the coding of the systems and their overall design.

Similarly, online courts offer the opportunities for enhanced efficiency in the delivery of public services in the form of the justice system, allowing enhanced understanding of rights for individuals and enhanced and affordable access to justice. But the new systems have to

---

38 [2019] SGHC (I) 03.
39 The case is going on appeal.
40 Para. [210].
41 C. Harlow and R. Rawlings, "Proceduralism and Automation: Challenges to the Values of Administrative Law" in E. Fisher and A. Young (eds), *The Foundations and Future of Public Law* (2020, forthcoming), ch. 14.
42 Harlow and Rawlings (n. 39), 297.

allow space for the procedural values which are at the heart of a fair and properly responsive system of justice.[43]

(3) The interface with politics and democracy.

A number of points should be made here. The tech world clearly places our democracy under pressure. Law is both the product of democracy, in the form of statutes passed by Parliament, and a foundation of democracy, in the form of creating a platform of protected rights and capacities which legitimises our democratic procedures and enables them to function to give effect to the general will.[44] I have already mentioned the dilemma identified by David Runciman, namely the problem of disconnection between democracy and technical control in a public space dominated by code. There are plainly other strains as well. Here I am going to call attention to four. Time does not allow me to explore solutions in any detail. As a society we are going to have to be imaginative about how we address them. The task is an urgent one.

First, we are witnessing a fracturing of the public sphere. Democracy of the kind with which we were familiar in the twentieth century was effective because Parliament worked in the context of a communal space for debating issues in the national press, television and radio, which generated broad consensus around fundamental values and what could be regarded as fact. Jürgen Habermas, for example, gave an attractive normative account of democracy according to which legislation could be regarded as the product of an extended process of gestation of public opinion through debate in the communal space, which then informed the political and ultimately legislative process and was put into refined and concrete statutory form by that process.[45] But information technology allows people to retreat from that communal space into highly particularistic echo-chamber siloes of like-minded individuals, who reinforce each other's views and never have to engage or compromise with the conflicting views of others. What previously could be regarded as commonly accepted facts are denounced as fake news, so the common basis for discussion of the world is at risk of collapse. In elections, the detailed information about individuals harvested by computing platforms allows voters to be targeted by messaging directed to their own particular predilections and prejudices, without the need to square the circle of appealing to other points of view at the same time. We need to find ways of reconstituting a common public space.

Secondly, Jamie Susskind points out that the most immediate political beneficiaries of the ongoing tech revolution will be the state and big tech firms:

> "The state will gain a supercharged ability to enforce the law, and certain powerful tech firms will be able to define the limits of our liberty, determine the health of our democracy, and decide vital questions of social justice."[46]

There is already concern about the totalitarian possibilities of state control which are being illustrated with China's social credit system, in which computers monitor the social behaviour of citizens in minute detail and rewards or withholds benefits according to how they are marked by the state. But Susskind argues that digital tech also opens up possibilities

---

43 See generally R. Susskind, *Online Courts and the Future of Justice* (2019).
44 See P. Sales, "Legalism in Constitutional Law: Judging in a Democracy" (2018) Public Law 687.
45 J. Habermas, *Between Facts and Norms*, trans. William Rehg (1996), ch. 8; C. Zurn, *Deliberative Democracy and the Institutions of Judicial Review* (2007), 239-243; P. Sales, "The Contribution of Legislative Drafting to the Rule of Law" [2018] CLJ 630.
46 *Future Politics* (n. 6), 346

for new forms of democracy and citizen engagement, and that to protect people from servitude we need to exploit these new avenues to keep the power of the supercharged state in check.[47] In relation to the tech companies, he argues for regulation to ensure transparency and structural regulation to break up massive concentrations of power. Structural regulation would be aimed at ensuring liberty for individuals and that the power of the tech companies is legitimate.[48]

Thirdly, James Williams, in his book *Stand Out of Our Light*,[49] identifies a further subtle threat to democracy arising from the pervasiveness of information technology and the incessant claims. that it makes on our attention. According to him, the digital economy is based on the commercial effort to capture our attention. In what he calls the Age of Attention, information abundance produces attention scarcity. At risk is not just our attention, but our capacity to think deeply and dispassionately about issues and hence even to form what can be regarded as a coherent will in relation to action. He points out that the will is the source of the authority of democracy. He observes that as the digital attention economy is compromising human will, it therefore strikes "at the very foundations of democracy", and that this could "directly threaten not only individual freedom and autonomy, but also our collective ability to pursue any politics worth having."[50]

He argues that we must reject "the present regime of attentional serfdom" and instead "reengineer our world so that we can give attention to what matters."[51] That is a big and difficult project. As Williams says, the issue is one of self-regulation, at both individual and collective levels. [52] It seems that law will have to have some part to play in supporting achieving it, perhaps through some form of public regulation. We have made the first steps to try to fight another crisis of self-regulation, obesity, through supportive public regulation. Similarly, in relation to the digital world, as Williams points out, it is not realistic to expect people to "bear the burdens of impossible self-regulation, to suddenly become superhuman and take on the armies of industrialized persuasion".[53] But at the moment, it is unclear how public regulation would work and whether there would be the political will to impose it.

Fourthly, the law has an important role to play in protecting the private sphere in which individuals live their lives and in regulating surveillance. For example, the case law of the European Court of Human Rights[54] and of our own Investigatory Powers Tribunal[55] sets conditions for the exercise of surveillance powers by the intelligence agencies and provides an effective way of monitoring such exercise.

(B) The challenges of Artificial Intelligence

Some of the challenges to legal doctrine in relation to AI will be extrapolations from those in relation to algorithmic programming. But some will be different in kind. At the root of

---

47 *Future Politics* (n. 6), 347-348 and ch. 13, "Democracy in the Future".
48 According to Susskind's vision, the regulation would implement a new separation of powers, according to which "no firm is allowed a monopoly over each of the means of force, scrutiny, and perception-control" and "no firm is allowed significant control over more than one of the means of force, scrutiny, and perception control together": *Future Politics* (n. 6), 354-359.
49 J. Williams, *Stand Out of Our Light*, (n. 1).
50 *Stand Out of Our Light* (n. 1), 47.
51 *Stand Out of Our Light* (n. 1), 127.
52 *Stand Out of Our Light* (n. 1), 20.
53 *Stand Out of Our Light* (n. 1), 101.
54 E.g. *Liberty v United Kingdom*, app. 58243/00, ECtHR, judgment of 1 July 2008.
55 E.g. *Privacy International v Secretary of State for Foreign and Commonwealth Affairs* [2018] UKIP Trib IPT 15_110_CH 2 and related judgments.

these is the interposition of the agency of machines between human agents and events which have legal consequences. An example which is much discussed is that of a driverless car which has an accident.

Existing legal doctrine suggests possible analogies on which a coherent legal regime might be based. The merits and demerits of each have to be compared and evaluated before final decisions are made. We should be trying to think this through now. There is already a burgeoning academic literature in this area, engaging with fundamental legal ideas. Legislation at the EU level is beginning to come under consideration, stemming from a European Parliament Resolution and Report in January 2017.[56] On the issue of liability for the acts of robots and other AIs, the resolution proposes[57] including a compulsory insurance scheme, compensation fund and, in the case of sophisticated AIs, "a specific legal status for robots in the long run".

On one approach,[58] sophisticated AIs with physical manifestations, such as self-driving cars, could be given legal personhood like a company.[59] However, types of AI differ considerably and a one-size-fits-all approach is unlikely to be appropriate.[60] It may be necessary to distinguish between ordinary software used in appliances, for which a straightforward product liability approach is appropriate, and that used in complex AI products.[61]

A contrary approach is to maintain the traditional paradigm of treating even sophisticated AIs as mere products for liability purposes.[62] A middle way has also been proposed, in which some but not all AIs might be given separate legal personality, depending on their degree of autonomous functionability and social need;[63] but may be denied "[i]f the practical and legal responsibility associated with actions can be traced back to a legal person".[64] There are concerns about allowing creators or operators of AIs to enjoy a cap on liability for the acts of such the machines, which Jacob Turner calls the "Robots as Liability Shields" objection.[65]

---

56 European Parliament, *Report on civil law rules of robotics* (A8-0005/2017) (27 January 2017) and European Parliament, *Resolution on civil law rules of robotics* (P8_TA(2017)0051) (27 January 2017).

57 Para 59.

58 58 See e.g. Jiahong Chen and Paul Burgess, "The boundaries of legal personhood: how spontaneous intelligence can problematise differences between humans, artificial intelligence, companies and animals" (2019) 27 Artificial Intelligence and Law 73-92. See also G. Hallevy, *When robots kill: artificial intelligence under criminal law* (2013); S. Bayern, "The Implications of Modern Business-Entity Law for the Regulation of Autonomous Systems" (2016) 7(2) European Journal of Risk Regulation 297-309; Bayern et al, "Company Law and Autonomous Systems: A Blueprint for Lawyers, Entrepreneurs, and Regulators" (2017) 9(2) Hastings Science and Technology Law Journal 135-162.

59 59 The common factors being (1) physical location, (2) human creation for a purpose or function and (3) policy reasons for anchoring liability back to other natural or legal persons: Chen and Burgess (n. 58), p.81.

60 Chen and Burgess (n. 58), p. 74.

61 Chen and Burgess (n. 58), p 90.

62 S. Solaiman, "Legal personality of robots, corporations, idols and chimpanzees: a quest for legitimacy" (2017) 25 (2) Artificial Intelligence and Law 155-179. Solaiman objects to extending the corporate model to sophisticated AIs, principally on the grounds that this would serve the undesirable aim of exonerating the creators and users from liability where significant harm to humans can or has been caused by AIs and the inability to apply a rights-duties analysis.

63 Robert van den Hoven van Genderen, "Legal personhood in the age of artificially intelligent robots" in Woodrow Barfield and Ugo Pagallo (eds), *Research Handbook on the Law of Artificial Intelligence* (2018: Edward Elgar), ch.8.

64 Van Genderen (n. 63), 245.

65 Jacob Turner, *Robot Rules: Regulating Artificial Intelligence* (Palgrave Macmillan: 2018), 191-193.

However, legal personality for AIs could be used in conjunction with other legal techniques, such as ideas of vicarious liability and requirements for compulsory insurance.[66] These are familiar ways of distributing risk in society.

Conclusion

It is time to conclude. Algorithms and AI present huge opportunities to improve the human condition. They also pose grave threats. These exist in relation to both of the diverging futures which the digital world seems to offer: technical efficiency and private market power for Silicon Valley, on the one hand, and more authoritarian national control, as exemplified by China, on the other.

The digitisation of life is overwhelming the boundaries of nation states and conventional legal categories, through the volume of information which is gathered and deployed and the speed and impersonality of decision-making which it fosters. The sense is of a flood in which the flow of water moves around obstacles and renders them meaningless. Information comes in streams which cannot be digested by humans and decisions flow by at a rate that the court process cannot easily break up for individual legal analysis. Law needs to find suitable concepts and practical ways to structure this world in order to reaffirm human agency at the individual level and at the collective democratic level. It needs to find points in the stream where it can intervene and ways in which the general flow can be controlled, even if not in minute detail. Law is a vehicle to safeguard human values. The law has to provide structures so that algorithms and AI are used to enhance human capacities, agency and dignity, not to remove them. It has to impose its order on the digital world and must resist being reduced to an irrelevance.

Analysing situations with care and precision with respect to legal relationships, rights and obligations is what lawyers are trained to do. They have a specific form of technical expertise and a fund of knowledge about potential legal solutions and analogies which, with imagination, can be drawn upon in this major task. Lawyers should be engaging with the debates about the digital world now, and as a matter of urgency.

---

66 See Lord Hodge (n. 4): "The law could confer separate legal personality on the machine by registration and require it or its owner to have compulsory insurance to cover its liability to third parties in delict (tort) or restitution".

Manifesto for Responsible AI

A blueprint for an ethical, legal and regulatory framework

We are at a tipping point, on the precipice of a future so detached from the security of the past that it makes the previous seismic shocks that have shaken our societies look like the most inconsequential of parochial difficulties.

It may sound like hyperbole, but despite living through cataclysmic social events such as the Enclosure Movement, the Industrial Revolution or even the horrors of two World Wars, we have always retained control of our human destiny; the position of humanity secure.

Now – perhaps fittingly, in the much-heralded twenty-first century – we are simultaneously facing a potentially dislocating detachment from the physical world we have been rooted in throughout our evolution and an existential threat caused by technological development.

Within the past 30 years we have seen the development of the internet, the emergence of robots, the Internet of Things, virtual reality and the advent of quantum computing and the maturing of machine learning. More recently and just as seismic, has been the announcement of the Metaverse, a fusion of many of these technologies that will enable the development of a 3D virtualised digital copy of the world that will empower governments and companies to model events, buildings and plans in a 'cyberspace' before building them in the real world. At the moment it is being presented as a positive but the potential ramifications for social control and manipulation are huge and will need to be guarded against.

These developments are going to change our lives so profoundly that the dislocations of the industrial revolution will pale into insignificance by comparison and the ensuing social changes will have enormous consequences for our lives, our ideas of humanity and the world at large.

At the heart of this lies AI technology, upon which we will become increasingly reliant to survive; technology that will sustain our lives in the future and technology that will safeguard our world for the future.

To prevent climate change, to feed our people and to prevent massive social disaster, we will need AI. To control sustainable power systems, such as offshore windfarms, AI will be vital. We will depend upon AI to establish efficient and cost effective food supplies, which humans will not be able to produce at a scale and

317

speed to meet increasing demand. We will need AI to develop and invent ever more efficient industrial systems and cities.

AI will enable us to venture into space and to create the next generation of satellite communications systems which will provide high-speed internet communications anywhere on Earth.

It is an image of a future world that public relations companies are falling over themselves to project but one that as always could hide a very sinister reality that will allow control over and surveillance of the Earth's population in ways that we would never have thought possible. One area of huge concern is the complete takeover of the military by AI and the potential for the development of hybrid soldiers and robot armies. It will also lead to the wholesale destruction of large sections of the job market as AI systems replace workers in manufacturing, building, mining, farming, accountancy, the law and a whole host of other areas. This will lead to one of the greatest social changes, the development of new types of employment and the development of AI systems whose purpose is to look after the interests of the individuals they serve – a process known as augmentation.

This process is so fraught with dangers that politicians at the EU and academics such as Professor Sherry Turkle warn it must be strenuously policed in order to avoid dependence on AI and the development of misconceived human-AI relationships.

It is a world that Professor Stephen Hawking warned was laden with peril: suggesting that whilst the primitive forms of AI developed thus far were very useful, the consequences of creating something that can match or surpass humans was a very real possibility:

> 'Humans, who are limited by slow biological evolution, couldn't compete, and would be superseded.'

It is not only Hawking and prominent members of the scientific community who have called for caution in the development of AI. Leading business figures such as the former Microsoft boss, Bill Gates, and Elon Musk are equally concerned. Musk warned MIT in 2014 that AI was probably humanity's 'biggest existential threat'.

Ironically, given his role as a co-founder with Demis Hassabis of DeepMind, possibly the world's most famous AI business in the world, Shane Legg stated flatly that, 'I think human extinction will probably occur, and technology will likely play a part in this.'

To deal with this very real possibility we propose a Manifesto for Responsible AI, which lays out a framework to allow the development of AI in a way that presents as little risk to humanity as possible and ensures a co-existence between the technology and people. Crucially, it seeks to calibrate the inevitable tension between creating an environment, which supports and harnesses innovation and one that minimises the societal and personal risk posed by the technology.

So how can this be done?

When most people consider the relationship that we should have with robots and any form of AI they almost inevitably turn to the Laws of Robotics laid out by the science fiction writer and Professor of Biochemistry Isaac Asimov as a starting point.

On the face of it Asimov's Laws – which were set out and discussed in Chapter 9 – appear eminently sensible, but suffer from three significant shortfalls. First, they were conceived as a way to test conflicts which became the plots for many of Asimov's science fiction short stories and novels; secondly, they apply to the deployment of robotic systems and do not consider the development of AI systems working within networks or production lines. Asimov's deliberate attempt to avoid definitions left him with the concept of a robot first popularised by Karel Čapek in *RUR*. The robots that will do most harm to people are far more likely to be AI programs working in a network than a mobile autonomous system. Finally, although these Laws have not been incorporated into any regulatory framework, they have already been broken. The deployment of AI into the design and automated production of weapons systems clearly breaches Asimov's rules.

How then can we ensure that AI systems deployed by large organisations operate in our interests? How can we introduce accountability over systems that far exceed our intellectual ability to follow their calculations and did so from their very beginnings, whose workings we do not understand and whose objectives are just as remote?

In a world where the politicians responsible for creating the regulations needed to control the machines know very little about technology it is essential for a more informed debate about AI and Big Tech to take place. This is because it is now fundamentally important that the interests of the person on the street can be properly asserted against companies whose assets exceed those of many of the largest countries in the world. At the start of 2022, for example, Apple's value briefly exceeded $3 trillion dollars for the first time, over twice the annual GDP of Spain.

There is hope though. It is notable that at the same time that people are stressing the huge profits that are now possible for Big Tech, a new and more social dimension has begun to be stressed by companies. In 2019 the US Business Roundtable, a group of the largest companies in the country, surprised many people when it ameliorated the statement of the purpose of a corporation and for the first time stated that corporations have a social obligation as well as a duty to their shareholders. Just as striking, and as mentioned several times in this book, was Sundar Pichai, the head of Google's parent company Alphabet, asking in an editorial in the *Financial Times* for the European Parliament to draw up regulations on AI governance.

Against this backdrop and to this end we assert:

1. Transparency is essential to establishing trust

Those seeking to engage in AI will be required to describe what a given AI product or service is seeking to do; why a decision has been taken to use an automated process; and how such a process occurs.

Through the use of AI Impact Assessments, the potential risks of the technology must be identified at the outset, as well as its impact on the rights and freedoms of individuals, society and the environment.

To achieve this, it will be fundamentally important for those engaging in AI to be able to explain why they have selected particular datasets, how they ensured the accuracy of those datasets, how their algorithms have been coded or devised to use those datasets and how they are protected.

To meet the diversity challenges we have outlined in this book, it is essential that the technology is designed to operate fairly in and across society in general. It must not undermine the protected rights and characteristics of individuals and citizens.

We consider this to be the minimum level of transparency needed to establish trust and unleash the true power of the technology for humanity.

2. Establishment of an independent supra-national AI oversight agency is vital

We call for significant restrictions to be placed upon the current practice of road-testing so-called 'beta' versions of AI products and services through the creation of an independent supra-national AI oversight agency (Agency).

The role of the Agency will be to assess the potential risks and wider impact of any roll-out of technology identified in AI Impact Assessments, testing where appropriate in a sand-boxed environment. Higher risk applications should necessarily attract higher degrees of scrutiny.

We recommend the introduction of a certification or licensing system to provide assurance to the individual and to establish wider stability of the technology environment. We anticipate that such a system will be adopted by the insurance industry as a pre-requisite of any cover being provided.

To ensure that the wider interests of society and businesses are considered, based on the evidence we have taken, the Agency should as a minimum have representatives safeguarding ethical and philosophical as well as legal considerations.

The Agency should also operate as an advisory body to governments, legislators and regulators alike and as a potential guardian of training qualifications for those developing the technology.

We recommend that it could be funded by contributions from the largest software companies in the world.

3. Ongoing monitoring of performance is required – a black box for the black box

Once certified we recommend that the performance of the technology be monitored through a requirement to maintain logs and an ability of 'interested' third parties or the Agency at suitably determined trigger points to audit and verify performance.

The aim is to create snapshots of the performance of the AI technology in order that, in the event of a system failure and similar to the role of the black box in the aviation industry, investigators can determine what went wrong. In a more than ironic reversal of its linguistic use – the 'black box' in AI refers to where the system carries out calculations at scale and speed and in a manner which might otherwise be entirely impenetrable and incapable of reverse engineering. It is essential that the performance is captured and subject to audit to gain further trust in and ensure that there is greater transparency of the technology in operation.

Further consideration should be given to encouraging and/or requiring companies to provide a statement of compliance of AI technology against its confirmed objectives, in line with the emerging trends of companies on ESG, carbon emissions and diversity statistics.

4. Liability should support innovation and lead to improving standards

AI is not sufficiently well-developed or understood to ensure that the promulgation of a holistic AI law, whether nationally or internationally, will succeed or indeed support wider innovation. Rather the focus should be on ensuring that existing laws, policies and procedures are sufficiently flexible to embrace and capture the emergence of new technology.

It is essential that liability is approached in a neutral manner, so that the law responds to an activity carried out by a human in an 'analogue' or 'off-line' environment in the same manner as it would in a 'digital' or 'on-line' environment. Any distinction in approach will serve to undermine the wider liability regime and will lead to evasion or avoidance behaviours.

Whilst we recognise that an AI incorporated into a product might rightly be brought within the strict liability regime of product liability, this is insufficient and inappropriate to cover AI delivered as a service. Accordingly, we consider that fault-based liability be the appropriate standard for assessing liability.

Urgent work should be undertaken to determine whether the development of a liability regime based upon imposition and acceptance of fiduciary duties might align better with the future evolution of the technology.

5. Primacy of interest must be respected and device sanctity assured

In circumstances where a number of different stakeholders have an interest in a device which incorporates AI capability, we need to ensure that any value derived from that device respects and protects the interests of the individual it serves and who requested the use of the AI agent. Devices need to be 'loyal' to the individual who owns them and the primacy of the individual's interest needs to be protected.

We recommend that there is a need to reinforce what we call 'device sanctity'. Devices considered to have a human interest need to be properly protected against incursions from both state and cyber criminals; a protection enshrined in law.

Consent should be sought from the individual on an opt-in basis if their device (or any of its contents) is to be solicited or used by another party. The implications of such consent should be made clear, including that a technology company might have an active presence on such device. This necessarily goes wider than personal data. The role of Internet of Things devices and their implications will have to be spelt out.

6. Personality and personhood for AI should be limited and treated as exceptional

There are considerable dangers caused by anthropomorphising AI. We should therefore approach any attempt to confer personality onto technology with extreme caution and the lines of demarcation between human personality and legal personality should at all times be clear.

We recognise that there may be limited circumstances where it might be appropriate to consider conferring legal rights on an AI. AI is presently defined

321

and described by computing power and statistics, possibly bounded by some form of encryption. It could, however, be redefined by reference to its creator. These scenarios will be limited and exceptional.

Although AI systems can invent processes and systems, the default position should be that ownership of those processes and systems should be conferred on the AI's owner. The relationship should properly be analogous to the antiquated rights conferred upon slaves to transact on behalf of their masters, which developed towards the end of the Republic in Ancient Rome.

7. Prohibitions

The advent and evolution of new technologies will present use-cases, which should be resisted. We recommend that these should be identified at an early stage in respect of AI. Any encroachment on these areas must be supported by legal sanctions.

At the time of promoting this manifesto, at least three prohibitions should be given strong consideration for moral and ethical reasons.

First, any move to augment human beings physically or fuse them with AI must be strenuously protected. This applies equally to able-bodied as well as disabled individuals.

Secondly, the use of AI in military technology requires careful definition by international standards and must be tightly prescribed if we are going to halt a systematic and gradual erosion of the virtually universal condemnation of the use of AI in warfare.

Thirdly, the deliberate use of algorithmic collusion – where one algorithm effects another algorithm with the intent of either harm or unethical gain to the detriment of individuals and wider society – should be resisted in the absence of some lawful justification.

AI promises huge benefits to humanity and the possibility of a fairer and more equable society. It is essential that AI is guided to work for the greater good. In an age where even legislators are not in full command of the technology, which is about to become the bedrock of the world in which we live, however, it is critical that there is widespread education in AI and ethics.

It is our engagement with and our thirst to understand the technology which will not only provide the ultimate safeguard against its excesses, but crucially empower us to unlock and leverage its manifold promises for the good of humanity.

Index

[All references are to page number]